The
Producer

The Producer

●

**JOHN HAMMOND
AND THE SOUL
OF AMERICAN MUSIC**

Dunstan Prial

FARRAR, STRAUS AND GIROUX / NEW YORK

Farrar, Straus and Giroux
19 Union Square West, New York 10003

Copyright © 2006 by Dunstan Prial
All rights reserved
Distributed in Canada by Douglas & McIntyre Ltd.
Printed in the United States of America
First edition, 2006

Library of Congress Cataloging-in-Publication Data
Prial, Dunstan, 1963 –
    The producer : John Hammond and the soul of American music / Dunstan Prial.— 1st ed.
        p.   cm.
    Includes index.
    ISBN–13: 987-0-374-11304-9 (hardcover : alk. paper)
    ISBN–10: 0-374-11304-1 (hardcover : alk. paper)
    1. Hammond, John, 1910–   2.Sound recording executives and producers—United States—Biography.   I. Title.

ML429.H26P75 2006
781.64′092—dc22

                                                            2005012666

Designed by Jonathan D. Lippincott

www.fsgbooks.com

1   3   5   7   9   10   8   6   4   2

This—like everything else—is for Amy

CONTENTS

PREFACE

The only time I ever saw John Hammond was in October 1984, when he walked onto the stage of Carnegie Hall to introduce Stevie Ray Vaughan and Double Trouble. He cut an incongruous figure that night—gaunt and elegant in jacket and tie—squinting out into the raucous crowd. He was seventy-three years old and in declining health, and it showed. After shuffling to the microphone, he rambled for a moment before growing conscious of the crowd's impatience. Then he quickly got to the point. Tellingly, he introduced the group as "Double Trouble," calling attention first to the drummer, Chris Layton, and then to the bassist, Tommy Shannon. The gesture made it clear that the performers were part of a cohesive band, that Vaughan was not a solo act backed by an anonymous rhythm section.

When Hammond finally introduced Vaughan, the grin on his face was that of an exuberant child. It was a compelling scene—this elderly man dressed like a college professor gazing admiringly at Vaughan, who was wearing a brand-new mariachi outfit made expressly for that performance. Hammond was still beaming as Vaughan tore into the opening notes of "Scuttle Buttin'," a lightning storm of circular blues scales played at earsplitting volume.

Watching from my seat about ten rows from the stage, I wondered, "Who on earth was *that*?"

John Hammond was best known for his uncanny and perhaps unprece-
dented ability to spot musical talent at its earliest, rawest stage. The list
of artists whose careers he supported is well known: Billie Holiday,
Benny Goodman, Teddy Wilson, Count Basie, Charlie Christian, Pete
Seeger, Aretha Franklin, Bob Dylan, George Benson, Leonard Cohen,
Bruce Springsteen, and Stevie Ray Vaughan.

But there were a number of other signature traits. He wore his hair
in a neatly cropped crew cut even through the 1960s and 1970s, when
everybody was growing their hair long. He was rarely seen without a
thick stack of newspapers and magazines stuffed under his arm. And
he described everything he liked as "mah-velous, mah-velous" long before comedians turned the exaggerated pronunciation into a buzzword.

Yet ask anyone who knew John Hammond to describe him and one
of the first things they mention is his smile. "The smile, yeah, the smile.
It just kinda washed all over you," recalled Bruce Springsteen. It was a
giant horsey grin, so big it practically closed his eyes in a squint and left
deep creases down each side of his face. It left exposed nearly all of
his teeth, top and bottom rows, as well as the pink of his gums. It was
utterly unself-conscious and thoroughly full of joy.

It may well have been the defining characteristic of a man who re-
solved early on to spend his life using the thing he loved most, music,
to promote the cause for which he was most passionate, equality among
the races. Over the course of his seventy-seven years, Hammond's success
in pursuit of that singular endeavor left him with plenty to smile about.

Springsteen smiled a lot himself during a lively discussion of Hammond one evening a few years back. Deep within the bowels of the
Dunkin' Donuts Center in Providence, Rhode Island, on a bitterly cold
night, he recalled the morning in May 1972 when he first auditioned
for Hammond in Hammond's office at Columbia Records in midtown
Manhattan. Although he was just twenty-two years old at the time and
virtually unknown outside the insular music scene along the Jersey
Shore, Springsteen said Hammond treated him with respect and took
his music seriously from the very start. Indeed, Hammond, the same
man who had discovered Bob Dylan, Aretha Franklin, and Billie Holiday, had treated him as an artist.

Quite a bit of water had passed under the bridge in the ensuing thirty years, but Springsteen's recollections of Hammond were vivid and personal. He clearly enjoyed digging back into his memory to a time when he had to hustle just to get a gig in a small Greenwich Village club. In less than an hour, he and the members of his E Street Band were due onstage to perform in front of another sold-out arena. His legs were thin and his face was sort of craggy and lined, but now in his mid-fifties he was still wiry and athletic. And intense. Relaxed and friendly, but always intense. Sitting forward with his elbows on his knees, his hands clasped tightly in front of him, Springsteen threw himself into his memories of his old friend and mentor. It was rather touching.

Laughing, he did imitations. (Nearly everyone who ever met John Hammond has his or her own version.) "That's mah-velous, mah-velous, Bruce," he mimicked in Hammond's signature Brahmin accent. He also described a kindly, protective figure in a business known for predators. "I always felt that my music was safe with him," Springsteen recalled. "It was just a wonderful way to be introduced to the music business. If there's anything like it today—and I don't think there is anymore—I would wish it on anyone who was just getting started like I was."

Springsteen was touring in support of his latest album, *The Rising*, whose songs were written in the aftermath of the September 11, 2001, terrorist attacks and whose themes reflected an angry, confused, but still hopeful nation. The album served as a sort of rock-and-roll salve for a nation in shock. Few popular artists could have attempted such a sensitive mission—that of embracing unspeakable and unprecedented tragedy within the context of celebratory rock and roll—without coming off as either exploitative or simply maudlin. Springsteen pulled it off with aplomb.

Despite its potentially limited commercial appeal given its often-raw subject matter, *The Rising* was clearly an album Springsteen felt he had to make. In other words, it was exactly the kind of album John Hammond would have appreciated.

Certainly that passion for writing and performing songs that express universal experiences through a personal and singular point of view was one of the characteristics that Hammond found compelling in Springsteen more than thirty years ago.

The roster of artists with whom Hammond is most closely associated is staggering not only for the success of the figures on it but for the diversity of their talents. All of them might fairly be recognized as geniuses in some form or another. But their talents were expressed in markedly different ways. For instance, Charlie Christian was a prodigy, almost savant-like in his ability to play a guitar unlike anyone who had ever played it before. Hammond recognized that and made certain millions of jazz fans got the opportunity to hear Christian play.

Yet the genius that has inspired Bob Dylan—and Bruce Springsteen, for that matter—is far more subtle and subjective, not nearly as obvious as a guitar player with brilliant chops. But when Hammond saw it, raw and unpolished as it was with Dylan in September 1961, and again with Springsteen more than a decade later, he recognized it immediately and promptly set about ensuring that others heard it.

Many of the figures on that list have emerged as icons of the past century, their renown reaching far beyond the popular-music realm in which they first became famous. For Americans of the World War II generation, the music of Benny Goodman and Count Basie was as ubiquitous as advertisements for war bonds. And the swing jazz they played was seen as a symbol of America's blustery freedoms. A generation later, the music of Aretha Franklin, Bob Dylan, and Bruce Springsteen has similarly become a part of the American landscape. And their music, while a product of more ambiguous times, is nevertheless equally infused with a uniquely brash American worldview.

Was it merely a coincidence that the same man provided the springboard for such a diverse and lasting array of talent? Hardly. Time and again Hammond proved eerily prescient in his awareness of seismic change that loomed ahead for American society, and in how that change would manifest itself through popular culture, in particular through music. He seemed to know what America wanted to hear before America knew it.

Thus in the early 1930s, when Hammond began championing a brilliant but unknown young black piano player named Teddy Wilson, eventually pairing him with Benny Goodman, he did it not only because it made musical sense—the results were sublime—but also because he sensed that America was ready to hear black and white musicians make beautiful music together. Thirty years later he angrily defended Bob Dylan's intangible gifts to Columbia executives who couldn't see for themselves and who wanted to drop Dylan from the label.

In early 1987, a few months before Hammond's death, the jazz writer John McDonough published a profile of Hammond that, perhaps more than any other of the many profiles of him over the years, captured Hammond's legacy and the lifelong sense of purpose that built that legacy:

> Musical styles may come and go, but the dynamics of social change are eternal, notwithstanding periods of eclipse. Hammond could hear the important voices no one else could hear in the '30s, the '60s and the '70s because he was the only figure in the commercial recording industry who was so profoundly in touch with the underlying intellectual, social and revolutionary forces driving those times. Hammond's incredible string of insights from 1932 to the present simply cannot be explained as luck. His ears respond to new music as soundings of social change. He understands instinctively the equations between politics and culture.

I came to John Hammond backward—that is, in reverse chronology. My serious musical education began in the mid-1970s with the release of Dylan's *Blood on the Tracks*, the album that tied together for me the disparate but visceral messages I had been absorbing for a number of years from an artist who had recorded many of my favorite songs: "The Times They Are A-Changin'," "My Back Pages," "Like a Rolling Stone," "Stuck Inside of Mobile with the Memphis Blues Again."

Then Bruce Springsteen released *Darkness on the Edge of Town* in 1978. It's still probably my favorite of Springsteen's albums. These were mature songs, gritty and realistic, that told me life may not always be fair but that I can maintain a sense of hope and dignity. "It ain't no sin to be glad you're alive," he sang. Indeed. It's an adult message that has infused much of Springsteen's work since.

Finally, in the summer of 1984, Springsteen became the property of the entire world, and it was time for me to quench my musical thirst in some other, less crowded well. That was when I turned on the radio and heard Vaughan for the first time.

Two years after the 1984 show at Carnegie Hall, I attended another concert in New York City featuring Vaughan and his band, this one a tribute to Hammond at Lincoln Center. Hammond had recently suffered a stroke and was unable to attend. It was quite an evening: Benny Goodman made a surprise appearance to the delight of the silver-haired, black-tie crowd. Later, to the dismay of that same faction and the delight of the black T-shirt crowd (myself among them), Vaughan jammed with George Benson on Vaughan's "Couldn't Stand the Weather," a smoldering bluesy rocker.

At the time, I was vaguely aware of Hammond's reputation as the man who had "discovered" Dylan, Springsteen, and Vaughan. I knew nothing else about him. Inside the concert program, however, I learned that Hammond's legacy reached all the way back to 1932, when he first encountered Billie Holiday. And I learned that his footprints crisscrossed the country from New York City to Oklahoma City, and from the hills of rural North Carolina to the nightclubs of Los Angeles, Chicago, and Kansas City. I also learned that this scion of the Vanderbilt fortune had dedicated his life to finding exactly the kind of passionate and authentic American music that had instilled in me a wonder for these United States—and continues to do so. More important, I recognized then that I shared with John Hammond a belief and a faith that music that came from the heart could inspire others to act from the heart.

Later that night I said to my father, "Someone should write a book about that guy." "Why don't you?" he responded. Here it is.

The
Producer

THE BASEMENT ON
EAST NINETY-FIRST STREET

In a home fit for a king, John Henry Hammond, Jr., found sanctuary in the basement with the servants. It was always warm and cozy
down there, and the servants, usually so stiff and formal upstairs,
laughed and joked with the boy when he came downstairs to visit them.
But, as Hammond would recall, both in his memoirs and in countless
interviews, the main attraction, the thing that drew him downstairs
again and again, was the music. The year was 1918, and among the
songs the seven-year-old boy heard on the servants' battered old
Grafonola was Sir Harry Lauder's raucous "Roamin' in the Gloamin'."
It became his favorite song, and he learned every word. "Music, especially music on records, entered my life early to become the catalyst for
all that was to happen to me," he wrote many years later. "In the
grooves of those primitive early discs I found in my house, I discovered
a new world, one I could enter easily and as often as I pleased simply
by winding the handle of a phonograph."

It wasn't as if the rest of the family disliked music. To the contrary,
music was a constant presence throughout the house. It was just that
Hammond didn't like the music the rest of the family was listening
to. On the upper floors of the Hammonds' majestic five-story mansion
just off Fifth Avenue in Manhattan, the boy's mother, father, and four
older sisters listened to the great opera tenor Enrico Caruso, as well as
to standard classics by Beethoven, Brahms, and Mozart. The music

wafted like a soothing breeze up and down marble staircases and in and out of oak-paneled rooms. A brand-new Victrola record player, the latest advancement in early-twentieth-century audio technology, ensured the highest-quality sound. It was enough to make the boy more than a little sleepy.

Down in the basement, the mood was decidedly more upbeat. According to Hammond's sister Rachel Breck, John was often found perched on a chair in the corner of the servants' quarters, his feet dangling well above the ground, one toe tapping instinctively to the bouncy rhythms of the early blues and jazz records favored by the mostly black household staff. Hammond himself would often recall his fascination with the servants' emotional response to the music, which ranged from laughter to tears, or perhaps an impromptu dance. It was, he said, his first exposure to the visceral power that popular music could wield.

When John Hammond, Jr., was born on December 15, 1910, the Hammond family lived in one of the more spectacular private homes in Manhattan. The Hammonds—John; his mother, Emily; his father, John senior; and four older sisters (Rachel was three years older, Alice five years older, Adele seven years older, and Emily nine years older)— resided at 9 East Ninety-first Street in a limestone mansion located a half block to the east of Central Park between Fifth and Madison avenues, an area that remains to this day one of the most exclusive in the world. Mrs. Hammond's sister, Florence Adele Sloane Burden, lived with her family in equally grand accommodations next door. The girls had received matching mansions as wedding presents. John Hammond's cousin Frederick Field, who grew up in a Vanderbilt-funded mansion on Fifth Avenue a few blocks south, would later note acidly that the Hammond and Burden homes "boasted an elegant feature which our house lacked: a drive-in entrance so that you could walk into the house from your coach or automobile without exposure to the stares of the less privileged."

The Hammond mansion was designed to re-create the ambience of a European château. No extravagance was overlooked: eighteen-foot ceilings and marble stairways, paneled walls and gilded moldings, rooms furnished with heavy damask curtains, crystal chandeliers, tapestries, and Oriental rugs. A suite of reception rooms on the second floor included a library, a ballroom, and a music room that could hold as many as three hundred guests. The suite was often filled to capacity with Mrs. Hammond's society friends, who came to hear duets performed by John on violin and his mother on piano. Elevators were located in the front and rear of the home, but the children were cautioned to use them sparingly. John Hammond, Sr., issued frequent reminders that each ride cost twenty-five cents in electricity.

The museum-like surroundings were more than a little oppressive. "You had to have a sense of humor about it while growing up in these luxurious surroundings or else you could go a little crazy," said Rachel Breck. The home also included a regulation-size squash court on the fourth floor with a balcony for spectators and a locker room where players could change into their athletic togs. Instead of squash, the Hammond sisters used it for roller-skating and as an impromptu art gallery after an afternoon of painting.

Because the home was a gift from his wealthy in-laws, John Hammond, Sr., always considered the mansion something of an embarrassment. "It was one more reminder that he was married to a wealthy woman and expected to live in a house he could never have afforded to buy himself," John Hammond, Jr., observed many years after his father's death. While the father may have had little say over his family's living arrangements, or even the furnishings of their house, he was determined to raise his children how he saw fit. And he was adamant that his brood not fall into the vicious cycle of idleness and extravagance that sent a handful of his Vanderbilt in-laws into early graves.

A principled and hardworking man, John senior dedicated himself both to his family and to helping maintain the Vanderbilt fortune in his various roles as banker, lawyer, and railroad executive. One of six children, he was born in 1870 in Louisville, Kentucky, to a Civil War hero. After the war, the family moved to St. Paul, Minnesota, where General Hammond became a land speculator. As a teenager, John Hammond, Sr., won scholarships to Phillips Exeter Academy, then to Yale, where as a sophomore in 1889 he learned that his father had died unexpectedly. Despite his being the younger of the two Hammond sons by about a year, John senior took on the role of head of the family even as he earned a law degree from Columbia University.

Family pictures taken when he was in his mid- to late thirties reveal a handsome man just under six feet with a bit of a paunch and light brown hair that gradually receded into baldness. As a respected lawyer and executive, John senior rose each morning, took a carriage down Fifth Avenue to his law offices in lower Manhattan, and stopped most nights on the way home for a cocktail—a man apparently comfortable in his role as a Gilded Age captain of industry.

In the summer of 1919, when John Hammond, Jr., was eight, the family boarded a private railroad car in New York and headed west. John's father had been asked by the board of the New York Central, the huge railroad founded by Cornelius Vanderbilt, which he served as a director, to determine whether the company needed a spur across the northern region of the Grand Canyon. Determined that his children should share in the experiences common to children outside the family's rarified circles, John senior brought the whole family along, ostensibly to expose them to the hardships of Western travel.

"Hardship" is a relative term, of course. The Hammonds' private car included lavishly upholstered living quarters and a huge master bedroom for the mother and father. The first stop west of Chicago was St. Louis, where a handful of railroad executives and their wives, all of them dressed in their summer finest, anxiously waited for the wealthy family from New York. Rachel Breck, who was twelve at the time, recalled the thermometer hitting 112 degrees that day. "The only way to cool off the car was to open all the windows," she remembered. "But that allowed in all the soot and dust from outside, and the family all wound up hot and filthy." The crowd gasped when the Hammonds stepped off the train looking as if they'd ridden the last hundred miles on horseback.

From St. Louis, the family continued west across the Great Plains and into Utah, where they swam in the Great Salt Lake, then headed into the picturesque desert just north of the Grand Canyon. Since the area was federal land that had only recently been opened to the public, there were no lodging facilities available, requiring the family to sleep on cots inside Army tents. The children all responded with gusto except for John, who remained aloof throughout the trip, expressing no interest in roughing it like the cowboys of lore. In his autobiography, he wrote that the only part of the trip that had any lasting impact on him occurred during a stop in the southern Utah mining town of Kanab. One Sunday morning, as Mrs. Hammond was reading a Sunday-school lesson to the girls, the boy discovered a player piano at the inn where the family was staying. Incredibly, the piano somehow emulated the sound of a banjo. "I ran to the piano to find out how this was done and discovered that the instrument had been manufactured by Wing & Son of New York," he later recalled. "I took off the front panel and there was a row of little jangles which the piano hammers struck when the middle pedal was depressed. I thought that piano was the most intriguing instrument I had ever heard."

The trip further exposed a growing rift in the household. The father and his daughters seemed tolerant of life's foibles, more willing to let go and have a little fun than the mother and son. "I was very much like my father," Rachel Breck recalled. "I love peace and quiet and I hate arguments and fights. John lived to be a critic of every kind. Even when he was tiny, he would go to church with Mother, who was very religious and very intense, and he would say, literally, he was about four or five, 'Mother, how can you take me to a church where the first soprano was singing off-key?'"

In his autobiography, Hammond recalled an uneasy distance between him and his father and cited the forty-year difference in age as the primary cause. His sisters believed the emotional chasm had everything to do with their brother's strong artistic inclinations. The elder Hammond was an eminently practical man; his son was almost defiantly impractical.

The boy's love of "race" or "popular" music set him apart from his sisters from an early age, and his mother encouraged his curiosity, initiating violin lessons well before Hammond reached his teens. His sister Rachel recalled playing with the other wealthy children who lived in the neighborhood, sometimes tossing balls from rooftop to rooftop. Her little brother usually went off on his own, absorbed in his music, usually the blues and jazz he was hearing in the basement. "My sisters and I always said that John grew up in a different house than we did. He saw the house from such a different point of view than all of us. It was extraordinary. We wouldn't have known that we grew up in the same place."

Musical curiosity turned to passion, and passion soon bordered on obsession, a predicament that sometimes led to conflicts between the children. There was the time the boy's collection of piano rolls disappeared while he was away at camp, for example. Hammond, an avid collector before he reached his teens, also began collecting the piano rolls that were inserted into a player piano located on the fourth floor of the family home. According to Hammond's version of the story, he spent the summer of 1921, when he was ten years old, at the Lone Pine Camp in the woods of New England. Left behind in Manhattan was an "irreplaceable" collection of piano rolls by such keyboard luminaries as Lem Fowler, James P. Johnson, and Fats Waller. When Hammond returned from camp at the end of the summer, he was horrified to learn that his sister Rachel had given the rolls away to the Salvation Army. "It broke my heart, but she just didn't appreciate their value. She understood her strange little brother no better than her sisters," he recounted. Eight decades later, Rachel Breck disputed her brother's version of the story. As she tells it, the fire department arrived for an inspection one day while her brother was away. The inspector told Mrs. Hammond that the stacks of loose piano rolls created a fire hazard and something needed to be done. Mrs. Hammond solved the problem by giving the rolls away to charity.

None of the Hammond sisters was musically inclined, and their father was tone-deaf. Emily Hammond and her son, meanwhile, were passionate about music.

Hammond also inherited from his mother a blunt sense of self-righteousness. When he thought he was right, nothing could persuade him otherwise. And, like any passionate crusader, he came to think that if you weren't with him you were against him. Emily Hammond and her son "lived on another plane," according to Rachel Breck. "They were gifted in their own way, and they were privileged in their own way, and because they could afford to be their own person, I believe, maybe they didn't see the world as realistically as perhaps it is."

Emily Vanderbilt Sloane Hammond was the great-granddaughter of Commodore Vanderbilt, who at his death in 1877 was by far the richest man on earth. Emily's mother was Emily Thorn Vanderbilt, the daughter of the Commodore's oldest son and primary heir, William Henry Vanderbilt. Notwithstanding the Commodore's penchant for referring to him as a "blatherskite," William, or Billy as he was known, doubled his family's fortune in the ten years after his father's death. But if Emily Sloane ever feared that her Vanderbilt inheritance wasn't enough to sustain the lifestyle to which she was accustomed, she could always tap into the fortunes of her father's family. William Douglas Sloane, John Hammond's maternal grandfather, had earned the right to marry a Vanderbilt girl by being born into the family that founded the upscale W. & J. Sloane carpet and furniture retail chain, furnisher of many of New York's most luxurious Gilded Age mansions.

Like most rich families of that era, the Hammonds split their time between the city and a country home in Westchester County about thirty miles north of New York City. The property was a working farm with barns for dozens of Guernsey cows, as well as poultry houses for chickens and several acres for vegetable gardens. But John, who suffered from severe allergies, was a city child from his earliest days and was always happiest on the tiny bustling island of Manhattan. There were no antihistamines in those days, and allergy sufferers did just that—suffered. So instead of joining the family in tennis, track and field, and swimming, he hid away in his room on the top floor of the huge home listening to records on his private Grafonola, even in winter when the room was unheated.

By the time Emily Sloane married John Hammond, Sr., on April 7, 1899, at the age of twenty-four, she was already a "prodigious woman . . . considered odd by her friends, terribly earnest and undaunted by any challenge," as her son would later describe her. "When she wanted to do something, she did it even though it was often difficult and sometimes strongly resented." Growing up, Emily shunned the debutante balls and endless society gatherings that permeated the lives of her girlfriends. Emily's idea of a good time was playing the piano at Sunday school. Family members recall how in Lenox, at the Vanderbilts' country home in western Massachusetts, the teenage Emily would haul herself up onto a stump in the woods and preach sermons to her brothers and sisters.

Emily Hammond's faith was always a driving force in her life, and members of her family were prominent among the upper crust of Protestant clergy in New York City. Her first cousin Henry Sloane Coffin gained a reputation as a forceful speaker and an eloquent writer while leading the Madison Avenue Presbyterian Church from 1905 to 1926. He later served for twenty years as president of the Union Theological Seminary, a repository for distinguished liberal theologians, where he fought for improved educational opportunities for immigrants and equal rights for women and blacks. Coffin was eventually elected moderator of the General Assembly, the highest position within the American Presbyterian Church.

In stark contrast to many of her Vanderbilt relatives, who attended church each week in their Sunday finest, Emily was fiery, not ostentatious, in her religious practice. "We prayed every morning on our knees as a family to make the world a better place," one of her daughters recalled. Religion offered Emily an opportunity to assuage her apparent guilt at being arbitrarily born into such wealth and splendor while just a few blocks away the poor and unwashed masses lived in squalor.

Emily Hammond wasn't the first Vanderbilt woman to channel her prodigious energy into social reform. One of her role models was her aunt Alva Vanderbilt, who, after growing bored in her role as undisputed queen of New York and Newport society, became a powerful force behind the woman suffrage movement. Alva married Willie Vanderbilt, one of the Commodore's much-sought-after grandchildren, in 1875, but later divorced him when she got word of his philandering. Not one to live out her days as a rich, lonely martyr, she was well into her fifties when she found her true calling—that of social reformer. Unlike her aunt Alva, however, Emily never became politically active. Instead, she preferred personal crusades against smoking and drinking alcohol, a cause of constant conflict in the family.

Hammond believed his mother accepted the social and racial conventions of her era because her sheltered life essentially isolated her from reality. "Racial minorities were beyond her reach," he wrote. "Blacks were porters and laundresses. The poor existed and were to be helped, yet even the dispensation of charity must begin, if not at home, within the circumference of familiar territory." Consequently, Emily was comfortable establishing a home for young white Christian girls who had come to New York to perform in the theater. But she gave no thought to helping to eradicate teenage pregnancies or to addressing any of the myriad other social ills that plagued the immigrant tenements a few blocks to the east on Second Avenue.

While her only son's religious fervor largely faded as he grew older, Emily's faith never wavered, and her energies found a number of different outlets over the years. When five-year-old Rachel came down with a bad ear infection, Emily, on the advice of a friend, turned to Christian Science, which advocates prayer in lieu of medical treatment. Miraculously, Rachel got better, and Emily immediately started attending Christian Science meetings, and to the dismay of some family members she took her young son with her. She would remain a practitioner of Christian Science well into her old age, shifting allegiances only after her husband died in 1949.

Hammond's affiliation with this unconventional religion pushed him even further away from his classmates, who thought it odd that he had not been vaccinated against the common illnesses of the day and that he, sneezing and coughing in the dead of winter and clearly in the throes of a bad cold, prayed to God for a swift recovery.

One of the few things about Christian Science meetings that Hammond enjoyed was the movement's singers—one in particular, a black woman named Nevada Vanderveer, whom he heard in a church on West Ninety-sixth Street. Something else he took away from the Christian Science movement was the way in which followers believed in their ability to determine their own fates. He would later claim to find that aspect of Christian Science distasteful, but anyone who knew him in his adult years recognized right away that here was a man who believed wholeheartedly that he could determine not only his own fate but also the fates of those he sought to help. It was a personality trait not everyone found attractive.

Hammond spent his early teens absorbing the doctrines of several branches of Protestantism while circulating between Henry Sloane

Coffin's Presbyterian services, his grandmother's Episcopal services, and his mother's Christian Science services. Although he eventually drifted away from organized religion, he always remained aware of the powerful influence his mother held over him as a child, and he summed up his early years as follows:

> Until I went away to school I lived the life of a coddled little rich boy, tolerant like my mother of weaknesses and sins in others, intolerant of any fall from grace in myself, ignorant as Mother was of the world beyond our island of social and financial equals, except to realize that there were people out there who were not like us. I shared her religious fervor, her prejudices, and her saintly resolve to set an example for others, then to forgive them when they failed to measure up to it. Like her, I was already the reformer, fired with her energy, certain in the right, oblivious to physical infirmities which all right-minded flesh could overcome, an inheritor of the guilt and therefore the obligations of wealth.

In the early 1920s, as Hammond was approaching his teens and around the same time he was embarking on a spiritual search, he began explorations of a more secular nature. Not yet out of grade school, he started making his first excursions into Harlem. "The house [on East Ninety-first Street] was so big the family never knew whether I was in or not and I used to sneak out of school and either walk or take the trolley to the middle of Harlem and just roam around and look at the theaters and everything," he once said. "I was too young to go to a nightclub or anything. I didn't smoke and I didn't drink and I was a complete boyscout. But I got to meet musicians. They used to look at me and think I was crazy—white kids weren't supposed to like music like that."

Consider the image: a boy not more than ten or eleven standing on the corner of Madison Avenue and Ninety-sixth Street. He was wearing a pair of thick corduroy shorts, knee-high blue socks, black patent leather shoes, and a blue blazer with matching cap, both emblazoned with the ornate insignia of St. Bernard's School. He was smaller than his classmates, and when they walked past going to Central Park, the boy studiously avoided eye contact. When they asked him to join them, he always declined. His disdain for childish pursuits caused them to regard him as a serious, solitary child. How could they think otherwise? After all, the boy had once written "Harding for President" on the blackboard, and he was fond of quoting from the Bible.

John Hammond peered down Madison Avenue and saw the uptown bus approaching. He stole a glance in both directions to make sure there were no teachers or other nosy adults watching, then jumped aboard and dropped a nickel in the fare box.

Recalling these memories years later in a radio interview, Hammond clearly relished describing his own extraordinary sense of adventure.

The bus headed north along Madison Avenue, lined at the time on either side by dingy tenements filled with refugees from unpronounceable places across Eastern Europe or from the overcrowded slums of the Lower East Side. The neighborhood was only a few blocks from East Ninety-first Street, but it may as well have been separated by an ocean. Somewhere north of 120th Street the faces turned from white to brown. When the bus pulled to the curb at 135th Street, the boy could hardly contain his excitement. He climbed down onto the sidewalk—and all around him was Harlem.

This was the Harlem that would inspire Carl Van Vechten's bestselling novel *Nigger Heaven*, the Harlem of W.E.B. Du Bois and Langston Hughes, and, most important to a young music lover, the Harlem of the conductor James Reese Europe, the cornet player Johnny Dunn, the singer Mamie Smith, and the songwriter Noble Sissle, each of them early and influential practitioners of the romping new music known as jazz who would soon be joined in Harlem by Louis Armstrong, Fletcher Henderson, and Duke Ellington. This was the Harlem that set young John Hammond's heart racing.

Harlem was first settled by Dutch farmers in the mid-seventeenth century and remained sparsely populated up through the American Revolution. Located about ten miles north of the village of New Amsterdam at the southern tip of Manhattan, Nieuw Haarlem could be reached via an Indian trail that veered slightly to the west as travelers headed north from Wall Street. Large sections of the trail were used to establish the path of what would later become Broadway. The completion in the 1830s of the Harlem Railroad, which connected upper and lower Manhattan, was the first catalyst for rapid development. Another boost came in the 1880s, when construction of the elevated railroads along Second, Third, Eighth, and Ninth avenues was completed. For a brief period in the late nineteenth century, Harlem was one of the most fashionable neighborhoods in the city. German immigrants arrived and built the brownstone homes that remain one of Harlem's defining characteristics.

By the start of the twentieth century, many blacks had discovered that Harlem offered an opportunity to escape the violence and discrimination they encountered downtown. Real estate agents who were looking to fill the apartment buildings that had risen along Lenox Avenue north of 110th Street proved surprisingly color-blind. They sought only to find tenants who could afford the rents, a factor that helped create in Harlem a core community of middle-class African-Americans. Still, the neighborhood remained populated predominantly by Eastern European Jews until World War I, when overcrowded conditions led to an exodus to newly developing neighborhoods in the Bronx, Queens, and Brooklyn. At that point blacks replaced the Jews en masse. During the 1920s the black population of Harlem more than doubled from 80,000 to about 200,000. Many of the newcomers arrived from the South, former sharecroppers in search of jobs and a place where they could act as they pleased.

Nigger Heaven, published in 1926, caught the mood and atmosphere that attracted so many blacks:

> It was the hour when promenading was popular—about eleven o'clock in the evening. The air was warm, balmy for June, and not too humid. Over the broad avenue, up and down which multi-hued taxicabs rolled, hung a canopy of indigo sky, spangled with bright stars. The shops, still open, were brilliantly illuminated. Slouching under the protecting walls of the buildings, in front of show-windows, or under the trees, groups of young men congregated, chattering and laughing. Women, in pairs, or with male escorts, strolled up and down the ample sidewalk.

Van Vechten described middle-class blacks in his novel, and they were reveling in a neighborhood that allowed blacks a sense of opportunity and freedom of expression heretofore unknown in America. The Harlem Renaissance was in full swing.

Starting on 135th Street near Lenox Avenue, Hammond would pass in front of the Lincoln Theater. Too timid to buy a ticket or to sneak inside, he would huddle near the door, unnoticed since he barely reached the waists of most of the theater's patrons. Heading west along 135th Street, he would drift in and out of music stores, spending his small allowance on the jazz and blues records that had become his obsession. Shortly he would come to the upper reaches of Seventh Avenue, home to several other large theaters that catered primarily to black patrons. Turning south on Harlem's version of Broadway, the boy would pass the massive Lafayette Theater at 132nd Street. Right next door was Connie's Inn, an elegant basement club where white gangsters mingled with the city's top black entertainers. Bending over into the stairway entrance to get a closer look, Hammond saw only his own reflection in the mirrors and polished brass. Everything else was darkness and smoke, and his imagination was fired.

Hammond didn't know it at the time, but he had reached "The Corner," the intersection of 131st Street and Seventh Avenue, or quite simply the vortex of all that was happening in Harlem. At 126th Street the boy would pass in front of the Alhambra Theater, where in 1927 he would hear the blues singer Bessie Smith for the first time. Turning east on 125th Street, Hammond would soon find himself in front of the Apollo Theater, whose doorman, a kind young black guy who admired the boy's sense of adventure, began to keep an eye out for him and, according to Hammond's sister, made sure he got back downtown on the right bus.

It turns out John Hammond wasn't the only jazz hound checking out Harlem for the first time in the early and mid-1920s. In fact, most of the top musicians at this time were beginning to make their way east from Chicago to New York, where the clubs paid better and the music, like the city, seemed a little more adventurous.

Jazz's journey to New York began early in the twentieth century in

New Orleans, where men such as Jelly Roll Morton, Freddie Keppard, King Oliver, Kid Ory, Zutty Singleton, Johnny Dodds, and eventually Louis Armstrong turned traditional marching-band music on its ear. One of the first legends to emerge from this period recalls how in 1916 Keppard and his Original Creole Band rejected an offer to record their down-and-dirty songs. Keppard was said to be afraid that other musicians would steal his style. His reluctance proved significant: it meant that the first jazz recordings weren't made by a black band. A year later, a group of white musicians called the Original Dixieland Jazz Band made a series of records that caused a sensation and are now considered the earliest recorded jazz music.

By the early 1920s, the scene had shifted to the South Side of Chicago, where discrimination was less of an issue than in New Orleans. It was in Chicago in 1925 that Armstrong put together an all-star lineup to record his classic Hot Fives and Hot Sevens records, now regarded as perhaps the finest jazz recordings ever made. The crowds at Chicago's jazz clubs included a group of white teenagers, several of whom attended the same high school, Austin High, on the city's West Side. Among this group there were the future musicians Frank Teschemacher, Bud Freeman, Jimmy McPartland, and a bespectacled young whiz on the clarinet named Benny Goodman.

But by the end of the decade—an era later dubbed the Jazz Age—Harlem was the place to be. The clarinetist Mezz Mezzrow (best remembered for turning Louis Armstrong on to marijuana) recalled:

> Just on Seventh Avenue alone, going north from 131st Street, the line-up was: a barbershop, a drugstore, the Performers and Entertainers Club and under it Connie's Inn, then the Lafayette Theatre, then a candy store, the Hoofers' Club down in the basement, and finally Big John's famous ginmill. Around on 132nd Street were Tabb's Restaurant, and next to it the Rhythm Club, where you could call any hour of the day and night and hire a musician. And back on 131st Street, soon as you turned into it, you found a fine rib joint called the Barbecue, the entrance to a gang of upstairs halls where top bands like Armstrong's and Count Basie's and Jimmy Lunceford's and Cab Calloway's and

Erskine Hawkins' used to rehearse, and a speakeasy and night club called the Bandbox. Most important of all, there was an areaway running all around the corner building there, a wide alley with entrances from both Seventh Avenue and 131st Street. This alley led to the Lafayette's backstage entrance and also to a special bar in the rear of the Bandbox, and here it was that most of our social life was spent . . . [A]ll the cats from the show[s] would come out in the alley and mingle with the other great performers of Harlem who were appearing at the Lafayette, and they would be joined by visitors from all over, including a lot of white musicians.

And at least one nonmusician—a tall, skinny white kid, always impeccably dressed in a Brooks Brothers sport coat, button-down oxford shirt and tie, and well-pressed khaki slacks. In interviews after he became well known, he liked to contrast his youthful appearance with those of the musicians he was meeting. His prep-school manners, he said, cut an incongruous figure, to say the least, in Harlem night-life. Nevertheless, sipping lemonade, he became a familiar figure at the Alhambra and Lafayette theaters, Connie's Inn, and Small's Paradise, hearing the likes of Bessie Smith, Luis Russell, and J. C. Higginbotham.

If the early history of jazz is a quilt pieced together with equal parts fact and fancy, the same might be said of Hammond's early forays into Harlem. He told the stories many times, and over the years embellishments often became the foundation for further embellishments. But the main thrust of his accounts is true: that he ventured alone into neighborhoods not generally frequented by rich young white kids, searching for the music from the records he had heard in the basement on East Ninety-first Street. "I started as a record collector when I was about ten years old in 1921," he said in a 1981 television interview. "And I found a record by a piano player called James P. Johnson, and James P. Johnson wrote, well, the original 'Charleston,' and he was one of the great piano players of all time. He had a record called 'Worried

and Lonesome Blues,' which he made on the old blue label at Columbia Records in 1922, and this is the record that changed my life."

Hammond would later recall that he had to travel to Harlem to
purchase records made by his favorite black artists because none of the
downtown record stores carried them.

Emily Hammond was an enthusiastic amateur piano player, and the
Hammonds owned a box at the Metropolitan Opera House, where
the family, dressed in their evening attire, would attend productions.
Hammond was also taken to Carnegie Hall to hear classical performances by the New York Philharmonic. But he simply found something
lacking in classical music. By his own account, it didn't hit him in the
solar plexus, didn't make the hair on the back of his neck stand up, like
the raw and emotional blues of Bessie Smith. It didn't make him grin
and tap his foot, like the rollicking boogie-woogie piano of James P.
Johnson.

Jazz was having another effect on him as well, an effect that was
more cerebral than emotional. As Hammond observed in his memoirs,
as well as in numerous interviews, he sensed from an early age that
there was a reason this music was as deeply passionate as it was. It was
uniquely American music, written by and played for people who had
known the harsher realities of life firsthand. In particular, it was music
by and for people whose skin color kept them perpetually at the bottom rung of American society. Listening to this music helped awaken
Hammond to the vast class differences that separated him from the
servants in the basement.

Hammond graduated from St. Bernard's School in 1923. After a short
stint at Browning, another elite private school, Hammond, now fourteen years old, announced that he was ready to start making his own
decisions. One of his first (and one that he would later call one of the
most important of his life) concerned where he would spend the next
four years preparing for college. Already an iconoclast, he rebelled against
the plan for him to follow in his father's footsteps, first to Phillips Exeter
Academy, and then on to Yale. Hammond wanted to attend Hotchkiss,
a slightly less renowned prep school in Lakeville, Connecticut, tucked

away in the northwest corner of the state. In laying out his argument in favor of Hotchkiss, he offered up the following points: first, Exeter was too far from home, and its location in the mountains of New Hampshire promised bitter-cold winters; Hotchkiss was only two hours from New York by train. Second, his cousins Osgood and Frederick Field, his neighbors from a bit farther down Fifth Avenue, had attended Hotchkiss and returned with glowing reviews. Finally, Henry Sloane Coffin had recently moved to Lakeville, and often graced the Hotchkiss chapel with his eloquent and impassioned sermons. John Hammond, Sr., relented, and in the fall of 1925 John Hammond, Jr., began life as a Hotchkiss "prep."

Hotchkiss, founded in 1891 on about sixty-five acres of bucolic countryside in the foothills of the Berkshire Mountains, has sought over the years to separate itself from other prestigious New England prep schools by emphasizing its liberal curriculum, one that stresses personal enlightenment over individual accomplishments. "Whom do we hope to meet on the afternoon of the last commencement?" asks the rhetorical question posed in one piece of Hotchkiss literature. "Do we look for a man or a woman who has learned to trust the unique and specific value of his or her own mind? . . . Do we mean to discover individuals on the order of Thomas Paine, Thomas Jefferson or Archibald MacLeish, or do we want somebody who thinks that the sum and zenith of all human experience is a killing in the bond market and a house in Palm Beach?"

At the time Hammond attended, no one embodied the school's high-minded sense of purpose more than a young English teacher named John McChesney. Hammond and Frederick Field praised him extensively in their respective memoirs. Like his cousin, Hammond found McChesney's charismatic mix of devil-may-care insouciance and intellectual depth extremely stimulating. An avowed socialist and agnostic, McChesney took delight in challenging his students to think and live beyond the sheltered lives into which they had been born. Frederick Field wrote: "He influenced a whole generation of Hotchkiss boys. He never said, 'Get going. Grow up. Spit that gold spoon out of your mouth before you choke on it. Find out what the world is all about. Get started on your own and your friends will do all we can to help.' But without saying so in so many words, he conveyed that message."

Another role model was George Van Santvoord, the school's new headmaster, a Rhodes scholar and veteran of World War I. Upon arriving in Lakeville, a bastion of old-money Republican conservatism, Van Santvoord promptly became chairman of the local Democratic Party. These were the types of men whom John Hammond would admire throughout his life, and on whose actions and philosophies he fashioned his own persona.

Hammond played first violin in the Hotchkiss orchestra, and in the banjo club he played something called a mandobass. He was also a member of a jazz club called the Society Syncopators. During his senior year, and apparently at his urging, the banjo club performed a concert with a spiritual tinge titled "Plantation Echoes."

During his first two years at Hotchkiss, Hammond was content to adjust himself to life at boarding school while pursuing his musical education under the auspices of the school's violin instructor. But he was never entirely satisfied with his progress, and he eventually asked Van Santvoord for permission to make regular trips into New York to take lessons from Ronald Murat, a teacher in whom he had more confidence. The headmaster relented in the fall of Hammond's third year, and the teenager was allowed to take a train into the city every other weekend. "This was an unprecedented liberty. No Hotchkiss student had ever been allowed to leave school except for vacations, or to accompany his family to a nearby restaurant on Sundays," Hammond recalled. The fact that he didn't drink, smoke, or chase girls probably played an important role in Van Santvoord's decision.

As far as the headmaster knew, every other Saturday Hammond took a cab into the nearby town of Millerton, where he caught an afternoon train into New York. After arriving in the city, he dutifully attended his violin lesson, and then went home for a quiet dinner with his family. The next morning he returned by train and was back in Connecticut by early afternoon.

Inevitably, though, Hammond sneaked off to Harlem to listen to jazz. He would later claim that on the way to his very first lesson in the Morningside Heights neighborhood, south and west of Harlem, he happened to pass the Alhambra Theater, and as luck would have it, Bessie Smith was on the bill. "After my two hour lesson I went home to dinner at 91st Street, then, telling my family I was off to play string quartets, hurried uptown to hear Bessie. I had her records by then, and I considered her the greatest blues singer I had ever heard. I still do," he wrote years later. The story has been disputed by at least one biographer of Smith, who said it's unlikely that she appeared at the Alhambra during that period. It's a good story, nevertheless.

For the next two years, Van Santvoord's leniency made it possible for John to gain an unmatched musical education. "Every two weeks I traveled to New York for my lesson, then discovered the Lafayette Theater, the Club Saratoga . . . every jazz joint and speakeasy where jazz was played. I also became a much improved violinist. Needless to add, George Van Santvoord became my Hotchkiss hero."

At fifteen, Hammond sat for a photograph with his violin cradled in his lap. He looks every bit the sensitive musician. Pensive, he gazes straight ahead through soulful brown eyes set widely apart on either side of a prominent nose. His full lips reveal no trace of a smile. Wavy hair is combed to the side, held firm by handfuls of gel.

An interesting character portrait of the young man can be drawn from his senior yearbook. Hammond received one vote as "most likely to succeed" and seven votes as "most pious" and was voted far and away the "most pessimistic." He also received five votes for being "in the biggest fog," one vote for being the "most absentminded," and one for being the "class sleuth." And he was the landslide winner as the school's "worst woman hater."

One quotation under his picture in his final Hotchkiss yearbook reads: "His religion is at best an anxious wish." The other quotation reads simply, "Rationally speaking." The blind faith espoused by his mother had apparently been replaced by a wistful curiosity tinged with skepticism and born of a newfound sense of self-assurance in his own intellectual capabilities.

On a dewy late-spring morning in June 1929, the graduating class of Hotchkiss and their families gathered with the faculty in the school's chapel for a final ceremony together. While many of his graduating classmates were preparing to board cruise ships bound for Europe in order to spend a few final carefree weeks touring the Continent before entering college, Hammond had already packed his bags for a trip to Portland, Maine, where he would spend the summer working for a small newspaper. It was during those several months as a reporter in Maine that his instinct for aiding the underdog came to full bloom and he first learned to cast a critical eye in the service of one noble cause or another.

AN EDUCATION

The reporters on the *Portland Evening News* were for the most part high-school graduates, born and raised in close proximity to Portland's rough-and-tumble waterfront. Many had started out on the paper setting type, had worked their way up to the newsroom by way of a two-year stint as a copy boy, and now dreamed of covering City Hall. To these men the eighteen-year-old John Hammond must have presented an incongruous figure. Here was a wealthy New York City kid with a penchant for khaki slacks and blue blazers, driving an Oldsmobile convertible, just recently graduated from one of the nation's finest prep schools, newly arrived in their harbor town to spend the summer working for the grand sum of about twenty dollars a week.

One of the first places Hammond visited in Portland was a barbershop. There he requested the removal of nearly all of the tangled, gooey mess that was his hair and walked out sporting a crew cut, a style that wouldn't become popular for another twenty years.

At the *Evening News*, Hammond received no special favors, he recalled in his autobiography. He started out as a proofreader, checking reams of copy for misspellings and stray commas. He pored over society columns, wedding notices, and obituaries to make sure some prominent local figure's name wasn't spelled differently from one paragraph to the next. (Obituaries needed particular attention, he learned. Misquoting the mayor was far less egregious than misspelling the name of some recently deceased local.) His editors rewarded his diligence by sending him out of the office to cover Rotary Club breakfasts and Chamber of Commerce luncheons, as well as the usual assortment of fires, car wrecks, and criminal disturbances that make up the bulk of a small-town newspaper's police blotter. The pace was frenetic, the hours long, and the pay horrendous. Hammond loved every minute of it. "I traveled all over the state looking for stories and got my share of scoops," he wrote.

It was here along the rocky coast of southern Maine that John Hammond began actively seeking answers to the troubling questions of social justice. Years later he would recall with pride an article he wrote that summer that described the terrible conditions in which Maine's indigenous Indian tribes were forced to live. Like any eager young reporter, after hearing accounts of the Indians' plight, he decided to go out and see for himself if what he had heard was true. So he drove his Oldsmobile into the dense forests west of Portland, up muddy, unpaved roads onto the reservations of the Penobscot and Old Town tribes. What he found there appalled him. The Catholic priests who essentially ran the reservations lived in relative luxury and preached in impressively constructed churches. But the Native Americans to whom the priests' sermons were delivered lived in virtual squalor with no electricity or running water.

The situation infuriated Hammond, and his path was established; casting a critical eye in the service of one crusade or another appealed directly to his instinct toward rebellion and reform and would remain a lifelong vocation. "I did an exposé of the situation which made the front page of the paper and I learned something about myself: I write best when I am angry, when protesting injustice, criticizing bad music or uncaring musicians," he wrote years later.

The man responsible for bringing Hammond to Maine was the *Evening News*'s editor, Ernest Gruening. Hammond had written to Gruening seeking a job after reading an article about Gruening's efforts to keep the reform-minded paper afloat in conservative southeastern Maine. A Hotchkiss man himself, Gruening invited Hammond up for the summer. With the advantage of hindsight, it seems hardly a coincidence that the two took a shine to each other. Like Hammond,

Gruening came from a wealthy background and was a maverick thinker and a passionate risk taker. Gruening was born in 1887 to a well-to-do family in New York City. After graduating from Harvard Medical School, he decided against following his father into medicine and instead chose a career in journalism. During the 1920s, he wrote for and served as editor of two of America's leading progressive publications, the *New York Tribune* and *The Nation* magazine. Toward the end of the decade he moved to Portland to help breathe life into the fledgling *Evening News*.

The course of Hammond's life was indelibly altered by the few short months he spent chasing down stories as a poorly paid cub reporter in the Maine hinterlands. When he arrived at Yale that September, he felt the experience had set him apart from most of his classmates. In his rather harsh judgment, they were frivolous, blissfully immersed in an endless routine of football games and fraternity parties. He was a young man with a sense of purpose, even a mission—a mission that Yale came to stand in the way of.

A legendary Depression-era story that has been passed on from writer to writer and historian to historian goes something like this: Not long after the stock market crash in October 1929, a group of wealthy Harvard undergraduates gathered in the basement of a tiny Boston tavern to bid one another farewell before heading home for the holidays. It was a cold and blustery evening, and thick snowflakes blew in swirls past the window of the pub. Inside, the young men, dressed in the finest wool and cashmere, made merry around a large oak table placed strategically in front of a tall and roaring fireplace. They braced themselves for the cold by downing healthy portions of single-malt scotch whiskey and rivers of expensive French wine. "This is all too good to be true," one exclaimed, lifting his glass in a toast. "Yes, yes, I heartily agree," another concurred. Then, in a moment of sardonic genius, a third conceived of a way to put their splendid moment into proper perspective. "I've got it. I've got it. I know just what's missing," he uttered, then rushed out into the cold and on a nearby corner found two young beggars, a brother and sister, no more than eight or nine years old, shivering and dressed in rags. As the story goes, the wealthy young Harvard man paid them a dollar each to stand outside the window, runny noses pressed to the glass, so that the young merrymakers inside could gaze out upon them now and then and recognize their own good fortune.

The story is almost certainly just a story. But what's interesting about it is that the student who came up with the idea of posting the two beggars at the window was said to be Frederick Field, Hammond's cousin and role model—an assertion Field strongly denied.

Always at pains not to be labeled a member of the idle rich, Hammond arrived at Yale in the fall of 1929 determined to stand out. "After my summer in Portland, returning to formal education and the society of my contemporaries was a letdown. My classmates were interested in sports, in girls, in undergraduate weekends. Once again I was the oddball in the group. I believe I am the only Yale undergraduate who never saw a Saturday football game, who never attended a postgame dance."

Hammond would drop out of Yale, much to the consternation of his father, after less than two years in New Haven. A recurring case of jaundice forced him to withdraw mid-semester in the winter of 1930. The prospect of having to repeat a semester of classes contributed to his decision not to return: that and the fact that on weekend visits to New York a musician friend, the bassist Artie Bernstein, had begun introducing him around at the Manhattan music studios.

Hammond may not have been at Yale long, but he used his time there to explore an area of his ancestry that would remain something of an obsession with him for the rest of his life: namely, the belief that his family tree included a branch or two of Jewish blood. At a New Haven appearance of the Boston Symphony for a performance of Ravel's *Boléro*, Hammond met a young rabbi named Edgar Siskin, recently arrived in Connecticut from the Hebrew Theological Seminary in Cincinnati. The two hit it off, and Siskin invited Hammond to make what was his first visit to a synagogue. Hammond described the visit in his memoirs:

I went in and sat down to see what would happen. Spotlights came on, illuminating the Arc [*sic*] of the Covenant and, as he stepped to the pulpit, the rabbi himself. He was lit up like a vaudeville star. Later he explained that because the synagogue was so unattractive and because the services were usually at night, when no one could see a stained glass window or much of the architecture, he had hired Alexander McCandless, the lighting expert of the Yale drama school, to install indirect lighting. The $10,000 he had been allowed for renovation of the building was insufficient to make much improvement, so McCandless illuminated the congregation's best-looking asset—Rabbi Siskin.

The rabbi's clever nod to show business impressed Hammond, and the two became fast friends, spending long hours during Hammond's first year at Yale discussing jazz and classical music.

It was through Siskin that Hammond finally met his Mount Kisco neighbors the Meyers. Eugene Meyer, a wealthy businessman (he would later own *The Washington Post*), had purchased the plot of land next door to the Hammonds in the mid-1920s and promptly built a gigantic house that needed a water tower to operate its indoor plumbing. The eyesore offended the Hammonds, and the two families remained standoffish for years. On a weekend visit to the Hammonds, Rabbi Siskin mentioned to John that he was teaching one of the Meyer boys the history of the Jewish faith. It turned out that Bill Meyer was also a student at Yale, and the rabbi arranged a social gathering so he and Hammond could meet. They did, and John and the Meyer children remained friends for decades thereafter. In particular, Hammond was impressed by the athletic Katharine, who, after marrying a young newspaper executive named Phil Graham, would become one of the great newspaper figures of the century. Shortly before her death in 2001, she recalled Hammond's iconoclasm. "You know John always had to be in opposition to everything. I think he wanted to go in the opposite direction of his family. He used to tell people he was Jewish. He was overtly against everything establishment, and he sort of nourished that. He liked to shock."

After dropping out of college, Hammond moved back to his parents' home on East Ninety-first Street and began to pursue a career in the music industry. First he needed a couple of months to fully recover from the illness that had weakened him in New Haven. But soon he was establishing himself as a regular within New York City's flourishing jazz scene. He tagged along with Artie Bernstein, a close friend with whom he played viola in an amateur chamber music group, when Bernstein worked as bassist on jazz recording sessions, and at night the two made the rounds of the hot Harlem nightspots. A favorite was Small's Paradise at 135th Street and Seventh Avenue.

Hammond's wealth allowed him to travel abroad in search of opportunities as well. During a trip to England in the summer of 1931 to visit his sister Alice, who was married to a member of Parliament, Hammond met the English critic and bandleader Patrick "Spike" Hughes. The two jazz enthusiasts hit it off immediately, and Hughes would later recall being charmed in particular by Alice Hammond Duckworth. Despite their wealth and status, Hughes found the brother and sister anything but stuffy. At Alice's country estate outside London, Hughes, John, and Alice listened to Bessie Smith records and passed the time in lively conversation. Hughes eventually asked Hammond to serve as American correspondent for *Melody Maker*, a widely read English jazz magazine for which Hughes served as chief record critic.

Upon returning to the United States, Hammond decided he was ready to make the leap from obsessive fan to actual record producer. At age twenty, he had been listening to and collecting jazz records for ten years. And through his visits to recording studios with Artie Bernstein and his forays into Harlem, he was developing contacts with a growing number of the city's working musicians. What's more, he was getting paid to proffer his opinions on jazz for a well-respected music publication. But he still felt like he was on the outside looking in. "I fervently wanted to enter the record business," he later wrote of that period. "But I had no experience and no idea where to begin. My credentials were no more than a love for jazz, a growing acquaintance with many of its players, and a toehold as a writer for an English music publication." So he took matters into his own hands. He withdrew several hundred dollars from the bank and purchased a block of time at a New York recording studio operated by the Columbia Phonograph Company. For $125 he could record four record sides at five minutes each. In his memoirs, Hammond said he chose Columbia for no other reason than that it was the company for which Bessie Smith recorded. At the time, Columbia was one of three record companies—RCA Victor and Brunswick were the others—that dominated the industry.

As his first protégé, he chose a flashy gay pianist named Garland Wilson. Hammond had met Wilson in a Harlem nightspot called the Covan, whose front door was near the stage entrance to the Lafayette Theater, and the two recorded together in a Manhattan studio for the first time on September 11, 1931. The songs were never released. Undaunted, Hammond returned to the studio with Wilson in February 1932. In one of his earliest columns for *Melody Maker*, published in March 1932, he wrote of the second Wilson sessions: "I was in the studio at the time he made them and can testify to their worth." The comment is noteworthy for two reasons: first, because he failed to mention that he underwrote the recordings, which would have revealed an obvious conflict of interest; second, because it was apparently the first time he used the phrase "I was in the studio at the time" in print. He would use it so much over the next few years it became a running joke among his friends and associates. The sessions produced another batch of forgettable tunes, but Hammond's technique must have been improving—Columbia released the songs on its subsidiary Okeh, which specialized in so-called race records, geared toward blacks.

It may be that Hammond was unimpressed with the sides, since in interviews years later he didn't refer to himself as producer of the Garland Wilson recordings. He saved that distinction for his first sessions with Fletcher Henderson. Held on December 9, 1932, the Henderson sessions marked the beginning of an important relationship between the two men, one that would have significant impact on the direction of jazz. It is no wonder that Hammond liked to think his career had started with them.

"My first recording session as producer was with Fletcher Henderson's band for the American Columbia Phonograph Company in a studio at 55 Fifth Avenue," he recalled. The session was scheduled for 10:00 a.m., he remembered, "and the last guy finally straggled in at 12:40 p.m." Hammond was furious, but not in a position to scold Henderson and his band. Besides, Hammond had prior knowledge of Henderson's maddeningly enigmatic approach to his music.

Henderson is generally regarded as the architect of the big-band sound that had emerged in the late 1920s and was coming to be known as swing. Henderson's application of bright and energetic rhythms to the same orchestral arrangements played oozingly by hugely popular orchestras led by white bandleaders caused a sea change in the direction of popular music. The bouncier new style essentially split the popular-music world down the middle: on the one side stood the so-called sweet bands led by men such as Paul Whiteman and Guy Lombardo, and on the other the hot bands led by Henderson and his disciples, including Chick Webb and later Benny Carter and Don Redman, among many others. Henderson was by most accounts a lackadaisical bandleader and an even worse businessman. Jazz historians argue that he never fully recovered from a serious auto accident in 1928. That, coupled with the difficult economic times—for black musicians in particular—had by late 1932 left Henderson and his bandmates in dire financial straits. Consequently, they were eager to accept a recording offer from an up-start producer. As with the Garland Wilson sessions, Hammond rented the studio time and paid the musicians' salaries. Columbia, or one of its subsidiaries, would arrange for distribution if it deemed the records commercially viable.

When the last of Fletcher's musicians finally arrived, there was only forty-five minutes of rented studio time left. They made three sides, one of which was the well-known Fats Waller tune "Honeysuckle Rose." In addition, Catherine Handy, the daughter of the blues song-writer and promoter W. C. Handy, sang a song called "Underneath the Harlem Moon." (Hammond hated the song for its racist lyrics, which refer to cotton pickers and "darkies" who do little but drink gin. He later joked that Henderson must have been bribed by a song promoter to record it.)

It was on the third song recorded that day that Fletcher and his bandmates fully reminded Hammond why he took the trouble to or-ganize the session. The band's smoking version of "New King Porter Stomp" is considered by many one of Fletcher's finest efforts in a recording studio. Hammond noted presciently (but again without mentioning his own involvement) in his *Melody Maker* column a few months later, "Not so long ago Fletcher and his band made 'King

Porter's Stomp' [*sic*] . . . If that comes out, it may rightly be considered one of the most important discs ever made."

On the occasion of his twenty-first birthday on December 15, 1931, Hammond asserted his independence by moving out of the family mansion and into a small apartment in Greenwich Village. He was determined not to follow the well-traveled course of other affluent young men whose wealth was handed down generation to generation—fancy prep school, Ivy League degree, law school, and, finally, Wall Street boardroom. The mentors Hammond had sought out at Hotchkiss, men who had urged him to think and act independently, had kindled an already-active spark of self-reliance. Earning a paycheck as a reporter in Maine had only strengthened that inclination. His brief stay at Yale further convinced him that the knowledge he sought couldn't be found in a classroom.

Of course, Hammond's independence was bankrolled by a Vanderbilt-channeled annual trust-fund allowance of about twelve thousand dollars a year, quite a bit of money during the lowest point of the Depression—around the same amount high-level corporate executives were paid at the time. But the adult Hammond didn't view his inherited wealth with any measure of guilt or as a justification for idleness. To the contrary, he unself-consciously used his inheritance to create opportunities for himself, and he never shrank from the charge that he had used his wealth to buy his way into the music industry. Indeed, he made light of it. The staff at Columbia whom he approached about renting studio time for his earliest recordings "must have thought I was a nut," he wrote, "albeit a nut with money who should not be ignored while the company was struggling for survival." Hammond viewed the money as a tool, which, if used properly, would enable him to pursue his two great obsessions—making music and promoting social reform.

AN EMERGING VOICE

A s a wealthy young dilettante with no steady job, Hammond was able to throw himself into the vibrant mix of art, literature, and politics that infused Greenwich Village in the early 1930s. He became a regular at parties attended by such progressive literary luminaries as Theodore Dreiser, John Dos Passos, Edmund Wilson, and Malcolm Cowley, where he felt at home among like-minded intellectuals who viewed the arts as a means of achieving social reform. At the same time, he was becoming ubiquitous within the city's burgeoning jazz scene.

It was a frenetic lifestyle, perfectly suited to his interests and boundless energy. As the jazz writer Otis Ferguson put it a few years later, "Drop into almost any night club, uptown, downtown, or across, any recording date or broadcast or audition or rehearsal, and if you stick around long enough, you are almost sure to see John Henry Hammond, Jr., in the flesh, if briefly."

There he was in the front row of a battle of the bands at the Savoy Ballroom in Harlem, teeth bared behind a giant horsey grin, his head bobbing in time to the music as Chick Webb, the leader of the Savoy's house band, vanquished another challenger—Fletcher Henderson's band perhaps, or maybe Don Redman's outfit. Afterward, he might head off to hear some new singer or piano player at a downtown nightclub, where one of two things would happen: he would either enthusiastically applaud the performance or bury his head behind that day's *New York Times*, a technique he often employed to show disdain for a performer. He was rarely indifferent. Later the same night, he might be found at an intimate speakeasy in some less frequented section of Harlem watching two horn players joust in a "cutting contest" during a late-night jam session. The next day, there he'd be again, leaning against the wall of a midtown recording studio, arms folded across his chest, listening intently to many of the same musicians he had seen perform onstage the night before.

But what Hammond really wanted was to solidify a niche of his own, a place where he could actively participate in the creative process while at the same time satisfy his yearning to help bring about social reform. He knew that the entertainment industry—music, specifically— would be the broad mechanism by which he would seek to effect these changes. What he was looking for was the most effective tool within that larger apparatus to assist him in implementing his plan. There would be a couple of false starts before things began falling into place for him.

In early 1932, Hammond used part of his inheritance to join two other investors in opening a vaudeville-style theater in Manhattan. Their original plan was to open a theater in Times Square, and Hammond was quick to promote the idea to his *Melody Maker* readers: "There have been some exciting tales about a permanent Negro theater to be established on Broadway . . . This theater, if it ever materializes, should become enormously successful, and change many things in the music world." Hammond and his partners hoped to create a splash, but there was apparently very little water at their disposal. First, Louis Armstrong declined an offer to perform on opening night. Next, the investors decided to move from heavily traversed Times Square to avoid a head-to-head competition with a burlesque hall offering "very cheap prices" that was opening directly across Broadway. They eventually settled on an eighteen-hundred-seat venue called the Public Theater, located downtown at Fourth Street and Second Avenue. Hammond was determined to showcase talented black musicians for a downtown audience not familiar with the Harlem music scene. He especially hoped to stage performances that would jettison much of the conventional vaudeville song-and-dance shtick that, in his opinion, had long since passed from cliché to parody. In its place, he proposed shows whose focus was on the music rather than on tired slapstick gags and scantily dressed showgirls.

In his memoirs, Hammond claimed that his efforts to redefine the vaudevillian variety show were rebuffed by a business partner who was more concerned with profit margins than social agendas. Disgusted, Hammond backed out of the partnership, he said, shortly after the theater opened on April 15, 1932. But there was apparently much more to the story. Under the headline "The Negro Theater Flops," Hammond's June 1932 *Meloddy Maker* column reported that the venue shut down after just two weeks, having been "grotesquely mismanaged for the most part." He complained that the band he had hired, Fletcher Henderson's orchestra, once the toast of Harlem but by 1932 an undisciplined outfit struggling under Henderson's shaky leadership, showed up late most days and had to be fired after the first week. Moreover, just a few days after the theater opened, a mysterious fire broke out backstage—around the same time Hammond became aware of "a large shrinkage in the corporation's finances."

Did he quit in defense of a principle, or did the entire enterprise fail miserably on its own merits? Hammond would make a habit of citing some unacceptable social injustice whenever a job didn't work out. In any case, it was an inauspicious debut, but not without at least two redeeming aspects. The connection with Fletcher Henderson would prove to be valuable to both men. And Hammond struck up a friendship with the dissident Russian filmmaker Sergei Eisenstein, who showed up unexpectedly on opening night.

Next he tried radio. While promoting the Public Theater, Hammond had stopped by the Lower East Side offices of a radio station owned by the *Jewish Daily Forward*, a newspaper published for immigrants newly arrived in the United States. The station's call letters were WEVD, which stood for the initials of the five-time Socialist presidential candidate Eugene V. Debs. When Hammond paid a visit to purchase advertising time, the station's owners offered him a nonpaying job as a disc jockey. He accepted, and used his on-air time both to promote the Public Theater during its brief run and to spin selections from his extensive jazz collection. Soon he had introduced a live weekly jam session that was broadcast each Saturday night from WEVD's downtown studio. He was never shy about using his *Melody Maker* column to promote his own products. His July 1932 column read: "Over a small radio station in New York there is a weekly hour of race stuff which is pretty grand . . . There are no restrictions at all as far as the style is concerned; it is all strictly impromptu, and without regard for clock. With mediocre men such an experiment would be disastrous, but this programme over WEVD is anything but that."

The station managers allowed Hammond to do whatever he wanted, as long as he was willing to pay. Since he had no advertising sponsor, Hammond paid each of the musicians ten dollars per show out of his own pocket. It wasn't the last time he would use his own money to cover the costs of a musical enterprise he deemed worthy.

Now his nightly journeys across the city's jazz landscape were starting to pay off. By that time a regular at the Lafayette Theater, Connie's Inn, and Small's Paradise, he was starting to earn a reputation as a dedicated and knowledgeable jazz fan—and, perhaps more important, a fan with enough money to make sure the show went on. This reputation helped him recruit some top-notch talent for his weekly jam sessions. The bandleaders Fletcher Henderson, Chick Webb, and Benny Carter, the pianist Art Tatum, the saxophone player Chu Berry, and the bassist Artie Bernstein all performed on the show.

During Hammond's tenure at WEVD, the station moved its transmitting studio out of the Broadway Central Hotel downtown to the fancier Claridge Hotel at Forty-fourth Street and Broadway. According to Hammond, the Claridge management promptly barred the black musicians he hired for his jam sessions from using the hotel's front elevators. Instead, they had to use the service elevator in the rear. WEVD's owners couldn't afford to oppose the humiliating discrimination, so, by Hammond's own account, he quit in protest. "Down at WEVD we were developing a magnificent get-off band . . . But some very nasty incidents caused the cessation of the programmes through no fault of the station or the band," he wrote.

Hammond's version of his departure from WEVD fit an emerging pattern: he would take a job and seek to effect some societal change, only to be thwarted by others, usually due to their ignorance or out-right racism. It's difficult to verify the details of these accounts, but the formula didn't go unnoticed by his peers. Otis Ferguson saw it and wrote, "He has no job—or say he has twenty in the course of a year, some of them existing mainly in his anticipation, some going into an ac-tual matter of weeks . . . Every place he goes he presently spies the taint of commercialism in art or the sordid hand of capitalism clutching workers. He burns. He speaks out. And then he *is* out."

At a party attended by Hammond and his progressive literati friends in early 1932, an opportunity arose that led to his first active role as an advocate for civil rights. John Dos Passos and some other left-leaning writers were organizing a trip into the hills of southeastern Kentucky to deliver supplies to striking coal miners. The miners had been seeking to form a union to improve their dreadful working conditions. When the owners forbade it, the workers dropped their picks and shovels and walked out of the mines. The operators hoped to starve the striking workers back into the ground by preventing supplies from reaching them. Hammond was asked to join the delegation of writers head-ing south from New York to deliver food and clothing and to publi-cize the miners' plight. Unencumbered by a full-time job, he had time on his hands and, more important to the organizers of the trip, money and a car. "The fact that I had my own car made me especially welcome on the journey, and it was because of the car that we achieved what little we did," he wrote decades later. The group dubbed themselves the Delegation for Independent Miners' Relief Committee. Hammond's account of their trip is as follows: After pick-ing up supplies in Knoxville, Tennessee, the group, which included the critic Edmund Wilson and the novelist Waldo Frank, crossed the Ken-tucky border and headed up into the hills toward the mining town of Pineville. Sheriff's deputies, no doubt on the payroll of the mine oper-ators, stopped the caravan at the county line and confiscated food sup-plies intended for out-of-work miners and their families. When the Northerners protested, the deputies got violent and started making ar-rests. Hammond claimed he was able to escape back to Knoxville with a cameraman who had filmed the incident and, once in Knoxville, was able to get the film processed. The images, according to Hammond's version, were eventually seen throughout the United States, raising awareness and sympathy for the plight of the miners.

Edmund Wilson, who wrote of the trip in his diary just hours after the events occurred, told essentially the same story but in far greater detail. Fifteen years older and quite a bit more jaded than Hammond, Wilson viewed the experience more as a study in frustration than as a riveting tale of bravery. "The whole thing was very interesting for us— though I don't know that it did much for the miners," he wrote in a letter to Dos Passos.

By Wilson's account, the group spent several anxious days arguing with local officials over the Northern activists' constitutionally guaranteed rights, as well as other legal and philosophical matters that were apparently of little concern to the governing authorities in the mining towns of southeastern Kentucky. Several truckloads of food and supplies were eventually distributed, but not without incident. At one point, according to Wilson, Malcolm Cowley prevented a group of armed deputies from breaking into a truck that contained supplies of sugar. The delegation was eventually led out of town by a vigilante posse. "We're not going to harm ye, but we're going to take you out of Kentucky and we don't want ye never to come back again," one large, slow-talking local promised. Notwithstanding that promise, two members of the group—Waldo Frank and the labor lawyer Allan Taub— were beaten bloody when the vigilante escort reached the Kentucky state line.

Wilson characterized Hammond as "like somebody who had modeled himself on Proust, then received an injection of Communism," and as a careless driver who "missed his directions, didn't stop where he was supposed to and wait for the others and the trucks." Later, Hammond apparently argued with another member of the Northern delegation because he wanted to play a few songs on a jukebox and, for some reason not explained by Wilson, the others did not.

Whatever the results, the trip gave Hammond his first taste of frontline activism and opened other doors. His connections with progressive literary types brought him back into contact with his former editor Ernest Gruening. Gruening had left Maine and returned to New York and *The Nation*, a magazine written by the same progressives with whom Hammond now found himself socializing. Gruening introduced Hammond to Walter White, president of the National Association for the Advancement of Colored People. Hammond liked White immediately and agreed to donate money but declined White's offer to join the NAACP's board because, as he claimed years later, he doubted whether White's organization was militant enough in its opposition to segregation.

Early in 1933, Gruening asked Hammond to travel for *The Nation* into the Deep South to cover the second trial of a group of young black migrant workers charged with raping two white girls on a freight train outside Scottsboro, Alabama. One of the most sensational and well-publicized civil rights episodes of the past century, the Scottsboro trials were followed closely by Hammond's crowd of liberal activists. Again his car came in handy. In his autobiography, he recalled heading south in a brand-new Hudson with two other New York journalists. He was paid fifty dollars by *The Nation*, barely enough to cover his expenses. But what he didn't make in cold hard cash he would earn back through the exposure to a national readership; and, more important, the trial gave him an opportunity to see for himself the systematic mistreatment of blacks at the hands of the Southern power structure.

The dynamics of the Scottsboro case presented an almost-perfect forum for Hammond to air his views on ignorance, intolerance, and institutional racism. Here were nine black boys arrested, convicted, and sentenced to death for allegedly raping two white girls aboard a freight train rumbling through northern Alabama on the morning of March 25, 1931. The testimony of the two white accusers at the boys' first trial was, by most objective accounts, almost laughable in terms of the contradictions in their stories and the degree of implausibility given the physical evidence gathered by investigators. In the first place, neither girl showed any sign of being physically assaulted, yet both claimed to have been brutally and repeatedly raped. The girls positively identified each of the nine boys as participants in the attack, yet one of the accused was so racked with syphilis that he could barely walk let alone participate in a gang rape. Moreover, a doctor testified that neither girl seemed in shock, or even emotionally distraught, in the hours just after they claimed to have been attacked, an extraordinary level of composure given their accusations. It was obvious to Northern progressive observers that the two women had charged rape out of some misguided fear of a loss of reputation after being discovered riding the rails with a large group of black teenage boys. It was also obvious that one of the young women, a tough prostitute from Huntsville, Alabama, named Victoria Price, reveled in the attention. Price's friend and co-accuser, a far more reticent young woman named Ruby Bates, eventually recanted her story. Yet none of these factors prevented numerous Southern juries from repeatedly convicting the boys and sentencing them to death over a five-year period. As the appeals process ground forward all the way to the U.S. Supreme Court, the actual charges against the Scottsboro boys became almost beside the point. The Northern and international press portrayed the legal fray as nothing less than a struggle by an aging and anachronistic society to preserve its way of life.

Into this seething cauldron walked John Hammond, wearing an expensive suit and carrying a stack of his favorite left-wing magazines—*The New Republic, New Masses, The Nation*—under his arm.

The retrial of the Scottsboro boy Haywood Patterson opened on March 27, 1933, in Decatur, Alabama, having been moved from Scottsboro at the request of defense attorneys. Right after lunch, Hammond joined the other white newsmen at a hastily constructed table set up just in front of the spectators' section and off to the side from the judge's bench. Nearby, at a separate table, sat two black newsmen covering the trial. For two weeks they all listened intently as the trial progressed toward its inevitable conclusion. On April 9, 1933, Haywood Patterson was once again found guilty of raping the two white girls and was sentenced to death in the electric chair.

When court was out of session, Hammond wandered the streets of Decatur, and in his *Nation* piece he characterized the place as "a quiet Alabama town, perhaps a little busier than the average . . . The town does not belong to the old South; its houses are modern and nondescript, as are its public buildings. Its upper class is not of the 'aristocracy.'" The piece attempted to illustrate Hammond's decidedly

Northern point of view, which held that the Southern landscape might be moving forward with the advance of time but the Southern mindset was not.

Hammond's reporting appeared in *The Nation* on April 26, 1933. "The South Speaks" ran alongside a full-page editorial cartoon in which a black man, his head slung low, stands before a stern-looking jury of twelve white men, while in the rear of the jury box stands a man wearing a white hood bearing the words "race hatred." The caption underneath the cartoon reads, "The Thirteenth Juror." Hammond and *The Nation* made no attempt to hide their outrage and frustration. In a passage used by historians to illustrate the heavy odds against the defendants, Hammond described one of the prosecutors, a big country lawyer named Wade Wright, as

> a huge individual, blustering and bullying, a perfect barometer of the less enlightened Decatur opinion. When he speaks his face becomes purple and he imparts his frenzy to the court hangers on. Until Wright spoke, many of the newspapermen felt that there was an outside chance for acquittal, at least a hung jury. But Wright registered to perfection the repressed feelings and prejudices of the twelve good men. From then on the defense was helpless.

Notwithstanding the outcome, Hammond sought to find some good in the episode. Thus he portrayed the trial as a catalyst for black activism in the face of an egregious miscarriage of justice. He argued, for example, that Decatur's working-class blacks showed increased confidence after several members of the town's black elite took the stand to discredit Alabama's jury selection process, which systematically barred African-Americans from participation.

The experience in Alabama had a profound effect on Hammond. The impact was clear in the tone of his *Melody Maker* column, written in the days immediately after he returned to New York from covering the trial. The boyish enthusiasm so evident in much of his early music criticism was replaced—temporarily at least—by a seething indignation. "For the last two weeks I have been down in Alabama, watching one of the most ghastly travesties of justice our country has ever known—the trial of the Scottsboro boys. The jury's verdict of guilty, though expected, has shocked me out of my usual equanimity, and I am writing on the subject with far too much vigor in a local sheet."

His anger would serve him well. The *Nation* articles, well written, sharply analytic, and clearly opinionated, helped put John Hammond on the map.

One of the first black musicians with whom Hammond developed a close friendship was Benny Carter, a former Fletcher Henderson sideman. Impressed by Carter's ability on the alto saxophone, Hammond in the spring of 1932 asked him to play in an all-star pickup band— "almost the best band ever, an interracial affair," was his own description—he was pulling together for a Memorial Day dance "in a snotty country club" near the Hammonds' country home in Mount Kisco. It was the first such all star lineup that Hammond assembled, and it was hardly by chance that the band consisted of both black and white players. He was determined to push integration from his earliest involvement in music. Joining Carter for the gig were three other black musicians, the piano player Fats Waller, the trumpet player Frankie Newton, and the drummer Zutty Singleton, and three white musicians, Artie Bernstein on bass, Pee Wee Russell on clarinet, and Eddie Condon on guitar.

Carter, a talented composer who excelled on several instruments, had recently stepped out on his own and was rehearsing a new band that he planned to lead. Hammond liked what he heard at the first rehearsals he attended in July. Employing the hyperbole that would emerge as his signature voice as a critic, he predicted in his *Melody Maker* column that Carter's new band might soon prove more popular than Louis Armstrong's. "If I were not ashamed of my enthusiasm I should pour out countless superlatives about this group."

In Carter, Hammond found a willing tour guide to places that might have otherwise proved inaccessible to a white man. Hammond had grown proficient at mingling with black musicians on their turf, but there were limits to his access. Some black musicians and club owners would simply never trust a white man without his first being vouched for by another black man. Hammond's friendship with Carter helped to break down those few remaining barriers. A bond developed that transcended the color of their skins and their musical ambitions. Among his black friends, only Carter shared with him "things that nobody else that I knew would tell a white guy." "[He] had as much influence on me as almost anybody that I knew," Hammond recalled. In Hammond, Carter found an enthusiastic fan and supporter, and one who could open a few doors of his own. In addition to the Mount Kisco country club gig, Hammond arranged for Carter's new band to appear in a star-laden lineup during an October 1932 benefit held in Harlem to raise money for the defense of the Scottsboro boys. Duke Ellington, W. C. Handy, and the blues singer Monette Moore also appeared. Hammond quickly became a regular at Carter's recording sessions as well. "I was down at Victor last week when Benny Carter made some sides," he wrote. "They are good, but the drums were placed right next to the microphone, with the result that Sidney [Catlett] had to play down. So if there isn't enough swing, blame it on the recording officials."

Hammond got the chance to record Carter himself on a handful of sides for English Columbia in March 1933. The songs are memorable for no other reason really than that they represent Carter's first recordings made with a band that he himself had organized and led, and because they were just the second recordings on which Hammond served as producer.

As a critic, fledgling producer, and go-to guy when local concert organizers were looking for a quality pickup band, Hammond was starting to gain a firm footing in the music industry. He would soon add another title to his résumé—that of talent scout. It was the maturation of that final element, an intangible quality that can't be purchased with a trust fund, that by the end of 1933 would allow Hammond to orchestrate some of the most important recording sessions in the history of jazz.

DISCOVERY

On a cold, clear night in February 1933, Hammond went out on the town alone in search of music. Heading up Broadway toward Harlem in a Hudson convertible (he kept the top up in the winter), he fought traffic, but as he passed Columbia University, he was flying. At 133rd Street, he took a right and headed east toward Lenox Avenue. He pulled over after a few blocks and parked in a space a few doors up from a new speakeasy run by Monette Moore, the singer who had appeared with Ellington and Carter at the fund-raiser for the Scottsboro boys he had helped organize the previous fall. Moore had built a successful career in the 1920s, but the Depression had cut into sales of her records.

Hammond made the trip up to Harlem on this particular night, he later claimed, because he wanted to see Moore perform in the comfort of her own establishment. He was a fan of Moore's and had also recruited her to sing at his short-lived vaudeville theater on the Lower East Side. It's possible that Moore personally invited him up to her new speakeasy. Another version of this story holds that he headed to Moore's that night because his friend the singer Mildred Bailey had told him there might be some other interesting talent on the bill. In any case, it would prove a watershed evening for him.

Speakeasies, especially those in the rougher sections of the city, opened and closed with the same frequency as cargo ships pulling in and out of New York harbor. A club owner might open and close in several different locations within the span of a few months, usually one step ahead of the authorities. To get inside Moore's speakeasy, patrons walked down a flight of stairs and entered the dimly lit club through a front entrance manned by one or two large bouncers. The club hadn't been open long, and it wouldn't stay open much longer.

After rapping at the door a couple of times, Hammond waited a few moments while the bouncer on the other side gave him the once-over from behind a thin viewing slot cut into the door at eye level. The bouncer at Moore's that night didn't recognize Hammond, but the young white guy with the flattop crew cut waiting in the cold was well dressed and seemed at ease in his surroundings. The door opened and Hammond walked inside. He made his way to the rear of the club and ordered a brandy to warm himself. Glancing around at the other patrons, mostly well-dressed blacks from Harlem's upper crust but also a few white hipsters in Harlem for the night, he lit a cigarette and waited for the show to begin.

As it happened, Moore would not perform that night. She either was sick or had been called away as a last-minute substitute for Ethel Waters, for whom she was serving as understudy in a musical down on Broadway. But the sight of Moore's replacement, Hammond later said, took his breath away. She couldn't have been more than seventeen or eighteen years old. But her elegance and composure belied her youth. Dressed in an evening gown, she emerged from the dressing room and moved gracefully but with purpose across the floor through the array of small tables. She stopped at the piano, where she conferred quietly with her accompanist. Hammond was immediately struck by the young woman's abundant beauty. He was also greatly affected by her presence; she commanded attention—and she hadn't even begun to sing.

Then she did sing—and it was extraordinary. "I just absolutely was overwhelmed," Hammond told the disc jockey Ed Beach in a 1973 interview. One of the first numbers she did was a silly, slightly suggestive tune called "Wouldja for a Big Red Apple?" "She was not a blues singer, but she sang popular songs in a manner that made them completely her own. She had an uncanny ear, an excellent memory for lyrics, and she sang with an exquisite sense of phrasing. She always loved [Louis] Armstrong's sound and it is not too much to say that she sang the way he played horn . . . I decided that night that she was the best jazz singer I had ever heard."

When telling the story of how he "discovered" Billie Holiday, Hammond always cited serendipity as the primary factor in his chancing upon her that night. "My discovery of Billie Holiday was the kind of accident I dreamed of, the sort of reward I received now and then by traveling to every place where anyone performed," he wrote.

Holiday had been singing in small clubs around New York for at least two years before filling in for Moore that night in Harlem. Her first biographer, John Chilton, quoted a tenor saxophonist named Kenneth Hollon, who remembered playing club dates with her in a joint called the Gray Dawn on Jamaica Avenue in Queens in late 1930 or early 1931. Thus, despite her youth, she was an experienced performer at the time Hammond ran into her.

She was born in Baltimore on April 7, 1915, to teenage parents. The first paragraph of her 1956 autobiography reads famously: "Mom and Pop were just a couple of kids when they got married. He was eighteen, she was sixteen, and I was three." Her name was Eleanora Fagan, and her childhood was apparently marked by neglect and incidents of physical and sexual abuse. By the time she arrived in New York in her mid-teens, she was streetwise beyond the experiences of most other girls her age. Moreover, she was a big girl who carried herself with the poise of a much older woman. Thus it's easy to see how she was able to talk her way into professional singing gigs with much older musicians. She also had connections in the music industry: her father played guitar in Fletcher Henderson's band.

At some point, probably in her early teens, she smoked her first joint. Apparently she liked it. It helped take the edge off an otherwise harsh existence. Liquor and, later, heroin also worked—for a while. But these weren't factors when Hammond first heard her.

Her performance at Moore's speakeasy struck Hammond with the force of a Dempsey haymaker. She was, he observed, tall, full-bodied, and voluptuous to distraction. And her face was equally striking. The high, forceful cheekbones and broad, wide forehead recalled America's ethnic history of the past two centuries, a story of generations of racial mingling among Negro slaves, white slave owners, and Native Americans. Her skin was the color and texture of fresh-brewed coffee, light with cream and sugar. "She weighs over 200 pounds, is incredibly beautiful, and sings as well as anybody I ever heard," he wrote shortly after seeing Holiday for the first time. She also had magnificent bearing. Whatever the mood of the room, this singer was in complete control of it. It seemed to Hammond that she turned the traditional audience-singer relationship upside down. It was common at the time for singers to walk the floors of speakeasies and dance halls, accepting tips as they roamed from table to table. Singers generally acknowledged a tip with some small flourish, a slight bow, perhaps, or maybe a fingertip traced along the chin of a handsome man. Some singers might even linger and sing a few choice lyrics directly into the eyes of a blushing big spender. "Not Billie," Hammond called. "I mean everything was improvised and her mood changed according to the stiff or not so stiff people who were at the tables."

During a lush ballad her full, sensuous lips might shift slightly, offering a hint of a smile. Singing a more up-tempo number, she would fold her arms in front of her healthy bosom, and a scolding index finger might offer mock admonishment to an especially randy patron. The gestures were so easy and natural that they left Moore's patrons feeling grateful that this singer had deigned to accept their tips.

Incredibly, all of these qualities paled in comparison to her actual singing. Hammond noted that her voice slipped into his ear just slightly—almost imperceptibly—behind the beat, a style that suggested her singing was merely an afterthought, a spontaneous response to the chance hearing of a beautiful melody. It was as if the song had wafted in through an open window, perhaps, and Holiday had instinctively joined in. And the voice had the same range of emotion as the young singer. It could be forceful and confident one minute, then utterly vulnerable the next. It could be flirty and teasing, but always stopped well short of vulgarity. But it certainly wasn't the strength of her voice that made it distinctive. There were plenty of singers around who could shake the rafters. Rather, there was a delicacy to it that required the listener to pay close attention. And its effect was lasting. The nightclub owner Barney Josephson once observed, "She never had a really big voice—it was small, like a bell that rang and went a mile."

"She was seventeen when I first heard her, she was nearly eighteen," Hammond recalled. "She was just unbelievable, she phrased like an improvising instrumentalist. She was the first singer I ever heard do that. She didn't read music, didn't have to. To me she was unbelievable."

After that night at Moore's, Hammond immediately set about promoting his new find, both through word of mouth and in his *Melody Maker* column. "For this month there has been a real find in the person of a singer called Billie Halliday [*sic*], step-daughter of Fletcher Henderson's guitar player," he wrote for his English readers. He spent the next few months following Holiday around Harlem with the bass player Artie Bernstein. To his dismay, he found that not everyone was as instantly convinced of her talent. "It took months for me to persuade anybody that Billie could be recorded," he told Ed Beach many years later.

In the spring of 1933, Patrick "Spike" Hughes, the English critic who had hired Hammond to *Melody Maker*, arrived in New York. He slept on a couch in Hammond's Greenwich Village apartment, and the two were virtually inseparable for most of Hughes's two-month visit. Hughes, a handsome young man in his mid-twenties whose curiosity and passion for music mirrored Hammond's, quickly found himself immersed in his host's frenetic lifestyle. The duo was bound for Harlem just hours after Hughes's boat docked along the Hudson River. As much as anything else he saw on his first day in New York—the crowds, the lights on Broadway, the skyscrapers—Hughes was impressed with Hammond's car, in particular the powerful radio. In an effort to keep abreast of music being made across the country, Hammond had equipped the car with "a twelve-tube Motorola with a large speaker, unlike any other car radio in those days," that picked up stations from every corner of the United States. Their first stop was the Lafayette Theater to see Chick Webb. Hughes was familiar with Webb's reputation, but he had never met the diminutive bandleader in person, and he came away impressed by Webb's quiet charm. After the show, Hammond introduced Hughes to Benny Carter, who was also in the audience that night. Then Hammond, Hughes, and Carter left together for

a speakeasy called Big John's, where, according to Hughes, "the gin is
almost unbelievably unpleasant."

A few days later, Hammond introduced Hughes around the offices
of the powerful manager and promoter Irving Mills—"a hive of industry
if ever there was one," according to Hughes—where they bumped into
Cab Calloway. From Mills's office, they passed through bustling Times
Square to catch the show at the mammoth Roseland Ballroom. They
finished the evening at the Onyx Club on Fifty-second Street, an exclusive speakeasy that catered mostly to musicians. Hughes was pleased to
run into his old friends Jimmy and Tommy Dorsey. On another occasion, Hammond, Hughes, and the Hungarian violinist Joseph Szigeti
spent part of an evening drinking beer and eating salami in a midtown
speakeasy. After parting company with Szigeti, Hammond and Hughes
headed uptown to Small's Paradise in Harlem. A day or two after that,
they caught Duke Ellington's show at the Cotton Club.

The two managed to take some time off from listening to others
make music to make some of their own. In April and again in May,
Hammond pulled together a band made up mostly of men from Benny
Carter's orchestra, and the group made some records for Hughes's
record company, English Decca, under the name the Spike Hughes
Orchestra. Always blunt in his assessments, Hammond later complained that his good friend Hughes didn't know how to write music
that swung.

Hughes returned to England in June, pleasantly overwhelmed both
by the music that seemed to course out of every open window in New
York City and by the considerable energy and wherewithal of his host,
whom he thanked "for acting as the most perfect guide to Harlem that
one could wish for."

Hammond enjoyed the company. "There's an awful void now at the
Hammond household, not only because of Spike's departure but also
on account of the mysterious disappearance of some of [my] more elegant discs."

About six weeks after returning to New York from covering the
Scottsboro trial in Alabama, Hammond boarded an ocean liner bound
for England. The trip would serve as another example of how his mo-
bility worked to his advantage as he maneuvered his way into the music

industry. In 1933, the health of the American record industry mirrored that of the broader American economy, now entering the fourth year of the Depression. According to industry statistics, sales of records plummeted from 104 million in 1927 to a paltry 6 million in 1932. "Columbia's future is still uncertain," Hammond wrote in July 1932. "They have all but closed up their New York branch." So instead of waiting for the economy to recover in the United States, he headed across the Atlantic to England, where the economy was still strong enough to sustain a market for jazz records.

Also on board Hammond's ship was Louis Armstrong. Only Duke Ellington came close to approaching Armstrong's popularity at the time, and Hammond and the rest of the jazz press chronicled his every move. Thus Armstrong and Hammond were familiar with each other but not close. In his memoirs, Hammond claimed that he and Armstrong's manager, Johnny Collins, got into a fistfight over Collins's liberal use of the word "nigger" somewhere in the middle of the Atlantic Ocean. If the story is true, Armstrong never mentioned it. Yet the anecdote, true or not, reflects Hammond's view of Armstrong. He admired Armstrong's genius he thought nothing of driving on a whim from New York to Philadelphia to catch an Armstrong performance—and he recognized the impact Armstrong had had on popular music. But at the same time he believed Armstrong had allowed himself to be exploited by manipulative white handlers at the expense of his vast talent. And he was appalled by the amount of marijuana Armstrong smoked.

By the time Hammond arrived in England that summer, he had been writing his column for *Melody Maker* for more than a year, and English record executives were familiar with his name. So it was easy for Hughes and one or two other English contacts to arrange for him to meet with top executives at the Columbia Gramophone Company of England. It must have been apparent to these executives from reading Hammond's dispatches from New York that he was intimately familiar with the American jazz scene. What's more, Hammond had already produced several Fletcher Henderson records for Columbia that had been released with a modicum of success in England. So he had little difficulty arranging a contract with English Columbia to record a handful of American jazz musicians. There would be eight sides with a band led by Fletcher Henderson, eight more with Benny Carter's band, four with a rising clarinet player named Benny Goodman, and another four with a band led by the violinist Joe Venuti.

If Hammond negotiated any salary for himself as producer, he never mentioned it in his memoirs or in any of the interviews in which he talked about the contracts. It's likely that he accepted no fee, instead seeking only the access and experience that the sessions would provide. Furthermore, by declining a salary—if indeed that's what happened—he certainly made himself that much more attractive to the English Columbia executives with whom he was negotiating. In fact, he was so anxious to make the kinds of records he wanted to hear that, once back in the United States, he covered the train fare for the drummer Gene Krupa to make the trip down from Boston to New York for the Goodman sessions. As for royalties, it wasn't until very late in his career that he accepted any percentage of profits from the records he produced.

Hammond returned to the United States thrilled by the opportunity he had created for himself and determined to reach out immediately to the musicians for whom he had obtained contracts. He claimed to have been so excited that he tracked down Goodman at the Onyx Club on the very night he arrived back in New York. (Goodman's biographers suggest it was probably later than that.)

The only hitch to this otherwise promising enterprise was that Hammond had signed the contracts on behalf of the musicians without their knowledge. The Henderson and Carter sessions would be easy to pull together; he knew both men well and had already recorded with their bands. Goodman and Venuti might prove more difficult, however, since he didn't know either of them. He'd only met Goodman once before, briefly about a year earlier at one of Goodman's shows at the Woodmansten Inn, a popular nightclub in the Pelham neighborhood in the far reaches of the Bronx. To complicate matters, Hammond had described the Goodman-organized band he saw that night as "merely another smooth and soporific dance combination." Thus Hammond was stepping out on a rather thin limb a year later when he assumed the role of Goodman's de facto agent for a recording contract.

When Hammond and Goodman first agreed to work together in the late summer or early fall of 1933, neither was in a position to even think about making radical changes to the popular-music landscape.

Both men were simply trying to establish themselves in the industry. Hammond had a well-earned reputation as a musical gadfly who knew just about everyone and everything connected to the local music scene. But he had yet to prove that his many strong opinions on jazz could be translated into anything resembling commercial success. Goodman was twenty-four years old at the time, just a year older than Hammond, and already recognized as a virtuoso clarinetist. He had cut his teeth playing with some of the better-known big bands of the era, most notably Ben Pollack's band. By mid-1933 he was making a good living as a freelance musician in New York, working in Manhattan's recording studios and in the orchestra pits of Broadway shows, as well as in the relatively new medium of radio. Goodman was rapidly earning a reputation for being difficult to work with, however, and when Hammond tracked him down at the Onyx Club that night, Goodman was in need of a break.

Goodman had been raised in a Jewish ghetto on Chicago's West Side, one of twelve children to immigrant parents who had fled Russian-dominated Eastern Europe in the late nineteenth century to escape its brutal discrimination against Jews. David Goodman was from Warsaw and Dora Rezinsky, his wife, from Kovno, Lithuania. They met in Baltimore around 1890, then moved to Chicago, where David found work first in the stockyards and later as a tailor. Goodman recalled his hardscrabble early days in his 1939 autobiography, *The Kingdom of Swing*: "I can remember a time when we lived in a basement without heat during the winter, and a couple of times when there wasn't anything to eat, I don't mean *much* to eat. I mean *anything*."

At the age of ten, Goodman, with two of his brothers, joined a band organized by the neighborhood synagogue. He showed immediate promise as a clarinetist, and through a series of serendipitous events Goodman, despite his lack of financial resources, wound up studying with the brilliant clarinetist Franz Schoepp. In his early teens, he discovered jazz and fell in with a group known in jazz lore as the Austin High Gang. Other members of the gang were the future Goodman drummer Dave Tough, the cornetist Jimmy McPartland, and the clarinetist Frank Teschemacher. At fourteen, Goodman dropped out of school to immerse himself in Chicago's thriving musical nightlife. On nights when Goodman wasn't playing himself, he and his pals sneaked into famous

Chicago nightspots such as Dreamland and the Sunset, where they gazed wide-eyed at King Oliver, Louis Armstrong, and Earl Hines.

Two years later, Goodman left Chicago for Los Angeles to join Ben Pollack's band, now remembered as a sort of farm system; in addition to Goodman, it produced Glenn Miller, Harry James, and Jack Teagarden, the groundbreaking trombonist and vocalist. It was with Pollack's band that Goodman made his way east to New York in February 1928. He left Pollack after four years and thrived as a New York session man.

As his legion of biographers and discographers have made clear, Benny Goodman was neither a crusader nor a reformer. He was a businessman whose business happened to be music. When he decided in the spring of 1931 to put his own band together, he sought mainly to be his own boss, not to spark the civil rights movement.

According to Hammond, when he approached Goodman at the bar of the Onyx Club and told him of the English Columbia contract, Goodman responded, "You're a goddam liar." If there's any truth to the story (Hammond's version), it was a fitting start to one of the more tumultuous but ultimately productive and important partnerships in the history of twentieth-century American popular music.

The question that remains, and one that Hammond never fully answered in his lifetime, is why he singled out Goodman. In his early days as a critic and record producer, Hammond made no secret of his belief that jazz had been created by blacks and was therefore best represented by black musicians. "It is obvious that Negro blues and stomps are the basis for all modern 'swing' music," he wrote in a *Brooklyn Eagle* article. "Negros were the pioneers in developing it, even though New Orleans white musicians were the first to exploit it successfully." And in a not-so-subtle jab at technically proficient white musicians— musicians like Benny Goodman—he concluded, "The best of this art is usually simple, for when technique and virtuosity get in the way of real feeling the result is always dire." Some of his music industry peers thought he preferred black musicians almost to a fault. Otis Ferguson wrote that Hammond used the term "white musician" the way most people would use "greaseball."

So why Goodman? Goodman's biographer James Lincoln Collier has speculated, probably accurately, that Hammond's first motive in approaching Goodman was his respect for the clarinetist's talent. But, Collier has theorized, Hammond just as likely hoped from the outset to parlay that talent into the creation of a racially mixed Goodman band that would ultimately break down the racial barriers in popular music.

That a lasting partnership was formed at all between men with such different backgrounds and disparate personalities is surprising. Hammond's sister Rachel Breck, who knew both men well, summed up best their differences. Goodman, raised in dire poverty, never forgot what it was like to have nothing, she explained. His work ethic—he rehearsed his bands to the point of exhaustion and practiced several hours a day by himself—was rooted in a fear that he might one day lose everything. He was not inclined, therefore, to risk all he had gained to further some social agenda. Hammond's ancestral wealth, meanwhile, would always provide a soft cushion if he stumbled and fell. Knowing he had nothing to lose, he never feared taking risks.

And Hammond could be persuasive, as evidenced by his ability to convince Goodman to participate in a classical concert at the Hammond mansion on East Ninety-first Street in 1935. Hammond had exchanged the violin for the viola around the time he left Yale, after determining that the viola was easier to play, and had joined a string quartet that played together each week strictly for the fun of it. Goodman, of course, had had some classical training as a youth in Chicago and was now somehow persuaded by Hammond to run through some works by Mozart with Hammond's amateur group. Goodman found he liked the music, and a plan was hatched for him to debut his classical side at a performance at the Hammond mansion.

Gathered that night in the second-floor music room of the Hammond residence, a room that comfortably seated three hundred guests among the elaborate gilded moldings and cut-glass chandeliers, were the elite members of several New York worlds. There, perched on tiny rented whitewashed folding chairs, sat the wives and daughters of many of the era's most powerful industrialists, including Mrs. Andrew Carnegie, Alice Van Rensselaer, and Gertrude Whitney. Joining these grandes dames of society were Charlie Buchanan, the manager of the Savoy Ballroom in Harlem, and his wife, Bessie; Fletcher Henderson and his wife, Leora; and Walter White, the executive director of the

NAACP, and his wife, Gladys. Hammond loved the contrast between both skin colors and pedigrees.

It turned out to be a splendid evening, with smiles and polite applause all around. The musical highlight was probably a duet of a Handel sonata featuring Hammond on viola and his mother on piano. Goodman covering Mozart was received warmly, but the concert was hardly a revelation. (He would dabble in classical music throughout his career, but the response from critics and fans was consistently lukewarm.) The evening may have been best remembered for Mildred Bailey's inadvertent one-liner to one of Mrs. Hammond's friends. The bandleader Charlie Barnet apparently stretched his long legs a little too far, knocking the legs out from underneath the chair of a plump society gal. When things had settled down and the woman was back in her chair, Bailey, also on the stout side and concerned for her own stability, sneaked a look over her shoulder and asked loud enough for others to hear, "How'm I doing?"

No sooner had Goodman agreed to record for English Columbia than Hammond suggested they put together a racially mixed group that would have included the black musicians Benny Carter and Coleman Hawkins. Goodman immediately balked. Instead, he asked Hammond to come to a rehearsal of the all-white band he had put together for an upcoming radio show. Unimpressed by the group, Hammond again proposed a mixed band, to which Goodman responded, "If it gets around that I recorded with colored guys I won't get another job in this town."

Goodman was telling the truth and Hammond knew it. Thus he gave up for the moment on an integrated band, and together he and Goodman organized an all-white band. On October 18, 1933, Hammond and Goodman worked together for the first time. Differences of opinion were apparent from the start inside the Columbia studio at Fifth Avenue and Twelfth Street. "There are lots and lots of stories behind this particular session because . . . Benny didn't want to have a swinging improvised date, the kind that I wanted," Hammond told a radio interviewer in 1973. "He insisted on having an arrangement. He

insisted on having an all-white band. He wanted actually for this session to have sort of a society-type band. I insisted that he use Jack Teagarden, that he get Joe Sullivan and Gene Krupa and a good rhythm
section . . . I wanted it to be a jazz band but it's not quite a jazz band."

The single released from the session, a catchy tune called "Ain't Cha
Glad?" proved a minor hit, selling some five thousand copies, according
to Hammond. The profits reaped by Columbia provided Hammond with
some leverage, which he used to obtain more studio time to record
Goodman. In the wake of the success of "Ain't Cha Glad?" Hammond
"was now driving himself like a peg into the record business with the
energy and force that characterized everything he did," wrote Collier.

Hammond continued to press Goodman about recording with
black musicians. His badgering paid off in November, when Goodman
relented despite the very real fear that he could lose the studio and
radio work that was his bread and butter. Reluctance turned quickly to
visceral stimulation, according to Hammond, and by the mid-1930s
Goodman had decided to risk being ostracized and was making regular
appearances at mixed-race sessions organized by Hammond. One in
particular stood out in Hammond's mind—a July 1935 date led by the
black pianist Teddy Wilson that produced the Billie Holiday classic
"Miss Brown to You." In that 1973 radio interview, Hammond gushed:
"You know, I'll never really be able to thank Benny Goodman enough
for making that session because, honest to Pete, I don't think he ever
played better, for one thing. And he was never stimulated so much as
by these guys. It was incredible. This is one of the reasons, I think, that
eventually Benny had the first truly integrated band in jazz in 1939 and
1940 because he realized, you know, just playing on a few of these sessions, how wonderful it was to have new sparks all the time. Benny,
after all, was the only white guy on the session and he was [musically]
not out of place."

Goodman recalled:

> It was during these months, around the end of 1933 and during
> the beginning of 1934, that I first began to make records with
> colored musicians. For this the responsibility must be given al-
> most entirely to John Hammonds [sic], who really put me back

in touch with the kind of music they could play. We went
around a lot together uptown, and in fact it was in a little dive
on 135th Street that we first heard Billie Holiday. Nobody had
to convince me, with my background in Chicago, about their
ability. It just happened that in working along as I had during
those seven or eight years, I had gotten out of touch with them,
except for hearing some band in a night club or on records. But
the idea of working with them had never come my way before,
nor, for that matter, had there been much opportunity.

In September 1933, Hammond had tuned his powerful car radio to
WMAQ in Chicago to hear the pianist Earl Hines, whose nightly show
was broadcast live from the Grand Terrace Café. Hines, who was already recognized as a giant for having participated in Louis Armstrong's
legendary Hot Five sessions in the mid-1920s, influenced a generation
of pianists who followed him, men like Art Tatum and Erroll Garner.
Hammond listened to the Grand Terrace broadcasts whenever his radio
picked up the signal. But on this particular evening, a different sound
emerged—"a cleaner, lighter, more elegant" sound, as he would later
describe it. "One night Earl Hines wasn't on, he was on vacation, and
there was another band on, a substitute band and they had a piano
player who just was absolutely fantastic. I couldn't believe my ears."
Hammond called the station the next day to get the piano player's name.

The pianist, he learned, was a classically trained twenty-year-old
named Teddy Wilson. Raised on the campus of Tuskegee Normal and
Industrial Institute in Alabama, Wilson began studying the piano at
seven or eight. At fourteen he first heard the music that would shape
his career—solos by Duke Ellington, Earl Hines, and Fats Waller.
After a year of studying music theory in college, Wilson felt he was
ready to turn professional. He quickly landed in Chicago, where he
played in bands led by, among others, Louis Armstrong and Jimmie
Noone. He was hired in 1931, while still in his teens, to fill in for Earl
Hines at the Grand Terrace when Hines took a vacation or went out on
the road. It was during one of those replacement gigs that he caught
Hammond's ear.

After learning Wilson's name, Hammond called Benny Carter. Carter agreed that Wilson, whom he was already familiar with, would make a splendid addition to his band. Hammond also planned to use his agreement with English Columbia to record Wilson by himself. "So I gave Benny some loot to go out to Chicago and pick this guy up," Hammond recalled. It turned out to be one of his better investments.

Few American musicians have personified grace and elegance like Teddy Wilson. He was lean, handsome, and self-assured, and he always dressed with impeccable taste. (No jazz musician before or since has ever knotted his tie with more precision.) With his quiet self-confidence and classic sense of understated style, he could easily have passed for a university president rather than the brilliant jazz pianist he was. If an off-color story exists with Wilson as the protagonist—perhaps a wild night in Chicago during Prohibition, or a hot little dancer hidden away in Kansas City—it's never become part of jazz lore.

It's been well documented how Branch Rickey specifically chose Jackie Robinson to break the color barrier in baseball because Rickey believed Robinson was the only athlete who had both the talent and the courage to succeed under such intense pressure. The same might be said of Hammond's gut feeling soon after meeting Teddy Wilson. "[H]e had the bearing, demeanor, and attitude toward life which would enable him to survive in a white society. I have always considered him a man of destiny, and I suppose my role in his later career reflects this confidence that he not only had the talent to make it in any surroundings, but the mental and emotional equipment to do so," Hammond wrote.

The manner in which John Hammond and Teddy Wilson came to know each other and work together raises the thorny issue of "discovery." Wilson's music came to Hammond's attention under very different circumstances from those that led to Hammond's revelation with Billie Holiday just seven months earlier. Teddy Wilson was already a road-hardened professional by the time Hammond heard him. And where did Hammond hear him? On a popular radio show. Unproven amateurs, after all, aren't hired to fill in for legends like Earl Hines. Musicians and club owners in New York needed to be convinced that Billie Holiday was special. That wasn't the case with Teddy Wilson.

Perhaps what Wilson benefited most from was Hammond's energy and enthusiasm. "John seemed to be everywhere where things that were worthwhile were happening in the jazz world, and his great quality was perhaps this unfailing acumen and discernment in things musical," Wilson wrote in his memoirs. "After Benny Carter he introduced me to Benny Goodman and after Goodman to Billie Holiday, and all these key contacts proved to be of decisive importance to my life and career as a musician."

Hammond first recorded Wilson in a studio on October 10, 1933, the very day Wilson arrived in New York from Chicago. The band, which consisted primarily of members of Benny Carter's group, recorded a handful of sides under the pseudonym the Chocolate Dandies. Wilson, who had recorded before as a sideman, thought of these sessions as perhaps the most significant of his career because Hammond allowed him to stretch out for the first time on a number of solos. The mellow, sophisticated sound of the Chocolate Dandies didn't make much of a splash at the time. But the recordings are remembered for having stood in stark relief to the symphonic blast of the big-band style that was growing more popular by the day.

Although just twenty-two years old and with barely a year of studio experience under his belt, Hammond in the fall of 1933 embarked on one of his most productive periods as a record producer. Not only did he make his first records with Benny Goodman, Teddy Wilson, and Billie Holiday, he also arranged and produced a session for one of his favorite performers, the blues singer Bessie Smith.

"I had been a Bessie Smith fan ever since I heard [her] first records," he explained decades later in a radio interview. "The first Bessie Smith records I ever heard were the ones I bought because Louis Armstrong was accompanying her. I wasn't really smart enough at the age of twelve to realize that this marvelous, lusty blues singer was probably the greatest popular singer we've ever had in America. And then suddenly, I guess when 'Baby Doll' and 'Young Woman's Blues' and those records came out [in 1926], I suddenly realized that this was not only the greatest pop singer but perhaps one of the greatest musicians that jazz had ever produced." He grew determined to record her.

Bessie Smith is remembered as much for her lust for life as for her singing prowess. She was very publicly a larger-than-life black woman whose songs—"'Tain't Nobody's Bizness If I Do," "Whoa, Tillie, Take Your Time," "New Orleans Hop Scop Blues," "Worn Out Papa Blues," and "Dirty No-Gooder's Blues"—suggested a way of life that cared little for conventional societal boundaries. She sang slowly, deeply, and with troubling purpose. The songs conjured images of blood, sweat, and other body fluids.

Smith openly carried on affairs with men and women alike. She figured if there was a full glass of gin on the bar, why drink just half? In the 1920s, she was reportedly the highest-paid black entertainer in the United States. Said the guitarist Danny Barker: "She dominated a stage. You didn't turn your head when she went on. You just watched Bessie. You didn't read any newspapers in a nightclub when she went on. She just upset you."

Smith's popularity waned toward the end of the 1920s, however, as musical tastes shifted from the blues to the peppier swing music. She hadn't recorded for more than two years when Hammond found her living in Philadelphia, working as a hostess at a nightclub. He convinced her to come to New York to record by offering to cover her traveling expenses, as well as the cost of the recording session. Thrilled by the prospect of recording with one of his heroes, he convinced Columbia to provide the recording space and used his own money to hire some of the top musicians working in New York at the time—Jack Teagarden, Chu Berry, and Benny Goodman, among others—hoping to see what would happen if he matched Bessie with some of the finest jazz improvisers.

Recorded on November 24, 1933, at Columbia's Fifth Avenue studios, the songs were released on the Okeh subsidiary, whose records sold primarily to black audiences. They didn't revive Smith's career as Hammond had hoped, perhaps in part because Smith refused to record any traditional blues songs. Stubborn as ever, she argued that it was the middle of the Depression and people wanted their spirits lifted, not ground further into the dirt. The song most often heard from those sessions is a novelty tune titled "Gimme a Pigfoot (and a Bottle of Beer)." It remains on playlists because Benny Goodman's distinctive clarinet can be heard briefly backing Smith on a couple of choruses. The song is meant to re-create the mood of a Harlem rent party, which tenants would throw to raise a little cash just before the rent was due. Revelers would pay a dime or a quarter for entry, and then listen to music while eating pigs' feet and drinking beer.

The song's lyrics were apparently reminiscent of the rehearsals held the night before in a Harlem railroad flat. (The lyrics include the verse "Gimme a reefer and a gang o' gin. Slay me, 'cause I'm in my sin. Slay me, 'cause I'm full of gin.") Hammond attended the rehearsal/party and hadn't forgotten the bash four decades later. Sputtering the anecdote through his hah-hah-hah breathy laugh, he recounted cryptically to the disc jockey Ed Beach that "wild things were going on" during the rehearsal, "but that's another story."

"The size of her voice was tremendous, and the spirit marvelous," Hammond recalled. The records died on the vine, but Hammond kept after Columbia for several more years in an effort to get Smith a recording contract. He claimed that in 1937 he finally finagled a contract for her with Brunswick, another Columbia subsidiary. But the agreement came too late. Smith was killed in a car accident on September 26, 1937, before she could sign the papers.

Just three days after the Bessie Smith session, in a studio in the very same building on lower Fifth Avenue, Hammond recorded Billie Holiday for the first time. Holiday's singing has since set the standard by which all other jazz singers are judged. Her lifestyle has proven no less important to her emergence as an icon.

Holiday's tragic story has always lent itself to much romanticizing, both by her fans and by writers determined to exploit society's perverse fascination with celebrity and tragedy—especially the dark places where those two powerful dynamics collide. Hammond was aware from the time he met Holiday that she was fond of marijuana and booze. (Her descent into opiates came after the two no longer worked together.) But Hammond never viewed drug addiction and other modes of self-destruction as necessary consequences of genius. In Holiday's case at least, he viewed them as a pitiful waste of talent.

In the fall of 1933, her talent had yet to be diminished by her dark compulsions, and Hammond used his burgeoning relationship with Goodman to get her into a recording studio for the first time, joining a group to back the singer Ethel Waters. Goodman had become a fan of Holiday's after traveling with Hammond several times up to Harlem to hear her sing. In fact, in her autobiography Holiday said her first recording sessions with Goodman came at the bandleader's, not Hammond's, insistence, but gave Hammond credit for introducing her to "Joe Glaser, the big agent and manager. He was handling Louis Armstrong, Mildred Bailey, and practically everybody who got to be anybody. Glaser signed me up on the spot." She continued: "Benny Goodman came around plenty, too"—it was said that they dated—"and eventually he asked me to make my first record with him. I'll never forget it. Benny came up to get me and took me to the studio downtown. When we got there and I saw this big old microphone, it scared me half to death. I'd never sung in one and I was afraid of it."

The sessions are now considered significant for reasons other than their being Holiday's first recording date. They marked the first time Goodman served as leader of an integrated studio band—Hammond's doing. Joining the white trombonist Jack Teagarden in the brass section was Shirley Clay, a respected black trumpet player who was a member of Don Redman's popular band, to replace the white trumpeter Manny Klein. Goodman's biographer Collier has suggested that Hammond brought Clay in for no other purpose than to further his own reformist agenda: "Clay was a good jazz musician, but there was no reason to use him in place of Klein; it was all part of Hammond's campaign to integrate the music industry."

Black and white musicians regularly jammed together in clubs, speakeasies, and after-hours joints. But they rarely mixed in the studio. Many white bandleaders and musicians shied away from recording with black musicians for fear of being barred from lucrative radio work by racist producers. As Lewis Erenberg noted in his study of the period, *Swingin' the Dream*, the studios kept the ban on black players firmly in place because radio executives knew that the sponsors would pull their ads if they believed their products were being associated with black players. But this was 1933, the lowest point of the Depression, and white musicians needed whatever work they could get. "Benny didn't dare do it but he did on this one. He used Don Redman's wonderful trumpet player Shirley Clay and this young girl whom I persuaded [him to use] . . . I twisted his arm but I made him record her. He never liked her as much as I did but he was willing to try her on records. Benny was very well organized and to Benny's way of thinking I don't think he thought Billie was commercial at all," Hammond recalled.

Nevertheless, Holiday was called in for one of the last cuts of the day—a fun and energetic but otherwise nondescript pop song called "Your Mother's Son-in-Law." Hammond was not overly impressed. "A spirited arrangement," he called it, "not too good a tune." But he was wowed by Holiday's singing. "She was eighteen when this was cut, and of course everybody was just gassed by her in the studio—the musicians."

Critics writing of "Your Mother's Son-in-Law" down through the years haven't been as kind, faulting her singing as nervous and halting, a far cry from the confidence and ebullience she exuded just two years later during the first of her extraordinary sessions with the pianist Teddy Wilson. The musicologist Michael Brooks, who worked with Hammond in the 1960s on reissues of classic Columbia recordings, has written: "Listening to this primitive first effort can be compared to seeing a beautiful woman through her ugly duckling childhood photographs, where everything is there, but in the wrong proportions . . . the instinctive musical subtleties her fans grew to admire are largely absent and she comes across as just another band singer."

In any event, Holiday was impressive enough that Hammond brought the group together again two weeks later for a second date, at which Billie performed a song called "Riffin' the Scotch," another upbeat but forgettable pop tune.

No one knew it at the time, but Holiday's first recording date, just three days after Bessie Smith's last session, represented a passing of the torch from one legend to another—by way of Hammond. The last week of November 1933, then, proved more than just productive for a young record producer still considered by some little more than a dilettante: it was quite literally historic.

$$\binom{5}{}$$

CONVERGENCE

On June 22, 1933, Judge James E. Horton stunned a crowded courtroom in his hometown of Athens, Alabama, by throwing out the conviction of the Scottsboro boy Haywood Patterson. In a lengthy and wholly unexpected ruling, the judge offered his own point-by-point renunciation of the accusations against Patterson. Horton apparently thought his own sound judgment and long-standing credibility would be enough to convince prosecutors to drop all of the cases against each of the Scottsboro boys once and for all. But he was wrong. The charges against Patterson were immediately refiled, and a new trial began in November.

Hammond took time off from the record sessions he was producing in New York to return to Decatur to cover the trial for *The Nation*. In his second report, "Due Process of Law in Alabama," which appeared on December 20, 1933, he cut right to the chase. "Alabama has been anything but shrewd," he wrote.

> After Judge Horton's reversal of the Decatur jury's verdict . . . the wise thing to do would have been to nolle-pros [dismiss] the whole case. In this way the entire blame would have rested on the courageous judge; Tom Knight, the Attorney-General, could have pointed to his success at having obtained a conviction; Alabama might have emerged as the great liberal Southern State; and Morgan County could have escaped the tremendous

cost of a new trial. But Alabama felt that it was necessary to
show the world that alien influences could do nothing to affect
its justice.

In short, Hammond argued that Alabama had missed a genuine
opportunity to rid itself of this ongoing albatross in such a way that all
the participants could have claimed victory. Instead, the state chose a
spiteful course, one that led to additional appeals and more spurious
convictions and ultimately did little more than cast an unyielding spotlight on Alabama's racist power structure.

Hammond concluded the report with an amusing account of Decatur's big Thanksgiving Day football game against its state rival Hartselle. "The natives were out to see a smashing victory," he wrote. "But
the referee was a Hartselle man. Time after time he penalized their
team. The crowd became more and more furious. Finally it shouted at
him: 'Leibowitz, Leibowitz!'" Samuel Leibowitz had become a household name in Decatur. He was the New York lawyer who had defended
the Scottsboro boys.

After returning to New York, Hammond sought to seize the momentum generated by his string of productive recording sessions a
month earlier by heading straight back into the studio to record the
drummer Chick Webb. By now, he had adopted many of the characteristics that would come to represent the Hammond persona for the rest
of his life. Dressed casually but conservatively in tweed over a blue oxford shirt and a matching tie, he arrived at the studio each day looking
more like an English professor than a record producer. Permanently
tucked under one arm were at least a half-dozen newspapers and magazines. As the band tuned their instruments, Hammond would sit with
one long leg crossed over the other, his face buried in *The New York
Times*. When it was time to record, he would put the paper down and
move into a corner of the studio where he could observe the entire
band. Then he would lean one shoulder against a wall, fold his arms
across his chest, and cross his legs at the knees. Motionless and
wrapped around himself like that, he looked like a well-dressed bar-
ber's pole.

Once the band was warmed up, Hammond would grow more animated, nodding his head and tapping his foot in time to the music. A

particularly tasteful solo might produce a grin that left him squinting, his molars clearly visible somewhere back near his ears. "That's mah-velous. Just mah-velous," he would say.

The gem that would emerge from the Chick Webb sessions, which ran through the spring of 1934, was "Stompin' at the Savoy." Other lasting tunes from these dates include "Let's Get Together," "Darktown Strutters' Ball," and "Blue Minor." But "Stompin' at the Savoy" became an anthem of the swing era, first among the Harlem dance hall fanatics by way of Webb's energetic rendition, and then again four years later as a mainstream hit for Benny Goodman, who recorded a far tamer but apparently more accessible version.

Webb is remembered as a man who never had a bad word for anyone. His pleasant demeanor, however, belied a fierce set of chops and an inner strength capable of tremendous resilience, not to mention a fiery competitive spirit. Congenital tuberculosis of the spine stunted his growth, leaving him hunchbacked and tiny as a dwarf and almost always in poor health. Yet his physical ailments never stood in the way of his becoming a first-rate musician—a genius, in fact, by many accounts.

Webb arrived in New York around 1925 as a teenager with his friend the guitarist John Trueheart. Two years later, Webb and Trueheart were fronting a band that appeared regularly at Harlem's legendary Savoy Ballroom. For much of the 1930s, Webb was leader of the house band at the Savoy, where he presided over some of the most famous battles of the bands of the swing era. These legendary competitions were widely promoted and breathlessly anticipated by the patrons who jammed the Savoy and other large Harlem dance halls.

In one of the Savoy's most famous battles, a 1937 affair at which several thousand fans were turned away at the door and the overflow snarled traffic for blocks near the busy intersection of Lenox Avenue and 140th Street, Webb and his bandmates vanquished Benny Goodman's orchestra at the height of Goodman's popularity. A year later, during another legendary battle, Webb's boys pounded Count Basie's star-studded orchestra into submission. Of course these were highly subjective competitions, determined by the ferocity of the audience's applause. Thus visiting bandleaders generally took their Savoy defeats in stride. Webb was, after all, the home team and revered by the Savoy patrons with a passion that bordered on worship.

Not surprisingly, Hammond was a regular at these events. The producer Jerry Wexler, then a twenty-year-old record collector, recalls seeing Hammond at an epic clash held in 1938 at a dance hall in the Bronx, the Fordham Club, between the Count Basie orchestra and the trumpeter Bunny Berigan's big band. "All the cats turned out for that one," Wexler recalled. As a prolific jazz columnist, record producer, and concert organizer, Hammond was highly regarded among the group of young jazz fanatics with whom Wexler prowled the nightclubs and record stores of New York. "John was *the man*. He was like a demigod to us."

Inside the mobbed Fordham Club, Wexler and his buddies crowded near the bandstand to get a better look at Basie's crew, which at that time included such stars as Jo Jones, Buck Clayton, and Lester Young. Berigan's rhythm section was paced by the top-notch drummer Dave Tough. The bands jousted back and forth for several hours, much to the delight of the frenzied crowd, according to Wexler. Eventually, though, Basie's guys pulled it all together and blew Berigan's band out of the water. There, in the front row, crew cut bobbing in time to the beat, was John Hammond. "He looked exactly like he always would down through the years," Wexler recalled decades later. "That was my first Hammond sighting."

By the summer of 1934, Hammond had successfully thrust a foot inside the door of the music industry. His *Melody Maker* column had earned him a bit of notoriety in England, as well as among musicians in the United States, and a handful of the records he had produced as a freelancer for Columbia had turned a small profit, enough at least to earn him additional studio time. But he was hardly an industry insider, and when that opportunity presented itself in the form of a job with Irving Mills, he quickly accepted. In his myriad roles as a talent manager, promoter, song publisher, plugger, and sometime lyricist, Mills was a dominant figure in the music industry during the 1930s. He seems to have derived his business acumen from the robber barons of a half century earlier in that, like Carnegie with steel and Rockefeller with oil, Mills had a vision that took in the entire landscape of the

music business. Cognizant of the profit potential in every aspect of the business, he sought to keep the profits for himself. Hammond explained Mills's approach in his memoirs: Mills and his brother Jack owned Mills Music, a major publisher of sheet music, which at the time accounted for a significant portion of an entertainer's revenues. By frequently adding his own name as a lyricist to songs written and performed by entertainers he promoted—a stable that included Duke Ellington and Cab Calloway—and then publishing those songs through his own company, he double-dipped on the profits, earning money both on royalties on sales of records and on sales of sheet music. So it was in Mills's best interest to publish and record as many of his performers' songs as he could. Thus, as noted by Hammond, in the depths of the Depression, when even record companies lacked the money to make discs, the Mills machine remained profitable by virtue of the popularity of its performers and its unique system of self-generating revenues.

Hammond joined Mills's music factory in mid-1934 as associate editor of a magazine published by Mills to promote his performers. Given the job description, which Hammond had to have known would at some point require him to write nice things about someone for whom he had nothing nice to say, it's not surprising the job lasted only four months. The pattern he had established two years earlier thus resurfaced: he quit or was fired (he didn't clarify which) after refusing some directive that offended his sense of right and wrong.

He didn't leave Mills embittered, though. To the contrary, he later expressed gratitude to Mills for giving him an invaluable look into the inner workings of the music business. Besides, Mills's highly profitable publishing ventures made him one of the few people in the industry at the time who could afford to make records. Realizing an exceptional opportunity when he saw one, Hammond used Mills's money to supervise a number of recording sessions in the summer of 1934 with, among others, Benny Goodman, Red Norvo, and Norvo's wife, the singer Mildred Bailey.

Around the same time, Hammond was beginning to gain notoriety as a jazz critic. The growing popularity of jazz among American college kids created an insatiable demand for gossip and other tidbits of information on the top musicians. These mavens followed their favorite bands as fervently as their fathers followed their favorite baseball teams: Was Benny Goodman or Artie Shaw tops on clarinet? Was the horn player Bunny Berigan emerging as the new Bix Beiderbecke? Was Jack Teagarden number one on trombone? What about this new fellow Harry James? Was Gene Krupa the real deal on drums, or was he all greasy hair and chewing gum?

The American magazines *Down Beat* and *Metronome*, quick to recognize this competitive spirit, sought to stir the fire by publishing annual fan polls. As it became obvious to the fans that the jazz critics got to hang around the bandstands and recording studios, the men who covered the jazz scene—writers such as George Frazier, George Simon, and Otis Ferguson—became figures almost on par with the musicians themselves. Hammond relished this competitive mix and threw himself energetically into the fray.

Hammond's dual roles as writer and producer were also starting to earn him a reputation among musicians as a critic with no scruples about praising in print the same players he was promoting and recording. In the July 1934 issue of *Melody Maker*, for example, he noted that Benny Goodman had put together a band to play the opening of Billy Rose's Music Hall, a big new venue on Broadway. "Although the names of the guys are all but unknown, with few exceptions, the bunch will probably have more swing than any whites in New York. In other words, it's a helluva good band," Hammond crowed, not saying he had helped Goodman organize the band and was producing its recording sessions for Columbia.

Hammond seems never to have considered the issue of his own conflicts of interest. Indeed, he seems to have believed that since he had no need to make money, he was above reproach. Others in the business strongly begged to differ, however. Among them was Duke Ellington.

A series of articles, the first of which appeared in *Melody Maker* in the summer of 1934, shows the incestuous nature of the jazz world and the press that covered it, and shows how Hammond used his typewriter to further his own agenda, if not necessarily to line his pockets.

In addition to Hammond's glowing reviews of Goodman's work in *Melody Maker*, the magazine's feature pages touted the imminent departure of an integrated band made up of some of the best American jazz musicians for a historic tour of England. According to the stories, Benny Goodman was going to lead an orchestra that would include Jack and Charlie Teagarden, J. C. Higginbotham, Benny Carter, Chu Berry, Teddy Wilson, and Gene Krupa. One front-page headline fairly shouted: "Black, White American Stars Form Greatest Outfit Ever." It was pure Hammond, although the article did not include a byline. A few weeks later, Hammond went so far as to announce an opening date. "The spirit of the guys is swell," he wrote in the August 25 issue. "Jack Teagarden could hardly be more excited, and Benny Goodman has a new idea every moment. The rest are equally happy, and I suspect that October 15 is going to be something in the history of swing music." Strangely, *Melody Maker* was the only jazz magazine to carry stories on this ostensibly groundbreaking event, and just as suddenly as the story had emerged it died.

Goodman's biographer Ross Firestone has speculated that Hammond made up the tour, then set about trying to will the idea into reality:

> Nothing remotely like this had ever been tried before. Black and white musicians might casually sit in with each other now and then, but an interracial orchestra, even one formed on a temporary basis, was absolutely unheard of. And quite apart from race, the logistical problems were all but overwhelming. Most of the listed musicians were featured sidemen working in different parts of the country. Leaves of absence would have to be negotiated, suitable replacements found, schedules adjusted and readjusted before they could even be brought together to start rehearsing. Labor permits would also have to be obtained to allow the band to work in England, and the right sort of bookings arranged. This was a high-priced package of talent, and only the largest halls would be able to handle the expense.

When *Down Beat* finally picked up the story in October 1934, it was only to mention that the tour had been canceled, supposedly because the organizers couldn't obtain labor permits for the musicians. "The whole affair [has] cooled off, and now nobody knows or seems to care when the 'black and white fantasy' leaves, if at all."

Then, in the spring of 1935, *Down Beat* ran a laughably self-serving "interview" in which Hammond blamed the collapse of the so-called Black and White Band on an English promoter named Jack Hylton. The headline promised "the lowdown on why the black and white band idea took a 'brodie.'" In a tone angry, sonorous, and slightly rambling, Hammond laid blame for the tour's failure squarely at the feet of Hylton, concluding: "Hylton broke a definite promise to me, and I, for one, will never forgive him for it."

The editors of *Melody Maker* were not amused. "John Hammond is a young man of means who has devoted much of his life to the cause of the oppressed Negro in the U.S.A, and his intense enthusiasm for the cause undoubtedly results in him conceiving schemes sky-high and almost as unattainable," they wrote. They refuted Hammond's account point by point, explaining that Hylton had ignored Hammond's phone calls and cables after learning on a trip to the United States in the summer of 1934 that the Black and White Band was a fiction.

Undaunted, Hammond simply moved his column from *Melody Maker* to *Down Beat*. Far from being dampened, his desire to organize the first integrated jazz band only grew stronger.

As it turned out, the decision by *Down Beat*'s editors to rehash the soap opera was little more than a prelude to introducing Hammond as *Down Beat*'s newest columnist. His first bylined column appeared in the very next issue, published in June 1935. Little wonder, then, that the editors had generously described him as a "brilliant young music critic." Indeed, not yet twenty-five years old, Hammond was proving remarkably adept at drawing attention both to himself and to his causes—on both sides of the Atlantic.

Down Beat was the brainchild of a Chicago insurance man named Al Lipschultz. From its debut issue in July 1934, it was geared toward professional musicians, but that wouldn't last long. Legend has it that the head of Chicago's professional musicians union, concerned that Lipschultz was muscling in on his territory, told him that he could either sell insurance to local musicians or publish a magazine, but not both. Lipschultz heeded the warning and stuck to what he knew best. He sold the magazine to one of his early partners, an ex-musician named Glenn Burrs, for fifteen hundred dollars. Burrs quickly set about recasting the magazine for a broader audience. Written by hepcats for hepcats, *Down Beat* soon became required reading for musicians and swing fans alike.

Hammond joined *Down Beat*'s staff in the spring of 1935, introducing himself with a doozy of an article. "One of the greatest disappointments of the winter has been the musical fizzle of Ray Noble's orchestra, which should certainly have become one of the most distinguished in America," he wrote. "It pains me to say this, as I consider both Ray and Bill Harty, his drummer, very fine guys. There is no ensemble in any of the sections, let alone in the band as a whole. The tone of the violins, particularly the first, is ugly in the extreme, and the intonation frequently false. There is not even good rhythm, to say nothing of swing, in the orchestra, and the blame for this can be divided equally between the arrangers, leader and rhythm section." He remarked: "I defy anyone to play Noble's American records critically and still call the band first rate by any standards." Then he recast his provocation as constructive criticism, concluding: "I have a suspicion that Noble himself is by no means satisfied, which will ultimately mean considerable improvement in the orchestra, I'm sure."

In the same issue he took several long strides toward earning the reputation to which Ferguson would later refer—that of "the Critic, the Little Father, the Guardian Angel, and the Big Bringdown of dance music." Hammond bemoaned what he saw as a lack of original swing music emanating from the New York and Chicago jazz scenes. He had also begun writing for the *Brooklyn Eagle*, and later that summer he ripped into the commercial jazz being played by Paul Whiteman and the hugely popular Casa Loma Orchestra. He called it "upper class snob stuff, played by bands in small spots for refined and exquisite people who dislike noise or pronounced rhythm. At best this is castrated music which cannot be well played even by the best of musicians because of the limitations of the audience." Not only was he insulting musicians who played music he found distasteful; he was alienating many fans as well.

In the same *Brooklyn Eagle* article, Hammond expounded on one of his deepest-held beliefs—namely, that music, specifically improvised jazz, could and would serve as an essential catalyst for realizing integration in America:

The last and least appreciated class is our "swing" or "hot" music, played by musicians who would rather improvise collectively than eat. It is music which has had curiously little appreciation in this country, although it is probably nearer to real folk music than any other music type. Its appeal is so strong that it has succeeded in completely breaking racial bars, even in certain places in the South. It is a not at all uncommon sight to see the finest of white musicians sitting in with colored bands in order to get their only real pleasure of the day. In no other kind of music is such a thing true.

Later that summer, Hammond left the jazz scene behind and went on a long trip. After stopping in England to visit his sister, he traveled east through Europe and into Russia, where he spent a few days in the company of Sergei Eisenstein, the dissident Russian filmmaker. The two had met three years earlier at the opening night of Hammond's short-lived Public Theater. Through a common friend who lived in Russia, Hammond was invited to the set of a film Eisenstein was shooting on location outside Moscow.

"Our first night together Eisenstein took me to dinner. He chose a Georgian restaurant where the music was played very loud—loud enough, he explained, so that no one could overhear our conversation. We arrived at the restaurant about eight o'clock and left at five the next morning, time enough for him to tell me what it was like for an artist in the Soviet Union," Hammond recounted in his autobiography. An ardent Trotskyite when the two first met in New York in 1932, Eisenstein in the intervening years had grown critical of the strict authoritarian rule within Communist Russia, especially the constraining effect this heavy-handed control was having on Russia's arts and culture.

The encounter, according to Hammond, confirmed in him a growing suspicion that Communism as it was being practiced in Russia was little more than a hammer used to brutally suppress the civil rights of Russian citizens, and, moreover, a hammer wielded mercilessly by Joseph Stalin and his henchmen as a means of extending their power.

Hammond didn't really need further convincing that Communism wasn't the answer to the world's social ills. It would have been easy to assume in the mid-1930s that he was a card-carrying member of the Communist Party. He wrote for left-leaning magazines, he traveled in progressive circles, and he was affiliated with numerous liberal causes. He had traveled to Kentucky to help striking miners organize a union, and he was outspoken in his support of the Scottsboro boys, whose defense costs were underwritten in large part by the American Communist Party. So it's fair to say that he held common ground with the Communists on many of the leading social issues of the day. What kept him distanced from the Communists was the party's position on integration, Hammond's most cherished cause. The Communists wanted to create a new country for blacks somewhere in the southwestern United States. Moreover, he knew equality among the races was secondary in their primary goal of overthrowing capitalism and the party leaders in the United States weren't shy about manipulating the race card to further that agenda. Hammond had seen firsthand how the Communists used the Scottsboro case to blindly advance their dogma, frequently to the detriment of the defendants. Thus his trip to Russia served to solidify beliefs already taking form within him.

Hammond's matching of Teddy Wilson with Billie Holiday in the summer of 1935 is widely regarded as one of the most inspired pairings in the history of jazz. Wilson's piano is tasteful and restrained, full of high-register sprinklings that rise through the air like so many bubbles floating upward in a glass of champagne. Billie's vocals are perhaps at their warmest. She never sounded more at ease. "I Wished on the Moon," from a July 2, 1935, session, with its jaunty Dixieland feel, captured the musicians' buoyant spirit. Wilson and Benny Goodman trade solos around a supremely confident Holiday vocal. Nearly two years after her first recording dates, at which she was admittedly nervous, Holiday's voice on these sessions registers her comfort at sharing a recording studio with these virtuoso musicians. Goodman's biographer Collier has described this collection of recordings as "one of the finest small bodies of work in jazz history."

Goodman, at Hammond's urging, sat in on many of these early Wilson-led sessions. Naturally, Hammond was doing his best to promote the burgeoning musical relationship. "There should be a great future somewhere for Teddy Wilson. His reputation, which was helped by his solos on records, has grown by leaps and bounds so that he is considered both in America and Europe, as the finest orchestra pianist in the profession. Benny Goodman goes even further and places him at the top of the jazz virtuosi," he wrote in a June 1935 column.

By the end of the summer, Wilson, Goodman, and Gene Krupa on drums had recorded a handful of records as a trio. It was these records, sophisticated in the extreme, elegantly subdued, and more reminiscent of European chamber music than swing, that set into motion the chain of events that led directly to the fulfillment of Hammond's vision of an integrated music industry.

The matching of Wilson, Goodman, and Krupa as a trio was as much the product of serendipity as it was a natural evolution for musicians who were playing regular studio dates together and frequently socializing outside the studio. But the idea emerged on its own; no one gave voice to it. And the three did not first play together on an arranged date. The seed was planted at a party in July 1935 at the home of the singer Mildred Bailey and her husband, the jazz xylophonist Red Norvo. The story sounds almost too good to be true, but apparently it happened just the way it's been told and retold. Hammond and many of the top jazz musicians in New York regularly attended dinner parties at the Forest Hills, Queens, apartment of Bailey, a large woman who liked to cook for her friends. (Southern fried chicken was one of her specialties.) On this particular evening, Goodman and Wilson began to jam, accompanied by Bailey's cousin, a test pilot and amateur drummer named Carl Bellinger. Bellinger played the whisk brooms on either a chair, a handy suitcase, or a spare drum set (depending on who was telling the story).

Since Goodman and Wilson had recorded together on many occasions, their impromptu jam didn't initially strike anyone as significant. But, according to Hammond, there was something exceptional to their playing, a singular intimacy that was missing from their prior studio dates. Everyone at the party quickly stopped what they were doing to listen. The next day, Hammond set up a recording date for Wilson, Goodman, and a drummer to be determined, and on July 13, 1935, Wilson, Goodman, and Krupa recorded together as a trio for the first time. The results were stunning. "Body and Soul" from that first session for RCA Victor sounds like the first conversation in a long time among three old friends. Goodman and Wilson, already at ease with each other from the recent Billie Holiday sessions, trade relaxed— even playful—solos, while Krupa keeps time like a metronome behind them.

Hammond started touting the trio two weeks later in the *Brooklyn Eagle*: "Victor has just assembled a three-piece combination which, although it may not break any sales records, provides an excellent example of what swing music can be. The pianist is Teddy Wilson, an extraordinarily sensitive young Negro with tremendous lift, Benny Goodman, the superb clarinetist, and Gene Krupa, a surpassingly fine drummer."

The response to Hammond's public excoriation of Ray Noble's orchestra in the pages of *Down Beat* was swift, and the magazine's editors squeezed the controversy for all it was worth. An angry letter written by one of Noble's band members appeared on the front page of the next issue (July 1935): "If [Noble was] independently wealthy and [didn't] care what the public or musicians think of him, he can try to please the Boogie Man. Ray Noble isn't independently wealthy. All he wants is to make a living." *Down Beat* decided to add a little fuel to the fire by weighing in with a lengthy editorial:

> There were a few discerning musicians who thought that Hammond was right, a great many who disagreed with him heartily, and some who thought his criticism intelligent but biased. And a few individuals asked us why we printed it. Although we thought Hammond a bit severe, we published the article because we considered his criticism sincere, and because we believed it would be of interest to our readers. Hammond is a boon companion of some of the finest swing men in the business, a great friend of Benny Goodman, Gene Krupa, etc., and represents a type of thinking that may not always be correct but it is honest and sincere—and we believe stimulating.

For his part, Hammond made light of the controversy. "I had considered making an early visit to Radio City to hear the band once again," he wrote, "but I am a bit timid when it comes to fifteen simultaneous frigid stares. One member of the band now refers to me as the boogie man."

No sooner had the Noble furor died down than Hammond took on a genuine American icon, Edward Kennedy "Duke" Ellington. Upon the release of "In a Sentimental Mood" and "Showboat Shuffle" in May 1935, Hammond, writing for *Down Beat*, turned his caustic pen toward Ellington, calling the records "a great disappointment." The records, he wrote, suffered from "entirely too much of exhibitionist [cornetist] Rex Stewart, too little of [trumpeter] Cootie Williams, and hardly any of the old time Ellington sincerity and originality." A month later, in his *Brooklyn Eagle* column, his criticism continued: "I'm afraid I was too kind to the Duke Ellington records. All are considerably below the composer's standards and I urge you to buy some of his older gems as an antidote."

Then, on November 3, 1935, Hammond published an article in the *Brooklyn Eagle* under the headline "The Tragedy of Duke Ellington." The headline must have jolted readers. What tragedy? Was Duke ill? Had he been in an accident? It turned out to be nothing quite that serious. Hammond, like many other critics at the time, had simply had enough of Ellington's attempts to move beyond straightforward, uptempo dance music. Ellington had followed "In a Sentimental Mood" and "Showboat Shuffle" with a ruminative piece titled "Reminiscing in Tempo," released in the fall of 1935. The song was innovative on a number of levels, eschewing any pretense of a typical jazz structure and running nearly thirteen minutes, or about four times the length of a standard three-minute dance tune. Written shortly after the death of Ellington's mother, the piece has more in common with a Brahms concerto than a Benny Goodman "killer diller," the hepcat jargon for the bombastic crowd-pleasers such as "Sing, Sing, Sing" that became emblematic of the swing area.

This time Hammond used his displeasure with "Reminiscing in Tempo" to issue a sweeping broadside at Ellington for, as he saw it, deliberately ignoring the plight of downtrodden American blacks. After blasting Ellington for allegedly turning a blind eye to his own exploitation at the hands of white promoters—"Ellington is fully conscious of the fact that Broadway has not treated him fairly, knowing many of the sordid details. And yet he did not lift a finger to protect himself because he has the completely defeatist outlook which chokes so many of the artists of his race"—Hammond painted what he saw as the big picture. And it wasn't pretty.

He wrote:

> But the real trouble with Duke's music is the fact that he has purposely kept himself from any contact with the troubles of his people or mankind in general. It would probably take a Granville Hicks or Langston Hughes to describe the way he shuts his eyes to the abuses being heaped upon his race and his original class. He consciously keeps himself from thinking about such problems as those of the southern share croppers, the Scottsboro boys, intolerable working and relief conditions in the North and South, although he is too intelligent not to know that these all do exist. He has very real fears as to his own future, and yet he has never shown any desire of aligning himself with forces that are seeking to remove the cause of these disgraceful conditions.

In Hammond's view, this social stance had musical consequences: "Ellington's music has become vapid and without the slightest semblance of guts . . . The Duke is afraid even to think about himself, his struggles, and his disappointments and that is why his 'Reminiscing' is so formless and shallow a piece of music."

The article—reprinted on the front page of the next issue of *Down Beat*—was both a courageous and an appalling move on Hammond's part. There was an element of truth in what he wrote insofar as Ellington had grown both rich and famous as the leader of the house band at the segregated Cotton Club, where he performed his sublime numbers for all-white audiences on an elaborate set built to resemble an old Southern plantation. The blacks working that "plantation" would naturally have been slaves, and the symbolism could not have been lost on Ellington and his musicians. And Hammond seems genuinely to have felt Ellington could have used his position as one of the most popular bandleaders in America—black or white—to further the same civil rights causes that so consumed him. Yet hubris hardly begins to describe the mind-set of a twenty-four-year-old heir to a Vanderbilt fortune who would take to task a hugely successful, extremely hardworking black man for looking out for his own in the Jim Crow years of the Depression-era United States.

It has also been suggested that Hammond blasted Ellington because Duke had paid no attention to him. Hammond had offered frequent and unsolicited advice to Ellington in his columns prior to the scathing November 1935 article. "Without doubt the band is unequalled," he had written in 1932. "But there could, and should be, improvements, for there is much that ails the rhythm section." Hammond very likely offered these same suggestions on the several occasions at which the two had met in person. Ellington, already immensely popular and needing help from no one, paid no attention to Hammond's advice. The writer and historian Albert Murray, who knew and respected both men, noted wryly, "Duke wouldn't let anyone mess with his music and John Hammond liked to make suggestions."

Ellington refused at first to publicly acknowledge the attack. He waited almost four years before issuing his response. It came in a series of articles for *Down Beat* in which he decried swing music as a "stagnant" art form and defended his orchestra's attempts to transcend popular formulas.

The Ellington articles also covered the increasingly hostile relationship between jazz musicians and the critics who wrote about them. Here, uncharacteristically, he targeted one of his critics specifically: "The swing critic who perhaps has stirred up the greatest resentment, while at the same time was earning the deepest gratitude of others, has been John Henry Hammond Jr., son of a prominent New York family and possessed of wealth in his own right."

But rather than defend himself point by point, Ellington took Hammond to task for flagrantly violating conflict-of-interest standards:

To properly judge the "modus operandi" of Hammond, it is necessary to devote some thought to the man himself. He appears to be an ardent propagandist and champion of the "lost cause." He apparently has consistently identified himself with the interests of the minorities, the Negro peoples, to a lesser degree, the Jew, and to the underdog, in the form of the Communist party. Perhaps due to the "fever of battle," Hammond's judgment may have become slightly warped, and his enthusiasm and prejudices a little bit unwieldy to control. Whether or not that may be the case, it has become apparent that John has identified himself so strongly in certain directions that he no longer enjoys an impartial status which would entitle him to the role of critic. He has continued to publicise his opinions of musical units other than those to which he has been attached, freely condemning and condoning, ignoring the fact that he has forfeited the right to do this. Such tactics would not be tolerated from the business man and they are doubly unappreciated when employed by one whose name and position allow him to remain immune from counter-attack.

Legend holds that Duke Ellington's disdain for Hammond prompted him to leave Columbia Records for Victor in 1940, not long after Hammond joined Columbia as a full-time record producer. But Ellington never said as much. Others, including Hammond, claimed Ellington left Columbia because the company had recently signed Count Basie and Ellington preferred to be the only black artist on whichever label he was recording for. Only Ellington knew the real reason.

The same belligerent position that, by Hammond's thinking at least, justified his attack on Ellington had also left him frustrated with the NAACP, which favored a cautious and patient approach to the ultimate goal of integration. But in 1935 he changed his mind and joined the civil rights organization at the urging of his friend and former editor Ernest Gruening. A deciding factor occurred when Louis T. Wright, a black surgeon, was named NAACP chairman. Hammond felt the fiercely independent Wright, whom he knew through Fletcher Henderson, was more militant, which is to say more in keeping with his own worldview, than past NAACP chairmen. "Louis Wright had no worries about labels," Hammond wrote. "He didn't care who called him a Red or leftist. All he cared about was that there should be real progress in race relations." Hammond agreed to join the NAACP's board alongside such notables as Eleanor Roosevelt, Adam Clayton

Powell, Sr., and the former New York governor Herbert Lehman. "The organization was changing," he wrote years later. "It was losing some of its middle-class, middle-of-the-road caution. It was no longer content with small victories and slow progress. It was becoming more aggressive and a champion of all blacks." He would remain affiliated with the NAACP as one of its most vocal and visible members for the next thirty years.

Even as a member of the increasingly militant NAACP, Hammond, in the mid-1930s, remained convinced that music was his most effective tool for opening the door to integration, and most of his focus was concentrated in that arena. The door had opened a crack in late 1933, when Benny Goodman began recording regularly with black musicians. It opened a little wider when Goodman, Wilson, and Krupa began recording as a trio. It would swing all the way open on Easter Day, 1936.

The Chicago Rhythm Club was one of many similar clubs that organized in cities across the United States in the 1930s as swing music swept the nation. These groups were made up mostly of upper-middle-class college kids who had the time and resources to indulge their obsession with so-called hot jazz. Helen Oakley, an energetic and resourceful young woman who knew many jazz musicians and wrote regularly for *Down Beat*, was the leader of the Chicago Rhythm Club. Oakley had already produced a successful Benny Goodman concert in Chicago in late 1935, and early the following spring she asked him to return. Only this time Oakley, a big fan of the Goodman trio records, had something a little different in mind. She asked Goodman if he would consider bringing Teddy Wilson to Chicago so that the trio could perform a short set during the intermission of Goodman's regular show.

At first Goodman hesitated, just as he had two and a half years earlier when Hammond suggested he start recording with blacks. Goodman, after all, was still basking in the glow of his first taste of success on a national scale. Eight months earlier, during a series of dates at the Palomar Ballroom in Los Angeles, the young fans exhibited for the first time a frenzied appreciation for Goodman's innovative, revved-up approach to jazz. (The Palomar shows are cited by many jazz historians as the dawn of the swing era.) Goodman's popularity virtually exploded in the months after he returned to New York from California, and he wasn't looking to fix what wasn't broken. Helen Oakley described Goodman's reaction to her radical idea in an interview with Goodman biographer Ross Firestone: "Benny was extremely dubious. He was not an adventurous person and certainly wasn't interested in sticking his neck out. He just wanted to go along doing what he knew how to do best and try to make a success out of that. Racial integration was not a personal cause with Benny . . . Not that Benny was against it. He just couldn't envision what might be and was only interested in cold, hard facts, and he was afraid that if he and Teddy played together in public, it might not be found acceptable."

Goodman relented despite his misgivings, and according to numerous accounts the live set by the trio on April 12, 1936, proved at least as magical as their studio performances. The set was successful on a number of levels. For instance, even the teenagers who traditionally spent much of the time at a Goodman show either howling for the so-called killer-diller numbers or ogling members of the opposite sex were transfixed by the sublime artistry of the trio's sound. "Both Benny and [Wilson] seemed entirely oblivious of the surroundings and played for their own enjoyment," Hammond wrote. "The result was not so far from perfection." Based on the success in Chicago, the trio's set became a standard part of Goodman's show.

Down Beat took notice immediately with an editorial titled "Fine Sportsmanship":

> In a world sick with carbuncles of hate, ravished with fevers of race discrimination and nauseated by dictatorships based on persecution and disciplinary rule of the masses by force, it is refreshing as all hell to witness an example of fine sportsmanship in any line of endeavor. Conditions in the music world are not as discouragingly bad as they are in some other worlds of endeavor, but there are plenty of instances of talent suffering because of race and color, and plenty more because of unjust and disgusting exploitation. It is then with a great deal of pleasure that we noted a colored boy of great talent employed with a group of white musicians and playing to generous applause night after night on the sole basis of his merit as a musician.

The editorial went on to praise Goodman's regular white pianist Jess Stacy for giving up his piano bench to Wilson each night: "This was not just a noble gesture of solitary occasion, mind you, but a regular nightly stepping aside. It is civilized intelligence appreciating a rare gift of talent on the basis of its own worth."

While Hammond probably didn't write the editorial—it's unlikely he would have made the reference to "a colored boy of great talent"— the principles were his. Indeed, in the very same issue Hammond described a cruel paradox then at work in Chicago in which discrimination enforced by the local musicians' union kept black musicians hungry while at the same time preserving the kind of gut-wrenching music Hammond loved.

According to Hammond, the jazz being made in New York was beginning to lose some of its primal energy, due in part to the strict enforcement of union wage scales, which made it hard for small clubs to hire local musicians. In New York, black musicians were allowed to join the union and therefore expected to be paid union wages. Moreover, rigidly enforced licensing fees for New York clubs that sought to employ bands and orchestras inadvertently kept music out of many smaller clubs that couldn't afford to pay the fee, Hammond argued. Consequently, Hammond predicted (inaccurately, as it turned out) a situation in which the only venues that could afford to hire bands would be the large clubs and ballrooms that catered primarily to upscale white audiences—in other words, places where improvisational swing jazz was rarely heard. The city's small nightclubs, where innovation and experimentation were encouraged, would eventually be squeezed out of the picture.

The opposite was true in Chicago, where blacks weren't allowed to join the union and their exclusion made it possible for nightclubs to afford to pay them. Unfortunately, many of the club owners took advantage of the musicians by forcing them to work seventy-hour weeks for horrendous pay, according to Hammond. "The only blessing that this vicious system brings is informal and unlettered music with an almost primitive wallop," he wrote.

A month later, Hammond targeted his old boss Irving Mills. "There are a few incidents around town that are worth recounting," he observed in his *Down Beat* column. "The Irving Mills office has just established a 'Jim Crow' waiting room for all colored folk who visit the office. Mills is branching out as a ballroom operator and big-shot producer. He does not wish to 'jeopardize' his position in the show world by being thought of as just a colored entrepreneur."

Just twenty-five years old, Hammond had emerged as arguably the strongest force behind the push for an integrated music industry. Little more than a fantasy just a few years earlier, Hammond's crusade was rapidly turning into reality.

6

FURTHER AND FURTHER AFIELD

It's doubtful that John Hammond's signature grin—the one that pulled back his lips, thrust forth his big teeth, caused lengthy dimples to crease the sides of his lean face, and made his eyes squint until they were practically closed—was ever any wider than the night in July 1936 when he walked into the Reno Club in Kansas City and saw a slightly plump, nattily attired man with a pencil-thin mustache seated at the piano. Hammond recognized the sound coming from the instrument straightaway. It was the same spare, relaxed, yet dynamic playing he had been listening to on the radio recently late at night and raving about in *Down Beat*.

The man at the piano, William Basie, had put on a few pounds since Hammond had last seen him in Harlem some four years earlier. He had also given himself a nickname: the Count.

The Reno Club was Hammond's kind of place—the kind of place where musicians made music to please each other rather than the patrons. "The Reno Club is not only not inferior to comparable spots in Chicago and New York, it is infinitely preferable to them," Hammond wrote. Located on Twelfth Street near Cherry, it was one of scores of nightclubs that dotted the black neighborhoods just to the southeast of downtown Kansas City. The first thing that caught Hammond's attention once inside was a giant mock-up of a peacock's feathers, ten feet tall and all aglitter, that served as a backdrop for the stage. Right beside the piano sat a grinning, life-size ceramic cat—the so-called kitty in whose mouth patrons were strongly urged to leave tips. Above the men's room sign to the right of the stage was a list of the club's specialty drinks: Manhattan, martini, Alexander, and sidecar. Each cost forty cents, at least a dime cheaper than in New York City.

Hammond decided to bypass the bar and forgo a table. Instead, he pulled up a chair right next to Basie's piano bench. "I didn't pay much attention to him at first, because actually that was something that used to happen very often, especially at the Reno," Basie recalled in his autobiography, *Good Morning Blues*. The young man grinned at him, according to Basie. Then he introduced himself. "Hi, I'm John Hammond." Hammond ordered Basie a drink—gin over ice—and then settled in for the rest of the show.

The players in Basie's band had no idea who Hammond was, let alone that he was in a position to propel them to the top rung of the music industry. But it didn't really matter. They played with the same passion and ingenuity every night, and that night they carried Hammond along for the ride of his life. "Of course, they completely destroyed me," he recalled nearly forty years later.

After Basie finished his show, he took Hammond out on the town to hear some blues. From the Reno it was just a few doors down to the Sunset Café, where the singer Big Joe Turner and his partner, the pianist Pete Johnson, held forth most nights. "Those two cats damn near killed [Hammond] because they were swinging so much. He just sat there shaking his head and slapping his hands," according to Basie.

A powerful bond was forged that night between the black bandleader and the young white record producer. Basie said his respect for Hammond stemmed not from the influence he wielded in the music business, nor from the fact that he had driven all the way from New York just to hear him play. Instead, Basie found himself astonished at the depth of Hammond's knowledge of American music. Hammond was familiar with virtually every musician Basie had ever met. And he wasn't just familiar with their names—he knew where they had played recently, with whom they were playing, and when they had last recorded.

Their evening ended long after sunrise with breakfast at Eleanor's, a well-known coffee shop frequented by Kansas City's black musicians,

where Hammond was introduced to fried corn, ham, and, Basie recalled, "some beautiful biscuits that I think he still remembers."

Opportunity abounded in Kansas City during those years, so much
so that it was frequently described as "a wide-open town." It was the
Kansas City of the Democratic machine boss Tom Pendergast, who for
nearly two decades used the mountains of cash he skimmed from the
city's highly profitable—but illegal—liquor, gambling, and prostitution
rackets to grease the city's political wheels. When it came to making
money, Pendergast believed in equal opportunity. If black club owners
on the city's east side could generate profits—a healthy percentage of
which were passed on to Pendergast's army of bagmen—by staying
open all night, then they had just as much right as any white club
owner to serve liquor, run their gambling tables, and keep their prosti-
tutes working for as long as customers were willing to stay and spend
money. Hammond wrote breathlessly of the city: "In Kansas City there
are no less than 854 spots with night life of some kind, whether it be orchestras, piano players, or nickel phonographs. Descriptions of the
place as the hotbed of American music are in every way justified, for
there is no town in America, New Orleans perhaps excepted, that has
produced so much excellent music—Negro, of course."

During Hammond's stay in Kansas City, Basie took him to all the
local hot spots. Along Twelfth Street there were the Reno, the Lone
Star Summer Garden, and the Sunset Café. And near the intersection
of Eighteenth and Vine there were the Cherry Blossom, the Paseo
Hall, and Lucille's Paradise. Basie introduced him to a couple of tough,
smart, and ambitious black businessmen, Jimmy Ruffin and Piney
Brown, who operated nightclubs and found Kansas City a conducive
place to prosper.

The freewheeling environment fostered a unique spirit among
Kansas City's musicians. They played as they pleased, unencumbered
by the constraints of the well-paid musicians who worked in the upscale clubs of Chicago or New York, where well-heeled patrons demanded to hear pristine versions of the latest dance tunes. The piano
player, writer, and arranger Mary Lou Williams once described the
scene: "It was a ballin' town, and it attracted musicians from all over
the South and Southwest, and especially from Kansas . . . In Kaycee,

nothing mattered. I've known musicians so enthused about playing that they would walk all the way from the Kansas side and attend a jam session. Even bass players, caught without streetcar fare, would hump their bass on their back and come running."

Improvisational jamming was the preferred style. The jamming soared above the short, rhythmic bursts of repeated melody known as riffs, and it was the riffs that provided the solid foundation from which the soloists took flight. Basie's "One O'Clock Jump" is perhaps the archetype of this style, with its dynamic BAH BAH BAH-buh-BAH riff serving as the ground over which Basie on piano, Buck Clayton on trumpet, and Herschel Evans on tenor saxophone performed their aerial feats of derring-do. Years later, Hammond recalled the first time he played "One O'Clock Jump" for Benny Goodman. "This is the thing that absolutely overwhelmed Benny Goodman . . . Benny realized immediately this completely free and easy riffing thing would be the next thing in jazz." Basie's smooth musical approach contrasted starkly with Goodman's often-bombastic arrangements. Listening to Basie might be likened to watching Picasso slowly and easily turn a canvas into a masterpiece, while Goodman's music conjured a sense of majestic precision, not unlike watching construction of some noble monument, perhaps the Empire State Building or the Brooklyn Bridge.

The path that led John Hammond to Kansas City in the summer of 1936 began earlier that year on a frigid night in Chicago in the front seat of his convertible. Restless after another evening of listening to Benny Goodman's band at the Congress Hotel, Hammond went out to his car to scan the radio dial for something different. Shivering in the cold, he worked the dial back and forth. Suddenly he came across something that caused him to warm up considerably. "I heard this faint sound on the very end of the dial . . . It was an experimental station called W9XBY . . . I found out that every night this W9XBY broadcast live from a little club called the Reno Club in Kansas City, and I listened to this unbelievable band."

Basie's name soon began appearing regularly in Hammond's *Down Beat* columns. The superlatives flowed from the typewriter. In one column, Hammond noted that Benny Goodman himself believed Basie's orchestra "has the most powerful drive of any band in the country." His praise for Basie's musicians was no less effusive. "I want to say categorically and without fear of ridicule that Count Bill Basie has by far and away the finest dance orchestra in the country," he wrote in the spring of 1936. "And when I say this, I am fully aware of Benny Goodman, Fletcher Henderson and Chick Webb . . . [Basie's band has a] driving rhythm section more exciting than any in American orchestral history." He went on to predict that if Basie could keep his men together for a few more months, the group would emerge as one of the top bands in the country.

Meanwhile, Hammond was writing to Basie in an effort to arrange a meeting. Basie claimed later that he ignored the letters because he had no idea who Hammond was, let alone any notion of Hammond's considerable influence in the music industry. By that summer Hammond had grown impatient at not hearing back from Basie, so in July he simply got in his car and drove to Kansas City to find him.

Basie's journey to the Reno Club began in the resort town of Red Bank, New Jersey, where he was born in 1904. In his memoirs, Basie recalled how as a child he had watched his mother as she washed the neighbors' clothes to earn extra money. That experience, he said, drove him to pursue a career in music, where someone with talent might find unlimited possibilities. He studied the piano in earnest and took his first professional job—filling in for the regular accompanist at the local movie house—in his early teens. A few years later, while working at a roadhouse called the Hong Kong Inn on the outskirts of Asbury Park, Basie was encouraged to try his luck in the clubs of Harlem. After moving to New York, he became acquainted with Fats Waller and Willie "the Lion" Smith, two of Harlem's most revered jazz pianists. Nightclub gigs soon led to a job in a traveling vaudeville show.

It was while touring with such a show around 1927 that Basie first traveled to Kansas City. During a stop in Tulsa, Oklahoma, on the same tour, he heard for the first time a band called the Blue Devils, an influential so-called territory band that traveled throughout the Southwest. The Blue Devils members Jimmy Rushing, a powerful blues singer, and Walter Page, the bass player, would join forces with Basie a few years later in Kansas City. As Gunther Schuller noted in his comprehensive study of the period, *The Swing Era*, the territory bands that crisscrossed America's dusty backroads during the 1920s and 1930s served as fertile training grounds for some of the greatest players in jazz. In addition to Rushing and Page, the saxophonists Lester Young and Charlie Parker and the guitarist Charlie Christian served apprenticeships in territory bands.

More important perhaps than the individual musicians who emerged from these bands was the manner in which these well-traveled outfits influenced the evolution of regional jazz styles. In the Southwest, for example, over time the bands adopted a bluesy edge to their sound, the result of playing gigs along the perimeter of the blues-soaked South. The style that emerged, a gumbo of soul-searching blues, conventional dance music, and gutbucket jazz, became known as "the Kansas City sound." Basie would become its primary ambassador.

Basie settled in Kansas City in 1929, joining Bennie Moten's orchestra. It was with Moten that Basie made his first studio recordings. And it was with Moten that he returned to New York to play the big Harlem theaters where Hammond recalled first hearing him. By 1935, the Moten band was running out of steam, and Basie was struggling to earn a living. Basie and some other members of Moten's group formed their own band and took up permanent residence in a new Kansas City club called the Cherry Blossom with Basie as leader. (Perhaps the move was fortuitous, for Moten died unexpectedly in 1935.) From the Cherry Blossom the group moved on to the Reno Club.

Hammond's arrival in Kansas City in July 1936 was marred by an unpleasant surprise—but one he probably should have expected. In his enthusiasm to alert the public to Basie's talent, Hammond had written extensively on him in *Down Beat*. The articles caught the attention of Dave Kapp of Decca Records, one of Hammond's competitors in the music industry. Kapp, apparently based solely on Hammond's rave reviews, made his way to Kansas City just ahead of Hammond and signed Basie to a three-year contract. When Hammond found out, he was furious. Kapp had not only stolen his prospect but also, according to Hammond, taken advantage of Basie's naïveté and limited financial resources. Kapp had signed Basie to a contract that paid the bandleader a straight fee of $750 a year to record twelve records annually, a pittance even during the Depression. What's more, the contract included no provision for royalties. Basie's musicians fared even worse under the deal. "It was a slave contract," Hammond declared angrily some three decades later.

Although Hammond couldn't get all the terms of the contract voided, he was able to convince Decca to pay the band members union-scale wages. There was nothing he could do about the lack of royalties, however. Basie recalled wistfully, "The thing about the whole situation was that the very reason that John had come out to Kansas City at that time was to tell me about a deal he had in the works for me with Brunswick Records. Naturally, it was a much better deal, and John had set it up just because he liked us and wanted people to hear us on records. There was no money at all in it for him."

Basie was a local star in Kansas City when Hammond arrived to whisk him away. From the remnants of the Moten band, the Count, as he was now calling himself, had formed a crack nine-piece unit that included the Blue Devils veteran Page on bass, Jo Jones on drums, Oran "Hot Lips" Page and Joe Keyes on trumpets, Dan Minor on trombone, and the saxophonists Buster Smith, Jack Washington, and Lester Young. The orchestra, sometimes called the Barons of Rhythm, was one of the most popular bands in the city. In fact, Basie's only real competition came from Andy Kirk's Twelve Clouds of Joy and Harlan Leonard and his Kansas City Rockets.

It's hard to say which of the three was the most popular. Andy Kirk's group opened a show for Fats Waller in July 1936, and later that summer shared the bill with the great pianist Earl Hines. And when the popular bandleader Don Redman passed through around the same time, Harlan Leonard's group was asked to open. But when Duke Ellington's band, one of the most popular in the country at the time, came to town early that fall, Basie's orchestra opened the show.

Hammond's role with Basie, then, was different from his role in promoting Billie Holiday. Holiday was a thoroughly unproven talent. Basie was not. What Hammond had in mind for Basie was success on a national scale, success on the same level as Duke Ellington and

Benny Goodman. On his own, Basie was unlikely to achieve that level of success. Hammond intended to use every bit of his considerable energy and influence to ensure that Basie did.

Basie had become Hammond's primary focus in the wake of Benny Goodman's phenomenal success. Goodman's orchestra had emerged as the most popular dance band in America after a triumphant engagement at the Palomar Ballroom in Los Angeles in August 1935. As Goodman's popularity grew in the months that followed, Hammond went in search of new challenges. But he still had Goodman's ear, and when he saw or heard something he thought Goodman might find interesting, he was quick to alert his friend. Both men found Lionel Hampton very interesting.

Nearly twenty years after the actual events, Hammond and Goodman's first encounter with Hampton was depicted in a movie based loosely on Goodman's life. In the film version, released in 1955, Hampton, playing himself, is working as a soda jerk at a snack shop on Catalina Island off the coast of Los Angeles. Goodman, played by Steve Allen, and some bandmates arrive at the snack shop and are waited on by an energetic black man, Lionel Hampton. After cooking and serving their food, Hampton, implausibly to say the least, begins to entertain the customers on his vibraharp. Soon, he and the Goodman band members all join in an impromptu jam. (Years later, Hampton laughed uproariously at the scene depicted in the movie.)

There's no telling why Hollywood felt the need to revise the story, since the actual events that led to Hampton's joining Goodman's band in late 1936 were dramatic in their own right. Likewise it's hard to say why more attention wasn't paid at the time to the fact that Goodman was creating the first integrated jazz band. Ten years later, America was riveted by the story of Jackie Robinson's debut as the first black major-league baseball player. Oddly, the addition of first Teddy Wilson and a few months later Lionel Hampton to the formerly all-white Goodman orchestra generated but scant attention outside the music industry. Maybe it was because the walls of segregation broke down gradually in popular music over the course of many months. Or maybe it was because most music fans knew that white and black musicians were already making records together and they didn't consider it controversial for blacks and whites to play together on the same bandstand.

In hindsight, however, Goodman's decision to add the two to his touring band was no less significant to American popular culture than Branch Rickey's decision to open baseball's doors to black players. Indeed, there are those who believe Goodman's decision made Rickey's a lot easier. Lionel Hampton thought so. "I think we opened the door for Jackie Robinson getting into major-league ball," he said more than sixty years later.

Hampton's addition to the Goodman band caused little more than a ripple in the jazz press. Goodman himself, so cautious just a few months earlier about playing in public with Teddy Wilson, welcomed Hampton into the fold virtually overnight. Of course, since Wilson had already opened the door, it was easier for Hampton to follow him through. But other forces were at work as well. Wilson's combination of poise and talent made him the perfect choice to take the initial plunge. Hammond had handpicked him for the role precisely for those qualities. Similarly, Hampton, a brilliant musician and wildly charismatic performer, was the perfect choice to follow in Wilson's footsteps. Hampton's talent and charisma seemed to transcend skin color—crowds just reacted to him.

After returning briefly to New York from his trip to Kansas City to woo Count Basie, Hammond in August 1936 turned right around and headed to California to join Goodman in the studio in Los Angeles. Hampton, who had been working in Los Angeles for several years by then, was holding court each night in a rough-and-tumble beer joint called the Paradise Club, at Sixth and Main streets in a dingy section of downtown Los Angeles. Word of Hampton's performances had spread among Los Angeles's knowledgeable jazz enthusiasts, and his shows were drawing large crowds. Hammond waited no more than a day or two after arriving in Los Angeles before he made his way out to the Paradise to catch a show.

Rare is the combination of real musical genius and truly inspired showmanship. Hampton was blessed with both, to spare. His music alone was enough to startle even virtuoso musicians of Benny Goodman's caliber. When Hampton's mallets struck the metallic bars of the vibraharp, a spray of notes burst forth. And each one made perfect sense, one note following another impossibly fast but never forced. Moreover, Hampton was a showman's showman, a pioneer in the art of working an audience into a frenzy. Grinning madly, wildly bobbing his head in time to the music, his mallets little more than a blur of motion, he was usually drenched in sweat midway through a set.

Hampton was born in Louisville, Kentucky, in 1908 but raised in Birmingham, Alabama. His family moved north to Chicago in the 1920s, and he became a member of the Chicago Defender Newsboys' Band, a musical group sponsored by Chicago's leading black newspaper. Hampton's first exposure to Chicago's jazz scene came through his uncle Richard Morgan, a well-connected hustler and bootlegger who achieved a certain immortality in 1937 for being at the wheel during the car crash that killed Bessie Smith. Hampton began playing drums professionally while still in his early teens. After moving to California while still in high school, he joined a band fronted by Les Hite, with whom he made a handful of records with Louis Armstrong. According to Hampton, it was Armstrong who first suggested he try the vibraharp. By 1932, Hampton was fronting his own band at a Los Angeles nightspot called the Red Car Club, whose clientele of sailors and cable car drivers was apparently less than discriminating when it came to music. (Hampton later credited the inattentiveness of the Red Car's patrons with allowing him the freedom to experiment on the vibraharp, an instrument similar to the xylophone but amplified by an internal motor to produce a loud, chiming sound not yet common in jazz.) Renamed the Paradise Club in the mid-1930s, it became a regular haunt for celebrities and various scenesters.

"John Hammond came down to the Paradise Club to hear me and my band play because we played jazz in Los Angeles, and of course you know John Hammond was crazy about jazz," Hampton recalled with a chuckle sixty-four years later.

Hampton said he hadn't noticed Hammond arrive but that one of his bandmates had. Hammond, according to the bandmate, appeared to be enjoying himself immensely. What happened next is part of jazz lore, and many of the details depend on who's telling the story. Hampton told it this way: "After about four or five nights [of watching the show from the audience], John Hammond came and introduced himself. We had heard of John Hammond and heard that he helped black musicians." The following night Hammond returned to the Paradise and brought Benny Goodman along. Impressed, Goodman returned the following night with Teddy Wilson and Gene Krupa. "We were playing so hard that Benny got up, took out his clarinet, and joined us," Hampton recalled. (The song on which they first played together was a jam called "Blues in D Flat," according to Hampton.) "John Hammond was really enjoying Benny playing with us, and it got so good that Gene Krupa joined us on drums and Teddy Wilson got on piano." Sensing the beginning of something special between the four stars, Hampton's regular bandmates drifted one by one away from the stage, leaving Hampton, Goodman, Krupa, and Wilson alone.

Hammond, according to Hampton, was ecstatic. He apparently determined right away that the Goodman Trio had been transformed that night into the Goodman Quartet. "John Hammond came up to the bandstand where we were playing up there and said, 'Oh, Benny, you've got to record this. This is great.' So Benny asked if I could record with them the next day in a Los Angeles studio at 10:00 a.m. I told him I'd be there at 9:00 a.m.," Hampton said. Two months later, Hampton packed his belongings and drove cross-country to join the Goodman band full-time.

Once back in New York, Hammond turned his full attention to Count Basie, whose departure from Kansas City was imminent. The band was scheduled to open a series of performances in Chicago in November and then move on to New York. Hammond needed to arrange additional dates so that the band could work between Chicago and New York.

The newspaper coverage of Basie's last days in Kansas City reveals the intelligent and mild-mannered bandleader as not only a popular musician but also a respected member of the community who would be missed. Basie's courting by both John Hammond and a representative from Decca Records had been reported in the press, and when word spread that fall that Basie would be leaving Kansas City to pursue a wider audience, local fans responded warmly. Indeed, fans threw bouquets onstage at a farewell dance attended by several thousand people at Kansas City's Paseo Hall on Halloween night. An article that appeared ahead of the dance in *The Call*, Kansas City's black newspaper, noted, "The Count and his band are one of the most popular units in this section. This will mark Kansas City's last official time to hear the Count for some time. He and his aggregation will play the latest tunes and play them as only Basie can play them."

A few days after the dance an article in *The Call* enthused, "Kansas City is eagerly watching Count Basie's bid for the big time." It wouldn't happen overnight.

Hammond's column for the November issue of *Down Beat*, written in October before Basie left Kansas City for Chicago, foreshadowed some of the difficulties the band would encounter as it emerged into the national spotlight. Observing that there was no pressure on Basie's men as the house band at the Reno Club, Hammond noted that expectations would be higher at Chicago's famous Grand Terrace, where Basie was booked for a string of shows that opened just a few days after the band left Kansas City. Adding to the pressure was the fact that Basie was following Fletcher Henderson's band into the Grand Terrace. Regular patrons, then, would be judging him against one of the best in the business. "I hope that the band can readily accustom itself to the more hincty surroundings of the Grand Terrace and play with the same ease and assurance" that were its signature characteristics at its Reno Club shows, Hammond wrote. "Basie's band is at its best when it is playing a single good tune for about twenty minutes, with the rhythm section exerting a drive unlike that of any other, and a couple of good soloists playing against brass figures which could only originate in Kansas City. Once it becomes mannered and pretentious the group will have lost its only reason for existence."

The band stumbled through its first few nights in Chicago. The Grand Terrace was essentially a high-end nightclub similar to New York's Cotton Club, and Basie's group was required to perform as part of an elaborate floor show. But since several of the band members couldn't read music, it was difficult for them to learn the songs that accompanied the show. What's more, Basie's Reno Club band was a nine-piece unit, whereas the typical dance band of that period consisted of fourteen pieces. Thus Basie needed to add five musicians before opening in Chicago, which meant those five musicians had just one week to adjust to the rest of the band and vice versa.

Basie thought he was going to be fired. "John Hammond came out to Chicago to be with us during that opening week and of course he was pulling for us." Hammond's relentless support, Basie recalled, helped restore the band's confidence.

Ultimately, all of the worrying proved unfounded. Hammond attended most of the shows in Chicago with his friends the singer Mildred Bailey and her husband, the vibraharpist and xylophonist Red Norvo. Together they watched as the band jelled over the course of the engagement. When it all came together, Hammond heard "music the like of which I have never before heard."

Unfazed by the band's shaky start, Hammond rented studio time in Chicago and gathered Basie and several of his top soloists to record a handful of sides for Vocalion Records. In later years, Hammond often referred to this session as one of his favorites. It's easy to understand why. Inside what Hammond once referred to as "the crummiest studio that I've ever seen in my life" were Basie, Walter Page, Jo Jones, Carl "Tatti" Smith, Lester Young, and the singer Jimmy Rushing. The session began at 10:00 a.m., and none of the musicians had been to bed. They had played the Grand Terrace until 5:00 a.m., grabbed a bite to eat, then headed straight to the studio. Hammond hoped the adrenaline from their performance the previous night would carry over into the studio. It was stuffy and the equipment was crude. The room was too small for a grand piano, so Basie played a battered old baby grand. The acoustics were so bad that vibrations emanating from the bass drum caused the recording needle to jerk back and forth. Jo Jones could use only his snare and cymbals.

But, according to Hammond, none of that affected the quality of the playing. In about three hours, the men recorded four sides—"Shoe Shine Boy," "Evenin'," "Boogie Woogie," and "Oh, Lady Be Good." All four were captured in one take each, and the spontaneity is evident. The records are now considered some of the finest jazz recordings ever made. It was "an absolutely perfect session," Hammond recalled. (Another aspect of the session that pleased Hammond was that Basie cut the records for Vocalion despite being under contract at the time to

Decca, a point that always seemed to tickle his appreciation for the mischievous. Basie's name went unmentioned, and the group was billed as Jones-Smith Inc.)

The session also marked the first time that the tenor saxophonist Lester "Pres" Young's innovative sound was committed to record. Young's unique tone is most often described as big, warm, and open, and jazz historians hold him in the same esteem as Louis Armstrong, Coleman Hawkins, and Charlie Parker. Young was also jazz's first hipster. Aloof and enigmatic, he seemed to live in his own world, even speaking a language of slang all his own. Introducing Young onstage one night in 1938, Hammond referred to him as "the greatest tenor saxophone player who's ever blown."

After wrapping up the Grand Terrace dates, Basie headed east to New York, performing a series of one-night stands along the way. Hammond waited in New York, where he had arranged for the band to be represented by Willard Alexander of the Music Corporation of America, one of the biggest talent management agencies of the era. Alexander, a highly respected agent who was as enthusiastic about Basie as Hammond was, had set up a series of dates at the huge Roseland Ballroom on Fifty-second Street beginning Christmas Eve.

By most accounts, the early shows were a disaster. The critic George Simon wrote famously that the band played out of tune. The trumpeter Buck Clayton didn't dispute the criticism, but offered an explanation: Basie had changed the ending to "King Porter Stomp," the band's big finisher. But some of the musicians forgot what Basie had done. "The result was total confusion," Clayton wrote. "We were so embarrassed that we didn't want to face anyone the rest of the night. John Hammond was so upset that he almost pulled all of his crew cut out. He had invited friends, critics, reporters and many others to hear this great band out of Kansas City and we had gotten screwed up on the ending of 'King Porter Stomp' and the band sounded like a cat fight at the end of the number."

Basie later shrugged off the criticism, attributing the band's early jitters to their trying to adjust to a new show for a different audience in a different setting. Part of the problem was that bands hired to play large dance halls were required to play popular songs, songs that patrons were familiar with and to which they could hum along mindlessly as they moved about the dance floor. That wasn't Basie's forte. His band jammed: they found a riff in which they were all comfortable, and then the soloists jammed on top of that riff. For his part, Hammond encouraged Basie and his men to retain their unique style and ignore the naysayers.

But even Hammond wasn't entirely satisfied with the band's sound. He felt it could be improved with some tinkering, and he began to do just that. The changes to the band's lineup that he oversaw led to bitter accusations—accusations that followed him for the rest of his career— that he "broke up" the Basie band.

Hammond had already earned a reputation as an opinionated meddler. Duke Ellington, for example, viewed him as someone who could and would help a musician's career, but only on his own terms. According to that view, a musician who agreed to work with Hammond in the studio would likely be told not only what songs to play but also what musicians to play with. That view only presents one side of Hammond, however. He could also be flexible when the situation warranted. And when he determined that his input wasn't needed, he blended into the scenery.

Hammond's occasional bossiness bothered some musicians but not others. Billie Holiday grew weary of it over time. Teddy Wilson and Count Basie, meanwhile, never complained. And while Ellington never recorded with Hammond, members of his band frequently participated in the all-star sessions Hammond put together for Brunswick in the mid-1930s. Still others, Fletcher Henderson and Benny Goodman, for example, learned to compromise with him and ultimately reaped the benefits of his uncanny skill at finding talented musicians and matching them up with other musicians of complementary abilities.

Whether Hammond actually "broke up" the Basie band is open to interpretation. He certainly helped retool it. But the truth is usually more complicated than bitter memories allow for. In the first place, the big swing bands of the 1930s were highly transitory outfits. Band members often clashed over musical philosophy, money, or women. Many of the musicians drank heavily and used drugs, and different bandleaders took different approaches toward employees who did so.

(Goodman ran a notoriously strict outfit; Basie was more tolerant.) Furthermore, bands often poached talented players from their rivals. Musicians were loyal but only to a point. A more lucrative offer was always a persuasive incentive to join a different band. This was, after all, the Depression. All of these factors contributed to high turnover rates within the bands.

It's also important to understand why Basie, probably more than any other major musician with whom Hammond worked, was generally receptive to his tinkering. Basie was an easygoing man who tended to avoid confrontation. But his relaxed demeanor masked a strong desire to see the band succeed, and Hammond was helping to make that happen. In fact, Basie had every reason to listen to Hammond. By touting him in his columns in *Down Beat*, Hammond had brought Basie to the attention of some of the most powerful names in the music industry and made it possible for him to leave Kansas City for more lucrative engagements in Chicago and New York. And it was Hammond who stood up for Basie after he naively signed an exploitative contract with Decca Records. Finally, Hammond did these things while asking nothing of Basie. According to Albert Murray, who helped the bandleader write his autobiography, Basie trusted Hammond without reservation. "The main thing [that impressed Basie] was that Hammond wasn't doing it for the money," Murray explained.

Still, it wasn't as if Hammond were manipulating puppet strings. Basie and his bandmates were experienced professional musicians who were open to suggestion but at the same time certain of their abilities. "Basie was the kind of slick guy who could make you think you were running things when you weren't," said Murray. "The [band members] wouldn't refuse to try something. In fact, sometimes they tried it just to satisfy him. [But] if Hammond made a suggestion and it worked, it worked. They'd leave it." Hammond was also tirelessly promoting the band, as well as lending the guys a few dollars when they needed it. "They had a very pragmatic attitude toward Hammond," Murray observed wryly.

Naturally, some of Hammond's suggestions left egos bruised and may even have derailed promising careers. But hindsight has shown that his instincts were almost always right, that the musicians he recommended to Basie usually proved beneficial to the band's long-term success. The addition of the guitarist Freddie Green is perhaps the best example. Hammond liked to hang around a little club on West Broadway in Greenwich Village called the Black Cat. He liked the six-piece jazz band, and he liked the ninety-nine-cent dinner that came with a free drink. He also liked the naked girl who danced on most nights. But he loved the band's guitar player. "I thought he was the greatest I had ever heard . . . He was the ultimate ensemble player I had always looked for."

The story that emerged from the night Hammond introduced Basie to Green has joined the annals of jazz lore. Like all these types of stories, what supposedly happened depends a great deal on who's telling it. But if Hammond's version is true (and it has never been disputed), it's a story worthy of its legend: In January 1937, while Basie was still playing the Roseland Ballroom, Hammond invited Basie, Lester Young, and several other members of the group down to the Black Cat to hear the house band and maybe sit in on a few numbers. Benny Goodman was also invited. Young, not yet popular among jazz fans but already well known by musicians, was the first to be invited onstage. When Goodman, who was already a star, arrived a short time later, the excitement was palpable. Goodman, according to Hammond, was particularly impressed with Young's playing. The memory of what happened during the ensuing jam session stayed with Hammond the rest of his life. He recalled: "What was so superb about it was that Lester had a beat-up old metal clarinet and Benny heard him and was terribly impressed with the way Lester played clarinet. And so, on the spot, [Benny] gave him his Selmer clarinet. It's the only time I've ever seen Benny give a clarinet away like that and it was sort of wonderful."

Soon Basie had taken over on piano, Goodman and Young were trading licks on clarinet, and Freddie Green was impressing everyone with his steady chops on the guitar. "It was quite a night," said Hammond.

There was, however, the issue of Basie's current guitar player, a competent veteran of the Southwest territory bands named Claude Williams. Williams was known as "Fiddler" because his primary instrument was the violin. While Hammond admittedly hated Williams's violin playing, he

had no issue with Williams's guitar work. He simply felt Green was better, and Basie evidently agreed. Green was hired after the band finished
the Roseland dates and was on the bandstand with them in Pittsburgh a
few weeks later. Williams was never actually fired, but he apparently saw
the writing on the wall and left the band shortly after Green arrived. The
experience left him embittered, and he never forgave Hammond. "You
know, this John Hammonds [*sic*] that took over Count's band, he didn't
want nobody in the band to outshine Count 'cause he was pushing
Count. Every time I'd take a solo or two, you know, I'd get a big round of
applause. So that's another reason he got rid of my ass," Williams told an
interviewer many years later. Basie, who felt bad enough about the incident to include an explanation in his memoirs, claimed that at the time
Green was hired, Williams was looking to leave the band to find a gig
where his violin would play a more prominent role. In any case, Hammond's methods may have been ruthless, but his instincts were correct.
Freddie Green remained with Basie's band for decades and is considered one of the top jazz rhythm guitarists ever.

And Hammond wasn't done tinkering. He convinced Basie to replace his lead alto saxophone player, Caughey Roberts, with Earle Warren, and the trumpeters Ed Lewis and Bobby Moore were brought in
from Kansas City to replace Joe Keyes and Carl Smith. Each of these
recommendations was vindicated over time as Basie's band gained
wider and wider acclaim. But not everyone in the band appreciated
Hammond's insight. Lester Young is said to have never trusted Hammond after watching as his bandmates—and friends—were dismissed
one by one. Young's biographer Douglas Henry Daniels wrote that Young
and Billie Holiday shared, among other things, a disdain for Hammond
rooted in their perception of him as a heartless meddler. (Ironically, it
was during a session organized by Hammond in early 1937 that Young
and Holiday first recorded together. The result was one of the most un-
forgettable pairings in recorded jazz. On classics such as "He's Funny
That Way" and "Sailboat in the Moonlight," Young's pitch-perfect solos
weave gracefully in and around Holiday's inimitable phrasing. It's been
said that, like a long-married couple, the two finished each other's musical thoughts.)

There are also those who offer a different description of Hammond's studio demeanor, one that contrasts sharply with his reputation as a meddler. Ahmet Ertegun, who recalled often bumping into Hammond inside various Manhattan studios during the 1950s, laughs at memories of finding him, time and again, seated in a corner quietly reading *The New York Times* while the musicians he had gathered made their music. "Those records from the thirties with Teddy Wilson, Benny Goodman, and Billie Holiday, no one needed to produce those records. Those people were talented professionals. They knew exactly what they were doing and didn't need much direction," Ertegun observed.

There is truth in both descriptions—the meddling Hammond and the laissez-faire Hammond. Nevertheless, his genius lay in his willingness to experiment, and in his uncanny success rate in making those experiments work. The list of musicians he brought together for recording dates in the 1930s is staggering. Contemporary jazz historians can only shake their heads at the thought of walking into a studio in midtown Manhattan and finding Billie Holiday, Benny Goodman, Lester Young, Teddy Wilson, Buck Clayton, Freddie Green, Walter Page, and Jo Jones. (Imagine a baseball team with a lineup that included Ted Williams, Joe DiMaggio, Jackie Robinson, Stan Musial, Willie Mays, Hank Aaron, and Mickey Mantle.) But such was the case in late January 1937, when Hammond organized a session at Brunswick's studio at Broadway and Fifty-seventh Street for a record that was later released under the unassuming title *Teddy Wilson and His Orchestra*. "It astonishes me, as I look back, at how casually we were able to assemble such all-star groups. It wasn't that we didn't know how great they were. We did. It was simply a Golden Age," Hammond recalled in his memoirs.

During the winter and spring of 1937, Hammond logged many hours of studio time overseeing sessions of these all-star bands. At the time, he and Billie Holiday still enjoyed an amicable relationship, and these sessions resulted in some of her finest recordings—"(This Is) My Last Affair," "Moanin' Low," and "Foolin' Myself." That summer, at Hammond's urging, Holiday joined Basie's band as vocalist. This may have been the only bad advice Hammond ever gave Basie. Holiday stayed for a turbulent nine months or so. Several versions emerged of what happened. Holiday herself offered at least two. In the first, she quit over musical differences with Basie's handlers (including Hammond) and because of the racism she encountered on the road. In the second, she was inexplicably fired on orders from Hammond. Basie claimed Holiday left on her own to pursue more lucrative opportunities. (She joined Artie Shaw's band a short time later.) Basie's manager, Willard Alexander, a close friend of Hammond's, accepted responsibility for her firing, stating in a 1938 *Down Beat* article that Holiday was let go because of her poor attitude and inconsistent performances. Alexander defended Hammond's role: "It was John Hammond who got Billie the job with Count Basie, and he was responsible for Basie keeping her. In fact, if it hadn't been for John Hammond, Billie would have been through six months sooner." Whatever the actual circumstances, the episode drained once and for all whatever warmth may have still existed between Holiday and Hammond.

Meanwhile, Hammond worked tirelessly to get Basie before as wide an audience as possible. In January 1938, he convinced Benny Goodman to bring Basie and several of his sidemen onstage to jam during Goodman's landmark concert at Carnegie Hall. At the time, the concert was one of the most widely publicized events in the history of jazz. (Later that night, Basie competed against Chick Webb in a now legendary battle of the bands at the Savoy Ballroom in Harlem.) The following summer, Hammond and Willard Alexander arranged for Basie's group to perform at a small club on Fifty-second Street called the Famous Door. The club's owners balked at first, doubtful that Basie's fourteen-piece outfit would fit comfortably into the tiny room. Ever resourceful, Hammond famously convinced them to hire Basie by agreeing to pay for an air-conditioning system. More important, though, the club was wired with a radio hookup similar to the one over which Hammond first heard Basie from Kansas City. So it didn't really matter how many people came to hear Basie at the Famous Door—he was playing for a national audience every night.

It's no wonder, then, that if Basie ever expressed regret at the extent to which he allowed Hammond to influence his career, it was never done publicly. Indeed, he told an interviewer in 1971: "That John, he's been so good to me through the years. If he hadn't come out to Kansas City, God knows what would have happened to me. I might still be out there . . . I was just having so much fun with this little band in Kansas City that it hadn't dawned on me yet to think seriously about the band at all." Perhaps Basie's ultimate tribute to Hammond came during a recording session in July 1937, shortly after Hammond had assembled what amounted to his notion of the ideal Basie band. The song "John's Idea," named in honor of the man with the ideas, is a flawless, raucous, flamboyantly swinging piece, punctuated by driving horn crescendos, and an all-too-rare instance of the usually economical Basie flaunting his extraordinary talent as a pianist. It's a touching tribute.

There must have been a wonderful energy in the studio that day. "One O'Clock Jump," Basie's signature song, was recorded during the same session. It quickly emerged as an anthem for the swing era.

7

A MINOR REVOLUTION

A minor revolution took place in deepest darkest Dixie early in September when Benny Goodman's band invaded the South for the first time," Hammond wrote in the October 1937 issue of *Down Beat*. "Benny's boys were engaged for the purpose of pulling the Dallas Exposition out of the red, but the world at large was scared that if Benny attempted to foist Lionel Hampton and Teddy Wilson upon a typically Southern crowd, he would not only be a flop but would possibly goad the population to acts of violence."

Hammond's belief that music was the ideal forum for promoting an integrated society was founded in the conviction that most people just wanted to hear good music. Jazz fans, he felt, would reward good musicians and punish bad ones regardless of skin color. Nowhere was that conviction more fully realized than at the Dallas Exposition in September 1937. "On all sides Benny was advised to leave the two colored boys behind," he wrote.

> White folks told him Southerners detested Negroes even as entertainers, and that they positively would not stand for Negroes being presented before their eyes on terms of complete equality with white performers . . . All along I had the suspicion that if the trio and quartet made excellent music the crowd would swallow its prejudices and acclaim the artists. But just the same

I made it my business to be in Dallas on the day of the opening just to see what would happen.

After spending the afternoon under a blazing Texas sun at a Chamber of Commerce parade in honor of Goodman, Hammond was relieved to finally get indoors. Unfortunately, the casino on the exposition grounds where Goodman, recently dubbed "the King of Swing," was scheduled to perform that night didn't offer much relief. The hall was jammed with thousands of Goodman's fans, and it wasn't much cooler inside than out. The band took the stage promptly at a quarter after eight to the deafening shrieks of Goodman's worshipful admirers. A second show was scheduled for ten-thirty.

During the first set the band blasted through much of its most popular repertoire, charging through exhilarating performances of "King Porter Stomp," "Bugle Call Rag," and "Stompin' at the Savoy." As usual, the band's showstopper, "Sing, Sing, Sing," proved just that. When the drummer, Gene Krupa, his greasy black hair flipping wildly across his head in perfect sync with the gnashing and clenching of his gum-chomping jaw, began pounding out the song's familiar staccato rhythm—BOOM BOOM boom-boom BA BOOM BA BOOM—a palpable surge of energy swept through the crowd. The hysteria was contagious, affecting everyone from the squarest of awestruck teeny-boppers jammed into the darkest recesses of the hall to the coolest of hepcats pressed against the front of the stage.

None of this was new to Hammond. Ever since the shows at the Paramount Theater in New York City six months earlier, when the kids danced in the aisles and screamed so loud that the crack band could barely be heard above the din, Goodman's appearances had become events rather than music concerts. It seemed the only time the screaming stopped was during the intermission between sets, when Goodman, Krupa, Wilson, and Hampton performed as a quartet.

In Dallas, Hammond anxiously anticipated the crowd's response to the subdued proficiency of the quartet, so startling in its contrast to the grandiose bombast of the entire Goodman orchestra. When the first set ended and it became apparent that the quartet wouldn't be appearing, Hammond noticed some visibly disgruntled fans. He moved closer to eavesdrop on their conversations, and what he heard pleased him. The fans were grumbling not because Goodman had allowed two black men to join his band, but rather because he had decided to skip the segment of the show that featured the two black musicians. Goodman, apparently sensing what Hammond was hearing in the crowd, added the quartet segment to the second set, and Wilson and Hampton were greeted with thunderous applause. (Goodman later claimed that time constraints, not fear of a riot, prompted his decision to skip the quartet during the first set.)

Just as pleasing to Hammond as the crowd's acceptance of the black musicians was their response to the quartet's music. The same wild-eyed jitterbuggers who had been raising the roof just minutes earlier now quieted down in keeping with the level of subdued intensity displayed by the four artists onstage. The fans broke their silence only when prompted by Lionel Hampton's reflexive "yeah, yeah, yeah" as he took off on another astonishing run on his vibraharp.

The Dallas shows weren't without incident. On opening night, a fan sent a bottle of champagne backstage to Hampton and Wilson. The bottle almost didn't get to them, though, because one of the cops working the event said he wouldn't bring it back to the "niggers." "Teddy got mad and wanted to leave," Hampton recalled. "He didn't show up for rehearsal the next day, so Benny had the chief of police talk to Teddy and reassure him that things would be all right. The chief told all the band members, 'I'm the baddest guy in town, and if you guys give us the same performance you gave us last night, everything will be all right.'" The chief's boast proved prophetic. The band played and the fans responded with nothing but adulation.

Hampton said Goodman's enormous popularity helped take some of the pressure off the two black musicians because fans responded enthusiastically to almost anything Goodman did. "We were like the Beatles," he said. "We would get a fifteen- or twenty-minute ovation before we even played a note."

Wilson and Hampton's impact on broader society was felt immediately. Big nightclubs in large American cities that had refused to allow blacks inside could hardly refuse entrance to two members of the most popular band in America. (Of course, that didn't mean they had to let in black customers.) The landmark move also opened the door to other black musicians. Not long after Wilson and Hampton began appearing with Goodman, other popular white bandleaders such as Artie Shaw, Charlie Barnet, and Jimmy Dorsey also hired black sidemen. And it worked both ways. Soon black bandleaders like Fletcher Henderson, Lucky Millinder, and Earl Hines were hiring white musicians for formerly all-black bands, as Lewis Erenberg noted in his book *Swingin' the Dream*.

Reflecting back on events that helped set the stage for the civil rights movement of the 1950s and 1960s, Hampton regretted that Goodman and Hammond didn't get the credit he felt they deserved. "That was an important part of the history of our country. It was a turning point," he said. Each of the four men—Hampton, Wilson, Hammond, and Goodman—had a role to play. Wilson and Hampton had to set an example for other blacks, and they did so with aplomb. "We carried everything to new heights," said Hampton. "We played good and we weren't lazy. We acted professionally and we were the role models, and the black race knew us and they admired us." Goodman, as leader of the band, had to make the final decision on whether to challenge societal mores by allowing two black men into his band. Despite his pragmatic nature, he chose to act with courage. Finally, it was Hammond who initially believed it could be done and set about convincing a reluctant Goodman to allow it to happen. His perseverance paid off when Goodman relented. Hampton described Hammond's role succinctly: "John Hammond started a revolution."

Hammond hung around Dallas for a few more days just to make certain that opening night wasn't a fluke, that the Southern audiences were in fact genuinely more concerned with the quality of the music than the color of the musicians' skin. Satisfied that he had accurately gauged the fans' response, he returned to New York, concluding in *Down Beat*: "Most of the middle- and upper-class Southerners I spoke to about the use of Negroes with white musicians assured me there would be no objection to the mixture as long as the music they produced was superlative. It was only a few Southern white musicians who said that Benny could never get away with it, and I suspect that a Marxist would have no difficulty in analyzing their wistful thinking."

Just as Hammond had predicted in his 1936 columns, Count Basie's star had risen rapidly after the first difficult months of adjustment, and within a year of leaving Kansas City, his band was approaching Benny Goodman's in its popularity. The unintended result was that Hammond, in effect, had put himself out of a job. He had done all he could for Goodman and Basie, and now it was up to them to maintain the level of excellence fans had come to expect. Hammond still had his columns and his freelance recording work, which included his first classical recording, a session in February 1938 with the violinist Joseph Szigeti, who performed a piece by Mozart. But with Goodman and Basie out on the road reaping the benefits of their success, his studio work grew increasingly sporadic, since nearly all of the stellar musicians with whom he was accustomed to recording—Teddy Wilson, Lester Young, Walter Page, Buck Clayton—were otherwise occupied as touring sidemen. So in early 1938 Hammond turned his attention to fulfilling an ambition that had recently consumed him—that of producing a concert that would trace the history of American popular music from its current incarnation as swing jazz back through its roots in the blues of the Deep South and finally to its origins in African culture.

Hammond believed that virtually all popular music worth listening to had its roots in black culture. Yet he felt the people most responsible for creating the foundation for the music that would evolve into jazz were not receiving their just due. Thus he was determined to present a showcase for black roots musicians, one that would allow white audiences to follow the evolution of popular music from slave chants right up through the sophisticated, improvised jazz of Count Basie. The audience, he believed, would not only hear some great music; they might also learn an important part of American history.

The first order of business was to find financial backers. Hammond may have been independently wealthy, but he wasn't wealthy enough to cover the cost of renting a large hall in New York City. And he never seriously considered any venue other than Carnegie Hall. In addition, there would be promotional expenses, including fees for newspaper and radio advertising. There would also be printing costs for programs and for leaflets to promote the concert in advance, as well as traveling expenses to cover an extensive talent search and to pay to bring that talent back to New York City.

It seemed such a noble cause—to gather for an integrated audience on the nation's premier concert stage a collection of black artists whose music had helped shape American popular culture. These were artists who, despite the broad impact of their music, had seen their legacies largely ignored, or at best obscured by decades of systemic racism. For these reasons Hammond's first instinct was to approach the NAACP, which he viewed as an obvious prospective sponsor. Besides, he'd been sitting on its board of directors for three years. But the NAACP turned him down flat. In his memoirs, he claimed (somewhat condescendingly) that the "primitive black music" he planned to present at the concert he had titled "From Spirituals to Swing" was apparently "too unfamiliar to the middle-class leaders of the NAACP to be anything they could take pride in." The more likely reason, however, was that the NAACP simply didn't have the money to underwrite an event that didn't serve the dual purpose of acting as a fund-raiser for its own programs.

Next Hammond approached the International Ladies' Garment Workers' Union, which at the time helped sponsor an array of left-wing causes in New York City. The ILGWU also turned him down, probably for the same reason as the NAACP. Finally, and a little reluctantly, he turned to the Marxist literary magazine *New Masses*. Reluctantly, because Hammond was concerned the magazine's radical political message might distract from the message of racial equality he hoped to promote by presenting a concert featuring exclusively black musicians. Notwithstanding those concerns, he was thrilled when executives at the magazine agreed right away to back him.

Hammond was already a familiar face around the offices of *New Masses*, with its far-left mix of political essays, literature, humor, criticism, and reviews. In fact, at the time he approached the magazine for backing, he had been contributing to its pages for nearly two years under the pseudonym Henry Johnson. Moreover, the editors, authors, artists, and critics who filled the magazine's pages with long diatribes against Fascism and even longer defenses of Joseph Stalin's warped Communist vision were Hammond's intellectual and social peers. They included some of the most important writers of the day, among them Upton Sinclair, Erskine Caldwell, Richard Wright, James Agee, Ernest Hemingway, John Dos Passos, Theodore Dreiser, and Langston Hughes. Some were part of the same liberal/activist crowd with whom he had traveled to Kentucky in 1932 in support of the striking coal miners. But while Hammond identified with the passionate idealism expressed in the pages of *New Masses*, and while he reveled in its status as *the* iconoclastic literary voice of the era—the latest issue of *New Masses* was one of the many magazines he perpetually carried with him stuffed under one arm—his politics weren't based on any single economic theory. And he was a vocal critic of the Communist doctrine of separation rather than integration of American blacks.

Nevertheless, the resourceful and prolific Johnson/Hammond treated the readers of *New Masses* to more than one scoop. In one notable review in the March 2, 1937, issue, he remarked, "Before closing, we cannot help but call your attention to the greatest Negro blues singer who has cropped up in recent years, Robert Johnson. Recording them in deepest Mississippi, Vocalion has certainly done right by us in the tunes 'Last Fair Deal Gone Down' and 'Terraplane Blues,' to mention only two of the four sides already released, sung to his own guitar accompaniment. Johnson makes Leadbelly sound like an accomplished poseur." This brief mention was apparently the first time Robert Johnson's name was brought to national attention. Johnson's music so impressed Hammond that he imagined the guitarist as the cornerstone of the "From Spirituals to Swing" concert, which he began organizing not long after first hearing Johnson's records. Sadly, by the time Hammond eventually staged the show in late December of 1938, it was too late to showcase Johnson—he had died the previous summer. Murdered.

Despite his differences with Communist doctrine, it's easy to understand why Hammond sought to have his articles published in *New Masses*. Within its pages he found an outlet for his progressive reformist views. The same wasn't true in the pages of the music magazines where the majority of his articles appeared. (What's less clear is why Hammond wrote his *New Masses* column under a pseudonym.

Perhaps it stemmed from a desire to appease his bosses at *Down Beat*, who may have disapproved of his writing for a competing publication.) Most of Hammond's *Down Beat* columns were essentially well-written, opinionated diary entries, comprised of reviews of musicians he had heard recently, records he enjoyed or disliked, and his myriad thoughts on what popular bandleaders might do to improve their music. There were digressions into social reform—most notably his attack on Duke Ellington—but for the most part Hammond focused on music. *New Masses* allowed him far more latitude for proselytizing. In a column written in the fall of 1936, for instance, Hammond, writing under the Henry Johnson pseudonym, publicly vented his anger with the Decca Records executives who he felt had taken advantage of Count Basie. Threatening to hold Basie's contract up to public scrutiny, Johnson/ Hammond predicted the deal "will make a very interesting exhibit in the drive to rid the phonograph industry of the cheapest kind of chiseling." (Decca subsequently reworked several key aspects of the contract.)

Hammond also wrote a lengthy investigative piece for *New Masses* that would have been out of place alongside *Down Beat*'s steady fare of record reviews and musician profiles. Essentially a sweeping indictment of the record manufacturing industry, the article, published in the April 20, 1937, issue, described how deteriorating working conditions at American record factories had led to a dramatic decline in the physical quality of the records being sold to the public. The solution, he thought, was to allow trade unions to organize the record factories.

Hammond made a strong case for his position—and for him the issue was personal. Although still a freelance producer, he was working regularly for Columbia Records. Thus his views regarding the quality of Columbia's records were gained firsthand. Showing no reservations toward biting the hand that fed him, he targeted a Columbia manufacturing plant in Bridgeport, Connecticut, for particular scrutiny. With a keen eye for detail, he described the intense heat and foul smells generated by mixing the melted shellac used at the time to make records. Over time, these oppressive conditions wore down the factory workers, affecting their concentration, he argued. Former employees told him that the Bridgeport plant had been repeatedly cited for violations of

Connecticut's labor laws. And Hammond even finagled a tour of the plant to view working conditions for himself. He also used compelling statistics (albeit provided by labor union friends sympathetic to his conclusions) to back up his anecdotal evidence. In summary, he wrote, nonunionized record factories such as the Columbia plant in Bridgeport were forcing their employees to work too fast at the expense of quality. Meanwhile, RCA Victor was making the best-sounding records in the industry, he argued, noting that its factories had recently been organized by the United Electrical and Radio Workers.

Ironically, that critical article pointing up the miserable working conditions at a Columbia-owned plant led to Hammond's first full-time job with the company whose future he would later help shape. Angry about the allegations in Hammond's article, Columbia's president, Dick Altschuler, requested a meeting with the author. Hammond agreed, and the two hit it off. A short time later, in early 1938, Altschuler offered Hammond a job as sales manager for Columbia's classical division. The job lasted less than a month. In keeping with his now-well-established pattern, Hammond quickly got into a tiff with one of his superiors and quit, by his account, as a matter of principle after his secretary was fired without his authorization for trying to organize the other secretaries into a union.

The timing of the split proved fortuitous, though, because Hammond needed time to scour the South for the musicians he was planning to present at his "From Spirituals to Swing" concert later that year. After recruiting a new friend, a young classical music student named Goddard Lieberson, to join him, he set off in search of talent in the spring of 1938. Lieberson and Hammond met while both were studying with a composer and songwriter named Alec Wilder, who would later achieve international acclaim writing and composing for such luminaries as Frank Sinatra and Mabel Mercer. (Wilder is the author of numerous standards, including "I'll Be Around" and "Trouble Is a Man.") Hammond quickly determined that Lieberson was "the wittiest man I had ever met."

In Durham, North Carolina, the pair, aided by a local talent scout named Jimmy Long, found a blind harmonica player named Sonny Terry. Terry shouted—grunted, really—the blues and used his harmonica to huff and puff the narrative of his signature piece, "Fox Chase." Terry's performance was as raw and visceral as anything Hammond had ever heard. Yet "Fox Chase" was also infused with strains of the classical milieu in the way in which its tempo surged forward, growing stronger and stronger, until finally reaching its climactic ending, all the while telling a story through the music. This was organic folk music with its origins in the land. Hammond wanted his Carnegie Hall audience to hear how the source of Terry's music might have been the sound of the wind blowing through a tall grove of pine trees or the whine of a far-off train whistle. Those sounds, so familiar in the rural South, were then reinterpreted as song by local musicians, men who had been absorbing those sounds their entire lives. Terry was invited north to appear at Carnegie Hall in December.

Their next stop was along North Carolina's eastern coast in the tiny tobacco community of Kinston, where Hammond and Lieberson tracked down four young men who gathered each week in church to sing traditional spiritual songs a cappella. Hammond had heard recordings of them singing and had written glowingly of them in his *Down Beat* column. "It is just about the finest and most natural group singing ever recorded, as well as the first authentic spirituals I've heard on records. No arrangements, no accompaniment, complete freedom. Everybody who has been bored or disgusted by the castrated versions of spirituals we hear on the concert stage should get hold of this record," he wrote. The men called themselves Mitchell's Christian Singers. Hearing these four singers in person—the blending of their voices, at turns soaring and transcendent, at other times foreboding and spectral—within the clapboard walls of a whitewashed church off a dirt road just outside Kinston was a revelation. "Goddard and I agreed there could not be a concert without the Mitchell Christian Singers," Hammond wrote in his memoirs.

In Arkansas, they signed up William "Big Bill" Broonzy, a blues singer and virtuoso guitarist who was already a star for the Vocalion record label's race line. Broonzy, who had never appeared in front of a predominantly white audience, let alone in a venue the size of Carnegie Hall, was brought in as a replacement for Robert Johnson to demonstrate the raw, primitive power of acoustic country blues.

The lineup was now set. In addition to Sonny Terry, Mitchell's Christian Singers, and Big Bill Broonzy, Hammond planned to present the boogie-woogie pianists Albert Ammons, Meade "Lux" Lewis, and Pete Johnson; the blues singer Big Joe Turner; the pianist and Harlem legend James P. Johnson; the hymn singer Sister Rosetta Tharpe; Sidney Bechet, one of the founding fathers of jazz; and finally, to bring the music up to the present, the Count Basie Orchestra.

Evidence of Hammond's resourcefulness surfaced a few days before the concert when *The New York Times* published a lengthy article of his in which he praised the virtues of Negro music. The article also doubled as a brilliant promotional tool for the "From Spirituals to Swing" concert:

> But despite all this welcome discussion of Negro music, the fact is that [the average American listener] knows next to nothing about the authentic music of the American Negro. To be sure, the public has seen men of the highly publicized Negro jazz bands, some of whom have made serious concessions to white taste by adding spurious showmanship to their wares and imitating the habits and tricks of the more commercially successful white orchestras. They also have heard torch singers like Ethel Waters sing dreamy Broadway ballads such as "Stormy Weather," highly sophisticated groups like the Hall Johnson singers do arrangements of traditional Negro spirituals with harmonies carefully adjusted for delicate ears, and the magnificent trained soloists like Marian Anderson, Roland Hayes and Paul Robeson make of the primitive spiritual and blues something akin to the art songs of other nations, with unrhythmical and fancy piano accompaniment. All this, we believe, has very little to do with authentic Negro music.

The article was pure Hammond: well written, well intentioned, knowledgeable, opinionated, and slightly condescending. Hammond's critics often accused him of acting as if he were the first white man to acquire an appreciation for black music. This article did nothing to dispel their criticism. Hammond also couldn't resist throwing in a few digs at some of the black musicians who he felt had sold out to commercial tastes. Anyone familiar with Hammond's way of thinking, or who had read his columns in *Down Beat*, knew that when he wrote of "spurious showmanship" he was talking about Louis Armstrong. (Cab Calloway, another demonstrative showman, was also a frequent target of Hammond's ire.) Finally, Hammond somehow convinced the *Times* editors to run the piece in the entertainment section as a straightforward news article rather than as an opinion piece on the editorial page. Nowhere was there any mention that the author of the article was also the producer of the show being touted, an obvious conflict of interest that a newspaper of the caliber of *The New York Times* should have at least acknowledged.

Hammond was hardly oblivious to the various conflicts of interest in which he frequently placed himself. But he certainly didn't view them as blemishes on his integrity. To the contrary, he seems to have viewed his tactics for promoting "From Spirituals to Swing" in the same light that he viewed his methods for promoting the artists whose music he favored: as sort of a righteous mission of enlightenment. And even those who disapproved of his aggressive tactics were hard-pressed to suggest that his ostensible ethical lapses were committed in an effort to line his own pockets. It's abundantly clear from everything he ever said or wrote concerning the "From Spirituals to Swing" concert that he never expected to make a cent from it. And he didn't. In his view, the free promotional outlet provided by the *Times* served just one purpose: it was an effective method of drawing attention to the show. If it also served as a high-profile forum in which Hammond could lord his encyclopedic knowledge of American roots music over an ignorant readership—well, he wasn't afraid of offending.

Hammond's initial fear that the publishers at *New Masses* would use the concert to promote their Marxist agenda proved unfounded. That doesn't mean Hammond or his backers shied away from politics, though. The concert's twenty-page program was littered with information concerning the refugees of the Spanish civil war. In the late 1930s, the conflict, which pitted the Marxist-leaning Republicans against the Fascist, military-dominated Loyalists, was a leading cause célèbre among American left-wing writers and intellectuals. Ernest

Hemingway famously volunteered as an ambulance driver to aid the Republican effort and later used the experience in his novel *For Whom the Bell Tolls*. And Hammond had helped organize "Stars for Spain," a 1937 benefit concert featuring Benny Goodman intended to raise money for the Republican effort. On page two of the "From Spirituals to Swing" concert program, the number 3,715,000 stared out at the reader in bold black lettering an inch tall. The figure, according to the material, represented the number of "children in Loyalist Spain (who) are hungry and suffering from rickets and pellagra."

Hammond evidently approved of the pro-Republican propaganda. It was an issue on which he and the *New Masses* publishers shared common ground. But his motives for producing the show were founded in a domestic agenda focused exclusively on fighting racism and promoting integration among blacks and whites. He saw "From Spirituals to Swing" as an opportunity for a large number of influential Northerners— both black and white—to see and hear authentic black music as it sounded at its point of origin. Hammond figured the opportunity to see and hear how this music had influenced American popular music might prompt the audience to consider how much Americans of all colors had in common. Moreover, the artistry of the performers might give pause to the racist belief that blacks were inferior to whites in all manner of intellectual pursuits. Years later he summed up his mission: "To bring recognition to the Negro's supremacy in jazz was the most effective and constructive form of social protest I could think of."

Sometimes Hammond's passions got the best of him. When channeled properly, the energy he threw into supporting his convictions was capable of bringing about great change. But, left unchecked, his passions, while generally well intended, could also affect his ability to make sound judgments. His account of Bessie Smith's death in a car accident in 1937 was such an instance. He dedicated the "From Spirituals to Swing" concert to her memory, writing:

We are dedicating the program to Bessie Smith, who personifies the grandeur and warmth of Negro music. Bessie Smith was seriously injured in an auto accident in Virginia fourteen months ago. Taken to a hospital, she was denied admittance because she was a Negro. Before she could be taken to the *proper* hospital she was dead. In this story you have an example of the cruelties Negro musicians share with their fourteen million brothers in America.

It's a tragic story. There was one problem with it, though. It wasn't true. What's more, Hammond must have known it wasn't true by the time he wrote the copy for the concert program. He had published a similar account in *Down Beat* not long after Smith's death on September 26, 1937, and that version was promptly refuted by people familiar with the facts. Yet more than a year later Hammond was repeating the same misinformation. For starters, the wreck occurred outside Clarksdale, Mississippi, not in Virginia. More important, Smith *was* admitted to the first hospital to which she was taken. According to Chris Albertson, the author of the first comprehensive biography of Smith, the singer's arm was practically severed in the accident, and she was sped by ambulance from the scene to the nearest hospital, which was in fact a segregated hospital that treated blacks. Once there, Bessie received the best care available—the same care anyone in her situation would have received—but she died a few hours after surgery was performed to remove her mutilated arm.

The real version of Smith's death is no less tragic than Hammond's version, but far less controversial. Apparently, it better served his purposes if Bessie Smith died as a result of cruel and systemic racism in the South rather than in an accident that could have happened to anyone. The whole episode was an unseemly case of Hammond's not allowing the facts to get in the way of his good story. And he never fully backed down from his embellished account. In his memoirs published in 1977, long after the true facts had been meticulously patched together by Albertson, Hammond stuck to his version that nefarious racist forces had contributed to Bessie's death.

By any measure, "From Spirituals to Swing," held on December 23, 1938, was a resounding success. The musicians played to a sold-out theater, and reviews in New York papers were favorable.

In an introduction included in the program, the sponsors sought "one indulgence" from the audience. "Most of the people on the program are making their first appearance before a predominantly white audience; many of them have never visited the North before. They will do their very best if the audience will cooperate with them by creating an atmosphere of informality and interest. The most memorable hot music comes when the performer can feel his audience. May we ask that you forget you are in Carnegie Hall?" They needn't have bothered to ask.

After some initial technical problems that left Hammond standing onstage mouthing words that no one could hear—his voice was drowned out by a recording of African tribal drumming—the curtain rose and the performers took over. Albert Ammons, Meade "Lux" Lewis, and Pete Johnson kicked things off with some truly raucous boogie-woogie piano, music that seemed far more suited to a Kansas City cathouse than to the venerable stage at Carnegie Hall. Ammons played an old upright piano that Hammond had obtained specifically to re-create the rough-and-tumble mood of a whiskey-soaked barroom. Lewis and Johnson, in a wonderful display of showmanship—especially given the two men's sizable girth—shared a single Steinway. Left hands pounded in driving unison, creating the signature, undulating boogie-woogie rhythm. Right hands, meanwhile, had minds of their own, fluttering mischievously up and down the keyboard. The music had an irresistible infectiousness that left many in the audience bouncing in their seats. It was loud, sweaty, and slightly inebriated. And, like a good stiff drink, it served to loosen up the crowd for the rest of the show.

Next, Big Joe Turner strolled onstage, strutting his stuff with the same ease and flourish he exhibited behind the bar at the Sunset Café in Kansas City. Tossing a wink at Pete Johnson, his partner at the Sunset, Big Joe brushed a microphone away from his face and shouted loudly and clearly into the very back rows of the hall, "I ain't gonna be your low-down dog no more." And the audience believed him.

Sister Rosetta Tharpe followed. Virtually unknown to the New York audience, she astounded the crowd with dexterous guitar work (echoes of her rhythmic chording appeared a decade later on Chuck Berry's records) and with her big, confident voice. And her stage presence matched her musical talent. Her sound was more suited to church on Sunday morning than to a fancy concert hall on Friday night. The audience loved her.

Tharpe was followed by Mitchell's Christian Singers, Hammond's personal favorite. The group was made up of a truck driver, a factory laborer, a bricklayer, and the owner of a small coal and ice business—four mild-mannered men who quietly took the stage, and then proceeded to floor the crowd with stunning renditions of obscure spirituals heretofore unknown to Northern audiences. A cappella arrangements of "What More Can My Jesus Do?" and "Are You Living Humble?" were sublime. And when the lead vocalist, William Brown, declared in his rich, soulful tenor, "My poor mother died a-shouting" and the others— second tenor Julius Davis, baritone Louis David, and bass Sam Bryant—joined in, pleading, "Ain't that good news?" there was hardly a dry eye in the house.

Big Bill Broonzy abruptly shifted gears. As casually as if he were sitting on a front porch watching the sun set over his farm in rural Arkansas, Broonzy picked country blues and sang songs that appealed to the common man. "I dreamed I was at the White House, sitting in the president's chair," he sang. "I dreamed he shaked my hand, and said, 'Bill, I'm glad you're here.' But that was just a dream, Lord, just a dream I had on my mind." And the audience bellowed with laughter.

Sonny Terry followed with "Fox Chase," and the audience responded just as Hammond had hoped. Startled at first by the little man onstage who sang and shouted while simultaneously playing the harmonica, the crowd caught on quickly and got swept up in the musical narrative. They cheered Terry on as he led them closer and closer and closer, until it seemed the audience could almost see the fox's tail disappear into the bushes.

When the legendary saxophonist Sidney Bechet took the stage after Terry, he was accompanied by a group gathered solely for that evening's program. The audience could easily have closed their eyes and imagined themselves following a strolling Dixieland jazz band through the narrow streets of New Orleans's French Quarter. Bechet, a contemporary of Louis Armstrong's at the dawn of jazz, was joined by another Hammond favorite, James P. Johnson, on piano. Basie band members

Walter Page and Jo Jones held down the rhythm section on bass and drums, respectively.

Then it was time for the Count himself. By closing with the Basie band, Hammond hoped to demonstrate that all of the styles performed up to that point in the show—boogie-woogie, blues, gospel, spirituals—led inexorably, as streams to a great river, to the highly sophisticated form of jazz presented by Basie and his orchestra. He viewed Basie's music in an almost Darwinian light, seeing it as an example of the most advanced stage yet of an ongoing evolutionary process. Basie, who at the time was directing arguably his finest lineup—one that included Lester Young and Herschel Evans on tenor saxophones, Earle Warren on alto sax, Harry "Sweets" Edison and Buck Clayton on trumpets, Dickie Wells and Benny Morton on trombones, Freddie Green on guitar, Jo Jones on drums, and Walter Page on bass—delighted the crowd with romping and utterly flawless versions of "Swingin' the Blues" and "One O'Clock Jump."

"From Spirituals to Swing" represented a culmination of the ideals that Hammond had promoted so tirelessly during the past decade. Winnowed down to its essence, it was a simple message: good music played by talented musicians could and would transcend generations of ignorance and hatred by functioning as a vehicle for bringing people of all colors together. The concert itself, brash, eclectic, and laced with paradox, acted as a mirror held up to Hammond's character. He was all of those things, and the concert, his creation from start to finish, was nothing if not a direct extension of his extraordinary will and dynamic personality.

Otis Ferguson's pitch-perfect profile, written for *Society Rag* and published just three months before the concert, captured the Hammond of this period. Perhaps no better description of him exists:

> You can tell him by the crew haircut, which bobs approximately in time to the music, and also by a habit of standing with his legs crossed, and also by the fresh copies of the various trade, intellectual, and left-wing papers under his arm. Or just find the youngish chap with the crew haircut who is in the most earnest conversation with whoever is running whatever show it is, and

that will be John. Go forward to meet him and his head juts forward at you, slightly lowered as if to charge, but belying any seeming truculence by the open heartiness of his greeting. He is either spilling over with enthusiasm (Isn't it *swell*?) or only partly concealing his disgust (It's a *crime*, it stinks).

He is a little better than average height, under thirty, dark complexion, no fat, soberly dressed, hatless and coatless. Fairly voluble, socially at ease but with none of this greaseball heel-clicking. His enthusiasms, for or against, are gusty. He slaps his knee, he clasps his head in his hands, he strides out of places or sits with his head too far back and claps too heavily. In theaters he groans, snorts, slaps his knee again, explains to a movie critic the difference between a camera and Sergei Eisenstein (great director; stayed with him in Russia, you know), or holds a newspaper up high enough to read it in the dim light with pointed absorption. His laugh . . . is often a trial to the nerves, especially when used to stress a point not very funny. He is right and right with bells on; but if you happen to have the habit of stepping up and being right, too, he can take it.

John Henry Hammond (Junior) is known to practically everyone who ever mounted a bandstand, or plugged a song, or got on the free list for records and wrote articles using such phrases as gutbucket and out of this world and dig that stomp-box. He is known as the Critic, the Little Father, the Guardian Angel, and the Big Bringdown of dance music. But the point is, he is known.

Hammond would become even more well known in the decades to follow. But, unknown to him at the time he was basking in the success of his "From Spirituals to Swing" concert, he had reached a pinnacle, and it would be another two decades before his career would start to gain momentum again.

8

CAFÉ SOCIETY

When the show was over, Hammond and many of the musicians who had performed that night at Carnegie Hall headed downtown to Café Society, a new nightclub in Greenwich Village. The concert had been a tremendous success, and Hammond must have felt all of the blood, sweat, and tears he had put into it had been worth it. Just as he had hoped, the audience had responded viscerally to the diverse array of acts. The music had covered quite a bit of territory ranging from Sister Rosetta Tharpe's earthy gospel singing and the beatific and inspiring harmonies of Mitchell's Christian Singers to the raw, sexually charged boogie-woogie piano of Meade "Lux" Lewis, Albert Ammons, and Pete Johnson and the laconic country blues of Big Bill Broonzy. Finally, the matchless Count Basie Orchestra left the crowd on its feet, clamoring for more.

The three-hour concert, the culmination of months of preparation, had left Hammond emotionally drained. After making his brief introductory remarks, he had sidled off to a quiet spot backstage where he could watch the show unfold. Grinning broadly and nodding his head in time to the beat, he was content to let his stage manager, Goddard Lieberson, direct the musical traffic. When it was over, there was nothing left to do but celebrate.

Café Society was located in the basement of an apartment building across the street from tiny Sheridan Square. By coincidence, the club opened on the same late-December night on which Hammond presented "From Spirituals to Swing." The club's opening had been highly anticipated among the city's progressive intelligentsia, and the normally quiet neighborhood at the intersection of West Fourth and Barrow streets was bustling with activity that night. Each time Café Society's doors swung open, bright light sprayed out from within, illuminating darkened Sheridan Square, and the brittle still of a New York winter night was broken by the sharp din of conversation, laughter, and jazz.

Hammond's entourage, which included his parents and his sister Alice, was met at the bottom of the stairs by the owner and manager of the club, a diminutive and energetic young man named Barney Josephson. Josephson greeted Hammond as if he were visiting royalty, and the Hammonds were led through the buzzing club to a table near the bandstand, where Frankie Newton was leading a small orchestra made up of black and white musicians. It was a scene that would be played out again and again over the next decade: Hammond strolling through the Café Society crowd, stopping at practically every table to schmooze with many of New York's leading writers, artists, and show-business people, leaning over here to say hello to the *New Yorker* writer S. J. Perelman, stopping over there to shake hands with the screenwriter Budd Schulberg (who would later write *On the Waterfront*), then whispering something clever into the ear of the charming character actor Lionel Stander before offering a quick peck on the well-rouged cheek of the playwright Lillian Hellman. Unlike at other tony New York nightclubs of that period, at Café Society many of the tables were occupied by well-dressed black couples. At larger tables dashing young white couples could be seen laughing and sharing toasts with handsome young couples of all racial and sexual orientations. The club's patrons clearly reveled in the openly subversive environment.

Virtually every detail of Café Society was designed as a way of giving the finger to the all-rich, all-white Stork Club crowd uptown, whose regulars included the FBI director J. Edgar Hoover, already a pariah among New York's progressive crowd. Even the name—Café Society—was a clever play on words, a parody of the broad label "café society" used to describe the Stork Club crowd. To decorate the walls

of his club, Josephson commissioned several well-known artists—
among them the regular *New Masses* illustrators William Gropper,
Anton Refregier, and Adolf Dehn—to paint murals that mockingly
depicted the bona fide members of café society at play on the Upper
East Side.

From the outset, Josephson, a former shoe salesman from Trenton,
New Jersey, made it clear that his club would be integrated. He wanted
black performers to play for white audiences and white performers to
play for black audiences. Most of all, he wanted black and white performers to play for black and white audiences. Surprisingly, in New
York City in 1938 there was not a single club where black musicians
regularly performed onstage with white musicians in front of mixed-
race audiences. Groups of black musicians regularly performed for mixed
audiences in Harlem, and mixed groups of musicians frequently got together for after-hours jams in small out-of-the-way clubs, but it was
still taboo for mixed bands to headline shows at respectable nightclubs.
Josephson was determined to change that. He wanted to open a club
where black and white patrons could come to see the finest musicians—
period.

Josephson and Hammond met through mutual acquaintances in
the summer of 1938. One of Josephson's friends recommended Hammond as someone who could help procure talent for the new night
club. After realizing that he and Hammond had much in common in
the way of music and politics, Josephson turned over to Hammond
almost total responsibility for hiring the entertainment at Café Society.
It was a stroke of luck for him that Hammond was recruiting talent for
"From Spirituals to Swing" at the same time Josephson was preparing
to open the club. Throughout the fall of 1938 Hammond held rehearsals for the concert at Carnegie Hall, and Josephson was invited up
to sift through the assembled talent. "Barney didn't really have a policy,
he didn't really know what he was going to do for entertainment until
he came to a rehearsal of the concert, and he was so enchanted with
the people that he hired a gang of them, including Big Bill Broonzy,
Joe Turner, and Pete Johnson," Hammond recalled in a 1973 radio interview. Over the next decade, Hammond helped book some of the
biggest names in jazz into Café Society, among them Teddy Wilson,

James P. Johnson, and Billie Holiday. And he never accepted a salary. Instead, he took his payment in free meals and in the prestige that attended his position as the club's de facto musical director.

Josephson was able to scrounge up the initial seed money to open Café Society's doors, but he quickly ran out of cash to keep the club operating. Hammond was so infatuated with the idea of a fully integrated, politically charged nightclub—in particular, one where he could handpick the entertainment—that he invested five thousand dollars in cash and talked his friends Benny Goodman and Willard Alexander into contributing the same.

Hammond's enthusiasm may have been more important than his money. "The person most responsible for the club's success was John Hammond, Jr., a crew-cut young man still in his twenties, who found us the musical talent that was to become legendary," wrote the New York gadfly Helen Lawrenson. "His taste was infallible. It was what made the club." Lawrenson, a self-proclaimed Communist, spy, part-time lesbian, and pioneer feminist with connections in the publishing and public-relations fields, was brought on board early by Josephson to help promote the new club. In a memoir, she claimed to have thought up the satirical name Café Society, although most other accounts credit the writer and editor Clare Boothe Luce with coining the phrase. Lawrenson also claimed that Café Society was created for the sole purpose of raising money for the Communist Party. While there may be elements of truth to the claim—Josephson's brother was a well-known Communist, and Barney Josephson may have made contributions to the party—no evidence exists to substantiate a direct link between the club and the party's finances. The rumor hardly hurt business, however. To the contrary, it added cachet to the already-super-hip club, which advertised itself in elite magazines and on matchboxes as "The right place for the wrong people."

The club quickly emerged as something far more than simply a sanctuary where downtown hipsters could gather to thumb their noses at uptown squares. It became the de facto headquarters for the intellectual leadership of the progressive movements that had reached a critical mass in the United States by the late 1930s. Perhaps at no time in American history was liberal thought embraced by so many. President Roosevelt's New Deal had offered hope to a beaten-down nation in the depths of the Depression, and FDR's larger-than-life persona had helped swing much of the country to the left in a reflexive show of support for the man and his programs. Moreover, by 1939 the American Communists, who had initially opposed Roosevelt for not being radical enough, had softened their position and were seeking to make inroads into mainstream American politics. Thus there was room for millions under the broad banner of progressivism.

The leaders of the various progressive factions made Café Society their home away from home. And while they socialized there, they listened to jazz.

The music did more than merely serve as background noise, however. It played an integral role in helping to spread the progressive movement's concept of democracy. The left's adoption of swing for use as a political tool can be traced to 1935, just as swing was making an impression on the broad American psyche. In the case of the Communists, the decision to embrace jazz coincided with the party's decision to adopt a new worldwide strategy that rejected much of the old dogmatic, hard-line ideology in favor of a more inclusive policy. They called it a "popular front," and that's how the party came to be known in the United States in the late 1930s. The shift in policy stemmed from the Communists' inability to stanch the rise of Fascism in Europe. Party leaders were looking for a way to unite the many progressive movements around the world whose sympathies leaned toward Communism and away from Fascism. The popular front, therefore, would include Socialists, labor unions, and any other group that openly opposed Fascism. In the United States, the newly inclusive policy required many former hard-line Communists to reject the old rhetoric— the dogma that called for overthrowing the government by means of a worldwide revolution of the workers—and embrace Roosevelt's New Deal policies. The result was a series of political alliances among groups formerly at odds with one another. The Communists, the Socialists, and the members of various far-left labor organizations—the rapidly growing Congress of Industrial Organizations, for example— could now join forces.

The popular-front strategy proved highly successful in the United

States. By focusing on similarities rather than differences, the policy brought together like-minded, progressive-leaning Americans on areas of common ground, one conspicuous area being swing jazz. In an effort to capture the imaginations of young mainstream Americans, the erstwhile hard-line Communists promoted the concept that jazz music, especially the so-called hot jazz embodied by swing, had its roots in the proletarian working classes, specifically among the black working classes. The idea was to present a romantic view to millions of rebellious white youths who wanted to feel they were participating in something new, edgy, and authentic—something diametrically opposed to the "sweet" music favored by their parents.

The jazz critics, meanwhile, men like John Hammond, had always characterized jazz as a direct outgrowth of freedom and democracy—as an evolutionary culmination of the defining characteristics of American society.

The melding of left-wing politics and jazz allowed many of the country's most popular bandleaders to lend their names and their music to various causes openly supported by the Communists. Thus Benny Goodman, Teddy Wilson, and Count Basie, no doubt at Hammond's urging, all participated in benefit concerts to help refugees fleeing the various Fascist movements under way in Europe. The Scottsboro trials at home also served as a catalyst for a handful of benefits. No effort was made by concert organizers to conceal their ties to the Communists. Hammond helped organize several of these benefits a year, leading many to mistakenly believe he was a member of the Communist Party. Among those mistaken were investigators at the FBI, who around this time began compiling evidence in an effort to brand Hammond a Communist.

Café Society represented the best of both worlds for Hammond—a place that seamlessly blended his two passions. Barney Josephson shared his commitment not only to integration but also to providing a forum for showcasing the finest American musical talent. It was a mutually beneficial partnership with consequences that often caught Hammond and Josephson off guard. The response to Billie Holiday's rendition of the protest song "Strange Fruit," which she first performed at Café Society in early 1939, was one such instance.

Of all the many, many thousands of songs performed at Café Society during its decade in the limelight, none caused more of a stir than the incendiary "Strange Fruit." Written in the mid-1930s by Abel Meeropol, a Jewish schoolteacher from the Bronx, the song is a searing condemnation of lynching. The first line declares: "Southern trees bear a strange fruit." The "strange fruit" hanging from the trees, replete with "the bulging eyes and the twisted mouth," was, of course, a horrific metaphor for black lynching victims. The song's effect on the Café Society crowd was visceral and immediate.

In her autobiography, Holiday vividly described the first time she performed the song. She claimed her audience was so stunned by what they had just heard that for several long moments no one applauded. Then one patron began cautiously clapping, and little by little the rest of the audience joined in. Holiday clearly reveled in the song's effect, and she sang it almost every night during the year and a half or so that she performed regularly at Café Society. It was always the last song of her set, and she performed it with her typical flair. All activity inside the nightclub came to a halt. Waiters and busboys stood still in their tracks. The room grew silent and the lights went black save for a thin pale ray focused on Holiday's face. She sang the wrenching lyrics accompanied only by a light piano. After she was finished, she walked out of the hushed room without a word.

Hammond never liked the song. He felt its polemical message did more damage than good for Holiday's career. Specifically, he believed the attention garnered by the song, especially in left-wing intellectual circles, caused his former protégée to affect a style that wasn't hers. Hammond viewed Holiday as a brilliant interpreter of popular jazz tunes, not as a pious protest singer. When she sought to record "Strange Fruit" for Columbia Records, Hammond recommended against it, and the company sided with him. Columbia was nevertheless sympathetic to Holiday's desire to record the song, and she was allowed to step outside her contract to record it for an independent label run by Hammond's good friend Milt Gabler.

Gabler was a jazz enthusiast of the first order who owned the Commodore Music Shop, located first on East Forty-second Street across from the Chrysler Building and later on West Fifty-second Street. The Commodore also housed a small, independent record label, which Gabler eponymously named the Commodore Record Company. Gabler was a huge fan of Holiday's—he told an interviewer in the 1940s that he rarely went home at night without stopping off at a nightclub to see her sing—and he jumped at the opportunity to work with her in the studio. It proved a profitable arrangement for him, since the song went on to become a bestseller and by far the most popular ever released by his small record label. Gabler would later dismiss the idea that he recorded it as some noble gesture, telling a *New Yorker* writer in a 1946 profile that he recorded the song "for kicks."

The song has since attained iconic status in the pantheon of American popular music. (*Time* magazine in 1999 named it the best song of the past century—ahead of Irving Berlin's "God Bless America" and Woody Guthrie's "This Land Is Your Land.") Hammond never wavered in his opinion, though. He found the song pretentious in 1939, and he felt the same way nearly five decades later, long after the song had achieved its sanctified status. He was hardly alone in his opinion. The record producer Jerry Wexler expressed the view of many in the music industry when he told the writer David Margolick:

> Very few of us really liked that song. It's so un–Billie Holiday. It's got too much of an agenda. A lot of people who had tin ears and who wouldn't know a melody if it hit them in the head embraced the song only because of the politics. It's so polemical, and musically it has very little to recommend it in terms of a melodic line, and the melodic line was her meat. I absolutely approve of the sentiment. I think it's a great lyric. But it doesn't interest me as a song.

Hammond had never been personally close to Holiday, and now his critical view of her adoption of "Strange Fruit" as her signature song further poisoned an already souring relationship. It was Hammond who had arranged for Holiday to appear at Café Society in the first place. But her drug addiction soon proved a liability in terms of both her ability to perform and the unwelcome attention she drew from law enforcement. When Josephson was forced to let her go, Hammond didn't try to intervene. The mentor and his former protégée would have very little contact from the time Holiday stopped performing at Café Society in 1940 until her death in 1959.

Instead, Hammond concentrated on performers whose primary focus was on music rather than personal tragedy. Teddy Wilson, for example, was struggling professionally in 1940. The pianist had left Benny Goodman's band a year and a half earlier to start his own big band, but it never really caught on, and he found himself in need of a job. Wilson jumped at an opportunity presented by Hammond to lead Café Society's house band. "We had a happy time at the Café Society," Wilson wrote in his memoirs. "We were the house band and we played for the various acts that needed musical backing, for dancing and to open the show." One of the acts that Wilson's group backed was a gorgeous young singer named Lena Horne.

Horne was not yet famous when she was introduced to Hammond in 1939 through Charlie Barnet, a white bandleader who had been among the first to follow Benny Goodman's lead by hiring blacks. After completing a tour with Barnet, Horne was looking for something more stable, hopefully a job that would keep her off the road and in an environment where she could avoid the racism that all black performers faced when they toured with primarily white bands. Hammond thought he had just the solution—a steady gig at Café Society. Josephson, smitten by Horne's breathtaking beauty, was thrilled to have her. In her memoirs, Horne credited the politically charged atmosphere at Café Society with serving as the catalyst for her own extensive participation some two decades later in the civil rights movement.

If the success of Holiday's rendition of "Strange Fruit" puzzled and disturbed Hammond, the resurgence in popularity of boogie-woogie piano around the same time pleased him no end. The public's embrace of the music occurred directly as a result of the coincidence of "From Spirituals to Swing" and the opening of Café Society. The boogie-woogie musicians—Meade "Lux" Lewis, Albert Ammons, and Pete Johnson—were the uncontested fan favorites of Hammond's show. From Carnegie Hall the trio moved downtown to Café Society, where they proved just as popular as regular performers at Josephson's nightclub. Seeking to capitalize on their surprising popularity, Hammond booked a few hours of studio time in early 1939 to record the three. "There were only two pianos in that miserable old Brunswick studio," he recalled, "so we had to have the three piano players on two pianos." Ammons and Johnson doubled up on one because Lewis, although perhaps not as talented as the other two, had already attained a certain level of notoriety from his recording of the song "Honky Tonk Train Blues." "They were all enormous," said Hammond, adding that it was very difficult to fit all three in the same room, let alone two of them on one piano bench. The album that resulted from the sessions, *Upright and Lowdown: Boogie-Woogie, Barrelhouse, and Blues*, was a big hit for Brunswick. Only a cursory listen is necessary to understand why. The music is raucous, foot-stomping, good-time blues.

The success of the album prompted executives at the newly reorganized Columbia to offer Hammond full-time employment again. He agreed, returning to the label in 1939, just months after the company was sold to CBS as part of William Paley's $700,000 purchase of Columbia's parent company, the American Record Corporation. At the time, the Columbia Phonograph Company was the American Record Corporation's most important asset, and Paley believed, presciently as it turned out, that the record industry was about to make a comeback now that the worst of the Depression appeared over. Paley renamed the entire company the Columbia Recording Corporation and hired an experienced record industry executive named Edward Wallerstein as Columbia Records' first president. The next important hire was Hammond's friend Goddard Lieberson, who was brought on to run the company's classical music division. Hammond was hired a few months later as associate recording director at a salary of $105 a week. (Record producers worked strictly on salary in those days. Not until the 1960s did producers begin earning royalties—and getting very rich—on the records they produced.)

Lieberson, sophisticated, supremely charming, and always impeccably dressed, would rise steadily to the top of Columbia's executive chart and eventually serve two tours as head of the company before retiring in 1975. Columbia Records "soared" under his leadership, Paley wrote shortly after Lieberson's death in 1977. While concentrating primarily on his specialty, classical music, Lieberson also displayed a discerning ear for popular sounds, signing an unknown singer named Barbra Streisand in the early 1960s after hearing her sing in a Broadway musical. "He was an extraordinary human being," Paley wrote. "A handsome, elegant, dapper and meticulous man, he left behind him at Columbia Records a tradition and sense of good taste that is with us yet."

Lieberson had another important role at Columbia that was never mentioned in any official version of his job description—that of providing cover for his far more mercurial friend, John Hammond. Hammond, frequently stubborn and always outspoken, would earn a reputation in the company as something of a spoiled brat for his habit of circumventing Columbia's corporate chain of command and going straight to Lieberson to get what he wanted. Over the years, all of Hammond's immediate supervisors were keenly aware not only of his close relationship with Lieberson but also of his willingness to leverage that friendship. The two shared a unique personal and professional relationship that would last for forty years.

Hammond's first projects after joining Columbia as a full-time producer were a mixed bag of popular froth and the improvisational jazz that he preferred. He tolerated the former in order to concentrate on the latter. One day in the early summer of 1939, while working on some Mildred Bailey recordings, Hammond was talking with the piano player Mary Lou Williams when he blurted out his unhappiness with the guitar player on the session. It seems the guitarist not only played through an electric amplifier—practically unheard of at the time—but also used a piece of metal to produce a sort of shrieking effect. The technique, known as slide guitar, is now fairly common, but Hammond hated it. When he grumbled about it to Williams, she replied: "If you really want to hear an electric guitar played like an acoustic guitar, you've got to go to the Ritz Café in Oklahoma City, where Charlie Christian works. He's the greatest electric guitar player I've ever heard." That was all the recommendation Hammond needed.

When Mary Lou Williams vouched for the talent of another musician, Hammond listened. The multitalented Williams is the only woman in the pantheon of jazz greats who wasn't a singer. Starting with Andy Kirk's territory band in the early 1930s, she made a name for herself not as a pretty ornament with a decent voice but as a piano player, composer, and arranger. She wrote arrangements for early jazz giants such as Louis Armstrong and Earl Hines, and she composed original songs for swing era heavyweights like Benny Goodman. In the early 1940s she would join a handful of other restless musical souls in Harlem for late-night jam sessions that would ultimately move jazz in a challenging and esoteric new direction.

In fairness to the guitarist at the Mildred Bailey sessions, Hammond's disdain for his technique was probably not based on a lack of talent. In fact, the guitarist was more than likely a better-than-average musician, or he would never have been asked to play on the recordings. The problem was that Hammond, like most others in the music industry at the time, didn't yet think of the guitar as an instrument to be showcased, at least not within the conventional structure of the typical large swing band. Hammond's ideal jazz guitarist up to that point was Freddie Green, the brilliant rhythm player he convinced Basie to hire. Players like Green kept the rhythm by chording their instrument, or strumming a collection of notes in time with the rhythm of the song. Few guitarists back then picked single strings to create streams of melodic notes. Like the bass, the guitar helped build the foundation over which the band's soloists performed, and the soloists were generally the horn players. That was about to change.

Based on his conversation with Mary Lou Williams, Hammond altered his travel plans for a trip he had scheduled to Los Angeles later that summer to supervise Benny Goodman's first recording sessions for Columbia. Goodman, at Hammond's urging, had left the RCA Victor label earlier that year in favor of Columbia. Normally, Hammond would have driven to California. But he decided to fly instead in order to make a stop in Oklahoma City to check out Williams's tip on the talented guitarist working there. In those days, a detour by plane from Chicago to Oklahoma City took fifteen hours and was broken up by no fewer than eight stops along the way.

Hammond survived the ordeal, and at the airport waiting for him in Oklahoma were a half-dozen or so black musicians, all of them members of Christian's band. In a region where the Ku Klux Klan held more than a little sway, Hammond's greeting party turned a few heads. Nevertheless, the group piled into a big Buick sedan and, after dropping Hammond's bags off at his hotel, headed to the Ritz Café, located on the first floor of an all-white hotel in downtown Oklahoma City. Christian's band played the Ritz several nights a week, with each musician taking home about $2.50 a night.

Hammond described the scene in numerous interviews: It started out like any other audition. Sitting at first motionless, one long leg thrown over the other, his arms folded across his chest, he listened as the band's music filled the large room. He was grimy and exhausted from his trip. But he quickly realized that something unique was happening: the sound of the other band members gradually faded to the point where he heard virtually nothing but the stream of notes pouring forth from Christian's guitar. It was happening again, and Hammond knew it immediately. There it was, staring him right in the face. Welling up inside him was a rare form of elation that came whenever he knew he was witnessing something truly special, something that was going to change things, something that was going to last.

"Charlie . . . had put a pickup on a regular Spanish guitar and hooked it up to a primitive amp and a twelve-inch speaker," Hammond recalled in a magazine article written years later.

He used amplification sparingly when playing rhythm but turned it up for his solos, which were as exciting improvisations as I had ever heard on any instrument, let alone the guitar. He was carrying on his shoulders a pretty sad combo, including his brother and some other Texans, but the contrast between the never-ending inspiration of Charlie and the mere competence of the others was the most startling I had ever heard. Before an hour had passed, I was determined to place Charlie with Benny Goodman, primarily as a spark for the depleted Goodman quartet.

Christian may have auditioned for Hammond in the Ritz Café, an all-white club in an all-white hotel in segregated downtown Oklahoma City, but that's not where he honed his considerable skills, according to local historians. At the Ritz, Christian and the band played the popular numbers of the era, songs with which the well-heeled customers were intimately familiar. In other words, the musicians weren't allowed much leeway in terms of improvising and experimenting with music more to their liking. At the Ritz the songs had to be played a certain way. If they weren't played that way, the band was replaced. The house policy was fine with Christian and the other men. It was an easy gig, and the Ritz paid better than any other club in Oklahoma City. But once the show was over, usually around midnight, the band members broke down their gear, packed their instruments into their big Buick sedan, and drove a few blocks east to Ruby's Grill on Second Street. Once at Ruby's, they would set it all up again and play whatever music inspired them for as long as they felt like playing.

The clubs on Second Street, more commonly referred to within Oklahoma's black community as the Deep Deuce, were open all night. Margretta Christian Downey, Charlie Christian's childhood girlfriend, recalled the thriving scene: "Everybody had a little dive around there. They would pop up and last a little while. Then someplace else would open, and *it* would be the big thing. Anything you wanted was down at the Deep Deuce. Everything was down there—everything but the church."

Situated hard off the southeastern spur of the Santa Fe Railroad tracks, the Deep Deuce—also known as Deep Two and the Deuce—was tucked into the bottom of a small hollow bordered to the west by Oklahoma Avenue and to the east by Stiles Avenue. The area served as the commercial and cultural center for Oklahoma City's black residents from the early twentieth century until the early 1960s, when much of the district was razed under the city's urban-renewal program. In the 1930s, when Charlie Christian was a regular at Ruby's, Second Street was home to a hardware store, a bookstore, a music store, the city's first black newspaper, *The Black Dispatch*, and not one but two funeral homes, as well as two drugstores, two hotels, a rooming house, and Slaughter's Dance Hall. All of these businesses were owned and operated by black entrepreneurs.

The historian Anita G. Arnold, who has written extensively on Oklahoma City's black community, believes the Deep Deuce deserves a place alongside other American jazz landmarks, iconic spots like the French Quarter in New Orleans, the South Side of Chicago, 131st Street and Seventh Avenue in Harlem, and Eighteenth and Vine streets in Kansas City. The Deep Deuce was to the Southwest what those other locales were to their respective regions, according to Arnold. "Thursdays were special on 'The Deuce,'" she wrote.

> It was maids day off in Nichols Hills and Northtown [white neighborhoods in Oklahoma City]. Those ladies from the services industry would spend all day shopping, going to the beauty shop, and getting ready for "The Walk." Preparations for "Dragging the Deuce" always took place on Wednesday and Thursday morning . . . Every Thursday they started on the north side of Second Street and walked in their finery from Stiles to Central then crossed over to the south side of the street. Then they strutted their strut, showing off their clothes, their hairstyles from Central back up to Stiles. This continued all afternoon into the night . . . It was an occasion for families to load up the car, once again, and go to Second Street to watch these "Fashion Plates" walk and talk. This happened every Thursday night for years.

At night, the people's attention turned to entertainment. On the north side of Second Street was the Aldridge Theater, founded by Zelia Page Breaux, a local entrepreneur and an influential music instructor whose pupils included a young Charlie Christian. When big-name black acts came to Oklahoma City—acts like Cab Calloway or the Blue Devils—they played at the Aldridge. The blues singer and Oklahoma City native Jimmy Rushing worked at his father's restaurant next door to the Aldridge. He supposedly met his Blue Devils bandmates while taking a break in an alley that ran behind the theater.

Second Street was also a launching pad for talented regional musicians. Other influential Oklahoma-bred musicians who passed through the neighborhood in the 1930s were Jay McShann, the bandleader and pianist who grew up in Muskogee, and Oscar Pettiford, the innovative bassist who was born on an Indian reservation near the small town of Okmulgee.

The writer Ralph Ellison, a native of Oklahoma City, once bemoaned the lack of attention given to prominent black jazz musicians' roots, complaining:

> The jazz artist who became nationally known is written about as though he came into existence only upon his arrival in New York. His career in the big cities, where jazz is more of a commercial entertainment than part of a total way of life, is stressed at the expense of his life in the South, the Southwest, and the Midwest, where most Negro musicians at least found their early development. Thus we are left with an impression of mysterious rootlessness, and the true and often annoying complexity of American cultural experience is oversimplified.

This was certainly true of Charlie Christian. Christian's life prior to meeting Hammond in 1939 might have been summed up in one famous line uttered by Teddy Hill, the manager of Minton's Playhouse, the Harlem nightclub where modern jazz was born. According to legend, when Hill first heard Christian jamming with other musicians, he blinked a few times in astonishment and asked: "Where did he come from?"

Christian was born on July 29, 1916, surrounded by cotton fields in the bustling small town of Bonham, Texas, just south of the Oklahoma border. When Charlie was about two, his father, Clarence Christian, came down with an illness that eventually left him blind. Unable to work, Clarence took his family—his wife, Willie Mae, and his three boys, Edward, Clarence, and the baby, Charlie—north to Oklahoma City, where a handful of relatives and friends had already settled.

The Christians were a musical family, according to Margretta Christian Downey. Clarence Christian had led a small orchestra in Bonham and could play almost any instrument. Willie Mae Christian sang and played piano. The two older Christian boys began playing instruments when they were old enough to hold them, and Charlie quickly followed suit. In Oklahoma City, the Christian men made a little extra money by roaming the streets playing their instruments, and by the late 1920s Edward, the oldest of the sons, was an established professional musician. In 1929, while Edward was playing piano in Don Redman's orchestra, thirteen-year-old Charlie Christian joined the band onstage one night and knocked out solos on "Sweet Georgia Brown," "Tea for Two," and "Rose Room," according to Peter Broadbent, the author of a book on Christian's life.

Around the same time Christian was making his debut with his brother's band, he and Downey met at Douglass High School and began dating. (It was only by coincidence that Christian is Margretta's maiden name. She and Charlie were not related, and although they had a child together—Billie Jean, born in 1932—they never married.) According to Downey, as a teenager Christian played whenever and wherever he could—at barbecues, on street corners, and at occasional gigs arranged by his brother. Downey recalled Christian soaking up disparate influences like a sponge and then synthesizing them into his own voice. Their daughter's birth occurred just as Christian's growing reputation was earning him full-time work as a musician, she said. Since he put his music first, he faltered in his responsibilities as a father. After Hammond arrived in town and convinced Christian to leave Oklahoma City to join Benny Goodman's band, Downey and Christian rarely saw each other. For the last few years of his life the two kept in touch mostly through letters, she said—letters she sent care of John Hammond. "He was very excited about his career. He mentioned Lionel [Hampton] and Benny [Goodman] quite a bit. He said Benny could be hard to work for. And he always spoke very highly of [singer] Peggy Lee. He just insisted that Peggy Lee was the greatest," she recalled.

Charlie Christian was hardly the first person to play the electric guitar. In the late 1920s and early 1930s, as Christian was learning to play, the instrument was gaining popularity among western swing guitarists.

Christian was exposed to these players both in Oklahoma City and while traveling throughout the Southwest in various territory bands. The writer Rudi Blesh, who knew Christian while growing up in Oklahoma City, observed: "Most guitarists were at first afraid of [the electric guitar], and many spurned it as an 'illegitimate' instrument. Charlie embraced it and quickly probed its possibilities." By the time Hammond arrived in Oklahoma City, Christian had mastered the instrument and was a sought-after professional musician. A picture taken at some point in the mid-1930s shows Charlie, resplendent in black tie, posing as a member of Leslie Sheffield's Rhythmaires, one of Oklahoma City's top orchestras.

Once again, the powerful dynamic that enveloped virtually all of Hammond's protégés began to pull Christian into its wake. Christian, not unlike Teddy Wilson when he filled in for Earl Hines at the Grand Terrace in Chicago, or Count Basie during his tenure in Kansas City, was an extraordinary local talent who had begun to make a name for himself on a regional basis. But, as is often the case with local talents, a catalyst is sometimes needed to push them through to the next level. For Christian—as for Teddy Wilson and Count Basie—that catalyst arrived in the person of John Hammond.

After listening to Christian play for an hour or so, Hammond wasted no time in calling Benny Goodman to alert the bandleader to his find in Oklahoma City. "I've just heard the greatest guitar since Eddie Lang. He plays electric and . . ." At that point, according to Hammond, Goodman cut him off: "Who the hell wants to hear an electric guitar player?" It took some quick thinking and faster talking, but Hammond was able to convince Goodman to at least give the young guitarist an audition.

Before leaving Oklahoma City, Christian was sent off in grand style by his friends and fellow musicians. A party was thrown for him at Ruby's Grill the night before he left, and a number of friends and family gathered at the train station the following day, August 14, 1939, to see him off. A picture printed a few days later in the *The Black Dispatch* shows Christian, a broad grin splashed across his face, shaking hands with the band member James Simpson. Edward Christian, his face awash in pride, looks on. It appears from the picture that Christian had packed little more than his guitar, which is set down alongside him.

The caption in the newspaper read, "From Ruby's Grill to Benny Goodman's Band."

But if Goodman had had his way, it might never have happened.

Christian's debut with the Goodman orchestra in Los Angeles in August 1939 is one of the most celebrated and lovingly recounted anecdotes in the canon of jazz lore. It's a story that deserves to be retold, and many of the details handed down over the years are actually true.

Christian apparently had misgivings about leaving Oklahoma City. He had just turned twenty-three and hadn't traveled much outside the Southwest. Now he was being asked to audition for the most popular band in the country. It was hardly surprising, then, that he felt a little apprehensive. Hammond desperately wanted Christian's music to reach a wider audience, but he didn't want to scare Christian off by seeming pushy or intimidating. So he turned to Mary Lou Williams, who stepped in and encouraged Christian to make the move. Christian relented, and after arriving in Los Angeles, he headed straight to the studio in West Hollywood where Goodman was making his first recordings for Columbia Records. It was there that things got a little dicey. Hammond had told Goodman that Christian was coming, but Goodman, preoccupied as usual, apparently forgot about the audition and was rude to Christian when reminded of it.

Hammond himself seems to have embellished parts of the story. For instance, part of the Christian legend—an aspect perpetuated by Hammond—holds that when Christian arrived at the studio that day, he was dressed like a fool, wearing "a large hat, his purple shirt and yellow shoes," according to Hammond. This description seems highly unlikely. Scores of photos were taken of Christian during his brief career, including candid shots and staged publicity photos, and if any exist in which he is not tastefully attired, they have never surfaced. Moreover, people who knew him, as well as others who have closely studied his career, dismiss the tale as rubbish. Margretta Christian Downey recalled a disarming man who, when not performing, preferred to blend into the background. "It just isn't true," added the musicologist Michael Brooks. "Everything I've ever learned about him indicates he was always quiet in his clothes and demeanor."

Regardless of how Christian was dressed, Goodman supposedly

didn't want to listen to him play. The bandleader glanced at Christian, then turned to glare icily at Hammond, fixing on him the infamous Goodman "ray." He went back to doing whatever he was doing before Christian arrived. At the end of the recording session, Hammond approached Goodman and reminded him that he'd promised Christian an audition. At that point, the bandleader reluctantly gave in but came away unimpressed after hearing Charlie chord the rhythm for "Tea for Two." Christian never even got a chance to plug in.

Undeterred, Hammond decided to take matters into his own hands. Enlisting his longtime friend Artie Bernstein, who was playing bass in Goodman's band at the time, he set into motion a plan intended to make certain the bandleader would hear Christian play later that night during Goodman's gig at the popular Victor Hugo nightclub. Before the show began, Hammond and Bernstein wheeled Christian's amplifier onto the stage. Then, during the dinner break as Goodman was schmoozing the crowd, they pulled a chair up onstage and directed Christian to sit in it. When Goodman returned to the stage to prepare for the quintet segment of the show, there was Christian already plugged into his amplifier and seated alongside the current lineup of Bernstein on bass, Fletcher Henderson on piano, Lionel Hampton on vibraharp, and Nick Fatool on drums. Goodman found Hammond in the crowd and visited upon him another of his legendary glares, a look so frightening that accomplished professional musicians making lots of money were known to quit Goodman's band for no other reason than fear of the "ray." Hammond, however, was not so easily intimidated.

According to the legend, Goodman, thinking he would outsmart Hammond by humiliating the country-bumpkin guitar player, called for "Rose Room," a complicated piece and one he felt certain would stump Christian. But Christian played as if he'd been waiting for years for Goodman to call the song. Astounding everyone on the bandstand, Christian reeled off one sparkling lead after another. By some accounts, his solo lasted for more than twenty choruses as Goodman and the other musicians listened and followed him rapturously.

That part of the story is also very likely an embellishment. In the first place, it's hardly surprising that Christian was familiar with "Rose Room." In fact, it would have been surprising if he hadn't known it.

(Peter Broadbent claimed Christian soloed on the song many years earlier as a teenager while standing in with his brother's band in Oklahoma City.) Moreover, like any good musician, once Christian had found the key in which the other musicians were playing, he could solo over practically any song. Professional musicians don't necessarily need to know a song note for note in order to play along with the rest of the band. Finally, the musicologist Brooks is highly skeptical of the twenty-chorus version of the story. A solo of that length might have gone on for ten minutes or longer, he noted. Regardless of how impressive Christian's chops may have been that evening, it's unlikely either Goodman or the audience would have remained enraptured for that long.

What's left after the corny embellishments are eliminated from the story is simply the quality of the solos played by Christian. That's clearly what impressed Goodman and convinced him to hire the young black guitarist. When "Rose Room" ended, the audition was over, and the Benny Goodman Quintet was rather suddenly the Benny Goodman Sextet.

Charlie Christian proved just the spark Hammond had hoped for, the one that helped reenergize the depleted Goodman orchestra in late 1939. Teddy Wilson, Gene Krupa, and Harry James had all left recently to form their own bands, and Goodman needed a new creative voice to rejuvenate the small groups—the Quartet, the Quintet, and now, with Christian on board, the Sextet—that had grown so popular with the fans. Christian blended in seamlessly with the rest of the men.

An indication of how well and how quickly these musicians fit together came just weeks after Christian joined the group. On October 2, Hammond supervised the first recording sessions of the Goodman Sextet, and an instant classic emerged from the session: the Christian-conceived "Flying Home." Christian's snappy, confident solos are every bit a match in both quality and inventiveness with the solos offered by Goodman and Hampton. The song quickly became a staple of the Goodman repertoire.

Christian's career with Goodman would last just three years. Fortunately for jazz fans, however, those years coincided with what may have been the peak years of Hammond's influence in the jazz world. Hammond's reputation allowed him to bring together remarkable groups of musicians for recording sessions and live performances, and Christian became a staple of these all-star sessions. On Christmas Eve, 1939, for example, during a second "From Spirituals to Swing" concert, Christian performed at Carnegie Hall with the Goodman Sextet, as well as with a group called the Kansas City Six, which featured Christian on lead electric guitar with several of Count Basie's players. A week later— New Year's Eve—Hammond supervised a session for the singer Ida Cox that included Christian, Lionel Hampton, and the pianist James P. Johnson. Throughout 1940 there were recordings with the Metronome All-Stars, featuring Harry James, Jack Teagarden, and Gene Krupa, among others. It was pretty heady company for a twenty-three-year-old musician only months removed from Oklahoma City. But Christian more than held his own. Soon everyone wanted to hear the tall, skinny black kid from Oklahoma City who could spin out line after line of mesmerizing solos on his unusual instrument.

Meanwhile, Christian had met up with a group of less prominent musicians, mostly young sidemen like himself who were growing restless playing the same swing arrangements night after night. After their regular nightly gigs were over, these musicians would gather uptown late at night to jam at Minton's Playhouse on West 118th Street in Harlem. Christian and these other like-minded musicians—Dizzy Gillespie, Kenny Clarke, Thelonious Monk, and Mary Lou Williams—would ultimately restructure jazz and set popular music on a new course.

All the touring, late-night jam sessions, and high living as a member of the most popular band in America eventually took a toll on Christian. It's uncertain at what point in his life he was first diagnosed with tuberculosis, but musicians who worked with him in 1940 and 1941 recall hearing horrendous coughing spells and watching helplessly as Christian grew progressively weaker. Prior to being diagnosed, he was encouraged by people close to him to seek medical help, or at least adopt a healthier lifestyle. Their concerns were ignored. Finally, on the Midwestern leg of a 1941 tour with the Goodman band, Christian collapsed and was sent back to New York City. After several weeks at Bellevue Hospital in Manhattan, where his illness got worse, he was moved to Seaview Sanitarium on Staten Island. Recovery proved elusive, though, and Christian died on March 2, 1942, at the age of twenty-five.

Hammond's influence touched Christian in death as it had in life. It was another of Hammond's protégés—William Basie—who helped Christian's family through the difficult period following his death. Hammond had initially served practically as Christian's guardian during the early months with Goodman. But over time their paths diverged. Hammond was busy both in the studio and with his efforts to attract talent to Columbia. And he was always rushing around in furtherance of his various causes. Christian eventually carved out his own life for himself, finding his own social circles. Unfortunately, some of his new friends apparently shared with him a fondness for marijuana and alcohol, a factor that undoubtedly contributed to his early death. After Christian fell ill, many of the musicians he had met and grown friendly with while playing with the Goodman band apparently chose not to visit him in the hospital. The opposite was true of Bill Basie. Basie not only made sure that his own physician made regular visits to Christian at Seaview Sanitarium, the bandleader also saw to it that Christian's personal effects were in order when Christian's mother arrived in New York for the funeral. "Count Basie was a good friend to Charlie's mother," Margretta Christian Downey recalled. "When she got to New York, it was Basie who took her around and took care of her. He took her under his wing and made sure that she was able to pick up all of his personal belongings. He made sure she had everything she needed."

Hammond could hardly have known that Christian's music would go on to influence several generations of guitarists. But it has. In fact, of all the swing era jazz greats with whom Hammond worked in the years before World War II, only Billie Holiday has had comparable long-term influence on the generations of musicians who followed. Moreover, while the popularity of virtually every swing era giant—Benny Goodman, Artie Shaw, Tommy and Jimmy Dorsey, Glenn Miller—has waned over the years as musical tastes have shifted, Christian's reputation has grown. It's not hard to figure out why. In post–World War II America, a period sometimes referred to as the rock-and-roll era, the electric guitar has emerged as *the* iconic instrument in popular music. Whether it was Chuck Berry duckwalking to "Sweet Little Sixteen," Jimi Hendrix awash in a feedback of "Purple Haze," Jimmy Page massaging a "Whole Lotta Love" from his Gibson, or Stevie Ray Vaughan drowning his fans in a bluesy "Texas Flood," the electric guitar has been at the center of pop culture for over fifty years.

Ask any of these guitar gods where it all began, and more than likely each of them would respond, "With Charlie Christian."

9

A FAMILY

The one thing Hammond was apparently too busy for during the years he was building his career as a record producer and a jazz critic was a girlfriend. He was often seen out and about with women—sometimes beautiful women—but the dates always seemed platonic rather than amorous. Lena Horne was one such companion when she first began singing at Café Society shortly after it opened. But she and Hammond weren't really dating. They were out together to see and to be seen. So consumed was he with his various passions that he apparently had no time for passion of that sort. Otis Ferguson wrote of him: "As for girls, he never seems to be cluttered up with them unless they are music critics, in which case it doesn't count."

All that changed in early 1940 at a party in Manhattan thrown by the socialite Frieda Diamond and her wealthy husband, Barry Baruch, where Hammond met a beautiful young aspiring actress named Jemy McBride. Hammond later told Jemy's sister, Isobel Fisher, that he was struck literally speechless the first time he saw her and that he had set out immediately to win her over. His strategy included introducing himself not as a record producer and the scion of a Vanderbilt railroad fortune, but rather as a reporter for the *Brooklyn Eagle*. "He said he had never seen such a beautiful woman. And he said he wanted to be sure she wasn't a New York debutante who knew all about his background," Fisher recalled many years later.

After a courtship that lasted a little over a year, John Hammond married Jemy in a small ceremony in New Haven, Connecticut, on March 8, 1941. Only about ten close friends were invited. Among those notably missing were the mother and father of both the bride and the groom. While both sets of parents approved of the wedding, it seems each would have preferred a much larger ceremony. So rather than invite their parents to a ceremony that displeased them, the couple decided to flee New York and get married as quietly and discreetly as possible seventy-five miles away in Connecticut. The rabbi Edgar Siskin, Hammond's friend from his days at Yale, presided over a decidedly nondenominational affair. The guests included Benny Goodman and Hammond's sister Alice, who by that time were themselves romantically linked. Jemy's sister, Isobel, was also there with her husband.

Hammond's wedding was cause for one of his more extraordinary admissions. Although he was thirty years old, extremely well traveled, and independently wealthy, Hammond, in his memoirs, claimed to have been a virgin on his wedding night. He made this claim despite having spent the decade prior to getting married as one of the most visible figures (and eligible bachelors) in the notoriously licentious world of jazz. To be sure, Hammond was always an earnest iconoclast. It's entirely plausible that he professed his virginity simply to distance himself from other wealthy young men of his generation, whom he considered irresponsible playboys. The claim is also more than a little sanctimonious, and Hammond was not above sanctimony. Yet it seems likely that he was telling the truth. In any event, fumbling or otherwise, the young couple made it through their wedding night, and then sailed off to London for a brief honeymoon.

Jemy McBride was raised in a comfortable, upper-middle-class home in the small town of Batavia in upstate New York. Her father, Robert McBride, had emigrated from Ireland during World War I. Working as a boilermaker as a young man in the shipyards of Belfast, he had helped build the giant boilers for the *Titanic*. Landing first in Buffalo and later in Batavia in 1923, Robert McBride opened McBride Boiler Works in 1928. Subsequently renamed McBride Steel Plate Construction Company, the business quickly expanded beyond the construction of large boilers to include the lucrative manufacture of snowplows, a vital piece of equipment in the snowbelt region bordering the Great Lakes. The company eventually grew into one of Batavia's most successful local businesses.

The two McBride daughters steered clear of the family business and concentrated instead on more artistic endeavors. After graduating from Antioch College, a progressive liberal arts school in the bucolic small town of Yellow Springs, Ohio, Jemy headed for Los Angeles, where she won second place in a national talent contest and briefly dated the writer Irwin Shaw. She moved on to New York City a short time later to pursue a career on the stage. In New York, she roomed with Frances Heflin, the sister of the actor Van Heflin, in a small apartment on West Fifty-eighth Street. It was while living with Fra Heflin that she met the handsome and energetic young "reporter."

Isobel Fisher said Hammond's ruse was probably unnecessary since her sister wouldn't have been impressed by her future husband's ancestral fortune anyway. "She was doing just fine on her own," Fisher noted. Tall, confident, and blessed with a graceful, athletic build, Jemy wasn't lacking for suitors. Like the popular actress Frances Farmer, whom her friends said she resembled, Jemy wore her thick dirty blond hair in a sporty shoulder cut. Her high cheekbones, smoky blue eyes, and flawless pale skin made her a classic American beauty. "She was very beautiful, and she was not particularly impressed by her marriage to a Vanderbilt," Fisher recalled admiringly.

It's understandable why this intelligent and strikingly beautiful young woman, who undoubtedly had her pick of eligible young men, would have found Hammond impressive. He was good-looking, wealthy, and known in every nightclub in town. Yet he was neither a heavy drinker nor a ladies' man. He was mature and responsible, dressed neatly, drank and smoked little, and could be exceedingly charming when he chose to be. And he kept company with some of the most famous names in American show business.

Most impressive to Jemy McBride, though, was that despite his ancestral wealth, Hammond's success as a writer, jazz impresario, and record producer had come as a result of determination, hard work, and a willingness to take risks. According to Isobel Fisher, he earned her sister's hand in marriage in similar fashion.

Consider, for example, Hammond's success as a record producer, which was based in large part on his willingness to try just about anything. He loved nothing so much as bringing together talented musicians who had never before played together and seeing whether they jelled. If the right musicians were brought together under the right circumstances, anything was possible, he believed. His judgment was frequently sound, resulting in such sublime pairings as Teddy Wilson and Billie Holiday, Billie Holiday and Lester Young, Count Basie and Freddie Green, Benny Goodman and Lionel Hampton, and Benny Goodman and Charlie Christian, to name just a few. But occasionally a musical match that seemed like a good idea fizzled inside the studio. One such unfortunate pairing was that of Count Basie and Paul Robeson.

On September 29, 1941, Joe Louis defeated Lou Nova in a heavyweight title fight in New York City. At the time, Louis was unquestionably the most revered black man in America. A few days after the fight, on October 1, Hammond, Robeson, and Count Basie gathered in a recording studio on West Fifty-eighth Street to record a tribute to Louis with lyrics written by Richard Wright, the author of the recently published *Native Son*. Robeson, an accomplished athlete in college, a respected Shakespearean actor, and an outspoken political radical, was best known for his masterful renditions of spirituals. He and Hammond were good friends, both of them passionately dedicated to the cause of integration and both of them regulars at Café Society. And all three men—Hammond, Robeson, and Basie—were eager to celebrate Louis's achievements. With the Basie vocalist Jimmy Rushing coaching him, Robeson gamely attempted to shed years of classical voice training in an attempt to find the loose spontaneity needed to sing the blues. After several botched takes, Basie leaned over to Hammond and whispered, "It certainly is an honor to be working with Mr. Robeson, but the man certainly can't sing the blues." "King Joe, Parts 1 and 2" is one of the great novelty records of all time, but Hammond never again sought to broaden Robeson's musical reach.

The pairing of Robeson and Basie may not have worked, but Hammond never let his failures dim the enthusiasm that propelled him forward in pursuit of his goals. It served him well in his battles as a civil rights activist. It had fueled his goal of integrating the Goodman band in the mid-1930s, and it fueled him again in the early 1940s when he set his sights on integrating commercial radio. Despite Goodman's landmark decision, integration had yet to spread throughout the broader music industry. In 1941 the bands that provided backing for radio's live programming were all still lily-white, and Hammond set about to change that.

Integration was still an issue most people who made their liveli-hoods in the music business would rather have avoided, according to Harold Leventhal, a fixture in liberal music circles for decades. Inte-grating the radio bands was a particularly thorny issue, he recalled. "It was a big battle because it was also a battle with the unions. The Local 802 [the musicians' union in New York City] was segregated at the time, so you had a white local and a black local," he explained. Union officials, according to Leventhal, weren't interested in mixing the two. Consequently, Hammond was fighting not only radio executives who had no interest in integration but also powerful union foes. Through sheer persistence and resourcefulness, he succeeded in getting a hand-ful of black musicians hired to the CBS band.

Leventhal was plugging songs for Irving Berlin when he met Hammond in 1942. They worked in the same building at 799 Seventh Avenue. "We got to meet each other because I was aware that he was, in quotes, a left-winger and so was I. So we had that in common," Lev-enthal recalled six decades later. Leventhal enlisted Hammond's help in forming the Popular Music Committee for Russian War Relief, an effort to raise money for Russian war refugees during World War II. "Of course I was just a young kid at that point and he was older," said Leventhal. "John was able to get Benny Goodman to serve as chairman of the committee." Hammond also recruited Edward Wallerstein, who was then president of Columbia Records. Together, Leventhal and Hammond organized a successful benefit concert at Carnegie Hall that featured Duke Ellington.

Hammond, by Leventhal's description, was an easily recognizable figure, due to his suits and omnipresent reading matter. But what really made him stand out among New York's left-wing activists, according to Leventhal, was his penchant for looking beyond the political and economic issues that were the primary focus of the popular-front supporters. Instead, Hammond focused on civil rights issues. Leventhal had a similar worldview. "Nobody talked about that at that time," Leventhal said. "As we know, he was instrumental in Goodman making his mixed group, he was on the board of the NAACP and was very active in that, and he was close with Paul Robeson at that time. And so he and I had a lot in common; we were the rarities in those circles." Leventhal would remain a fixture in progressive musical circles for decades, eventually managing the careers of both Woody Guthrie and Pete Seeger. His and Hammond's paths crossed often.

"The fact that Hammond came from a wealthy background temporized his reputation [as a troublemaker] because he was also recognized as an intellectual," Leventhal observed. "Not too many of these [music industry] people were coming from an intellectual background. The musicians, the people in the record business at that time, [and the people] in the agencies, they weren't intellectuals, they weren't politically oriented. They knew how to make money. It was the era of Tin Pan Alley. So he was the odd guy out. The fact that he came from this old American background kind of stabilized him."

The jazz bassist Milt Hinton was working with Cab Calloway in 1942 when Hammond recruited him for the breakthrough band at CBS. "John was out front on the race issue at least twenty years before it became a fashionable thing. He was looking for talent, period. Skin color had nothing to do with it. Naturally, with his connections he could get away with things most other people couldn't," Hinton later wrote.

In other words, Hammond's pedigree gave him entrée where others from less august backgrounds had none. And Hammond wasn't shy about using that entrée to achieve his goals. Indeed, he leveraged his family connections in his battle to integrate radio orchestras. In his memoirs, he recalled that around the time he was targeting radio bands, a Vanderbilt cousin was married to a CBS executive. Hammond turned a family gathering into an opportunity, taking his cause directly to the in-law. Surprisingly, the executive agreed to let Hammond recommend a handful of black musicians for a new band CBS was putting together. As a result, the drummer Cozy Cole, the trumpeter Emmett

Berry, the trombonist Benny Morton, and the bassist Israel Crosby all found full-time jobs with CBS.

It was probably inevitable that Hammond, like so many others in his professional and social circles, would eventually fall under the watchful eye of the FBI director, J. Edgar Hoover. Hammond was never a member of the Communist Party, but he had organized the entertainment for dozens of benefit concerts and fund-raisers for causes supported by the popular front. For his efforts, his name popped up regularly in the pages of *The Daily Worker*, the Communist Party newspaper, as someone who was at least sympathetic to the cause. Moreover, he allowed his name to appear on the letterheads of numerous left-wing organizations, either as an actual member or as a donor. Among them were the National Committee for the Defense of Political Prisoners, the National Committee for People's Rights, the American Council on Soviet Relations, the Citizens Committee for Harry Bridges, and Russian War Relief Inc., just to name a few. All of these groups were undoubtedly viewed by the FBI as thinly disguised Communist fronts.

Hammond did nothing to conceal these affiliations. Indeed, had he known he was under Hoover's surveillance, he almost certainly would have been flattered. But Hoover was wasting his time. Hammond was not a Communist. He disagreed too strongly with too many of their core doctrines. To be sure, he had great admiration for the passion and idealism exhibited by many of his Communist friends. He idolized his cousin Frederick Field, an outspoken Communist who was jailed in the 1950s for his affiliation and was later forced to flee the United States for Mexico. Even so, Hammond didn't necessarily agree with his cousin's politics. In fact, he viewed much of the Communist Party leadership as so many opportunists cynically manipulating events—the Scottsboro case, for example—in an effort to achieve their own myopic ends. He claimed in his memoirs to have told an FBI investigator in the 1950s, "I think it's important to tell the absolute truth, because not only was I never a member of the Communist Party, nor would I be a member of the Communist Party, nor am I a member of the Communist Party, I could not be because I am interested in civil rights and it is not. Throughout the years the Communists have done flip-flops, and if I had been a member of the Party I could never have made the kinds of waves I did."

Hammond was also not a revolutionary. To the contrary, he believed in American democracy and its attendant benefits, not least of which was freedom of thought and expression.

J. Edgar Hoover apparently never thought to ask Hammond his views on politics. If he had, he might have discovered Hammond's opposition to much of what the Communists were trying to achieve. Nevertheless, in 1941 the FBI began compiling information on Hammond. The file is both comical and chilling. Ultimately, it reveals a lot more about the prejudices and petty vindictiveness of Hoover's street-level investigators than it does about any clandestine subversive activities on the part of its subject. The first entry, dated June 11, 1941, and obtained, according to the memorandum, from an "outside unknown source," describes Hammond as "so typical of the caviar cocktail crowd." The crux of the memo is to suggest that by virtue of Hammond's involvement in a committee formed by Orson Welles to assist the West Coast labor leader Harry Bridges against charges brought by the U.S. government, the committee must be a Communist front. It reads:

> Hammond is the son of an important corporation lawyer. He is wealthy in his own right. For a long time he has been associated with the *New Masses* and other Communist activity . . . Through his money and his myriad connections, we are informed by those who know, he is in a position to make or break musicians and bands, both classical and jazz. Only a few weeks ago swing leader Artie Shaw joined a West Coast Bridges Defense Committee and then signed the American Peace Mobilization call.

The eerily cryptic—"we are informed by those who know"— memorandum, which apparently originated at the FBI's Washington, D.C., headquarters, seems to suggest that Hammond used his influence to pressure well-known bandleaders into becoming fellow travelers. Using Shaw as an example of a bandleader easily influenced by

Hammond is especially ironic, however. Had the writer of the memorandum ever met Artie Shaw, he would have discovered that Shaw was an even more devout iconoclast than Hammond and not inclined toward succumbing to pressure of any kind.

Hoover himself took a special interest in Hammond, personally requesting in July 1941 that the bureau's New York office conduct an investigation "to determine whether this person should be considered for custodial detention . . . in the event of a national emergency." Over the next year Hoover sought several times to obtain an update on the Hammond investigation and was quick to express his anger when none was forthcoming. At least three letters related to Hammond and signed by Hoover were dispatched from FBI headquarters in Washington to the agency's New York office between July 3, 1941, and May 27, 1942.

The investigation that resulted from Hoover's requests, conducted mainly through the use of "confidential informants," revealed little that Hammond wouldn't have gladly acknowledged had someone thought to ask him. Thus an FBI memo dated February 1942 concluded that Hammond "has been affiliated with many reported Communist front organization [*sic*] since 1934 and may be considered a so called 'fellow traveler,' [but] there is no information indicating that he is a member of the Communist Party." Despite this seemingly conclusive finding, the FBI would continue to keep tabs on Hammond for another two decades, filling a thick file with the names and dates of his social engagements but offering no evidence that he was involved in anything even remotely resembling subversive activity.

The Hammonds' first year of marriage was an exciting one; the attractive couple spent countless nights at Café Society listening to jazz and socializing with the elite of New York's artists and intellectuals. Early in 1942, Hammond and his wife took their first cross-country road trip. It may have been the happiest, most carefree time they ever spent together.

On January 16, 1942, Hammond supervised what would be his last recording date for Columbia Records for nearly four years. It was an all-star session made up of that year's most popular musicians as voted

on by the readers of *Metronome* magazine. The group included Benny
Goodman, Count Basie, Gene Krupa, Benny Carter, Cootie Williams,
and J. C. Higginbotham. No one knew it then, but the session marked
the last time Hammond would work with such an elite group of jazz
musicians while each was either at or near the peak of his popularity.
For Hammond, the session would be the last of the swing era. In fact,
unknown to any of the men present at that recording date in New
York, the attack by the Japanese on Pearl Harbor six weeks earlier,
on December 7, 1941, would mark not only the beginning of World
War II for the United States but also the beginning of the end of the
swing era.

Two weeks later, Hammond was out on the open road in his convertible with his wife. He had requested the time off to pursue his myriad
other interests. Specifically, he wanted to devote more time to further-
ing integration in the various trade unions with which he was affiliated
in New York, particularly the American Federation of Musicians Local
802, which, despite his best efforts, remained segregated well into the
1940s. He also spent time helping to start a short-lived jazz magazine,
Music and Rhythm, whose express purpose was to fight discrimination
in the music business.

But before throwing himself into his various reform causes, he
wanted to take a long road trip to explore America with his wife. He had
made this trip before many times and was usually impatient to reach
his destination. But this trip was special, and for a change he wasn't in
a hurry to get anywhere. The trip wasn't special because of some significant musical discovery along the way. Indeed, he didn't stumble across
some phenomenal new trumpet player during a quick stop at White's
Emporium on Garfield Boulevard in Chicago. Nor did he happen
upon a marvelous new pianist at, say, the Boone Theater near Eighteenth and Vine during the short stopover in Kansas City. The trip was
special not because of anyone he met along the way but because of the
person he had brought with him.

Jemy was the perfect traveling companion. Seated next to him hour
after hour as the convertible sped across mile after mile of two-lane
highway (the big six-lane interstate highways didn't come along until
the 1950s), she shared his interests in music, literature, politics, and re-

ligion. They whiled away the hours agreeing and debating, agreeing
again and then debating some more. The couple was ultimately headed
to Los Angeles, where Hammond had scheduled some meetings to
promote his new magazine. Their journey was interrupted only by a
handful of overnights in big cities and a few daily pit stops at roadside
diners. Jemy, according to her sister, was impressed at the breadth of
her husband's renown. He had close friends in every city through
which they passed. He knew the owners of the toughest clubs and chicest
theaters and the managers of all the biggest record stores, and they all
knew him. He knew the most influential newspaper editors and the
slickest-talking public-relations men. And, of course, he knew all the
best musicians.

On the outskirts of Albuquerque, New Mexico, on the western
fringe of the Sandia Mountain range, the scrubby overgrowth of the
high desert began to give way to rudimentary civilization. That stretch
of Route 66 had been open for nearly five years, and Albuquerque was
eagerly reaching out into the desert to greet a steadily increasing flow of
tourists, businessmen, and other road-weary travelers. The Depression
was finally over and America was restless. After emerging from Tijeras
Canyon, Hammond could see the hazy outline of downtown Albuquerque off in the distance to the west. A roadside café offered coffee
and pie for a dime, up from the nickel they cost just a year or so earlier,
when much of the traffic on this same dusty stretch of highway still consisted of the last remnants of Steinbeck's dust bowl refugees. Now their
relatives, the ones who had remained in Arkansas, Oklahoma, and the
northern Texas Panhandle, were following that very same route. But
these migrants were heading west under markedly different circumstances; this latest wave had a sense of optimism and purpose, characteristics strikingly lacking among their earlier brethren. The difference
lay in the thousands of jobs—steady, good-paying jobs—awaiting them
in the shipyards and defense plants of Los Angeles and farther north in
the San Francisco Bay Area as America prepared for war in Europe and
the Pacific. These were the men and women John and Jemy Hammond
met as they crossed America just eight weeks after the attack on Pearl
Harbor. The Hammonds shared their sense of optimism.

On a flat swath just east of Albuquerque's Nob Hill neighborhood, emerging at the time as the city's first suburb, the roadside kitsch for which Route 66 will be forever remembered was springing up like so much wild sagebrush. The Iceberg Café (shaped like an iceberg, naturally) sold ice cream cones, cold drinks, and gasoline. A restaurant shaped like a Mexican sombrero offered tacos, enchiladas, and huevos rancheros. Neon signs flashed VACANCY—VACANCY—VACANCY from a string of roadside motor courts, one of which boasted a playground with several large tepees, perfect for rowdy games of cowboys and Indians between restless children cooped up for too long in the backseat of a car. Hammond drove past the tepees, stopping a little farther down the road in the unpaved parking lot of a tidy-looking establishment that sported a neo-pueblo motif.

Climbing out of the convertible, dusty and sunburned from the trip over the mountains, Hammond was glad to be away from the congested, grimy streets of New York. He was, according to his sister-in-law, completely relaxed. Far from the pressures of studio deadlines, record company budgets, and musicians' egos, he was looking forward to a few days of downtime with Jemy in Albuquerque, where they would stay with her sister, Isobel, who was married at the time to a professor at the University of New Mexico. The couple was renting a small house in the foothills of the Sandia Mountains, and Hammond and Jemy stayed nearby in the small, rustic motor court that Hammond had spotted on Route 66.

Isobel Fisher told an interviewer many years later that John and Jemy were clearly in love and extremely happy together during their stay in Albuquerque. Hammond tended to be preoccupied with big ideas and sweeping visions, Fisher observed, and he sometimes neglected to pay attention to life's smaller details. According to Fisher, that's where her sister took over: Jemy made sure her husband cut the price tags off a new sport coat before he left the house wearing it, and she made sure his pants were zipped before they entered a restaurant or a cocktail party.

On the day Hammond and Jemy arrived in Albuquerque, the two couples relaxed for a while reading "the fifty pounds of magazines and newspapers that John always surrounded himself with," Isobel Fisher recalled, laughing at the memory. Then Hammond got restless and headed downtown to stop by the offices of the local orchestra and the editor of the newspaper. On the way back to the motor court, he stopped by the train station and picked up all the local papers. Later that evening, while Isobel's husband taught a night class, Hammond took the women to the movie theater to see the new John Ford film, *How Green Was My Valley*, a poignant depiction of the everyday struggles of a Welsh mining family.

Hammond, usually "high-strung and a little nervous," according to Isobel Fisher, seemed uncharacteristically relaxed during the two or three days he and Jemy stayed in the little motor court. Perhaps it was the surroundings and the circumstances. No one knew where they were, so no one could reach them. The view from outside their room was dominated by majestic purple-tinged mountain ranges. At night the only sounds came from an occasional car whizzing by on Route 66, a screen door slamming shut in the wind, or the call of a wild animal off in the foothills. It was as far away from the hustle and bustle of New York City as Hammond was likely to find himself. And it seemed to agree with him, at least temporarily. He was happily married to the most beautiful woman he'd ever met, and he was out from under the stress of his job as a music industry executive. "They seemed very happy. A load seemed to have fallen off of John's shoulders since he left Columbia," Isobel remembered.

Hammond spoke excitedly of his plans for *Music and Rhythm*, which he hoped would one day compete with *Variety* as the publication of record for the music industry. But, typically, he wanted *Music and Rhythm* to take a hard-hitting approach to political issues—specifically racism and integration—that *Variety* tended to ignore. (Music fans apparently weren't interested in an overtly political magazine, however, and *Music and Rhythm* quickly folded in the face of stiff competition from *Variety* and *Down Beat*.)

And, naturally, the earnest young couples spoke of politics. Isobel Fisher said her curiosity got the best of her one night and she stopped her brother-in-law in the middle of a long discourse on the current state of affairs, both in the United States and abroad, to ask him point-blank why he had never joined the Communist Party. "He said he'd never really considered it," she recalled. And then, reviewing notes she had made in her journal that very night in 1942, she quoted Hammond directly. She said he told her, "It would be impossible to adhere to the party line and to condone the considerable amount of lying that goes on among the comrades." Satisfied with that answer, Fisher let him carry on.

These were carefree hours spent breathing fresh air, soaking up the bright sunshine, taking walks on crisp, starlit nights, and enjoying stimulating conversation with close friends. For Hammond and Jemy, not even married a year and still unburdened by the responsibilities of parenthood, it was truly a mountain oasis.

Not long after the couple returned to New York from their cross-country excursion, Jemy discovered she was pregnant. The news was cause for much joy in the Hammond household.

Around the same time, another event occurred that was also cause for great joy among the Hammond clan—all except for John, that is. Benny Goodman and John's favorite sister, Alice, had run off to Las Vegas and secretly gotten married. Goodman had first met Alice in 1934, shortly after Hammond and he began their professional collaboration. Nothing happened between the two, though, because Goodman was still quite the man-about-town and Alice was married at the time to George Arthur Duckworth, a member of Parliament whose ancestral lineage could be traced back in English history through the works of Shakespeare. The marriage was typical of many Vanderbilt marriages of that era in that it was intended to pair up English royalty with de facto American royalty.

More than any of his other sisters, Alice most closely resembled John in terms of both physical appearance and temperament. She was tall and a little gawky, and she had the same wide, toothy grin as her brother, a grin that broke easily and often across her handsome face. Hammond's friend the English music critic and producer Spike Hughes told a Goodman biographer:

> There was a great spiritual affinity between brother and sister which, I suspect, often disconcerted Alice's English husband, who was plainly a little bewildered on returning from the House of Commons to his elegant house in Westminster on one occasion to find his wife entertaining Duke Ellington and me and

playing us records of Bessie Smith. I think Alice enjoyed her life
as [the wife of a member of Parliament] while it lasted, for she
was a good hostess, with that rare gift of making all sorts and
colors of people her immediate and devoted servants. But her
"liberalmindedness" which she shared with her brother must
clearly have perplexed a typically Conservative and Old Etonian
husband.

Rachel Breck, the sister closest to Hammond in age but perhaps
furthest apart in temperament (she says she hates to argue, while noting that her brother never encountered an argument he didn't gleefully
join), recalled that her family began noticing the similarities between
John and Alice when the two were still small children. "He and Alice
were totally brilliant. They had photographic memories. They had total
recall, and like all people like that they got bored to death with studies," she remembered. Neither John nor Alice ever needed to study in
order to do well in school, she added, and they read only the books
they wanted to read and only when they felt like reading them.

Alice also shared with her brother an innate distaste for the trap-
pings of wealth. According to Rachel Breck, she was far less interested
than the other Hammond girls in society dances and the debutante
events that tended to fill the lives of teenage girls who also happened to
be descendants of Cornelius Vanderbilt. "They were both really down-
to-earth," she said.

In the late 1930s, Alice's marriage to George Duckworth was ending, and she began spending more time back in New York with her
family. Hammond and Benny Goodman were still very close during
that period, and at some point Alice and the bandleader met again and
something clicked. The two began quietly dating while waiting for
Alice's divorce to become final. When a judge finally signed off on the
agreement, Goodman and Alice, with Rachel in tow, sneaked off to Las
Vegas, where the couple married on March 21, 1942. Because of the
secrecy surrounding the wedding, Rachel Breck was the only person to
photograph the ceremony. (Well into her nineties, she still kept the
grainy pictures of the smiling couple posing with the Las Vegas desert
as a backdrop.)

Hammond apparently didn't take the marriage very well. Rachel Breck confirmed the unflattering accounts of several friends from that period who recalled his initial disapproval. But instead of being openly critical, Hammond opted for an indirect but no less subversive approach. Specifically, he began suggesting that his parents, while publicly blessing the marriage, felt privately that Goodman was not quite fit to marry their daughter. According to Hammond's narrative, it didn't matter to his parents that the groom was Benny Goodman, one of the most celebrated musicians then living. What mattered was that Goodman, notwithstanding his talent, popularity, and wealth, was still a clarinet player from the Chicago ghetto.

Rachel Breck dismissed her brother's insinuations as little more than a projection of his own mixed emotions toward the marriage. "John was crazy about Alice, and he was jealous of Alice's relationship" with Goodman, she said. Contrary to her brother's take on events, her parents held Goodman in high regard and were proud to have him join the family. Breck's views on matters involving Goodman, her sister Alice, and her brother, John, are both reliable and significant since few people were in a better position to observe the complicated dynamics at work between Goodman and Hammond during the decade or so that the two worked closely together. During much of the late 1930s and early 1940s, Breck was single and spent a lot of time socializing with Goodman and Alice. In fact, it was she who discovered the master recordings of Goodman's historic 1938 Carnegie Hall concert stashed in a closet in a Manhattan apartment that she moved into after Goodman and Alice moved out. After the recordings were cleaned up, the album that was subsequently released became one of the biggest-selling jazz records ever.

Breck attributed her brother's version of events to his and Goodman's mercurial relationship, which was complicated and volatile long before Alice entered the picture. For instance, early in their professional relationship Hammond seemed to go out of his way to embarrass Goodman by publicly criticizing him in *Down Beat* and other magazines. "I'm more worried about Benny's band than I would like to admit," he wrote in 1937. "The loud, meaningless 'killer' arrangements which Benny instructs Jimmy Mundy to pound out in mass production each week are definitely detracting from the musicianship of the orchestra."

Thus Goodman and Alice's relationship only exacerbated an already sensitive situation. So it probably wasn't a coincidence that Hammond launched another broadside at Goodman in *Music and Rhythm* shortly after the marriage. In his very first column in the new magazine, he blasted Goodman for sacrificing musical integrity in the blind pursuit of commercial success. "Better an unpretentious sweet group that played as well as it knew how than a sloppy, insincere swing band that ground out riff after riff of uninspired junk in the hope of catching public fancy," Hammond wrote, alluding to some new Goodman material. For his part, Goodman, a notoriously prickly personality, kept his cool in the face of these assaults. According to Rachel Breck, he made a concerted effort to maintain peaceful relations with his new family after marrying Alice.

Still, Goodman was aware of the almost-constant tension between himself and his brother-in-law, and he spoke candidly about it to Breck. According to her, while he was always grateful to Hammond for helping him jump-start his career in the mid-1930s, he had grown to resent the perception—which Hammond did little to correct—that Hammond had essentially "discovered" him. "Benny always rather resisted the publicity that said that John had discovered him. He said to me once in private, 'You know, I had made a name for myself in Chicago before I ever knew your brother.'"

The root of their differences may simply have been a natural competition between two men with healthy egos, Breck speculated. Hammond and Goodman were only a year apart in age, and it was hardly surprising that they competed for success in the same way that two brothers might have in a similar situation, she observed.

Another cause of friction likely stemmed from their vastly different backgrounds, which Breck felt couldn't but lead to markedly different points of view on key aspects of their lives. Things that Hammond took for granted—regular meals, comfortable beds, more money than he knew what to do with, a mansion on East Ninety-first Street with sixteen servants ("Although I never counted more than fourteen," Rachel says with a laugh)—were inconceivable to Goodman. "Benny grew up in the ghetto, one of twelve children. He took nothing for granted," Breck explained. Thus it was incomprehensible to him that Hammond could have dropped out of Yale after a year and a half, thereby forfeiting an education from one of the finest universities in the world. Goodman dropped out of high school to help support his family. Hammond, meanwhile, considered his dropping out of college a matter of principle: he believed, perhaps correctly, that his education lay elsewhere and that an expensive Ivy League schooling was being wasted on him.

Finally, in discussions with Breck, the details of which she never shared with her brother, Goodman expressed a personal frustration with Hammond for implying more than once that Goodman had never fully lived up to his potential. According to Breck, Goodman believed Hammond would only have been satisfied had he also achieved widespread acclaim as a classical musician. In short, the relationship between the two men was always "very tenuous. There were times when they were devoted to each other and times when they weren't speaking."

In the years leading up to his marriage to Alice, Goodman had made a conscious effort to distance himself from John Hammond. Hammond still participated in many of Goodman's recording sessions, but Goodman's popularity had allowed him more leverage in decisions that affected his music, and he found that he no longer needed—or wanted—Hammond's help. At first the shift was subtle, manifesting itself primarily through Goodman's quietly disregarding Hammond's advice. Occasionally and inevitably, however, the shift in dynamics resulted in open warfare between the two. But these hostile exchanges were usually brief.

Notwithstanding Hammond's apparent misgivings, Goodman and Alice's marriage was long and successful. Goodman was a doting father, both to the two children he had with Alice and to Alice's three children from her earlier marriage. The record producer George Avakian, who worked with Hammond at Columbia Records and was also a good friend of Goodman's, told a Goodman biographer, "Benny was a very loving father. I could see it in his relationship with the kids. He was always extremely tolerant of their interruptions, and he spoke of them very often. He simply exuded being a good father. Benny didn't have close friends. He never wanted to get too close to anyone. But I think it was a close and loving family."

Meanwhile, the birth in November 1942 of Hammond and Jemy's first son, whom they named John Paul Hammond (Paul in honor of their friend Paul Robeson), was a thrilling occasion. It seemed like perfect timing. Life was comfortable yet still stimulating for the couple. Hammond was busy with his fledgling magazine and with various progressive causes. At the same time, the couple's social life was filled with the fascinating incongruities that marked much of Hammond's life. Sumptuous holiday celebrations in Vanderbilt mansions, magnificent Gilded Age structures that either towered over Fifth Avenue or sprawled across the New England countryside, were juxtaposed against the regular Saturday night outings to smoky jazz clubs in Greenwich Village and Harlem.

It was an enviable existence—indeed, one unimaginable to most Americans, people whose lives were still stinging from the deprivations brought on by the Depression and were just now sensing an entirely new type of uncertainty as the United States charged full throttle into World War II. Hammond's independent wealth had for the most part kept him immune from the economic upheaval of the 1930s. But hardly anyone—John Hammond included—would remain untouched by the war. As Hammond himself observed: "The first year of marriage was a happy one, as well as a year of comparatively normal life for me. I . . . enjoyed for the first time the combination of a satisfying regular job and a home filled with mutual interests and friends. It was too good to last."

10

AT WAR AT HOME

Hammond's decision to take a leave of absence from Columbia Records in early 1942 in order to step up his activism proved prescient. Years later, he said the decision to focus his energies outside the recording studio stemmed from a belief that with war looming in Europe and Asia, it was just a matter of time before he would be drafted. Sure enough, not long after the birth of John Paul, in November 1942, his prediction came true.

With time running out for him as a civilian, his pursuit of an integrated society became that much more urgent. At the time, Hammond, although still just thirty-one years old, had already been sitting on the board of directors of the NAACP for seven years. This was a period, however, when the civil rights movement had yet to really gain steam in America. Segregation was still widely accepted as a domestic policy in the South, and the races were practically kept apart in the North. What's more, the country was only just emerging from the Depression and teetering on the brink of another world war. Fighting for the civil rights of minorities simply wasn't a priority for most white Americans.

Not so for John Hammond. Despite his myriad responsibilities as a producer, writer, and all-around music impresario, he had found time to play an active role in many of the NAACP's projects. In 1939, for example, he voted with a majority of the board to create the NAACP

Legal Defense and Educational Fund. Formed initially as a tax shelter for donations that could then be used to fund the NAACP's legal battles, the LDF, as it came to be known, soon established itself as an effective tool against government-sanctioned segregation. Under the leadership of Thurgood Marshall, it spearheaded the fifteen-year effort that ended with the Supreme Court's landmark 1954 ruling in *Brown v. Board of Education of Topeka, Kansas*, which struck down legalized segregation in the nation's public-school system.

From his seat on the LDF's board of directors, Hammond clashed frequently with Marshall and the rest of the LDF leadership over what he considered the organization's slow progress. The seat on the LDF board was in addition to his seat on the board of directors of the parent NAACP. He also sat on virtually every committee charged with overseeing the NAACP's day-to-day operations. Notes taken at these meetings show that he not only attended religiously but participated vigorously. Indeed, he was habitually outspoken with his opinions and often downright provocative in his dealings with the NAACP leadership.

In particular, Hammond squabbled with Roy Wilkins, second in command to the executive secretary, Walter White, a good friend whom he had met through Ernest Gruening. Hammond had grown convinced that Wilkins was trying to undercut White by means of behind-the-scenes politicking. White either didn't view Wilkins as a threat or chose not to participate in office infighting. Whatever the case, Hammond apparently saw it as his responsibility to defend White and to disparage Wilkins when the opportunity presented itself.

The tension between Hammond and Wilkins surfaced publicly in the fall of 1943, shortly before Hammond entered the military. The skirmish began when Hammond openly questioned Wilkins's loyalty to White. But the seeds for the ugly quarrel that erupted between them were planted years earlier. Throughout the 1930s, Wilkins had served as editor of *The Crisis*, the NAACP's highly regarded monthly magazine founded in 1910 by W.E.B. Du Bois. Late in the decade a handful of board members led by Hammond decided that *The Crisis* wasn't providing timely information to the NAACP's full membership. Hammond and his like-minded colleagues believed (correctly) that *The Crisis*, given its format as a glossy monthly publication that needed weeks of lead time for articles to meet their deadlines, couldn't adequately respond to issues of immediate significance to the members. What was needed, Hammond and his cohorts determined, was a publication with more reach and flexibility. The solution they proposed was a free monthly newsletter for distribution to every member.

While the principles behind Hammond's reasoning were sound—no one could argue that the NAACP membership didn't need prompt updates on important issues—his motives, given his distrust of Wilkins, were perhaps not entirely pure.

The issue came to a head in 1940, when an investigation by the NAACP revealed that blacks were being barred from vocational schools where training was given for jobs in the nation's giant industrial plants. After the outbreak of war in Europe in the late 1930s, the U.S. defense industry, dormant throughout the Depression, had burst back to life. There was suddenly an abundance of good-paying, highly skilled jobs in American factories. Yet in a paradox that could exist only in a system steeped in racism, blacks found themselves excluded from these training programs. It seems the people who ran the vocational programs were refusing entry to blacks because none of the defense plants were hiring blacks anyway. The plant officials, in turn, claimed they couldn't find any qualified blacks to hire. And the vicious cycle went round and round.

It was a volatile issue with rapidly changing dynamics as more information emerged. *The Crisis* was ill prepared to keep up with the story, and the door was left open for a rival publication. The result was a pamphlet titled the *NAACP Bulletin*.

Over Wilkins's strenuous objections—he argued that the NAACP couldn't afford Hammond's pet project—the *NAACP Bulletin* began rolling off the presses in 1940. Hammond, who believed Wilkins simply wanted to undermine the project and eliminate the in-house competition, volunteered to pay half the publishing costs out of his own pocket.

Three years passed and the *NAACP Bulletin* fulfilled its objective of providing timely information to the members. Yet its success did little to improve Hammond and Wilkins's relationship.

On September 24, 1943, toward the end of a meeting of the NAACP's Committee on Administration, as the other members were tucking papers into briefcases and otherwise packing up their belongings,

Hammond lobbed a verbal bomb at Wilkins. According to the account received by Wilkins (which Hammond never denied), Hammond stated matter-of-factly, "The whole trouble is a split between Walter and Roy—it is a [personal] matter. Roy is jealous of Walter and his position and prestige and this is the root of the problem. Naturally, if Walter is going to be away from the office for several months he doesn't want to leave affairs in the hands of a man who cannot be trusted and who will take advantage of the situation because of his personal feelings."

Wilkins wasn't in the room at the time, nor, apparently, did he have any inkling that Hammond was going to lash out at him. There were, however, several NAACP staff members on hand, at least one of whom reported back to the assistant executive secretary what had been said. Wilkins was, quite naturally, appalled.

Interestingly, Hammond seems to have made his comments twice: once while Walter White was out of the room, and then again after he had returned. White certainly heard the remarks and understood clearly what Hammond had meant, yet he made no attempt to defend Wilkins. When Wilkins asked White about the remarks, the executive secretary, in keeping with his conciliatory personality, asked him to quietly drop the matter. White, a dignified, soft-spoken man, was inclined toward restraint rather than confrontation. Wilkins, also a dignified man but keenly articulate—some might say long-winded—was far more inclined to meet a battle head-on. Wilkins refused to ignore the inflammatory comments and fired off a letter to Hammond in which he staunchly defended himself. Copies were sent to the other board members, as well as to the NAACP president, Arthur Spingarn. "As an employed staff member of the N.A.A.C.P. I recognize your right as a board member to evaluate my work as an executive; but I do not grant that any man, board member or not, has the right to attack my character in the manner you are reported to have done. If I were the kind of man your remarks describe I ought not be employed by the N.A.A.C.P. in any capacity whatsoever," the angry but always-diplomatic Wilkins wrote. He called on Hammond to back up his assertions with proof.

In a separate memo to White, Wilkins recounted their ten-year history together battling racism and questioned White's silence following Hammond's remarks:

Of course I do not intend to let Hammond's attack pass. I will insist on everything being brought out where it can be examined. I do this because I must for the sake of my own self-respect. But I do not need to do it for my conscience's sake. My conscience is clear and my mind on this matter—serene. I have not joined in any office politics, board politics, or field politics. There are no Wilkins cabals. There are no plots, large or small. There is no direct mail pressure waiting to be signaled. I despise these things. I have always believed (naively, how naively) that a good job well done would bring, sooner or later, its own reward. But you know all these things, every one.

Wilkins's letter, notwithstanding the author's flair for melodrama, seems to have had little effect on White, who evidently wanted nothing to do with the flap. There is no record in the NAACP's files to indicate that White ever contacted Hammond to discuss his unfortunate remarks, and Hammond never mentioned speaking to White about them.

For his part, Hammond made no attempt to back away from or retract his remarks. Instead, he told Wilkins that his comments stemmed from a conversation they had had a year and a half earlier at a cocktail party in New York. According to Hammond, during that conversation Wilkins had elaborated broadly on the many ways he felt he could improve on White's work at the NAACP. Should Wilkins persist in pressing the matter further, Hammond said he would be happy to elaborate on the details of that conversation in front of the entire NAACP board.

Wilkins, in another long defense of himself, acknowledged that in past conversations with Hammond he had undoubtedly made suggestions as to how the NAACP could improve its operations. But he denied ever being openly critical of White, let alone plotting to undermine him. And he was not yet ready to back down. "I am still of the opinion that you were greatly mistaken and that you grossly misrepresented anything I may have said to you on any previous occasion," Wilkins wrote.

After about a week of back-and-forth correspondence, during which neither man would budge, Wilkins suddenly backed down. Reluctantly, and only on Spingarn's advice, he decided to drop the matter. Neverthe-less, he couldn't resist another opportunity to extol his loyalty:

> As I have written to Walter, there is not a single instance in my record of twelve years as Assistant Secretary which will support in the slightest degree your interpretation of a single conversa-tion. Moreover, there is no single act which has taken place since that conversation which supports your interpretation. On the contrary, the record is overwhelmingly in the opposite di-rection, and I know within myself, through incidents that are not in the record, how overwhelmingly in the opposite direction my actions have been.

Wilkins continued in earnest:

> I have tried vainly since this matter arose to account for your outburst. I have tried to place myself in your shoes. I have tried to reason out what could have caused you to make so serious a charge. For example, if the charge was valid and serious on Sep-tember 24, 1943, it was serious and valid eighteen months ago [when Wilkins supposedly made his remarks to Hammond]. An organization does not keep a plotter, a schemer, a jealous and untrustworthy person on its staff, especially in a key position. If a board member had what he considered to be good evidence of such a situation it would have seemed his duty to the Associ-ation to have disclosed it at once. This is one of the aspects that I have been unable to fathom.

Finally, Wilkins ended on a conciliatory note: "Again I wish you good luck [in the Army] and especially since you are to work on the question of Negro morale. Your sincerity, knowledge, and positive conviction on the type of justice which should be accorded the American Negro should make you a valuable person in this work."

By agreeing to drop the matter, Wilkins had given Hammond space to admit the whole messy affair had been his fault in the first place. Backed against the wall, Hammond was ready to continue the fight.

But now that Wilkins had blinked and the flap was ending, Hammond acknowledged his role. Retaining his practiced tone of casual aloofness, he wrote to Wilkins, "In the first place, I want to say now that my tactics in bringing this matter to a head now were mistaken. I still believe that my charges were entirely accurate, but I think it was less than fair of me to bring up an incident over a year old on which to base my charges."

It was a typical Hammond concession—that is, a concession without really conceding. He had perfected the technique in his jazz columns, most notably when, after touting a proposed tour of England by an integrated group of American musicians, a tour that turned out to be little more than a figment of his imagination, he blamed someone else rather than accept responsibility for the fiasco.

The quarrel, although trivial when viewed from the perspective of Hammond's thirty-year affiliation with the NAACP, sheds light on one of the darker areas of his personality: an inclination toward blunt outspokenness that tended to disregard other people's feelings. This behavior often took the form of a harsh critique of someone—usually in terms that could easily be interpreted as insulting—with little or no regard as to how his criticism might affect the unlucky target of his wrath. These attacks frequently served as a subterfuge; that is, they were employed to mask his anger over not getting his way in some other, perhaps unrelated matter. (His scathing public criticisms of Benny Goodman, which grew harsher as the bandleader disregarded his advice, come to mind.) Hammond usually justified this behavior by asserting that he was merely speaking the truth and that the truth often hurt.

Like many of Hammond's public scrapes, the flap with Wilkins seems to have been motivated for the most part by good intentions. In this case, his differences with Wilkins were born out of a belief that the NAACP needed a publication that provided members with a monthly overview of its wide-ranging activities. Hammond felt that *The Crisis*, while without question the premier venue for expressing the goals of the civil rights movement, was not reaching the NAACP's grassroots membership.

Moreover, he was genuinely concerned that Wilkins's personal ambitions were clouding his judgment on decisions that affected the entire organization. After working with Walter White for nearly a decade, Hammond had gained an immense respect for the man, and he resented what he perceived as Wilkins's attempts to subvert White's authority.

Ultimately, though, Wilkins's argument proved correct. Publication of the *NAACP Bulletin* ceased in 1949 because, just as Wilkins had predicted, it was too expensive to maintain. Still, despite its relatively short life span, the pamphlet remained a source of pride for Hammond for the rest of his life.

The skirmish with Wilkins in the fall of 1943 took place as Hammond was preparing to enter the Army. Although he had received his draft notice almost a year earlier, his induction had been postponed through a temporary deferment that allowed him to fulfill a prior obligation in New York—that of recruiting the cast for an all-black production of an opera titled *Carmen Jones*. Thus he had spent a good portion of the previous spring and summer conducting auditions in various U.S. cities in search of talented amateur African-Americans who might capably make the jump to Broadway. He found his Carmen Jones in a camera store in Philadelphia. Another key role went to a New York police officer. The show was based on the French opera *Carmen* but instilled with contemporary themes related to the plight of Southern blacks.

Carmen Jones opened on Broadway on December 2, 1943, to rave reviews. (Not everyone found it inspiring, though. The poet Langston Hughes, whom Hammond personally invited to a warm-up performance in Philadelphia, found the actors' attempts at black Southern dialect unseemly.) Hammond, however, was not on hand to bask in the limelight. Having fulfilled his obligation to the show's producers, he was now fulfilling his obligation to his country.

Hammond was nearly thirty-three years old in November 1943 when he left New York City by train bound for Fort Dix, New Jersey. After three weeks of military indoctrination at Fort Dix, he was shipped off to Fort Belvoir, Virginia, for six weeks of basic training. At a little over six feet and weighing around 170 pounds, Hammond was slim but hardly athletic. He had never participated in sports as a child, and as an adult he rarely got any exercise. Now, in the swampy humidity of rural Virginia, he was required to carry an eighty-pound backpack on daily seventeen-mile marches. Moreover, he was expected to keep up with the much younger men with whom he was thrown together in basic training. His recollections of his six weeks at Fort Belvoir, recounted in his memoirs, are nothing short of nightmarish. He quickly lost twenty-five pounds, came down with a nasty case of pneumonia, and spent most of his waking hours on the verge of collapse.

But these physical ailments were nothing compared with the mental anguish he was about to endure.

The Hammonds' second child, a boy named Douglas, was born in early 1944, while Hammond was still at Fort Belvoir. The exact sequence of events in the days following the child's birth is impossible to piece together with complete accuracy, but what is known is that Douglas came down with a serious infection about a week after he was born and that Jemy Hammond had difficulty reaching her husband to alert him to their son's condition. Hammond later claimed that he only learned of his boy's illness after he called home to New York from his barracks, where, according to his version, he was recovering from an exhaustion-induced blackout suffered during a long hike. During that conversation, Jemy told him that she had sent a telegram through the Red Cross summoning him home to be with her and the baby. Hammond said he told her he had never received the telegram.

Exactly what happened next is unclear, but Hammond somehow received a three-day pass that allowed him to return to New York. He arrived at the hospital shortly before the baby died.

Hammond would later recount that upon his return to Fort Belvoir, he asked his commanding officer why he hadn't received his wife's telegram. He said the officer told him he didn't think the situation was serious enough to pass on the information. The officer, according to Hammond, blandly apologized.

Hammond's recollection of the events, which he published in his memoirs, remains easily accessible. Jemy Hammond's recollections are harder to unearth. Her version, as recounted by her sister, Isobel Fisher, differs from her husband's in one important area: Hammond claimed he remained at Fort Belvoir for as long as he did because he was never told about the telegram summoning him home. There is no reason to dispute that version. Yet, according to Fisher, Jemy Hammond somehow concluded that her husband had been attending a concert the day the telegram arrived and chose to remain at the concert rather than return home. It's unclear how or why Jemy came to that conclusion, but, according to her sister, she clung to that version and her anger festered. "She was aware of his fondness for black music, and she decided that he preferred his music to his wife," Fisher recalled.

Jemy Hammond's recollections appear to have been based more on emotion than on fact. Hammond never mentioned attending any concerts while in basic training. And it's highly unlikely that his boot camp instructors would have allowed him to slip away from the daily monotony of hikes, calisthenics, and inspections for a few hours of jazz. Nevertheless, that was the memory Jemy Hammond carried away from the ordeal.

Whatever really happened to delay Hammond's arrival was, unfortunately, of little relevance to the inarguable facts: the couple's baby had grown critically ill and died, and Jemy had had to deal with this unspeakable tragedy alone, without her husband by her side. Regrettably, the gap between two people's recollections and the facts as they actually transpired is often the space where the seeds of guilt and resentment are planted. In this case, the husband and wife apparently dealt with the horrific event by forming memories that best supported their personal views of the facts.

The incident left Hammond with a profound sense of guilt, and Jemy with an equally profound sense of resentment. "Three weeks [after Douglas died] I completed basic training and was given another three-day pass. It was hardly time enough for Jemy and me to find our way out of the tragedy together. I was ridden by guilt. I felt I had failed both Jemy and Douglas. I was unable to console her and certain to be sent even farther away," Hammond wrote.

Although Jemy would later give birth to another son, the Hammonds, according to Isobel Fisher, "were never close again. [Jemy] was broken in pieces over [Douglas's death]. She never forgave him."

Rivulets of sweat poured down the face of the trumpet man King Kolax as he blew solo after solo after solo from the stage of the makeshift theater on the grounds of Camp Plauche just outside New Orleans. The few audience members lucky enough to hustle one of the seats arranged in front of the stage that night in April 1944 were on their feet now with the rest of the crowd. Kolax, known at the time as the "new king of trumpet," was a showman who knew how to work a crowd. Each time he tore off another regal blast from his horn, he saved just enough so that the next one hit even harder, raised the stakes a little higher. And when he wasn't personally pumping the crowd's adrenaline, he was enthusiastically exhorting the members of his seventeen-piece band to assist him. The packed crowd, made up almost entirely of soldiers, loved it. Many had stripped off their heavy fatigues, and their faded green military-issue T-shirts clung to their skin in the thick humidity. It was a typical steamy spring evening in Louisiana.

John Hammond was just one of several celebrities in attendance that night. Among the other noteworthy attendees, according to an account a few days later in the *Chicago Defender*, were the former orchestra leader Teddy Hill and a New Orleans boxing promoter named Louis Messina. Unlike the other visiting dignitaries, however, Hammond hadn't dropped by to help boost troop morale. With his trademark crew cut shaved practically to the skin and his customary Brooks Brothers sport coat traded in for a set of dull green fatigues, Hammond was now a private in the U.S. Army. As he stood admiring the swinging melodies of the King Kolax Orchestra, his fatigues were stained through with sweat, the same as every other GI crowded around the stage that night.

And it was a terrific show. The *Defender* reported that King Kolax, a Chicago-based bandleader whose brief celebrity—Charlie Parker sat in with the band on a short layover in Chicago in 1939—faded with the decline of the swing era, "proved his right to the crown that was placed on his head by the Camp's Pin-up girl, Miss Dorothy Lamb. John Hammond, now stationed at Camp Plauche in special service, was loud in praise of the king."

Hammond had arrived in Louisiana about six weeks earlier, after completing basic training. Home of the Army's Transportation Corps

John Hammond with his mother and sisters, 1911: (left to right) Alice, Rachel, Emily Hammond, John, Adele, and Emily.

Three generations of Hammonds: John (right), with his father, John senior, and sons, John Paul (crouching) and Jason.

A yearbook photo from Hotchkiss, c. 1926. Here Hammond holds a violin, the instrument on which he received his first musical training.

The Hammonds' five-story mansion on Fifth Avenue, where John spent his childhood. The building is now an embassy.
(Photograph by David Scull)

Hammond in his Columbia Records office, c. 1939. (Courtesy of the Frank Driggs Collection)

Hammond (far right) watches over a studio session with (left to right) Buck Clayton, Lester Young, Charlie Christian, Benny Goodman, and Count Basie. (Courtesy of the Frank Driggs Collection)

Hammond listens in on a conversation between Benny Goodman and Charlie Christian. Looking on is Columbia A&R supervisor Marty Palitz (standing, right). (Courtesy of the Frank Driggs Collection)

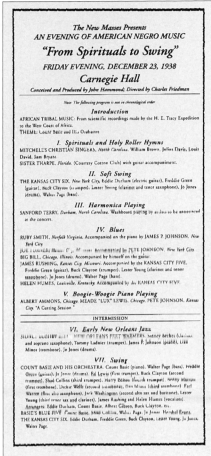

The cover and listings from the program given out at "From Spirituals to Swing" on December 23, 1938.

Hammond with his second wife, Esme.

BELOW: Hammond in the studio with Bob Dylan, 1961. (Courtesy of the Frank Driggs Collection)

After Hammond signed him to Columbia Records in 1972, Bruce Springsteen was soon touted as the next Bob Dylan. (© Fred Lombardi)

Hammond in Manhattan with Allen Ginsberg, c. 1981. (© Hank O'Neal)

Stevie Ray Vaughan (second from right) and Double Trouble were the last of Hammond's great discoveries. (© Hank O'Neal)

training center, Camp Plauche was situated on the eastern bank of the Mississippi River in the shadow of the Huey P. Long Bridge. The camp was named in honor of Major Jean Baptiste Plauche, who had helped General Andrew Jackson defeat the British in 1815 during the battle of New Orleans. To the likely dismay of the soldiers who trained there, Camp Plauche failed miserably to live up to any romantic expectations engendered by its evocative name. Like most Army camps established after the outbreak of World War II, Camp Plauche was a broad, flat, nondescript swath of land broken up only by small clusters of identically shaped Quonset huts.

Hammond's assignment at Camp Plauche was to help organize activities for the otherwise-idle black soldiers. While blacks during World War II had no trouble either getting drafted or enlisting in the military, it was often difficult for them to find anything useful to do. This forced idleness resulted directly from the reluctance of many white commanding officers to place blacks in positions of responsibility. Especially at military bases in the South, black soldiers often worked essentially as landscapers and maintenance men.

Hammond's role at the camp was to lift the morale of these frustrated black soldiers. He did his level best. But his disdain of large, inflexible bureaucracies, fervent long before he was drafted, was strengthened immeasurably during his tenure in the military. A letter written to his friends Phil and Kay Graham shortly after arriving at Camp Plauche fairly drips with cynicism:

Dear Phil and Kay,

Jemy wrote ecstatically about your visit and the sad news that you had been in Washington the last few weeks of my charming stay at Belvoir. God knows I called 1624 Crescent Place often enough for news of you, but I guess that they just slipped up on this most important of news.

Down here I've got the job of my dreams, after a few weeks of grind and disillusionment. Although it's in special service there's plenty of useful work to be done, and I've made several stabs at getting some activity started that will relieve the monotony and boredom of the race [black] troops stationed here. This office is fortunately short on crackers, which makes it all a bit easier than it might be. But timidity reigns supreme, which doesn't worry this particular buck private too much. It's pretty hard to bust a private.

I guess that Jemy told you of my tribulations when I first arrived. Nobody at the Port knew what the hell I was supposed to do, until a couple of letters dated the first week in January from Washington showed up in the files stating that [H]ammond had done much work in civilian life in helping our less fortunate brothers. These letters had been properly answered, stating that they had no need for anybody with my qualifications . . . but I was sent here anyway, much to a couple of guys annoyance. It's all worked out beautifully, however, and I feel very useful.

Intelligence works in great and mysterious ways. It seems that there is a great big plot participated in by Negro leaders and particularly newspapers to sabotage the war effort by raising a stink about segregation and discrimination. [Black e]nlisted men are carefully and secretly instructed to smoke the weed in order to get Section 8 discharges; because perhaps half of one percent of the men use the stinking stuff the story is that the great majority of them indulge in the vice. Southern Negroes are fine dumb, malleable souls. It's them Northern sonsofbitches that cause all the trouble by putting ideas into their heads. Why the hell should anybody raise hell about sitting in the back of buses bearing the signs Camp Plauche bus service. After all, if it's the law of the state who the hell are they to squawk.

The NAACP is subversive, all Negro newspapers are subversive, none can be sold at camp (which is normally over fifty percent colored), and only in the last two weeks have any of these papers been allowed in the jimcro library (*Journal* and *Guide*, *Crisis* with my name on the editorial board, and the local weekly). Result, naturally, is that the grapevine works its wonders, and marvelous juicy rumors start upsetting everyone. Since the camp has no newspaper (incredible for such a large installation) the colored troops have no information whatsoever of what their group is doing overseas, and are under the impression that our only labor battalions are at the front. The races at all costs must be kept apart, so that they can never know the other's reactions or understand them.

There's a much brighter side to the picture, however. The PX's are mixed, there have been no clashes between the races, and the mixed dance band, mixed jam sessions, mixed concerts and lectures I've conducted have led to no unpleasantness whatsoever. It's the first time at this place for any such activity, and it's been a boost to many of the whites and the blacks who feel very strongly on the subject. When the segregation order on camp buses was put into effect three months ago whites as well as blacks cooperated in destroying the signs on each seat; result is that the hated order has had to be painted on the roof. Intelligence tells me with straight face that I will soon be able to see the infinite wisdom of the southern attitude, and I do my very best to keep from arguing.

Would that you could come down here for a while, Phil. In a day or two you could straighten out the smirking young punk who considers himself so clever and doesn't understand a single one of the reactions of the colored group. If anything were to start these people would be utterly unable to find either perpetrators or causes, since they have absolutely no contact.

It's pretty distressing to see the utter lack of enthusiasm for the European War among almost all troops. The "Why We Fight" films are fine, but they are not followed up in any way by orientation, which seems to be non-controversial at any cost. It really wouldn't be too difficult to instill colored troops with real enthusiasm despite all the discomforts; but I've seen no effort to do this.

My furlough starts early in May and I hope to stop in Washington with Jemy at least on the way back . . .

I trust that I've been properly indiscreet and that the contents will shock any outside prying eyes that might see it before you do.

My love to you both.

John

The letter offers a vivid look into Hammond's worldview, with its seemingly incongruous philosophy that artfully blended a strong sense of suspicion for the powers that be—or those who would impose their will on others—with an innate sense of optimism steeped in the belief that human nature is essentially good. Hammond believed strongly that blacks and whites could and would get along if only they were given the opportunity to mix naturally in settings devoid of the racial tension caused primarily by ignorance. Whites who benefited from the status quo—which included, in his opinion, nearly every military officer—helped perpetuate that ignorance.

By attacking the status quo that had maintained segregated swing bands, Hammond had helped break down the racial barriers in popular music. Now, in lieu of firing an actual weapon, he hoped to attack the status quo in the Army. He made integration within the military his personal mission. His battlefields were the camps at which he was stationed, and the enemy the inflexibly segregated military bureaucracy.

He had his work cut out for him. The NAACP's archives contain hundreds of letters written by black soldiers during World War II that describe in bitter detail the racism pervasive in the military at the time. One of these, addressed directly to Walter White, was written by a relative of a soldier stationed at Camp Plauche around the time Hammond was there: "[Black soldiers] are treeten bad and the donot like that the want to be treete like people and the say the donot trete them right and the say the want someone to come to the camp and the camp in the city of new orleans at the camp plauche and the soldiers the donot trete the right the are no animals and the want to be trete lik peoples and this is all I have to say." (The letter was signed by someone, probably a parent, from the small bayou town of Jeanerette, Louisiana. Jeanerette is almost hidden among the miles of sugarcane fields that stretch across Cajun country in swampy south-central Louisiana. It's the kind of place where literacy, especially among blacks, was apparently not given high priority in the years preceding the civil rights movement of the 1950s and 1960s.) A black soldier from New York who was stationed at Camp Plauche in 1944 wrote a letter to his mother, who passed it on to the local NAACP office:

The other day, last Wednesday afternoon I was in charge of four men that went over to Service Club #1 to do some work there. I stepped into the cafeteria to purchase a package of cigarettes for one of the boys and the counter girl and the cafeteria hostess refused to serve me because I was colored. I immediately informed the men to stop work and we walked out. As witnesses they went with me to the commanding officer of Co. 2 where I explained to him what happened and told him, "We are all working together, we have to fight and die together. And this is not the kind of democracy we are fighting for. Since you and I and all of us are make [*sic*] the same sacrifice, we should have a democracy built on equality" . . . Either give me the address of the NAACP or get in touch with them yourself giving them my story. I can get the hostess' name. Along with a witness. I intend to break this damn mess up or die fighting this business of segregation.

These letters describe systemic racism. There were no lynchings at U.S. military bases during World War II, just the little day to-day humiliations black soldiers confronted while ostensibly in the service of their country. First at Camp Plauche, later at Camp Gruber outside Muskogee, Oklahoma, again at Camp Rucker in Ozark, Alabama, and finally at Fort Benning in Georgia, Hammond threw himself into efforts to eradicate this infected environment. He quickly discovered that fighting racism and segregation in the military was like fighting a forest fire one tree at a time. So that's how he fought it. He sought to have black newspapers like the *Chicago Defender* and *The Pittsburgh Courier* made available to black soldiers. He made a point of visiting black soldiers in their segregated quarters as a way of thumbing his nose at policies that kept black and white soldiers apart. And, reverting to his proven method of breaking down racial barriers, he used music as a battering ram, organizing concerts at which black entertainers performed for integrated audiences. He booked some terrific black acts into Camp Plauche—for example, Ella Fitzgerald, Louis Jordan, and Billy Eckstine, among others.

These efforts may not have led directly to codified changes in military policy, but they sent an important message. Similar to events in the late 1930s, when the integration of Goodman's band sent a ripple throughout popular music, Hammond's integrated concerts at segregated military camps opened the door to further interaction between the races. According to Hammond, shortly after the first jazz concerts were held at Camp Plauche, an integrated sports program was established for the soldiers. "Seeing integration finally become a reality at Camp Plauche was a high point in my army career. Segregation was demolished by sports and music," Hammond wrote.

As it turned out, his superiors at Camp Plauche were the most responsive to his calls for equality among the races. At subsequent stops at bases in Oklahoma, Alabama, and Georgia, when his efforts weren't ignored altogether, they got him in hot water. In his memoirs, he recalled being detained by military police while attending a Sonny Boy Williams show in the black section of Muskogee, Oklahoma.

Typically, he never grew discouraged by the rigidity and ignorance he encountered in the military. To the contrary, it emboldened him to fight harder and speak louder, regardless of the potential consequences. In fact, Hammond fired one of his final salvos at military segregation just a few weeks before he was discharged. He could have waited and taken aim from a vantage point beyond the reach of Army retribution. But he didn't.

The NAACP had been receiving detailed reports of discrimination at Fort Benning in Georgia throughout World War II. One black soldier reported in October 1944 that blacks were being treated like servants. Their duties included cleaning the fireplaces in the white officers' living quarters and waiting on tables and tending bar in the various officers' clubs. They also worked as "janitors, porters, farm hands and any number of things that do not come under Army Regulations," the soldier wrote. He concluded bitterly, "When inducted we were supposed to be American soldiers. Now look what they have us into now."

Fort Benning is one of the largest military bases in the United States and serves as headquarters for the Army's infantry training center. In other words, it's where the men who fight in the trenches are trained. As such, its commanding officers are held in high esteem by top Army brass at the Pentagon. That probably explains why a blind eye seems to have been turned toward the base where incidents of segregation and racism were concerned. In 1944, Walter White personally requested the War Department to conduct an investigation into allegations that a commanding officer at Fort Benning made racist comments and then threatened reprisals against anyone who complained. Not surprisingly, the War Department investigation determined that there was no truth to the charges. Indeed, the investigation found instead that the allegations had been distorted by a handful of soldiers and the local media. A letter to White informing him of the government's findings declared: "The War Department is anxious to investigate all matters such as this in order to take corrective action where it is appropriate. Thank you for bringing this matter to our attention."

Hammond arrived at Fort Benning toward the end of World War II and quickly determined that racism was more prevalent there than at any of the previous camps at which he had been stationed. After engaging in the usual battles with camp officers regarding segregationist policies during entertainment events, Hammond decided to take matters one step further. At a meeting of the NAACP's board of directors in December 1945, during a discussion focused specifically on the subject of discrimination at Fort Benning, he introduced a motion requesting that all materials forwarded to the NAACP related to discrimination and segregation at Army camps be made public at the earliest possible date. (It's unclear how he was able to attend the meeting while still serving in the Army. But he was nothing if not resourceful.) It was a provocative gesture, one that would undoubtedly embarrass the military —the same military in which Hammond continued to serve. The motion was approved by the board, but NAACP officials apparently weren't as anxious as Hammond to anger the U.S. military. There is no record in the association's archives to indicate that critical letters were either turned over to or sought by newspapers in an effort to raise public awareness of the issue.

Of course, Hammond wasn't alone in his efforts to root out discrimination in the military. Black entertainers such as Duke Ellington and Lena Horne were in unique positions to point out the irony inherent in asking a black American to fight a war against an enemy—the Germans—whose stated goal was to exterminate what it deemed an inferior race. Ellington, Horne, Count Basie, and others used their celebrity to remind Americans that blacks were playing an important role in the war effort.

An unintended consequence of World War II was the way in which it revealed the glaring hypocrisy of America's fight for freedom and democracy abroad while ignoring the flagrant mistreatment of its own black citizens. Civil rights activists in America pounced on this contradiction and used it as a rallying cry for improving conditions for blacks in the United States. "The black press and African American entertainers did the most to challenge the standard definition of the home front Americans were defending . . . When Ellington's orchestra was denied hotel accommodations, the [Pittsburgh] *Courier* said, 'It didn't happen in Tokio [*sic*] or Berlin, but right here in the good American city of Moline, Illinois, U.S.A.,'" observed the historian Lewis Erenberg. A number of civil rights–minded organizations, including the *Courier*, the Brotherhood of Sleeping Car Porters, and the NAACP, launched what they called their Double V Campaign, which stood for victory at home and abroad and, according to Erenberg, sought to contrast the U.S. war mission with the way blacks were treated at home.

The resentment wrought by this hypocrisy ultimately seeped into the music being created by those most directly affected by it. It was no coincidence that the bebop movement began to flourish during World War II in late-night jam sessions attended by a group of black musicians fed up with the status quo. Intent on turning jazz on its head as part of a larger statement on society, these players—primary among them the trumpeter Dizzy Gillespie, the saxophonist Charlie Parker, the drummer Kenny Clarke, the bassist Oscar Pettiford, and the pianists Thelonious Monk and Mary Lou Williams—were sending a message that they were no longer going to play by the rules.

In the years immediately after World War II, these iconoclastic pioneers would steer jazz far away from the by-then-tired clichés of swing, whose bombastic arrangements had come to symbolize American strength and which served as the de facto anthem for American patriotism. This new breed of musicians wanted nothing to do with flag-waving. On the contrary, with their dark sunglasses and berets, their flatted fifths, dissonance, and harmonic inversions, they rushed headlong into an uncharted musical territory that was intentionally chaotic and subversive.

Surprisingly, bebop was one of the few musical trends of the twentieth century on which John Hammond's stamp was minimal, especially given its origins in social discontent. While he appreciated the rebellion inherent in the music, musicians who worked with him during the period bebop was popular said he found the music itself impenetrable and ultimately pretentious. In any event, bebop's emergence at the cutting edge of popular music proved the deathblow for swing. Benny Goodman, Count Basie, Harry James, and Artie Shaw, all the top swing bandleaders, were starting to look and sound like relics. The same might be said of the critics, men like John Hammond, who had helped create the environment in which those bandleaders thrived. It would be another fifteen years before a new societal mood would emerge, bringing with it new musical tastes that would once again draw Hammond into the spotlight.

11

VANGUARD

The growing Hammond family—John, Jemy, and their three-year-old son, John Paul (nicknamed Jeep)—moved into a Greenwich Village town house on MacDougal Street between Bleecker and Houston after Hammond was discharged from the Army in January 1946. Their third son, Jason, arrived in February. Reflecting the progressive environment of the neighborhood and the liberal attitudes of its residents, the neat row of town houses operated as a sort of cooperative with a shared open courtyard running the length of Mac-Dougal behind the buildings. Mothers could look out their back windows at groups of children playing in the gardens below. On one of the first warm days of spring, residents would gather in the courtyard for "planting day," and during the winter holidays all the residents helped decorate a giant Christmas tree. The children participated in a holiday pageant, complete with costumes and carols. It was during one of these pageants that the family discovered that John Paul was a talented singer. According to Jemy Hammond's sister, Isobel Fisher, the boy performed an a cappella version of "We Three Kings of Orient Are" that resonated off the walls of the town houses.

On the surface, Hammond's life seemed the picture of domestic tranquillity. But there were cracks in the veneer. Hammond's absence during the war, especially at the time of his second son's illness and death, had left Jemy angry, and keeping house and watching small children left her isolated. If Hammond thought his returning home would lift her out of her emotional doldrums, he was wrong. Being a husband and father may well have been the hardest challenge he ever faced.

The popular-music landscape had also shifted during Hammond's three-year military stint, and he found that he needed to either adjust to new popular tastes or forge a new path. He chose the latter. Recognizing the decline in popularity of the big-band sound after World War II, Hammond, after returning to his job at Columbia Records in early 1946, went to his friend and boss Goddard Lieberson and asked if he could shift his focus from jazz to classical music. Lieberson, who personally oversaw Columbia's classical catalog, was less than enthusiastic about the idea, apparently seeing Hammond primarily as an authority on popular music. Never one to stew long in a situation where he was unhappy, Hammond resigned from Columbia rather than continue to record music he didn't like.

He moved to a brand-new small label called Majestic Records, where he felt he would have the independence to pursue his diverse musical interests. That job lasted less than a year, ending in mid-1947, not long after an unsuccessful bid to sign Count Basie to the label. Reflecting back years later on the failed negotiations, as well as on the larger subject of the complicated relationship between a onetime mentor and his former protégé, Hammond wrote, "Anyone who wants gratitude from or credit for a talent that already exists is a pain in the ass. If I expected Bill Basie to come to Majestic because I was there and wanted him, then I was a pain in the ass, too."

He moved on to Keynote Records, another small label on whose board of directors he had been serving for several years. Hammond's notoriety, which was based on his proven ability to cultivate talent and create extraordinary music, made him an attractive catch for an up-and-coming label like Keynote. When Keynote merged with another small, independent label, Mercury Records, in 1947, Hammond was named vice president of the larger, combined company.

His new role as a high-level executive with a small company brought with it responsibilities different from those he was accustomed to in his former jobs as merely a producer for a giant company.

The work was challenging but rewarding. It took him to Eastern Europe in the late 1940s, for instance, where he got another glimpse of totalitarian Communism. The revulsion he felt was the same as twelve years earlier when he had visited Sergei Eisenstein in Russia.

Hammond traveled to Prague in the summer of 1947 to secure for Keynote the American distribution rights to a number of classical pieces recorded by a German label prior to the end of World War II. The Germans had stashed the masters of these recordings in Prague while the war was still raging. After the Germans were defeated, the entire cache was seized by the Czech government. Hammond hoped to purchase the masters, bring the recordings to America, and release the music on the Keynote label. If successful, his plan would allow Keynote to compete for classical music fans in America while eliminating the considerable expense of recording its own classical catalog.

Prague in the years immediately after World War II was a surprisingly ebullient place. Natives of the Czechoslovakian capital had reason to celebrate. Nearby cities such as Dresden to the north and Budapest to the southeast had been devastated during the years of Nazi occupation. Prague, however, had survived the war virtually unscathed. As if to emphasize the palpable sense of relief felt throughout the city, the popularity of jazz soared. Like Americans a decade earlier, Czechs viewed jazz as an expression of freedom and open, democratic principles. The stodgy German patriotic songs that were ubiquitous during the war were replaced by the swinging sounds of Karel Vlach, Gustav Brom, and Emil Ludvik.

Classical music may have been the primary reason for the trip, but Hammond couldn't resist scouring the city's theaters and jazz clubs for talent. He found it in the person of Vlach, and he found Vlach onstage at the Karlin Theater, a giant mock-baroque venue built in 1881 to house circus performances. Located in a gritty working-class neighborhood a few blocks east of the cobblestoned byways of Prague's quaint Stare Mesto (Old Town), the Karlin, which seated well over one thousand people, was packed on any night Vlach and his orchestra took the stage. With a Goodmanesque knack for maintaining the swing, whether on powerful, full-orchestra arrangements such as "Hu a hu" or on gentler numbers such as "Provim to tancem," Vlach had emerged after the war as one of the most popular bandleaders in Eastern Europe.

Vlach's concerts reminded Hammond of the heady days of Benny Goodman's 1937 appearances at the Paramount Theater in New York, when the teenagers famously danced in the aisles. A palpable energy passed back and forth between Vlach and his audience. Hammond found his way backstage one night and convinced Vlach to record an album for Keynote. That same evening, after a stroll through the winding thousand-year-old alleyways of the Stare Mesto, he stumbled upon a nightclub just off Wenceslas Square. The Pygmalion Club, a cramped, dimly lit, smoky joint reminiscent of the Black Cat, Hammond's favorite Greenwich Village haunt, was home to Prague's burgeoning bebop scene, and Hammond got a unique opportunity to see how shifting trends in American jazz were influencing musicians around the world.

He left Prague after a stay of several days satisfied that his negotiations for purchasing the classical music he had gone in search of had been successful. But just as Keynote began receiving shipments of the European recordings, the Iron Curtain fell hard over Czechoslovakia. In February 1948, the Soviet Union began forcibly installing a new Communist regime in Prague. The coup came to both its literal and its symbolic conclusion on the morning of March 10, 1948, when the popular Czech foreign minister, Jan Masaryk, was found dead outside his apartment. He had either committed suicide by throwing himself from his bathroom window or been murdered.

Whatever the circumstances surrounding Masaryk's death, one thing was certain: the Soviet-backed Communists were now in full control of the country.

When Hammond returned to Prague in the spring of 1948, just six weeks after the Communist coup, he found himself in a markedly different country from the one that had so charmed him less than a year earlier. "I found a tremendous difference between the Czechoslovakias of 1947 and 1948. As far as a visitor could learn, there was no longer any personal freedom. Either the Czechs subscribed to the Communist regime, or they did not work or eat," he wrote years later.

Not surprisingly, the Communist officials now running the country took a different view of trade agreements forged with American companies prior to the Soviet takeover. The deal with Mercury was effectively dead, and with it went any remaining doubts Hammond may have had concerning his distaste for Communism.

Hammond's marriage, broken into pieces with the loss of the couple's second child, could never be repaired. Jemy asked Hammond for a divorce in early 1948. Family members familiar with the couple's relationship never doubted that Hammond loved his wife. And they are just as certain that Jemy loved her husband. But asked to describe Hammond's intimate relationships, people who knew him usually respond with virtually the same answer: "John could be difficult." The statement is usually accompanied by a knowing smile, suggesting that the words chosen don't thoroughly cover the subject. Pressed to elaborate, acquaintances will reluctantly (except for the thoroughly candid Rachel Breck, who wasn't reluctant at all) acknowledge that Hammond could be extremely selfish and stubborn at times, characteristics that frequently led him to put his causes and his career ahead of his family.

Hammond initially balked at Jemy's request. But eventually he relented. "At first, John refused to give her a divorce. He never really got over her," recalled Isobel Fisher. "It was John's father who persuaded him to give Jemy the divorce. He [Hammond's father] was very fond of her and thought there was no reason for John to make her miserable."

Jemy Hammond never remarried. Two separate tragedies apparently left her with such painful memories that she chose to remain single. The first was the death of her second child. The second was the death in 1954 of the famed war correspondent and photojournalist Robert Capa. Capa and Jemy had met through mutual friends in the late 1940s, around the time Capa founded Magnum, his Paris-based photo agency. The two began a relationship of such intensity that many believed the notoriously single Capa was ready to give up his wandering lifestyle to settle down with Jemy. He is believed to have expressed these feelings to her while on assignment in Vietnam covering the French Indochina War for *Life* magazine. "He wrote Jemy saying, 'I think this will be my last war. It's time to settle down and get married,'" said Isobel Fisher. Capa never made it home. On May 25, 1954, at the age of forty, after photographing some soldiers advancing across a rice paddy near the village of Thai Binh outside Hanoi, he stepped on a land mine and was killed. Jemy Hammond was one of a small group of people who attended a burial service for him at a Quaker church in upstate New York.

Hammond, on the other hand, didn't remain single for long. In early 1949, within months of his divorce, he met a graceful, dark-haired beauty named Esme Sarnoff. Born Esme O'Brien into a wealthy and politically connected New York family, she was a former debutante of the year in New York City. At the time she and Hammond met, Esme was married to Robert Sarnoff, the son of the radio and television pioneer David Sarnoff, who, as chairman of Radio Corporation of America, was one of the wealthiest and most powerful men in the United States. Hammond quickly learned two things about Esme: first, she shared his passion for good music and smoky nightclubs; second, she was planning to leave Sarnoff. After a trip to Reno that summer to finalize her divorce, and less than a year after meeting Hammond, Esme O'Brien became the second Mrs. John Hammond.

Shortly after the wedding, the couple moved into a fashionable (but modest by New York standards) building at the very far end of East Fifty-seventh Street. The location appealed to Hammond's inherent need for contrasts in his life. He liked to take the elevator downstairs in the morning, glance to his right at the tony high-rises soaring above the East River along Sutton Place, one of Manhattan's most exclusive neighborhoods, then hop across Fifty-seventh Street and squeeze aboard the crosstown bus bound for midtown with the rest of the hoi polloi.

His marriage to Esme was a bright spot in an otherwise-bleak period for Hammond. Family tragedies were starting to pile up. First came the death of his son. Next he was divorced. Then he lost his father. John Hammond, Sr., the same man who had convinced his son to grant Jemy her request for a divorce, was nevertheless profoundly troubled by the end of the marriage. According to his daughter Rachel Breck, the elder John Hammond loved Jemy for her energy and beauty and was proud to have her join the family. Now she was gone. Hammond, acutely aware of his father's distress, was excited about introducing him to Esme, an equally vibrant and beautiful woman. But they never got the chance to meet. John Hammond, Sr., died on a golf course at the age of seventy-eight while Esme was in Reno getting her divorce from Robert Sarnoff.

The death came as a shock to Hammond primarily because his father had never been sick a day in his life. Any bad feelings between the two over the younger Hammond's decision to drop out of Yale and pursue a career in music had long since dissipated by the time John senior died. In fact, a mutual passion for golf had served as the common ground for a genuinely warm relationship in the later years of the elder Hammond's life.

The central family issue confronting Hammond in the wake of his father's death, then, had nothing to do with emotional baggage left over from their once-strained relationship. Instead, it was his mother's increasingly erratic behavior that left him and his four sisters fumbling for answers. After her husband's death, Emily Hammond, now a wealthy widow, fell further and further under the spell of a clever and charismatic man named Frank Buchman. Buchman, a Christian evangelist, was the founder of Moral Rearmament, a society of reformers who believed humans could only experience real change and growth by undergoing a profound spiritual experience. (Many of Buchman's themes were used as the foundation for the twelve-step recovery program espoused by Alcoholics Anonymous.) Virulently anti-Communist, the organization experienced widespread popularity as the Cold War developed in the years after World War II.

According to family members, Buchman wasted no time in cozying up to the deeply religious Emily Hammond once her husband was buried. By some family estimates, before she died in 1970, Emily had turned over to Buchman and his organization somewhere in the neighborhood of three million dollars, as well as the family's country home in Mount Kisco. (The group's leaders were gracious enough to let her stay there after she had turned over the deed to them.)

The huge sums of money donated by Emily Hammond to Moral Rearmament were of no small importance to her only son. The divorce from Jemy had taken its toll on Hammond financially, requiring that he turn over a significant portion of his meager income from Mercury Records for alimony and child support. He paid it gladly and was never less than generous (he agreed with Jemy that both boys should attend private schools, regardless of the cost). But his generosity strained his resources. Throughout his adult life he had been accustomed to the security of a large family nest egg that had always served as a safety net and afforded him a level of independence unfamiliar to most working stiffs. But by the early 1950s, his mother had given enough money away that Hammond, now in his early forties, found himself for the first time in his life scrambling to make ends meet and uncertain as to how his bills would be paid.

In the spring of 1953, with financial burdens pressing in on him, he agreed to help organize an all-star tour featuring Benny Goodman and Louis Armstrong on the same bill. Hammond and Goodman had kept their professional distance for nearly fifteen years, but if they had forgotten during that time why they had stopped working together, their memories were soon jogged.

As with every story handed down in the annals of jazz lore, this one has as many versions as there were people involved. Some aspects are indisputable: Goodman was riding high at the time, enjoying a resurgence of popularity following the release a couple of years earlier of a recording of his hugely successful 1938 concert at Carnegie Hall. Energized by the public's renewed interest in his music, he decided to regroup some of the old band and take it out on the road. He asked Hammond to help out, believing, correctly, that Hammond would know how to go about tracking down and pulling together many of the guys from the old days. But the ever-cautious Goodman concluded that the safest way to ensure large crowds—and large profits—was to team up with another bankable star. That's why Louis Armstrong was asked along.

Another aspect people familiar with the tour agree on—including at least two of Goodman's biographers—is that Hammond, skeptical that he and his brother-in-law could ever work together harmoniously again, was reluctant to get involved.

Ignoring his own better judgment, Hammond signed on with Goodman. Money wasn't the only reason he did so, however. After six years as a vice president at Mercury Records, he was getting bored. Hammond was ill suited to life as an executive with a small record label, a job that required a lot of schmoozing and public-relations busywork. He liked to be near the music. To be sure, his years with Mercury allowed him to indulge in his passion for classical music. In fact, most of his recording work with Mercury was in the classical genre. (One of his first Mercury recordings was with a brilliant and bearded oboist named Mitch Miller, who became famous on television in the late 1950s with a remarkably popular program, *Sing Along with Mitch*.) A Goodman tour, though, would put Hammond back in touch with his first love—live swing jazz. So he left Mercury in search of a new challenge and the opportunity to make a lot of money quickly.

Hammond worked his magic and was able to recruit Gene Krupa, Teddy Wilson, Ziggy Elman, Helen Humes, and a handful of others from back in Goodman's heyday during the 1930s. At Goodman's request, he arranged two rehearsal shows solely for the orchestra at two venues in New England on April 10 and 11 so that the band could work out its kinks in front of a live audience but without the pressure of performing for expectant and discerning New York fans. Overflow crowds at both shows proved that Goodman still had a large national audience.

The trouble began a few days later at a closed rehearsal in New York, during which Goodman and Armstrong were supposed to figure out the logistics of presenting their dual show. Different versions have emerged over the years about what happened at that rehearsal. In one version, Goodman got mad at Armstrong because Louis showed up late with a giant, noisy entourage in tow. In another version, Armstrong got mad at Goodman because Benny kept him waiting for a prolonged period while he finished rehearsing his band. In any event, there was tension between the two stars well before a single note was played on their joint tour.

After a few shows, including two sold-out dates at Carnegie Hall, it was clear to observers that Goodman wasn't himself. Band members told two of Goodman's biographers that he acted erratically, that he was drinking more than usual, and that he seemed generally distracted. Finally, after driving to Boston from a show in Providence, Rhode Island, barely two weeks into the tour, Goodman apparently collapsed in his hotel room and had to be revived by emergency medical personnel. A week later he withdrew from the tour, citing health problems.

Few incidents in Goodman's career were cause for as much speculation as his decision to withdraw from the tour with Armstrong. Some believed he withdrew because he didn't like competing with Armstrong's huge stage presence. Others believed his claim that he was too ill to continue. Hammond fell into the former category and never forgave his brother-in-law for—in Hammond's view at least—walking out.

There is good reason to believe that Hammond was mistaken and that Goodman was in fact seriously ill. Hammond's sister Rachel Breck insisted that the bandleader was so ill that she was unable to reach him or her sister for several days after his reported collapse in Boston. According to Breck, she couldn't reach the Goodmans because Benny was recovering underneath an oxygen tent that had been placed in his hotel room because doctors were afraid to move him to a hospital. His wife, Alice, was at his side, and neither was taking calls.

When Goodman announced that the rest of the tour would have to be scuttled, Hammond was beside himself. At one point he even contemplated suing Goodman, to force him either to continue the tour or to compensate him for income lost due to the canceled shows. He soon changed his mind, however.

Rachel Breck believes her brother overreacted and used Goodman's withdrawal from the tour to further justify his long-held enmity toward Benny for marrying his favorite sister. Two decades later, Hammond's anger had barely abated. He managed to reopen all of these old wounds by recounting his version of the ill-fated tour in lurid detail in his memoirs. Naturally, Goodman was once again blamed for everything.

In an almost comical irony, Hammond's next contact with Goodman came two years later, when the producers of a film version of the bandleader's life sought Hammond's approval to portray Goodman in the movie. Hammond looked over a copy of the script and was appalled by what he read. It was loaded with ridiculous embellishments and outright fallacies. In an atypical move, Hammond demanded fifty thousand dollars to allow Universal International Pictures to include him as a character. A compromise was eventually reached that involved some revisions to the script and allowed him to pocket the far more reasonable sum of five thousand dollars. The Hammond character was eventually portrayed somewhat stiffly by Herbert Anderson, who would later star as Dennis the Menace's father in a popular television series.

Elaine Lorillard and her husband, Louis, a scion of the Lorillard tobacco empire, had grown bored of the standard Newport routine of
summer cocktail parties and debutante balls. So one day in the early
1950s they decided to "bring a little culture to Newport," as Elaine
Lorillard recalled fifty years later. "I said to Louis, 'Let's find something
to do other than canasta.' Well, neither one of us liked canasta, and
everywhere you went in Newport there were tables set up for canasta."
The wealthy couple set about arranging to have members of the New
York Philharmonic perform at the Newport Casino. It seemed at the
time a can't-miss event, one that would appeal to a wide array of Newport's tony summer crowd. But a funny thing happened. "Nobody came,"
Elaine Lorillard said, laughing. Rather than throw in the towel on
some form of summertime musical event, however, Elaine Lorillard
shifted gears a bit. Her next idea, she said, came to her like a ray of
sunshine bursting through the clouds: "Why not a jazz concert?"

As a Red Cross volunteer in Italy during World War II, the future
Mrs. Lorillard met a number of soldiers who were jazz musicians in
civilian life. When the musicians got together to play, the response
from the other soldiers—both American and Italian—was visceral.
"Boy, this is a music that people really love," Elaine Lorillard recalled
thinking at the time.

Nearly a decade later, in the months immediately following the dis-
appointing turnout for her classical music concert, Elaine Lorillard
began planning a jazz festival for Newport. "Louis said, 'If you'll run it,
I'll back it.'" And that's what he did, contributing about forty thousand
dollars in the first year alone.

Knowing very little about how to plan a jazz festival, Elaine Lorillard began casting about for help. The first person she called was a
friend from her days as a New York bohemian before World War II.
The friend, a well-known pianist and harpsichordist named Sylvia Mar-
lowe who was also familiar in New York left-wing circles, told her, "I'll
help you as much as I can, but there is a man in New York who I know
well who has roots in Newport." That man was John Hammond.

According to Elaine Lorillard, things immediately began falling
into place after Hammond came aboard as a personal consultant to her
and her husband (unpaid, of course). Hammond "was the one who had

the final word on everything because my husband [who held the purse strings] didn't know anything about jazz," she said. One of the first things Hammond did was give his blessing to the hiring of a Boston-based nightclub owner named George Wein to act as the festival's producer. Wein was something of a young Renaissance man in the jazz world at the time. A talented pianist in his own right and owner of a highly regarded club in Boston called Storyville, he had a reputation as an entrepreneur committed to delivering high-quality jazz to as wide an audience as possible. "John recognized in me the fact that I was a worker. John always respected the guys doing the work, and I was a dedicated producer who worked. And that was perhaps John's greatest talent—he was not impressed by bullshitters. He didn't care who we were or where we came from. He liked the people that would get in the trenches and do the work," Wein recalled.

Wein had met Hammond briefly a few years earlier at a party at Hammond's summer home in Connecticut. Aware of Hammond's reputation both in music and as a social activist before he actually met him, Wein said he came away impressed. "He paid attention. He paid attention to everything. He was aware of what was going on out there. He was one of these people that had so many varied interests."

Hammond's role with the Newport Jazz Festival would expand over the years as the festival grew into one of the premier live music events in the world. But for the first festival in 1954 his role was minimal—essentially limited to offering advice to the Lorillards on what musicians might be available and, more important, how best to present those musicians so that the audience was treated to a wide array of talent that represented the past, the present, and the future of jazz.

As VIPs at the premier event the weekend of July 17 and 18, 1954, John and Esme Hammond stayed with the Lorillards at their mansion, Quatrel, at the far south end of Newport's storied Bellevue Avenue. Quatrel is small by Newport's Gilded Age standards but still an impressive little "cottage" (as the locals like to refer to their mansions). The saxophonist Gerry Mulligan stayed in a room down the hall from the Hammonds.

A soft summer drizzle had evolved into a full-blown storm by the time Hammond and his entourage headed up Bellevue Avenue into town for opening night. On their immediate left they passed Belcourt Castle, the fifty-two-room "cottage" where Hammond's great-aunt the notorious Alva Vanderbilt lived after her divorce from her first husband, Willie Vanderbilt. A little farther on, just off to their right, was Aunt Alva's first Newport dwelling, the Greek-inspired, Corinthian-columned architectural masterpiece known as Marble House. Next the group passed signs directing tourists east along Victoria Avenue to the site of the Breakers, arguably the pièce de résistance of the world-renowned Newport mansions, and perhaps the single most glaring testament to the Gilded Age excesses of Hammond's Vanderbilt relatives.

Hammond made no mention of his family's formidable local legacy as the car headed toward the festival grounds. He didn't need to.

The traffic came to a virtual standstill near Narragansett Avenue, still three or four blocks away from the group's destination that evening—the Newport Casino, located just off Newport's busiest intersection at Bellevue Avenue and Memorial Boulevard. Crowds on foot only contributed to the congestion. Some folks wore rain gear and carried umbrellas, but most seemed unprepared for the weather. The latter group used their coats as tarps or tried in vain to stay dry under soggy newspapers. The crowds grew thicker nearer to the casino. Many simply milled about, content to absorb the energy emanating from the bustling street scene. Hundreds of others, meanwhile, had formed a line that snaked up Bellevue Avenue and around the corner at Memorial Boulevard. The entranceway to the casino, where the line either began or ended (it was hard to tell), teetered on the verge of chaos.

For nearly a century, Newport had been a gathering place for the cream of American society: summer repose of the Astors, owners of vast swaths of New York real estate; the Lorillards, who controlled the oldest tobacco company in the United States; the Drexels, founders of a Philadelphia banking empire; and, of course, the Vanderbilts. These were the folks one would expect to find strolling onto the grounds of the Newport Casino on a warm summer evening, possibly for a tennis match, or perhaps for an evening of classical music, the women resplendent in designer evening gowns and strappy high heels, the men smart in their blue blazers and well-pressed chinos.

Most of the crowd splashing about in front of the casino on opening night of the Newport Jazz Festival wasn't part of any high society, however. They were kids for the most part, dressed casually in T-shirts and blue jeans. Many of the guys wore dark sunglasses and sported goatees. Most of these young people had never been to Newport before and had descended on the town that weekend from points across America for the sole purpose of listening to jazz. No amount of rain could dampen their energy and enthusiasm.

Hammond and his entourage stepped out of the car in front of the broad archway that served as the casino's Bellevue Avenue entrance. Surveying the chaos around him, he couldn't help noticing that many people appeared to be strolling into the festival for free. (He learned later that he was right.) In hindsight, it wasn't surprising that festival employees were a little overwhelmed by the crowds, since no one had expected so many people to show up. The Hammond group threaded through the crowd and made their way inside the well-manicured grounds of the casino. They then headed toward a makeshift stage constructed above the casino's world-class lawn tennis courts. Six thousand seats had been arranged in front of the stage. But from the looks of the crowd already inside the grounds, as well as those still out on Bellevue Avenue, six thousand probably wasn't going to be enough.

As a VIP, Hammond was ushered into an exclusive box in one of the casino's picturesque piazzas overlooking the stage. From his perch above the grounds, he had a wonderful view of the somewhat-chaotic action below. Sipping a gin and tonic, he watched with amusement as some teenagers, apparently unhappy with the location of their seats toward the rear of the makeshift amphitheater, simply picked up their chairs and moved them closer to the front. He saw a Newport society dame grow frustrated with a pair of expensive-looking high-heeled shoes, two pointed heels sticking petulantly in the mud. She took off the shoes, handed them to her equally nattily dressed male escort, and walked off barefoot through the muck.

With all the excitement around them and below them, Hammond and his coterie hardly noticed that the start of the music was delayed by forty-five minutes. The weather and the unexpected throngs had contributed to the delay. But the real reason was that many of the musicians scheduled to appear that night were stranded in Jamestown on Conanicut Island, just across Narragansett Bay, waiting to be ferried across to Newport. The larger-than-expected crowds had created a bottleneck at every entrance to the city. Anxious Newport police offi-cials, wary of what thousands of impatient jazz fans could do to their lovely city, called over to the ferry operators in Jamestown and all but ordered them to allow the bus carrying the musicians to move to the front of the ferry line.

"The night opened with the appearance of Mayor John J. Sullivan, whose well-intentioned speech of welcome drew groans from some of the impatient 'cats.' The mayor worked his way through a scholarly prepared dissertation on the history of the jazz movement—which had as little attraction as a lecture on Etruscan pottery," noted a sardonic reporter for *The Newport Daily News*.

The wait proved well worth it. The musicians, apparently energized by the crowd's unbridled enthusiasm, were one after another magnifi-cent. The music inspired one fervent teenager to climb onto the top of the casino's clubhouse, where he performed a perilous Charleston on the wet, slanted roof until police ordered him down.

Festival organizers, under Hammond's watchful eye, had carefully arranged the performances to present the entire spectrum of jazz id-ioms, from traditional Dixieland to modern bebop. For the closing act on Saturday night, however, they decided to pull out all the stops and just go ahead and please everyone. Ella Fitzgerald, at the peak of her powers in 1954, simply held out her hand and allowed the thousands in attendance to crawl obediently into her palm. And not a single fan present was capa-ble of resisting her considerable charms. The seduction began with a smoldering version of "Lover, Come Back to Me." Next she brought them to tears with the bluesy "Angel Eyes." Then she carried them with her up into the night sky with a soaring "How High the Moon."

No one in the audience clapped louder than John Hammond. His signature grin fairly lit up the darkened box where he and his en-tourage were seated. As he stood there watching Fitzgerald perform below him, he couldn't help but notice that it wasn't just the old-timers who were wildly for Fitzgerald—the hipster kids loved her as well, the same ones who had arrived decked out in their berets and dark sun-glasses, hoping to get a glimpse of Dizzy Gillespie.

Having Fitzgerald close the show was a brilliant stroke. The eupho-ria that swept through the widely diverse audience in response to her performance instantly validated the festival organizers' belief that jazz belonged in Newport. Moreover, Fitzgerald single-handedly united a crowd as disparate as jazz itself had become. In the process, she also confirmed Hammond's belief that young music fans would appreciate the traditional jazz he so cherished if the music was performed as it was intended to be—with passion, energy, and creativity. Listening to much of the jazz that was popular in the mid-1950s, Hammond sometimes got the queasy feeling that his time had come and gone. For one night at least, Ella Fitzgerald restored his faith in the power of the music he loved.

By almost any measure, the festival was a huge success. "As for the music itself, the stuff was there and it was mellow. A million dollar array of all-star talent, representing the best in three decades of American jazz, delighted the crowd to the point of rapture. If the discords of the more extreme performers were beyond the ken of those unaccustomed to anything more subtle than the renditions of 'Lee' Liberace, the sessions were at least a liberal education in jazz," gushed one local reporter. Traditionalists were treated to Ella Fitzgerald, Gene Krupa, Teddy Wilson, and a depleted but still powerful Billie Holiday. ("She was very difficult. She didn't go around much with white people. But onstage she was fabulous," Elaine Lorillard recalled.) The modern movement was also well represented by, among others, the "high priest of bop" Dizzy Gillespie, the pianist Lennie Tristano, the saxophonist Lee Konitz, and the vibraphonist Milt Jackson.

The crowds, while larger than expected, were never out of control, and the only complaints aired afterward by locals and town officials were related to the traffic jams that clogged the city's narrow streets for the entire weekend. Festival organizers determined in short order that a larger venue would be needed if the concert was to remain in Newport as an annual event, and in the years to come, it was moved to Freebody Park, a large open space adjacent to the Newport Casino.

The Newport Jazz Festival was a landmark event in terms of the sheer number of musicians who participated and the scope of styles represented over the course of the weekend. It created the blueprint and set the standard for the countless outdoor music festivals that followed in its footsteps. "It was wonderful because it was fresh and new.

We were astonished at the success," Elaine Lorillard reminisced. Besides the great music, an aspect of the festival that never failed to thrill Hammond was seeing his black musician friends mingling freely within Newport's stodgy, self-consciously aristocratic, and, of course, lily-white society.

In the years that followed, as the festival grew in both size and stature into one of the most anticipated annual musical events in the world, Hammond never forgot who came up with the idea: "As far as I'm concerned, Elaine Lorillard should have the whole credit for the concept of the Newport Festival. I think it was the most important social concept of the fifties as far as jazz is concerned and I bless her for it."

The festival also served as the foundation for a long friendship between John Hammond and George Wein. When Hammond suggested adding a gospel segment to the 1957 festival, Wein went along with the recommendation, and the music proved hugely popular among the ostensibly myopic jazz fans. A couple of years later, Wein, again at Hammond's urging, reluctantly agreed to feature a flashy rock-and-roll guitarist named Chuck Berry. The fans howled their approval as Berry duckwalked across the Newport stage. "It was more than friendship— I learned from John," Wein recalled. "So John's influence in my life never really stopped while he was alive."

"As far as I know, ours is the first major attempt to return to natural sound through a single microphone. A lot depends on the hall, and we don't want anyone to know about it except us." John Hammond always knew how to work reporters. In this case, the target was a writer for *The New Yorker*, and Hammond was looking to plug his new project for his latest employer, Vanguard. The trick, Hammond knew all too well, was to make the reporter think he was being treated like an insider. It worked, and Hammond got his flattering write-up.

It was the summer of 1954, and somewhere in the vast sprawl of Brooklyn within the still and airy confines of a giant Masonic temple Hammond had gathered together a group of jazz musicians for a recording session. Having found himself out of work after leaving Mercury Records a year earlier to manage the ill-fated Benny Goodman comeback tour, Hammond was grateful when Vanguard's founders, the brothers Seymour and Maynard Solomon, came calling with an offer to record a handful of jazz albums. Vanguard, another small, independent label, was still known at the time primarily for its classical library. The Solomons had founded the label in 1950 and dedicated themselves to achieving the highest-quality sound for their recordings. After reading an article by Hammond in *The New York Times* in which he decried existing production standards on jazz records, the brothers asked him to join them in their quest. Like Hammond, they were interested in using technology not to alter sound but to purify it.

"Vanguard was struggling," he told the popular disc jockey Ed Beach in 1973. "It was a little classical company in those days. I was only doing it to help them out, to expand their [catalog]. The reason I did these things . . . was I was able to do completely uncommercial things." Hammond agreed to go to work for Vanguard for a minimal salary and aware that he would receive no royalties on the records he produced. He explained why he took the job: "Vanguard had marvelous equipment. The president of Vanguard was an engineer, Seymour Solomon, and he was his own control man. It was the greatest joy . . . Seymour was a classical musician." It was Seymour Solomon who had come up with the brilliant idea of using a Masonic temple as a studio. The building's stone walls, wooden floors, and high ceilings created almost perfect acoustics. Years later Hammond would say that the hall had the "most marvelous" acoustics of any place he ever recorded. But the brothers left it to Hammond to pick the right jazz musicians. As usual, he was up to the task. It had been at least a decade since he had participated in sessions as fulfilling and exciting as the ones he supervised in Brooklyn in the mid-1950s.

Breathlessly, he explained their mission to the *New Yorker* reporter, probably Whitney Balliett:

> Mitch Miller's a great guy, but ever since about 1948, when he started tricks with sound—making those horrible echo-chamber recordings, for one thing—all the record companies have been knocking themselves out to achieve phony effects. [By 1954 Miller was a top producer at Columbia Records.] Fun for the sound engineers, maybe, but tough on the musicians. What's the good of having every instrument in a band sound as if it

were being played in the Holland Tunnel? Anyhow, we're fighting all that electronic fakery and we've got just the place to fight
it in. Our hall has marvelous natural acoustics, thanks to perfect
proportions and a wonderful wood floor.

Hammond, playing to the reporter's desire to be in on the secret,
told him he could come along for the recording session, but he had to
promise not to divulge the whereabouts of the Masonic temple. (It was
on Clermont Avenue in the Fort Greene neighborhood.) It was a
clever ploy, and apparently effective.

The musicians for that particular session were Buck Clayton on
trumpet and Ruby Braff on cornet, Jimmy Jones on piano, Steve Jordan on guitar, Buddy Tate on saxophone, Benny Morton on trombone,
Bobby Donaldson on drums, and Aaron Bell on bass. Hammond called
the sessions "Buck Meets Ruby." Clayton was already something of an
icon. He had joined Count Basie's band nearly twenty years earlier and
had played on many of Hammond's all-star sessions in the late 1930s.
Braff, whom Hammond had first heard play in Boston through George
Wein, was just beginning to make a name for himself as a top jazz horn
player.

"It had thirty-five-foot-high ceilings and was just an amazing place,"
Braff recalled of the temple. "The purity of the sound there was sort of
the essence of John Hammond . . . he couldn't be talked out of anything. He had a lot of guts. Nothing scared him or bothered him." Braff
was aware that Hammond's reputation extended beyond the recording
studio, and he remembered being pleased and impressed to be working with the man who had helped integrate popular music. "He loved
jazz and he saw that many of these black musicians were wonderful
and they were getting the shaft," Braff said.

But Braff learned quickly that in order to stay on Hammond's good
side it was best to agree with him. Most of Hammond's difficulties with
famous musicians—Louis Armstrong, Duke Ellington, Billie Holiday,
and Benny Goodman, among others—began, observed Braff, when
Hammond's often-unsolicited advice was ignored. (Braff noted drily,
"He was trying to tell Duke Ellington what to do and it wasn't going
to happen.") Braff eventually had his own falling-out with Hammond

once he, too, stopped taking directions. Still, Braff, a blustery but easy-going fellow, said he could never stay mad at Hammond for long. "He was so enthusiastic, so boyishly enthusiastic about whatever he was working on. It was a wonderful thing to behold. I miss hearing his enthusiasm."

Hammond liked to find a seat in the middle of the temple while the musicians performed on a stage a good twenty-five yards away. During one especially sublime moment, Hammond, seated next to his young friend Nat Hentoff, leaned back, closed his eyes, and said, "Boy, is Benny Morton warm!" This was his kind of music and these were his kinds of musicians. Hentoff explained his and Hammond's rapture to the *New Yorker* reporter: "This is the rarest kind of jazz today. These [musicians] are caught in no man's land, somewhere between the people who think jazz died with Johnny Dodds and the people who think it began with Stan Kenton." In other words, it was more progressive than swing but far less esoteric than bebop.

Braff in particular shined during these sessions. Unlike the boppers with their self-conscious, jarringly complex riffs, Braff belted out one handsome solo after another with a relaxed confidence that recalled Joe DiMaggio gracefully running down fly balls in centerfield. Critics said they never saw DiMaggio dive for a ball. Admirers observed that DiMaggio never needed to. The same might be said of Ruby Braff's playing. He didn't need to be flashy to draw attention to himself.

Hammond cherished his time at Vanguard, savoring the independence that working for a small label afforded him. Almost single-handedly, from late 1953 through 1959, he built Vanguard's jazz catalog into a formidable competitor with the other small but influential labels that were producing jazz at that time, notably the Verve Records label run by Hammond's friend Norman Granz.

Overlooked and underappreciated by the broad record-buying public at the time they were made, the sophisticated records Hammond produced for the Solomon brothers have enjoyed a resurgence in popularity and a newfound appreciation in recent years. "For Maynard and Seymour, and also for John, the sessions produced for Vanguard caught a vital moment in American music," the jazz historian Samuel Charters wrote in liner notes when Vanguard recently reissued the Brooklyn recordings. "Although he chose to document jazz styles that were giving way to Bebop the albums had a decisive influence on the entire jazz era. The sound quality, and the freedom of the artists to extend their arrangements and to sort out the arrangements themselves, had a welcome tone of dignity and respect that the jazz world immediately recognized."

Hammond brought together a remarkable array of talent for Vanguard, recording musicians who adhered to the more traditional style of jazz he preferred. One of his favorites of this period was a brilliant pianist named Mel Powell, perhaps the only person with a claim as successor to Teddy Wilson as jazz's classiest pianist. The classically trained Powell clearly appealed to Hammond's intellectual side. He made Chopin swing. And just as important, he shared Hammond's sense of humor. A rollicking "California, Here I Come" recorded in 1954 is a three-minute nine-second tour de force. But it's also a hoot. Powell would eventually leave the rough-and-tumble world of jazz to pursue his love of classical music. (He won a 1990 Pulitzer Prize for classical composition.) "I had to twist his arm to do it, but I also recorded a classical sonata of his. We called him Melvin Powell on that one. He only plays jazz now when he's drunk, so one encourages him to drink," Hammond joked in 1973.

Some old friends also joined Hammond in the Vanguard studio, including Count Basie for a memorable reunion session in 1957. The following year Vanguard cleaned up and released recordings of Hammond's by-then-legendary "From Spirituals to Swing" concerts. Hammond was thrilled at the warm reception the album received from a younger generation of music fans.

Still, he had reason to feel older by the mid-1950s. The music landscape had changed dramatically in the ten years since he had been released from the Army. Benny Goodman, Teddy Wilson, and Count Basie, Hammond protégés and stalwarts of the swing era, were now regarded more as legends than as vibrant contributors to the contemporary scene.

Hammond's reputation had similarly faded over time. So much so that his diminished stature became fodder for up-and-coming jazz critics. "And anyway, a younger jazz fan might ask, who the heck is John

Hammond. I mean, is this some nut, some crackpot that we can just dismiss? I'm afraid not. It wasn't so long ago that he was described as 'America's Greatest Authority on Hot Jazz,'" the Boston disc jockey John McLellan wrote circa 1957. "All right. So he never was America's greatest authority. But John Henry Hammond Jr. was a pretty important figure in jazz. I say 'was' because his importance and influence in jazz have decreased markedly in recent years."

McLellan, whose feet were planted solidly in the modern jazz camp, had taken issue with a 1957 interview in *Esquire* magazine in which Hammond, with typical brashness, blurted, "I think the present Basie band stinks, and so does Basie." McLellan ripped Hammond for his hubris, and then questioned whether anyone even took notice any longer of Hammond's legendary acid tongue. "Maybe the jazz world is just passing him by. And there's nothing left for him but virulent attacks on some pretty fine jazzmen . . . There was a time when a Hammond attack would raise a hornet nest of angry rebuttal. I remember when he criticized Duke Ellington's band back in the '40s, [critic] Leonard Feather's answering article was titled 'Heil Hammond!' Nowadays, few seem to notice."

By 1959 Hammond's most influential work in jazz was behind him. By then, much of contemporary jazz had grown so insular that its fan base had been whittled down to only the most devoted of hipsters. Many young people had veered in the opposite direction, turning to a far more inclusive genre. Folk music acts like the Kingston Trio, the Chad Mitchell Trio, and the Brandywine Singers were on top of the popular-music charts. Hammond had little experience with folk, but was intrigued precisely because of the music's inclusiveness and immediacy. So when the phone rang in 1959 and it was his old friend Goddard Lieberson, now in charge of Columbia Records, calling to broach the subject of a job, Hammond, though reluctant to leave the cozy environment at Vanguard, saw in front of him a path back to the big time. Moreover, he viewed a return to Columbia as an opportunity to once more immerse himself in the contemporary music scene.

12

A SECOND ACT

I t hadn't occurred to him immediately. He had been too busy taking care of details—setting up microphones, taping wires to the
floor, adjusting dials on the recording equipment—to notice. But
when Hammond did notice, he was pleased: he and the sound engineer he had brought with him across the Hudson River from Manhattan were the only two white people in the building.

The Abyssinian Baptist Church, in the heart of Newark's Central
Ward, was jammed that warm spring day in April 1960. In order to
replicate the sound and feel of an actual Sunday morning service, Hammond and Abyssinian's musical director, Professor Alex Bradford, had
decided to record the church's choir with as much of the congregation
present as they could pack into the building on a weekday morning. It
proved an inspired decision. Spurred on by the presence of a live audience, the 120 members of the church's choir sang with such spontaneity, power, and pure joy that Hammond and Bradford couldn't resist
calling the final collection of recordings *Shakin' the Rafters*.

The Abyssinian choir recordings were Hammond's first sessions of
real substance after he came back to Columbia Records in late 1959.
His return to the company where he first made a name for himself in the
1930s was significant enough news in the music industry to warrant a
press release from Columbia. Hammond's old friend Goddard Lieberson, now president of the company, announced the hiring in a flattering

press release. "John Hammond is one of the deans of America's recording industry and we are happy to welcome him back to Columbia, where he made his first discs twenty-seven years ago," Lieberson enthused.

Notwithstanding this impressive buildup, Hammond agreed to return to Columbia, at the time one of the most profitable record companies in the business, at the paltry salary—even in 1959—of ten thousand dollars a year. Friends and family members could only speculate as to his reasons for working for such low pay. The most likely reason offered is that he enjoyed cultivating a reputation as someone who worked for love of music rather than love of money. Indeed, instead of complaining about how little money he made, Hammond liked to brag about his ridiculously low salary at Columbia.

Shakin' the Rafters wasn't a chart topper for Columbia: it barely sold enough copies to turn a profit. But it served at least one purpose for Hammond—that of establishing a sort of guideline, a moral compass as it were, which he planned to follow now that he was back at a large record label. In the 1950s, Columbia had virtually perfected the art of generating piles of cash from the sales of bland music. Hammond wasn't averse to helping Columbia make money, and he would produce banal hits if so ordered by his bosses, but he was determined to retain his reputation as a producer with a discerning ear whose desire for quality took precedence over churning out popular drivel. Making records like *Shakin' the Rafters* would certainly only enhance that reputation.

Hammond had never recorded with a gospel choir prior to his work at the Abyssinian Baptist Church. His inexperience recording large groups never became an issue, however. The group quickly lived up to its reputation as one of the finest in the nation. And filling the church with congregants contributed an incalculable dimension to the already supercharged atmosphere. The energy created by the audience was every bit as significant as the force generated by the choir. In pew after pew, eyes shut tightly, their heads swaying slowly in unison from side to side, the congregation members sat enraptured. During the gorgeous introduction to "Sweet Jesus," for instance, a moving ballad notable for Dickie Mitchell's ethereal organ work, so starkly in contrast with the grave and solidly earthbound piano of Willie James McPhatter (brother of the rock-and-roll pioneer Clyde McPhatter), exuberant audience members began loudly exhorting the featured soloist, Calvin White, to join in. White didn't disappoint. Earnest as a funeral, full-throated, and divinely articulate, he sang, "He's the sa-ame as the mo-on is to the ni-ight. He's the sa-ame as the da-ark is to the li-ight. He's as swe-eet as the honey falling from the tree."

Then, in an awesome display of the classic gospel call-and-response technique, some three hundred voices sang: "THAT'S WHAT HE IS TO ME-EE-EE-EE-EE-EE-EE."

"He Stays in My Room" was not so much a song as a sermon. "Let everyone say 'Amen,'" the soloist, White, urged the whooping, hand-clapping, foot-stomping congregation. "Let's say 'Amen' again." Next the full choir intoned, "He stays in my room," and White responded, "And then He gives me all of my medicine." Someone in the audience let out a pitch-perfect scream. White continued, preaching a bit now: "How many of you have ever been sick in here? I want you to raise your hands. Did the doctor ever give up on any of you?" It was a rhetorical question, and everyone in the church knew White wasn't talking about a medical doctor. "Well, all you've got to do is keep faith and He'll come in your room. He healed me one day and ever since that time [White was singing now] *He's been in my room.*"

The congregation didn't have to be told who "He" was.

Then, gloriously, the Reverend R. P. Means, with perfect rhythm and intonation, stuttering, and pausing for effect:

I-I don't ca-yare what else you've tried. I-I know we've tried a whole lot of things. Yeah! S-some of us have gone he-yare and yonder tryin' to find help. But-but I-I would like to recommend to you Jesus. YEAH! YEAH! He-He won't never leave ya! He'll ALL-WAAAYS be in your room. [Shouting now.] OHHHHH, Lord, yes, He will. I-I took Him in partnership a long time ago. He told me IIIII'd be with Him when the WOORRLD is against ya. OHHHHH, Lord, stay with Jesus.

This was no longer a recording session. This was church.

"Said I Wasn't Gonna Tell Nobody" is five minutes and thirty-one seconds of sheer jubilation—it could be stored in a time capsule and opened one thousand years from now to illustrate definitively the rousing call-and-response paradigm of gospel music. The song seemed to be winding down at about three and a half minutes. But extemporaneous shouts from the congregation lit a spark, leading to several more minutes of exultant exchanges between the callers (the featured singers, Calvin White and Margaret Simpson) and the responders (the choir and the audience).

It was the kind of session Hammond liked best; he simply turned on the tape and let it roll.

As for the music itself—song selection, the length of the songs, featured soloists—Hammond left that entirely in the eminently capable hands of Professor Alex Bradford. Bradford was an indispensable figure in gospel music during the second half of the twentieth century, a period that saw gospel seep out from the Baptist churches of the inner cities and the Deep South and into America's musical mainstream. Bradford was at the epicenter of that movement. The writer Dave Marsh credits him with influencing the styles of such artists as Little Richard, Ray Charles, and Sam Cooke. Bradford also had an eye for talent. From his perch as director of Abyssinian's renowned choir, he nurtured a slew of talented singers, including Cissy Houston, Dionne Warwick, and Judy Clay, all of whom carried their gospel roots with them when they crossed over into mainstream popular music.

Raised in Bessemer, Alabama, outside Birmingham, Bradford was a child prodigy who was performing on vaudeville stages at four years old. Committed to the church from an early age, he seemingly dedicated every waking moment of his life to gospel music. As a youngster, he was a talented singer and charismatic performer who pioneered the flamboyant stage persona later adopted by Little Richard. He excelled at both the organ and the piano and was a prolific composer, producer, and arranger: in fact, all of the songs on *Shakin' the Rafters* were written by Bradford. Much to Hammond's chagrin, though, Bradford couldn't sing on the album, because he was already under contract to another label, Savoy. So covetous of Bradford's talents was Savoy that, according to Hammond, the company's president sneaked into the church during the recording of *Shakin' the Rafters* to make sure Bradford's voice didn't inadvertently wind up on the record.

———

After resigning himself to the drawbacks of working for a giant company—for instance, the likelihood that he would have to record artists who bored him—Hammond hit the ground running in his first few months back at Columbia. By the time he recorded the Abyssinian Baptist Gospel Choir, he had already produced a couple of hits. The first artist he signed to the label following his return was a talented pianist named Ray Bryant. Hammond had been a fan of the pianist's since first hearing him play many years earlier in a club in Philadelphia when Bryant was barely out of his teens. During the 1950s Bryant had made a name for himself as a sideman with, among others, Miles Davis, Sonny Rollins, and Coleman Hawkins. Later he formed his own jazz trio, with whom he made several memorable recordings for some small, independent labels. Hammond kept tabs on him as the pianist moved from one project to the next. Then, in 1958, when Hammond was making a record for Vanguard with Count Basie's former drummer Jo Jones, he brought Bryant in to play piano.

What Hammond liked best about Bryant was his versatility; he was comfortable in virtually any setting, equally at home on peppy dance numbers geared to a jukebox audience and mixing it up live onstage with frantic beboppers. Bryant's first session with Hammond for Columbia, in 1960, yielded a catchy rhythm and blues single called "Little Susie." It wasn't exactly Hammond's cup of tea, but the song did well, cracking the Top 40 on the R&B charts. If nothing else, the success of "Little Susie" showed his new bosses that Hammond could produce moneymaking music. (Hammond's handwritten notes from the session indicate that he personally preferred a slow bluesy number called "Blues for Norine.")

A month or so later, Bryant was back in the studio with Hammond recording "The Madison Time," another catchy single. Irresistible to the ears but ultimately about as enduring as the flavor in a stick of chewing gum, "The Madison Time" spawned a brief dance craze in Baltimore in the spring and summer of 1960. (The filmmaker John Waters gave the song a brief second life when he used it in his 1988 film, *Hairspray*.) Perhaps the most memorable thing about "The Madison Time" was the promotional material that Columbia created and distributed to capitalize on the song's popularity. Teenagers who bought the single also received a pamphlet that included several elaborate diagrams intended to help novice dancers. The promotional copy that accompanied the diagrams could only have left Hammond cringing in embarrassment: "So get in line and dance 'The Madison'—the Newest—the Hottest—the Grooviest dance craze of the day! If you slip, if you slide, if you stumble, if you fall don't fret—You may have found another 'Madison' step."

Of course this sort of thing would have been unthinkable at Vanguard. But Hammond had made his decision to return to the big time, and he was well aware of how crass and commercial the industry could be when it set its collective mind to it. And in those days no one was doing commercial better than Columbia. Under Mitch Miller, the company adhered to a formula whose ultimate goal was to sell records that appealed to as broad a buying public as possible. It was music that offended no one and took absolutely no risks—and Columbia was practically printing money. In a memoir published in 1975, Clive Davis explained the formula:

> Columbia had coasted nicely through the previous decade with a solid middle of the road format, aided during the late fifties and early sixties by the immense popularity of the Broadway cast albums it recorded. *My Fair Lady*, for example, sold more than five million albums, *South Pacific* more than two million albums and *Camelot* almost as much. Equally important, the company had a solid stable of gifted MOR [middle of the road] artists—Ray Conniff, Doris Day, Percy Faith, Tony Bennett, [Barbra] Streisand, [Andy] Williams, Jerry Vale, Robert Goulet—all of whom could record compositions from the same musicals. In fact, it was written into their contracts that they had to record them. So we had it both ways. Rodgers and Hammerstein and Lerner and Loewe wrote successful musicals, and Columbia acquired the original cast album rights; then Williams, Streisand, Percy Faith and others recorded the songs again.

Hammond didn't concern himself with how Columbia made its profits. He simply bided his time until the right opportunity arrived, one that would allow him to do what he did best—nurture raw talent until it reached its potential. He didn't have to wait long. "When I got back to Columbia . . . I was supposed to be responsible for reissues," he told a radio interviewer in 1973, "but I started recording some artists I had used on Vanguard, and one of them was a superb piano player named Ray Bryant . . . And about the time I was recording Ray in 1960, a composer came into my office by the name of Curtis Lewis . . . He came in with a demo of some tunes of his, and one of them was 'Today I Sing the Blues.' There was a *fantastic* vocalist on the record, and it was of course—I asked him who it was—and it was Aretha Franklin, who was still in her father's gospel choir in Detroit."

Franklin was just eighteen years old when she signed with Columbia. Like that of most of the other young artists whose careers Hammond guided over the years, Franklin's startling talent had hardly gone unnoticed by others. Four years earlier, Chess Records, the Chicago-based independent label known mostly for its pioneering work with blues artists, released a collection of gospel songs sung by fourteen-year-old Aretha Franklin. The recordings were made during actual services led by Aretha's father, C. L. Franklin, a prominent minister in Detroit with charisma to spare. Franklin had made her debut as a soloist during a service at her father's New Bethel Baptist Church, one of the city's largest. Thus she earned her chops singing each week in front of the four thousand worshippers who regularly packed the church on Sunday mornings to witness one of the Reverend C. L. Franklin's high-voltage performances. And C. L. Franklin wasn't shy about promoting his daughter. Throughout her teen years, Franklin traveled back and forth across the country with her father's gospel caravan, singing at huge arenas and auditoriums in many of America's largest cities. Word of her talent spread quickly.

According to one of Franklin's biographers, the fledgling record producers Berry Gordy, Jr., and Billy Davis attended Sunday services at New Bethel Baptist Church for the sole purpose of listening to the young soloist with the awe-inspiring voice. Gordy had yet to form Motown Records, and he and his songwriting partner Davis were looking for talent to record their songs. "The impression that I had was that she was a child genius. Everything that she sang was with such emotion that you felt every word. She had just terrific control over her expressions. So, as far as I was concerned, she was a young genius," recalled Davis, who first heard Franklin sing around 1958.

Gordy and Davis hoped to work with Franklin, preferably as a rhythm and blues singer. But her father killed the idea because, according to Davis, he didn't want his daughter entering the music business at such a young age.

C. L. Franklin may have thought his daughter was too young to become a professional singer, but he couldn't prevent her from becoming a mother. While still in her teens, Franklin gave birth to her first child and dropped out of high school. She stayed at home, played piano, and dreamed of following in the footsteps of her idol, the blues singer Dinah Washington. This period of reflection apparently led her to conclude that she should pursue her dreams at all costs. In early 1960, she left her baby with relatives and set off for New York.

By 1960 Hammond's reputation in the music industry had been earned not only by being in the right place at the right time—he was at Monette's in Harlem in 1933 the night Billie Holiday performed there, he was at Mildred Bailey's home in Queens the night Teddy Wilson and Benny Goodman first jammed as part of a trio, and he was in Oklahoma City long enough to hear Charlie Christian knock out a handful of tasty guitar solos—but also for knowing what to do when opportunity came knocking. Indeed, Hammond seemed to be perpetually standing at the door, waiting and listening for the knock. Thus when the recording of "Today I Sing the Blues" with the astonishing vocal track landed on his desk, he knew instinctively that he needed to move fast if he wanted to sign the singer to Columbia Records.

Equally vital to this scenario was Hammond's recognition of his own unique ability to make things happen for an artist he liked. Few in the business could count as many industry contacts as Hammond, especially in the media. This fact was not lost on the managers of up-and-coming artists, who were attracted to his ability to get their artists' names in newspapers and magazines. Robert Altshuler, who served as head of Columbia's public-relations department for much of the 1960s, admired his skill at cultivating reporters. According to Altshuler, Hammond always promptly returned their calls, and he always made sure to stroke their egos, offering praise for a recent article. It was a dynamic that worked well for both parties. "It would have been very foolish [for any reporter covering popular music] not to call John Hammond. I mean, a lot of people accuse John Hammond of being self-seeking and of spending a lot of time getting PR for himself. But the truth is most of the calls to journalists emanated with the journalists. They knew a good source. He was an incredible source, and John knew how to use those opportunities that were given him." Certainly Hammond had more to offer Aretha Franklin in terms of bringing attention to her and getting her music heard than other, less-influential industry types, such as Berry Gordy, Jr., and Billy Davis, who had recognized her talent but lacked the resources to guide it toward a wider audience.

The opportunity to meet Franklin occurred not long after Hammond first heard her on tape. Hammond had told Curtis Lewis of his reaction to the vocals on "Today I Sing the Blues," and Lewis had in turn passed word of his interest on to Jo King, who was acting as Franklin's manager in New York. King promptly telephoned Hammond and invited him to meet and listen to Franklin. After meeting and hearing her for the first time in a small studio on Broadway, Hammond quickly determined that she was much better live than on tape. Franklin signed a six-year deal with Columbia a few days later.

Because of Ray Bryant's diverse background in gospel, blues, and jazz, as well as his proven ability to write a hit song, Hammond asked him to help supervise Franklin's first recording session for Columbia, held on the evening of August 1, 1960, in New York City. Also on hand, according to notes taken during the session, were Osie Johnson on drums, Bill Lee on bass, Lord Westbrook on guitar, and Tyree Glenn on trombone. Franklin was pleased with Hammond's selection of musicians. "Some of the best musicians in the business were on my very first session. Mr. Hammond surrounded me with the very best," she told her biographer Mark Bego.

Hammond would later recall Franklin's joy at the collaborative process that developed that evening. In the liner notes of a 1972 reissue of Franklin's first Columbia album, he wrote, "Aretha was barely 18 when she cut her first pop sides on August 1, 1960. It was an evening session that was one of the three or four most exciting in my life in recording. Aretha played piano when she felt like it; otherwise she let

Ray Bryant take over with his fine rhythm section and the trombone comments of Tyree Glenn. She had all the passion of a gospel veteran, along with humor and a natural vocal technique almost unknown in a jazz singer."

The session yielded four finished songs. Three of them, "Today I Sing the Blues," "Right Now," and "Love Is the Only Thing," were chosen by Hammond. The fourth, "Over the Rainbow," was selected by Franklin. As was Hammond's practice, all of the songs were recorded live without the use of overdubs to capture the intimacy and spontaneity that he desired in all his records.

There would have been no way for him to know it at the time, but that night may have represented the high point of Hammond's professional relationship with Franklin. Over the next eighteen months, the relationship would swiftly deteriorate.

Meanwhile, Hammond was busy helping Columbia make inroads into an area of music the company had up to then ignored—folk music. In early 1961, he signed Pete Seeger. Bringing Seeger to Columbia would ultimately prove fortuitous both for Hammond and for Columbia.

Seeger recalled that he was reluctant at first to sign with Columbia, home to Andy Williams, Ray Conniff, and Mitch Miller. "I had never had a desire to be a pop success," he said. "I'm not sure it's a good thing."

Nevertheless, the move was pure Hammond. He had pursued Seeger doggedly despite the singer's having been blacklisted in the early 1950s during the height of the McCarthy era. Seeger had been a close confidant and traveling partner of Woody Guthrie's back in the 1940s. But he was more of an intellectual than Guthrie and had far closer ties than Woody to the Communist Party. Not without consequence, however. At the time he was blacklisted, Seeger was a member of the popular folk group the Weavers. He and his bandmates were banned from recording at any of the large record companies, and also from appearing on radio, on television, and at many concert venues. When Hammond signed him to Columbia, Seeger was making money touring college campuses and doing an occasional recording for Moe Asch's

Folkways Records. Despite the blacklist, which had proven effective in limiting the audience his music could reach, Seeger's powerful populist message had lost none of its bite.

"You see, I had come back to Columbia about a year earlier," Hammond explained, "and I was distressed at the fact that we weren't into too many kids while Mitch [Miller] had been running the show. The first thing I did was to sign Pete Seeger—he was still under indictment for contempt of Congress, still being blacklisted by CBS, our parent, but I felt he would give Columbia a better image with the kids. And we were willing to take a chance on a controversial artist because he was obviously a great artist."

Hammond first met Seeger in the late 1930s, and their paths had crossed occasionally over the next two decades. Hammond had agreed to sit on the board of directors of People's Songs, a short-lived organization thought up by Seeger in 1946 to help promote the ideals of the folk movement through occasional performances and the creation of a library of protest songs, and the two had worked together on Henry Wallace's failed bid for the presidency in 1948. A trust developed between them.

"John was an upper-class left-winger, and to a certain extent I was, too," said Seeger. "John was dubious about the Henry Wallace campaign; he didn't think it would succeed. But he didn't just let his name be used; he was very active."

Ironically, it was Moe Asch of Folkways who convinced Seeger to leave him and sign with the major label. Asch, according to Seeger, told him that if he succeeded at Columbia, his music—and his message— would reach a huge audience, far bigger than the audience he would reach recording for Folkways.

If Seeger was reluctant to join the ranks of smooth crooners, the suits at Columbia were equally reluctant to welcome him aboard. Hammond was determined to sign him, however. First he had to convince some of the more conservative executives at Columbia that bringing Seeger to the label was a good business decision. "John went right to the top of Columbia and was told, 'Seeger is persona non grata here,'" the singer recalled. Hammond argued forcefully in Seeger's favor. Then an executive asked Hammond, "But do you think he'll sell?" Hammond, Seeger recalled, responded, "Well, I wouldn't sign him if I didn't think he'd sell."

"Well, then go ahead and sign him," he was told.

"I have to take my hat off to him," Seeger said, admiringly. "He was able to confront [the Columbia executives] head-on. As long as he didn't get them in trouble, he could do what he wanted."

For Hammond at least, just as important as Seeger's prospective record sales was his stature as a man of principle and moral authority. Yet in time, Seeger would sell many hundreds of thousands of albums for Columbia. A live album recorded during a 1963 performance at Carnegie Hall was a surprise hit and helped to popularize the civil rights anthem "We Shall Overcome." And in the decades since then, Seeger has emerged as an American icon every bit as revered as Woody Guthrie.

Hammond's decision to pursue Seeger despite the singer's political baggage would prove more than simply bold: it may have led directly to what was arguably the most significant signing of Hammond's career. "Bob Dylan went to Columbia because Pete was there," asserted Harold Leventhal. "I was close to Dylan at that time because of my relationship with Woody Guthrie. He wanted to know how Pete reacted to working with John and was he satisfied and we were. Anything we wanted or needed in terms of Pete recording, John was the guy you went to. I used to invite Dylan up to [Seeger's] recording sessions, and John was always there." Leventhal was himself a revered figure on the New York folk scene at the time in his role as manager for Seeger, as well as for Woody Guthrie, who was by then gravely ill. Thus it's not surprising that Dylan, given his reverence for Guthrie, would have sought Leventhal's advice before signing a contract with a major record label.

Many details of Dylan's early career have since grown cloudy. Countless retellings have caused times, places, and events to be thrown together in a stew of half-truths and misinformation. Until recently, Dylan himself had proven little help in clearing up his own history, often perpetuating myths or simply remaining silent. Much of that changed, however, with the release of his memoirs, *Chronicles, Volume One*, in which he offered a detailed account of his first meetings with Hammond and how he came to be signed at Columbia. It's a vivid recollection, and one that corroborates the versions of two of his most respected biographers, Anthony Scaduto and Robert Shelton.

"I had never really fixed my gaze on any big recording company. I would have been the last one to believe it if you'd have told me I'd be recording for Columbia Records, one of the top labels in the country and one with big name mainstream artists like Johnny Mathis and Tony Bennett and Mitch Miller. What put me there amongst that crowd came about because of John Hammond," Dylan wrote.

According to Dylan, he first met Hammond in the apartment of a singer-songwriter named Carolyn Hester, whom Hammond had signed to Columbia a few months earlier. (Dylan provided no date for the meeting, but his biographers have narrowed it down to the first week of September 1961.) Hester was an attractive young singer with lustrous brown hair who hailed from Texas. She had been a familiar figure in Greenwich Village folk circles, and Hammond had signed her ostensibly as Columbia's answer to Joan Baez, who had signed earlier with Vanguard Records and was quickly establishing herself as a standout on the folk scene.

Hester recently recalled those times and, specifically, the day she auditioned for Hammond: "In 1961 my hero, Pete Seeger, had recently signed with Columbia Records. There was a rumor around Greenwich Village that John Hammond and Columbia were possibly going to build a stable of folk musicians. It was a warm summer day [possibly late July or August] and I was going to get to audition for Mr. Hammond, thanks to my young manager, Charlie Rothschild . . . I had guitar in hand, and wore a green dress trimmed in black velvet latticework. Mr. Hammond was tall, warmhearted, and positive."

Hester said she was aware of Hammond's track record. "Mr. Hammond's wonderful reputation as a benefactor and mentor to artists in the jazz world really impressed me," she said.

After Hester had performed just one song—a tune called "Blackjack Oak"—Hammond stopped the audition, and then he and her manager made plans for her to record in a studio. The following week Hester met again with Hammond to sign her contract and discuss the sessions. That's when she suggested putting together a band for the recording dates. She said she wanted Bruce Langhorne on guitar and

Bill Lee on bass. Hammond agreed to hire both musicians for the session, which was scheduled for September.

"A month or so before [the session] I had a gig at Club 47 in Boston," Hester explained. "There is a story that Bob Dylan made it his business to get up there and talk the manager into letting him open for me. I don't really know that for sure, but he did open that night, and the next day we spoke at length about his business situation. He explained that though Dave Van Ronk and his wife, Terri Thal, were in overdrive trying to help him, he was needing more gigs and did I have any ideas. I told him that right now I wasn't moving around so much, as I was getting ready to make an album over at Columbia."

She said she told Dylan, "As a matter of fact, my dad played harmonica on my first album at Coral—maybe John Hammond would let me bring you in on harmonica. How about I try that?" To which Dylan replied, "I'll be there and here's my phone number."

Hester went on to describe the rehearsal at which Hammond and Dylan first met: "John Hammond wanted to hear my band. Bruce, Bill, and Bob. The three Bs. We had a get-together in Greenwich Village. Very informal. The kitchen and the living room—the great room, as they would say now—kind of a picnic table setup. John sat on the same side of the table as Bob. Bill Lee had his big stand-up bass. Bruce and I sat on the other side of the table with our guitars. John liked it. As a matter of fact, in years to come, people would acknowledge that we even swung! Bluegrass, Appalachian, Ladino, folk of all kinds. I felt like I was a song short, so Bob taught me 'Come Back, Baby,' a blues. John liked it a lot. And he liked Bob a lot. He asked him if he wrote songs or anything. A musical revolution was on the way."

At the time of the Hester rehearsal, Dylan had been on the Village folk scene for less than a year, having arrived in New York from his home state, Minnesota, in early 1961. He was already making a name for himself, though. By all accounts, it didn't take long for him to stand out among the legions of grimy young folk singers who congregated in such Village folkie redoubts as the Gaslight, the Kettle of Fish, the Bitter End, and Gerde's Folk City.

Dylan recalled that during the rehearsal, in addition to playing harmonica, he played some guitar and sang harmony vocals on a couple of songs. "Before leaving, [Hammond] asked me if I recorded for any-body. He was the first authoritative figure who ever asked me that. He just kind of said it in passing. I shook my head, didn't hold my breath to hear him respond and he didn't and that was that," he wrote.

Yet Hammond saw something he liked. He told Scaduto:

I saw this kid in the peaked hat playing not terribly good har-monica but I was taken with him. I asked him, "Can you sing? Do you write? Why don't you come up to the studio? I'd like to do a demo session with you just to see how it is." I was sitting there thinking, "What a wonderful character, playing guitar and blowing mouth harp, he's gotta be an original." It was just one of those flashes. I thought, "I gotta talk contract right away" . . . I was just waiting for somebody with a message for kids when I met Bob and I just had some good success. I had brought in Aretha Franklin and I was in fairly good shape at Columbia. I told Bob, "I don't have too many artists to produce, and I'd love to record you." So we made a date for him to come to the studio.

On September 29, 1961, an article by the music critic Robert Shel-ton was published in *The New York Times* that praised Dylan as "one of the most distinctive stylists to play in a Manhattan cabaret in months." Although in his memoirs Hammond doesn't mention having seen the article, Dylan recalled that he had. The article, according to Dylan, ran in the paper on the same day that Hester was recording for Hammond, and he suggests that Hammond was so impressed by Shelton's praise that he stepped up his efforts to sign Dylan. Dylan was also in the stu-dio that day, and when the session was over, Hammond asked to talk to him in the control booth, where he offered him a contract with Colum-bia. "It seemed too good to be true," Dylan wrote.

Hammond's version in his autobiography is slightly different. He claimed that after meeting Dylan for the first time at Hester's apart-ment, he invited Dylan up to his office to listen to him sing. He then offered the musician a contract based solely on hearing him play one song, "Talkin' New York," Dylan's clever autobiographical account of his first winter in the big city.

In any case, Dylan recalled that he was thrilled not only by the offer to sign with Columbia but by having been asked to do so by John Hammond. He wrote, "Hammond was a music man through and through . . . He talked the same language as me, knew everything about the music he liked, all the artists he had recorded. He said what he meant and he meant what he said and could back it all up. Hammond was no bullshitter."

Dylan said Hammond's offer was especially gratifying because "the folk labels had all turned me down." The Shelton and Scaduto biographies corroborate that account (Shelton wrote that Dylan was rejected by Elektra, Folkways, and Vanguard), as did George Avakian, a contemporary of Hammond's who was also working as an A&R (artists and repertoire) man at the time. Far from being impressed by Dylan's hobo shtick, Avakian was turned off by it. "I must say in the case of Dylan it was a very bold move to make at the time because . . . [when] Dylan first came to New York . . . I was doubtful as to whether to sign him or not. I got a feeling that, gee, this guy is a bit of a phony because he came out with a brakeman's cap and big work boots and, you know, looking like a real bum, and what he did was that twangy country singing about God knows what," he recalled four decades later.

Avakian, himself a top producer and talent spotter (he had helped coax Miles Davis off heroin and later signed him to Columbia Records), found Dylan's idiosyncrasies annoying. "I didn't see [Dylan] as somebody who could be big. He was just somebody who was so offbeat, and the mere fact that he looked so grubby and sounded so whiny made me think that he's going to appeal to a certain class of record buyer. But how big was the class? This big?" Avakian shrugged his shoulders dismissively and held his hands in front of him about six inches apart.

Hammond claimed to have acted on little more than instinct, telling Scaduto:

So he came in and made some demos. He did "Talking New York" as the first one, and when I heard him I flipped. I told him I wanted him to record for Columbia, and I had the contract drawn up. We sat in my office and I said, "How old are you?" and he said he was twenty (which was true) and I said, "I have to get your contract signed by your parents" and he said,

"I don't have any parents." I asked, "Do you have any relatives?" and he said, "Yes, I have an uncle who's a dealer in Las Vegas," and he added, "John, don't worry, you can trust me." He had a romantic point of view at this time. As Bob Dylan he had no parents. He said he had no manager and I told him, "I'll get you the best deal possible from the company. We usually start an artist at two per cent of royalties but I'll start you at four." It was unprecedented to start him at four. Seeger was getting five, and he was established.

Dylan described the same scene: "John Hammond put a contract down in front of me—the standard one they give to any new artist. He said, 'Do you know what this is?' I looked at the top page which said Columbia Records, and I said 'Where do I sign?' Hammond showed me where and I wrote my name down with a steady hand. I trusted him. Who wouldn't? There were maybe a thousand kings in the world and he was one of them."

During that same meeting, according to Dylan, Hammond gave him a copy of a Robert Johnson album that Columbia was about to release. The album had a profound effect on him, Dylan said. "From the first note the vibrations from the loudspeaker made my hair stand up," he wrote. He said he played the album over and over during the next few weeks, astonished by Johnson's guitar playing and transfixed by the complexity of the dark lyrics. (Dylan's experience was apparently shared by many. The album, *King of the Delta Blues Singers*, was a reissue of songs recorded by Johnson in 1936 and 1937. Produced by Frank Driggs under Hammond's supervision, the record has been credited with rekindling interest in country blues in the early 1960s, and with helping Johnson attain legendary status.)

Dylan's first album was recorded in November 1961, about two months after he and Hammond first met. The record was completed in just three or four recording sessions. Hammond told Robert Shelton that he essentially left Dylan alone to make his music. "I had no direction on him at all because I felt Bob was a poet, somebody who could communicate with his generation. Now, Columbia was not known for doing that at the time. I thought, the less a record producer interferes, the better results we'd get from Bob." According to Hammond's paperwork filed with Columbia, the album cost just $402 to produce. It's easy to see why. Dylan arrived for the sessions with his acoustic guitar, his harmonica, and his girlfriend, Suze Rotolo. Hammond's only instructions seem to have been to remind Dylan to stand back from the microphone so as to reduce the abrasive sound caused when Dylan pronounced words with the letter p in them. Dylan told an early biographer, "There was a violent, angry emotion running through me then. I just played guitar and harmonica and sang those songs, and that was it. Mr. Hammond asked me if I wanted to sing any of them over again and I said no. I can't see myself singing the same song twice in a row. That's terrible."

The quotation is impressive but untrue. Dylan may well have been a violent and angry guy in those days, but the performances don't necessarily reflect that. Indeed, only during "House of the Rising Sun" does he seem to emanate genuine anger. Instead, on "Talkin' New York" and "Pretty Peggy-O," there is abundant evidence of his ear for humor, and "Song to Woody" and "In My Time of Dyin'" are achingly sincere. Like most folk singers, Dylan tended to adopt whatever persona was required by the song he happened to be singing. Hammond also contradicted Dylan's description of the sessions, telling one of Dylan's biographers, "He was just a doll in the studio. He was completely inexperienced, popping every P, but he was so enthusiastic."

The part about Dylan refusing to do more than one take is also contradicted by Hammond's session sheets, which are included in his papers at Yale University. What remains of his notes taken during the sessions indicates that virtually all of the songs on the album required more than one take. The quotation does, however, capture the spare and spontaneous mood Hammond was seeking to create on vinyl.

The album, released in late February 1962 and titled simply *Bob Dylan*, contained thirteen songs, only two written by Dylan himself, "Talkin' New York" and "Song to Woody." The former, a story told by a rube arriving in New York City for the first time, is gloriously descriptive, sardonic without being bitter, and often flat-out hilarious.

Nat Hentoff, an old friend of Hammond's who by 1962 was writing regularly for *The Village Voice*, recalled getting a phone call from Hammond around the time *Bob Dylan* was released. "He really wanted me to listen to Dylan's first album. He wanted me to listen to the lyrics.

I saw something there, but it was only after John made me listen to the album that I started paying attention. The characteristics that John Hammond looked for in an artist were feeling and passion. He heard these things in Dylan. He heard something distinctive in Dylan—the message that came through the sound," Hentoff explained many years later.

Hentoff, it turned out, was merely one of the first of many people whom Hammond would badger before they would become as convinced as he was of Dylan's genius.

13

THE A&R MAN

S he flopped on Columbia—five years of mishandling," said the Atlantic Records founder Ahmet Ertegun, a longtime friend of Hammond's, referring to Aretha Franklin. "You see, John discovered her, but he was not really a producer. And the people who were producing her, or whoever was in charge, whatever they did, they did not understand where her greatness lay."

There is no single reason why Franklin's career foundered at Columbia. And if blame is to be correctly apportioned, it should be allotted evenly among Hammond and the handful of other producers with whom Franklin worked on the eight records she released for the label between 1960 and 1966, when she departed for Ertegun's Atlantic label. Simply put, no one at Columbia seemed to know what to do with her, so they tried everything.

Hammond and Franklin's working relationship was strained almost from the start, and it was over after working together on just two albums. Depending on who tells the story, Hammond either relinquished his role or was removed as her producer after the release of her second album in early 1962. But the writing began to appear on the wall just a few months after Franklin signed with Columbia. According to Hammond's Columbia correspondence, friction arose after he began to chafe at what he perceived as Franklin's immaturity. Talent wasn't the only characteristic he sought in the musicians he put his weight behind. He also demanded that they act as professionals, and he seems to have sensed early on from Franklin a lack of commitment and professionalism.

Hints of his concerns, couched in his typical ebullience, started to crop up in letters to Franklin's Detroit-based handlers as early as January 1961, just about six months after she signed with Columbia. "I'm happy to report that Aretha's new record, 'Won't Be Long,' looks as if it is going to be one of the biggest records in the country. In less than two weeks we have already sold 40,000 and it hasn't even begun to reach its potential. Last week we completed her album and all I can say is that everything she does turns to gold. There hasn't been a singer and performer like this in 20 years. The talent is all there, but of course it still needs very close supervision," Hammond wrote.

By early 1962 it had become clear that the two couldn't continue working together. During the previous twelve months, correspondence between them had grown increasingly terse because, according to Hammond, Franklin had missed numerous commitments, both in the studio and at live performances. The tension fairly seeps from a letter he sent to Detroit in early 1962: "Here is your royalty statement from Columbia up through Dec. 31, 1961. The sales of 'I Surrender Dear' [the first single from Franklin's second album] are not included in the statement so you will see that because of the heavy costs of recording sessions and the fact that we were unable to issue another album before now, you have not recouped your advances." The letter continued: "I must say you chose a very bad time to develop a throat problem. It has been very difficult to book you in New York after your not showing up for your first Apollo date and now you didn't show up for your commitment at the Village Gate. If you don't straighten up soon you will be a legend in the business and not one of the nice ones."

Franklin's response couldn't be located among Hammond's personal papers, so her precise wording is unknown. What is certain is that she no longer wanted him to work as her producer.

Now the gloves came off. Hammond wrote back: "I did not understand your telegram dismissing me as your recording agent since, of course, I have never been an agent of yours in any way, shape, or manner. I am employed by Columbia Records as a producer and I can assure you that Columbia intends to enforce all the provisions of its contract with you."

Then, in more conciliatory tones, he wrote: "We do hope to hear from you soon so that we can make more recordings without me as your producer."

Two things are clear from this correspondence. First, despite efforts by Hammond and Franklin over the next several decades to sugarcoat their conflicts while working together, it was a rocky relationship. Second, Hammond's own words contradict his often-asserted claim that Columbia arbitrarily replaced him as Franklin's producer while he and his wife, Esme, were away on a European vacation.

It's entirely possible that Hammond told his own version and skipped the truth and its more lurid details so as not to publicly embarrass Franklin. It's also possible that the truth was blurred to allow both him and Franklin to save face in the wake of a professional relationship that just didn't work. It was much easier, of course, for everyone involved to place the blame on a big, faceless corporation. Whatever the reasons for telling it, Hammond's version—as these stories have a way of doing—has been passed along over the years and accepted as fact.

Hammond elaborated a bit on his own embellished version in his autobiography, tying his removal as Franklin's producer to a perception among the younger executives at Columbia that his particular genius lay in finding talent, not necessarily producing it. Ironically, that was in fact the truth. Naturally, he didn't agree with this perception, and it's easy to understand why.

Hammond was by then considered among the top A&R men in the business, and not without good reason. As the record industry grew into a billion-dollar business in the four decades since its birth in the 1920s, the A&R man had become something of an iconic figure—and Hammond was the archetype. It was the A&R man's responsibility to go out and find the talent, sign that talent, and then nurture it to its full potential. By the early 1960s, Hammond had found, signed, and nurtured an impressive array of artists.

Thus a good A&R man was expected to spot the one talented singer among the hundreds performing nightly in the speakeasies that dotted New York City during Prohibition. He should also be able to hear the visionary guitarist in an otherwise dismal jazz band rambling around the Southwest. A good A&R man could also handpick the real poet among the scores of young poseurs smoking cigarettes and guzzling red wine in Greenwich Village in the early 1960s. This was the bar set by John Hammond.

Even Hammond's detractors, those who for whatever reasons felt he got more credit than he deserved, have never seriously challenged his uncanny ability to spot raw talent. But the perception that he didn't know what to do with that talent once he got in the studio was more widespread than he might have been aware. Indeed, several of his peers—some of them big admirers—thought as much. "John was involved with the music . . . [but] he was not a very good producer," observed the former Columbia executive Robert Altshuler. "And one of the reasons he never made big money in the music industry—and men were making big, big money—was because, although he had these incredible ears and the ability to recognize talent at its earliest stage, at its embryotic stage, he was not very good at producing."

A defining difference between the producers who emerged in the 1960s, men such as Jerry Wexler, Phil Spector, Tom Dowd, and Terry Melcher, and Hammond's contemporaries during his jazz heyday in the 1930s was that this new breed had far more input into how the final product sounded. In some cases, these men—Spector, for example—wrote the music and actually played on the songs. For their efforts, they received royalties, and some of them became very wealthy. That was not the case in the 1930s.

Besides, Hammond's talents were less quantifiable. Even Goddard Lieberson, one of Hammond's oldest and closest friends in the business, offered a backhanded compliment with regard to Hammond's unique gifts. In a 1968 memo requesting Columbia's PR people to generate articles on Hammond, Lieberson wrote, "The story, which I believe is an interesting one, should be told of his great gift for recognizing talent, and he should be described as the unique A&R man who is not tied to the recording studio (in fact, his time should not be spent there at all), but who is a man able to 'listen' and recognize the sounds around him."

Ahmet Ertegun recalled bumping into Hammond regularly in the 1950s at a Manhattan recording studio right across the street from Carnegie Hall. "After I started Atlantic Records and I was producing a lot of records then, I'd run into John from time to time. You know, we'd be in adjacent studios in New York. I remember he would be *produc-*

ing some singer or another. [Ertegun placed an exaggerated emphasis on the word 'producing' so that the listener would understand the word didn't really apply.] But he was not a *producer* producer. I'd walk in and the singer would be singing and he'd be reading *The New York Times*." Ertegun shook with laughter at the memory.

In defense of his friend, Ertegun noted that the role of the record producer in the early 1960s was very different from when Hammond had first made a name for himself producing jazz records in the 1930s. The person who supervised recording sessions for the likes of Benny Goodman, Teddy Wilson, and Count Basie, and later Ruby Braff, Buck Clayton, and Mel Powell, played a very different role in the studio, according to Ertegun, from the person supervising the raw talent that record companies were signing and promoting in the 1960s. Yet both people were called producers. "Nobody produced those [early jazz] sessions. That role emerged in the sixties," said Ertegun. "Back then . . . the bandleader would determine the introduction choruses, the solos, where Billie [Holiday] came in, and so forth. Benny Goodman and Teddy Wilson didn't need a producer."

Advancements in technology also put Hammond at a distinct disadvantage. The new crop of producers coming up in the late 1950s and early 1960s were not only familiar with such techniques as overdubbing—laying tracks recorded separately on top of one another to create a single, blended sound—most of them actually enjoyed fiddling with the knobs and mastering the ever more complicated soundboards favored by the large record companies. Hammond, meanwhile, was outspoken in his disdain for much of the new technology, dismissing it as gimmickry used to cover up a singer's or musician's lack of talent. He favored recording the old-fashioned way, the way he had always recorded—by placing a single microphone in the center of the studio and letting the musicians play.

One could also argue that because Hammond never envisioned Franklin as a pop star, it's unfair to criticize him for her failure to achieve superstardom under his tutelage at Columbia. According to a Franklin biographer, Hammond made it abundantly clear to both Franklin and her manager, Jo King, that he intended to cast her in the mold of a Billie Holiday or an Ella Fitzgerald—in other words, as a jazz/pop chanteuse. Yet despite a rival offer from RCA, whose producers wanted to record her as a rhythm and blues artist, Franklin jumped at the deal offered by Columbia, very likely prompted by the opportunity to work with John Hammond.

Notwithstanding the conflicts in their professional relationship, the fruit of their collaboration was a lovely if not necessarily coherent collection of jazzy and bluesy tunes that in no way detracts from Franklin's lengthy career as a popular-music icon. To the contrary, each of the twelve songs on her first album for Columbia, *Aretha*, serves as a powerful indicator of what would follow later in the decade. Taken individually, each performance reflects a maturity and sophistication well beyond the singer's years. "Won't Be Long" has a raucous brazenness to it that would have fit hand in glove on any of Franklin's late-1960s albums at Atlantic. "Love Is the Only Thing" is pure pop but memorable for its spare yet sophisticated arrangement. On "Over the Rainbow," Franklin's vocals glide easily over the gorgeous spare arrangement, highlighted by Ray Bryant's gently elegant piano. Franklin's version of this classic show tune holds its own against any of the countless others recorded over the years. It's pure jazz and pure Hammond. "Are You Sure?" takes Franklin straight back to her gospel roots in her father's church in Detroit.

Hammond's favorite of these first twelve was "Today I Sing the Blues," the song on which he first heard Franklin exercise her remarkable voice. The Columbia version is notable for the stinging blues guitar of Lord Westbrook, and the utter confidence with which Franklin mines territory once almost exclusively the terrain of Bessie Smith and Franklin's idol, Dinah Washington.

Despite the high quality of the recordings, *Aretha* didn't sell particularly well. The general consensus handed down over the years by pop-music historians and industry types is that record buyers were confused by the eclectic grouping of songs. "Columbia just couldn't find the handle. I thought they had made some beautiful recordings there. But they never found [Franklin's] essence. They tried the Vegas route, and they wanted her to be Judy Garland. What worked was simply to put her at the piano and frame her with a powerful rhythm section," said Jerry Wexler, the rhythm and blues producer credited with helping Franklin find her singular voice at Atlantic Records.

Following the release of *Aretha*, Franklin spent much of 1961 touring small jazz clubs. The unfamiliar setting made her uncomfortable, according to one of her biographers. She told Mark Bego, "I was afraid. I sang to the floor a lot."

Still, Hammond remained determined to groom her as a jazz singer. On her next album for Columbia, *The Electrifying Aretha Franklin*, he chose to back her on several numbers with a big band, presenting her this time as a direct descendant of Mildred Bailey, Helen Humes, or Peggy Lee. This was another collection of classy songs, each one an eminently suitable vehicle for displaying Franklin's remarkable ability. But, again, the lack of coherence proved distracting and the album sold poorly.

Franklin, working with at least three different producers after Hammond stepped away, would record another half-dozen albums at Columbia, and all of them were plagued by the same lack of coherence, an inability to create for her a signature sound, as her first two. Each new producer seemed to be asking himself, "Who is this artist?" Was she another Billie Holiday, another Judy Garland, or perhaps another Barbra Streisand? No one seemed to know.

Clive Davis recalled in his 1975 memoir the lesson he learned from Columbia's mishandling of Franklin while he was still a young attorney at the label:

> An artist can be extremely gifted and yet remain unsuccessful if he or she records the wrong music, or gets an image that confuses potential audiences. The best example of this was Columbia's painful inability to break Aretha Franklin . . . She was recorded by both black and white producers: everyone knew she was a brilliant talent. But nothing much happened. She was very young then and needed professional guidance: yet no one found the right songs for her.

With the Franklin debacle seared into his memory, Davis claimed that after becoming the head of Columbia in the late 1960s, he never signed an artist until he knew exactly what direction the label planned to take.

At Atlantic Records, meanwhile, Jerry Wexler let Franklin decide for herself who she was. In his autobiography, *Rhythm and the Blues*, Wexler explained:

> Clearly Aretha was continuing what Ray Charles had begun— the secularization of gospel, turning church rhythms, church patterns, and especially church feelings into personalized love songs. Like Ray, Aretha was a hands-on performer, a two-fisted pianist plugged into the main circuit of Holy Ghost power. Even though we produced Aretha in a way that we never produced Ray, she remained the central orchestrator of her own sound, the essential contributor and final arbiter of what fit or did not fit her musical persona.

For her part, Franklin has never spoken badly of Hammond in public, and she apparently doesn't look back with any regret at the years she spent zigzagging among genres at Columbia. She told an interviewer, "It wasn't selling, but I liked very much what I did at Columbia. When I went to Atlantic, they just sat me down at the piano and let me do my thing. The hits started coming."

Hammond also seems to have harbored no ill will toward Franklin for their disagreements during their eighteen-month professional relationship, nor did he ever publicly express resentment toward her subsequent success at Atlantic. To the contrary, he seems to have been genuinely happy for her, and their relationship flourished after they parted ways professionally. "You have always been a very special favorite of mine and I will never forget the excitement of those early days ten and eleven years ago," he wrote her in 1971. "Hope all goes well with you and I'm thrilled that you have found your proper home at Atlantic with my old friend Jerry [Wexler]. My very best to you, John." The two maintained warm relations right up to Hammond's death. In 1972, Hammond wrote the liner notes for what would emerge as one of Franklin's most popular and critically acclaimed albums. The pure gospel songs on *Amazing Grace* were recorded live inside a crowded church under the direction of the renowned choir director James Cleveland. Franklin had come full circle—she was back in church. Ironically, the album was precisely the kind of album Hammond was recording with the Abyssinian Baptist Gospel Choir in Newark around the time he began courting Franklin for Columbia. Perhaps their history together—and the history of pop music—would have been different if Hammond had simply invited Franklin to come along with him to Newark.

Although his critics like to cite Franklin's struggle at Columbia as a glaring example of a Hammond failure, Hammond himself found vindication in Franklin's eventual phenomenal success. He always felt she would become a star; it just didn't happen under his watch. Besides, once Franklin became a star at Atlantic in the late 1960s, Columbia wasted no time in capitalizing on her success by repackaging her recordings on two greatest-hits volumes and releasing several albums of old unreleased material that had been stored away in the company vaults. Thus Columbia benefited (and continues to benefit) rather handsomely from Hammond's decision in 1960 to aggressively pursue the then-unproven Aretha Franklin.

Meanwhile, Hammond's other top priority at Columbia, Bob Dylan, was also giving him headaches. Signing Dylan to Columbia proved to be the easy part. Keeping him signed was more difficult.

Albert Grossman was the primary reason. Grossman wasn't yet a factor in Dylan's career during the recording of *Bob Dylan* in the fall of 1961. In fact, Dylan had no manager, essentially trusting men like Hammond and Harold Leventhal. A talent manager originally from Chicago, Grossman arrived in New York in the midst of the folk revival. In short order, he was representing some of the biggest names in folk, including the hit-making trio Peter, Paul, and Mary. He would eventually become as well known as many of his clients, a larger-than-life figure who represented different things to different people. Some considered him little more than a hustler, intent on wringing from his artists' musical talent every dime he could possibly get. Others viewed him as a powerful force of nature who intuitively recognized genuine talent and had the will and wherewithal to get that talent heard—and possibly even make that talent rich. Perhaps the most widely held characterization of Grossman was derived from his appearance in *Don't*

Look Back, D. A. Pennebaker's incendiary documentary film of Dylan's 1965 tour of England. In the movie Grossman comes off as a monstrously arrogant Svengali, lording his influence with Dylan over cowering reporters and concert promoters.

According to at least two of Dylan's biographers, Grossman set his sights on the musician the moment he signed with Columbia. It didn't take him long to convince Dylan that he needed representation and that he, Grossman, was the man best positioned to perform that role. He became Dylan's manager in mid-1962, not long after the release of *Bob Dylan*.

Hammond's relationship with Dylan changed abruptly and dramatically as soon as Grossman entered the picture. In late September 1962, Hammond got a curt letter from Dylan demanding that his contract with Columbia be torn up and everything he ever recorded for the label returned to him because the contract had been signed when he was still a minor. Hammond was understandably startled by the request, since Dylan had never expressed displeasure with the contract.

After calling one of Columbia's lawyers for advice, Hammond invited Dylan over for a talk. The lawyer was Clive Davis, then a young Harvard Law School graduate who had migrated into the music industry in 1960 after growing bored with corporate law. Davis later recalled Hammond's anxious response to his legal opinion that yes, Dylan probably could void the contract if he had signed it when he was only twenty. According to Davis, he asked the producer how solid his relationship with Dylan was, and when Hammond said it was strong, he suggested that he use all his powers of persuasion to convince Dylan that Columbia was behind him. The day after he received the disturbing letter, Hammond was able to persuade Dylan in a private meeting to renounce his earlier demand to have the contract voided.

The matter wasn't exactly settled, though. A few days after the meeting, Dylan returned to Hammond's office, this time with Grossman. When they left, there was a brand-new, potentially far more lucrative deal. Hammond had agreed to tear up Dylan's existing five-year contract, which was by then a year old, and replace it with an amended five-year deal that increased Dylan's royalties from 4 percent to 5 percent. And Hammond agreed to this even though *Bob Dylan* was not selling well—about five thousand copies in its first year of release, or just enough for Columbia to recoup its expenses. Like him or not, Hammond had to acknowledge that Grossman was a savvy business-man. In a memo to his superiors at Columbia seeking approval of the new contract, Hammond noted that Grossman had made a strong ar-gument in favor of tendering a revised contract to Dylan. "Grossman made the following point," he wrote; "there is a statutory limitation of 3 years duration for contracts signed by minors in New York State." In other words, unless Columbia did something to appease Dylan, they risked losing him in two years.

In his memoirs, Dylan tells a different version. Grossman, he wrote, advised him to refute his original contract and tell Hammond that Grossman was ready to negotiate a new one. "I went up to see Mr. Hammond, but I had no intentions of doing that," Dylan wrote.

> Not if I had been offered a fortune would I have done it. Ham-mond had believed in me and had backed up his belief, had given me my first start on the world's stage, and no one, not even Grossman, had anything to do with that. There was no way I'd go against him for Grossman, not in a million years. I knew that the contract would have to be straightened out, though, so I went to see him. The mere mention of Grossman's name just about gave him apoplexy. He didn't like him, said he was as dirty as they come and was sorry Grossman was representing me, though he said he'd still be supportive.

At that, according to Dylan, Hammond called in Clive Davis and a new contract was produced, which he signed on the spot.

Still, there was no guarantee Columbia's top executives would sign off on the new deal. More than a few veterans of the label, men who had gotten rich maintaining Columbia's middle-of-the-road reputation, argued—not without some merit—that Dylan couldn't sing, couldn't play harmonica, and couldn't play guitar. Davis, in an early memoir, recalled, "[Dylan's] first album didn't sell well and, outside of Ham-mond and a few others, most people at Columbia thought he was a freak, at least a 'different' performer."

What Hammond knew that the others did not was that Dylan was a talented and increasingly prolific songwriter. According to Robert

Shelton, in the months following the release of his first album Dylan was encouraged by Pete Seeger to concentrate on a new genre of song-writing, a genre that would come to be known as protest music. "Blowin' in the Wind," "Masters of War," and "A Hard Rain's A-Gonna Fall" were all written during this period.

Thus, undeterred by his colleagues' skepticism, Hammond launched a campaign of support for Dylan. "I want to point out that Bob is a very hot song writer and Tennessee Ernie Ford and The Kingston Trio, among others, are recording his material . . . I have enormous faith in Bob Dylan and think he will be the most important young folk artist in the business," Hammond wrote on October 9, 1962, in a memo distrib-uted to his bosses. Reluctantly, Columbia signed off on the amended deal. But it would be another year or so before Hammond's absolute faith in this enigmatic young talent was shared by the label's decision makers. During this period, many of Hammond's colleagues at Colum-bia—even the younger guys who shared space with him in the A&R department—snickered behind his back and referred to Dylan fa-mously as "Hammond's Folly."

Colleagues recalled that when Hammond was enthusiastic about one of his artists, he tended to be adamant in his desire that others share his enthusiasm. According to Robert Altshuler, Hammond had talked up Dylan quite a bit to his fellow A&R men at Columbia, and some of them could not resist the opportunity to make fun of Ham-mond when Dylan did not immediately live up to his hyperbole.

In his own memoirs, Hammond recalled battling with his immedi-ate boss, David Kapralik, who, as vice president of Columbia's artists and repertoire department, had a great deal of influence over which of Columbia's artists got the label's full backing. According to Ham-mond, at some point early in Dylan's career, probably around the time of the contract dispute in the fall of 1962, Kapralik threatened to drop Dylan from the label. "Over my dead body," Hammond claimed to have responded.

In hindsight, Hammond looks like a genius and Kapralik comes off as the goat. But several people who worked for Columbia at the time have suggested that Kapralik was entirely justified in second-guessing some of Hammond's decisions. After all, despite Hammond's track record for finding raw talent, he wasn't having much success producing that talent and transforming it into record sales. Aretha Franklin was a glaring case in point. Her albums weren't selling well, and now Dylan's first album was gathering dust in record stores. Kapralik also had bosses, and they demanded that he keep an eye on the bottom line.

Fortunately for Hammond, Kapralik may have been his boss, but he wasn't Hammond's rabbi. That role was filled by Columbia's president, Goddard Lieberson.

"Goddard Lieberson was the head of the company, the legendary head of the company," observed Altshuler, who was in a position to know the depth of Hammond and Lieberson's relationship. In the early 1960s, Lieberson, according to Altshuler, was starting to get pressure from Columbia's parent company, CBS, to tap into the huge youth market that was spending its allowance on records. Columbia had all but ignored this lucrative market, targeting instead the parents. And Lieberson, who had spent much of the previous twenty years developing Columbia's classical catalog and knew next to nothing about rhythm and blues or folk, let alone rock and roll, was an unlikely person to spearhead the move. Moreover, his immediate underlings, the men who inhabited Columbia's corporate suites, were as decidedly unhip to the youth movement under way in America as he was.

The one person Lieberson did trust to go out and find artists who would appeal to younger audiences was his old friend John Hammond—the man with whom he had toured the South in the summer of 1938 in search of authentic American music, and, perhaps more important, the man who had helped him land his first job at Columbia. Lieberson not only never forgot the boost Hammond had given his career; he also never lost faith in Hammond's musical intuition. With Lieberson behind him, Hammond was free to take chances on artists whose appeal was not always obvious.

Johnny Cash, a big seller for Columbia in the early 1960s, also played an important role in the record company's patience with Dylan. "Johnny Cash was one of Dylan's big boosters at Columbia," Hammond told Anthony Scaduto. "Way back there in '62, whenever Dylan was in the studio or playing in town, Cash would come around. They hung around together back then. Johnny dug me because I brought Seeger to the company, and I brought Dylan to the company, and he was behind me all the way. Cash was behind Dylan every which way, everybody in the company knew it. Cash made it known he thought Dylan was a giant. There's no higher recommendation possible."

Hammond's Columbia peers may have been skeptical about Dylan's commercial potential because many of them had never seen him perform live. Thus they had never seen how Dylan mesmerized audiences with his unique mix of earnest passion, sly charm, and not-so-subtle provocation. Dylan has always preferred to challenge his audiences—at times pushing them to the brink of hostility—rather than gift wrap for them a comfortable evening of mindless entertainment. Audiences either loved him or hated him, and that's apparently what Dylan wanted. The skeptics at Columbia who may have witnessed a Dylan performance at some point or another simply didn't get it. These were men who, for better or worse, enjoyed Andy Williams and Barbra Streisand. Hammond, who recognized Dylan's visceral appeal both as an artist with a message and as a calculating and charismatic provocateur, got it right away.

Tapping directly into the unrest bubbling up among the youth of America in the early 1960s, Dylan seemed to reflexively blend a heady brew of earnest protest, an aloofness that was paradoxically magnetic, and a witty, Chaplinesque flair for slapstick. There was a little something for everyone. One of the more revealing anecdotes in terms of illustrating his consummate control over an audience is included in David Hajdu's book *Positively 4th Street*, which recalls the ambitious young musicians who sang, screwed, and smoked their way to the top of the folk scene in the early 1960s. (A slightly different version of the same anecdote is recounted by the folk singer Eric von Schmidt in Scaduto's biography.)

Dylan, according to the story, was hanging out in a pub in London with pals and fellow folk singers von Schmidt, Richard Fariña, and Ethan Signer when someone pulled out a bag of marijuana and offered them some. A short while later, Dylan, now exceedingly high and apparently unimpressed with that evening's performer, announced, "Fuck this. Let's go up and play." The musicians performed several songs together, but eventually the others melted away, leaving Dylan alone on a stool with a guitar. While fingerpicking the chords to a new tune, "Don't Think Twice, It's All Right," he began to mumble, "My fingers are moving sooo slooww."

The audience is captured now, both by the hypnotic rhythm of the rolling chords and by Dylan's mesmerizing balancing act between genuine performance and embarrassing mistake. The audience was uncertain which experience they were about to witness. Nevertheless, they had to have been thinking that whoever this guy is he's clearly got a lot of nerve while at the same time wondering if he was too loaded to pull it off. "Where are we—are we underwater?" Dylan sputtered. "We're all underwater. We're in a submarine." The audience seemed to be following Dylan into his murky, surreal vision. Then, almost as if on cue, a heckler shouted something at Dylan, jarring everyone back to reality, and Dylan used the shift in momentum to segue seamlessly into the first lines of the song: "Well, it ain't no use to sit and wonder why, babe "

While creating the illusion that he might spin out of control at any time, Dylan was in fact in total control, manipulating the crowd in order to maximize the emotional impact of his performance. It was virtuoso and seems to have been at least partly instinctual.

Another Dylan trick was to win over an audience by merging with them, in effect by creating the illusion that he was one of them and that any one of them could be him. One method for accomplishing this was to borrow a harmonica from someone in the audience. Dylan had learned the trick from other folk singers, and he had honed it in the small clubs in Dinkytown, the bohemian neighborhood near the University of Minnesota campus where he began his career. He later perfected the technique in Greenwich Village and Cambridge cafés, using it to create a feeling of intimacy and shared purpose.

These anecdotes point up the intangibles that have mesmerized Dylan's fans and confounded his skeptics for over four decades. Hammond had a gift for recognizing intangibles. So what that Dylan couldn't sing or play guitar or harmonica? He struck a nerve, a powerful nerve, and Hammond sensed it right away. "I always said one thing about John—that he was the youngest man in the record business right until the day he died. I always thought of him as a great, great example that age really doesn't mean a goddamned thing so long as you really have ears and you have enthusiasm," said Bruce Lundvall, a Columbia executive from 1960 through 1982. "John's credo really had nothing to do with commercial or pop records or anything like that. What John was always excited about was the original voice. Not only the singing voice but the original voice instrumentally as well. And when he heard something that excited him and that he felt was new and fresh and qualitatively very good, he just went for it. I learned from that, and he became my mentor in a very real way, one of two or three mentors in my life in the business. He taught me that when you hear somebody that has originality, you just sign him, you don't start asking questions about, well, can we sell enough records, how will we market this, will this get played on the radio—any of that nonsense. That means you're just doing pop confections. Dylan represented something really fresh and raw, and John heard that. He heard the lyrics; he heard what he was singing about. And he believed fervently in Bob and, of course, the rest is history."

Hammond didn't have to wait long for his vindication. It began early in 1963 when "Blowin' in the Wind," written almost a year earlier, became a big hit for the popular folk group Peter, Paul, and Mary. The song posed a number of searching questions, and its wistful refrain—"The answer, my friend, is blowin' in the wind. The answer is blowin' in the wind"—suggested that the solutions to those questions were elusive but ultimately there for the grabbing. People just needed to reach out and take hold. By the time *The Freewheelin' Bob Dylan* was available in record stores in mid-1963, the song, by now the centerpiece of every Peter, Paul, and Mary concert, had emerged as an anthem for the exploding civil rights movement.

Freewheelin' sold much better than Dylan's first album. According to Scaduto's biography, it sold about ten thousand copies a month through the second half of 1963. But there was another important difference between the two albums: all of the songs on *Freewheelin'* were written by Dylan. Here, then, was Hammond's faith fulfilled in approximately fifty minutes of music. "Blowin' in the Wind," "A Hard Rain's A-Gonna Fall," "Oxford Town," and "Masters of War" established Dylan as the songwriter of record for the civil rights movement, a visionary prodigy who saw through the establishment's lies. The love songs, meanwhile, "Girl from the North Country," "Don't Think Twice, It's All Right," and "Corrina, Corrina," revealed a vulnerable side to this earnest, articulate young troubadour—the vulnerable side in us all. The songs on *Freewheelin'* thrust Dylan into the role he would spend a good portion of the rest of his career trying to shake—that of the voice of his generation. It was the last album Hammond and Dylan worked on together.

It would be stretching things to suggest that John Hammond ever served as Bob Dylan's mentor. Bob Dylan never really had a mentor, notwithstanding perhaps his spiritual mentor, Woody Guthrie. He took what he needed from artists he admired and synthesized those à la carte items with his own unique vision. And he was driven like few other popular musicians of his era—or any other era, for that matter. It wasn't enough to be successful. He was successful by the time he was twenty-two. Bob Dylan was determined to expand his music beyond conventional standards. If his audience followed him, that was fine. But he was going there anyway. No A&R man, no producer, no record company executive—not even Albert Grossman—could have blocked his path.

Hammond recognized these unique qualities in Dylan and always held him slightly in awe, although at times that awe sounded a lot like wariness. The contract renegotiation probably contributed to Hammond's wariness toward Dylan, for he recognized early that Dylan was no wide-eyed babe in the woods and would do whatever it took to achieve his goals, be they social, musical, or financial. Hammond certainly admired those qualities, even identified with them. Nevertheless, for whatever reason, the two men never developed a close relationship. But then again, how many people can say they've developed a close relationship with Bob Dylan?

None of this altered Hammond's respect for Dylan's talent. Quite simply, he considered Dylan a genius. But it was a crafty kind of genius, a bit calculated, even manipulative, in any event different from the naked talent of a Billie Holiday or a Charlie Christian.

"Bob Dylan is a great and original artist and I doubt that he has ever been sincere in his life. Strangely enough that did not take away from his artistry although it does separate him from the completely sincere people like Pete Seeger and Woody Guthrie," Hammond wrote a curious Dylan fan in 1966.

I would say that Bob always had fantasies about himself. He told me [when the two first met] that he had no parents and that for the past years [*sic*] he had been bumming around on the road. The facts of course were quite different.

Bob was always a tremendously prolific writer and I think that the taste of money agrees with him perfectly.

I certainly was not surprised to see him become the founder of folk rock and I must confess that I like his performance on HIGHWAY 61 REVISITED better than on either of the albums that I produced. I think he is an important poet and I am not disappointed that he has sought a wider audience with his "electric sound." I will not be able to predict that the present Dylan is the final Dylan, but I can remember Pete Seeger saying three years ago that Dylan will be the most important folk singer in America if he doesn't burn himself out first.

Dylan never burned out, and Hammond was right—the Dylan Hammond was writing of in early 1966 was hardly the final Dylan.

Perhaps Hammond's most articulate summation of his admiration for Dylan came in his autobiography:

His genius has been the acuity of his vision of American life, his ability to internalize his observations and experiences, and his artistry in retelling them in a penetrating and dramatic poetry that overwhelms his hearers. With persistence and intensity he has opposed war profiteers, lynchers, racists, and all forms of injustice . . . He helped shape the attitudes of a generation, and God knows his unique and uncompromising albums transformed Columbia Records.

Indeed, the roster of youth-oriented popular artists who followed Dylan to Columbia in the mid-1960s is formidable: Simon and Garfunkel, the Byrds, Janis Joplin, Chicago, Blood, Sweat & Tears, Sly and the Family Stone, Johnny Winter, and Santana, among many others. John Hammond had made the jobs of the very A&R men who had mocked him just a few years earlier a whole lot easier. "Everyone knew that because of Dylan's presence on Columbia, we had a better shot [at signing] other important up-and-coming rock-and-roll artists," observed Robert Altshuler, who ran Columbia's public-relations department through much of the 1960s.

Yet despite Dylan's success and the new direction that success took Columbia—or perhaps because of those things—some older executives remained obstinately perplexed by Dylan's popularity. Altshuler recalled being summoned upstairs sometime around the release of *Highway 61 Revisited* to clear up some confusion over Dylan's name. Apparently, there were still people around Columbia who were referring to him as "Die-lan." Which was it, the executive wanted to know— "Die-lan" or "Dylan"? This was in 1965, when Dylan was almost single-handedly altering the sound of pop music, not to mention selling many hundreds of thousands of albums for Columbia Records. "He and his own people didn't know that it was Dylan," Altshuler recalled in astonishment. "I realized then and there this is not a very hip guy."

Hammond may not have always understood Dylan's specific musical decisions, but he understood well the larger motivation behind those decisions—he had always been decidedly hip to Dylan's ambition. His admiration for Dylan as an artist helped to maintain a respectful relationship that lasted long after their professional careers diverged.

Consider two men sitting together in box seats at Shea Stadium during the 1969 World Series. The courtly older man, sporting his signature crew cut and dressed in a rumpled tweed sport coat from Brooks Brothers, holds a stack of left-wing magazines and newspapers in his lap. He leans in close to his younger friend so that his words can be heard over the roar of the crowd. The younger man is wearing jeans and a black leather jacket, his mop of curly brown hair is partly concealed by a knit wool cap. John Hammond and Bob Dylan, eating hot dogs and Cracker Jack together while watching the New York Mets play the Baltimore Orioles on a crisp fall afternoon.

Hammond and Albert Grossman had butted heads throughout the *Freewheelin'* sessions (Hammond complained that Grossman was so controlling he even told Dylan where to stand while performing in the studio), and Grossman eventually lobbied successfully to have Hammond replaced as producer of Dylan's third album, *The Times They Are A-Changin'*. Thoroughly disgusted by Grossman's behavior, Hammond relinquished his role without a fight. A young African-American producer named Tom Wilson was asked to step in. Wilson had helped out on several of the tracks on *Freewheelin'*, most notably the songs on which Dylan began using electric instruments. (Robert Shelton called "Mixed Up Confusion," recorded during the *Freewheelin'* sessions with Wilson as producer, the very first folk-rock song. A backup band using electric instruments was also used on the song "Rocks and Gravel.")

In hindsight, the decision to replace Hammond was probably right. Hammond, by his own admission, would have been satisfied to have Dylan continue to record alone with his acoustic guitar. The way he saw it, a backup band using electric instruments detracted from rather than added to the raw power and emotion of an artist like Dylan.

Dylan, of course, had more elaborate plans.

Ironically, it was a song that didn't make it onto *Freewheelin'* rather than one of the scornful, acerbic, accusing songs that did that would haunt Hammond for nearly a decade. The song, "Talkin' John Birch Paranoid Blues," a scathing satire of the far-right-wing organization, was rejected by CBS lawyers, a move Dylan viewed as censorship. Hammond found himself impotent to do anything about it. But before the song was kept off the album, Dylan was told by the same CBS lawyers that he couldn't perform the song on *The Ed Sullivan Show*. That rejection prompted Clive Davis's first face-to-face meeting with Dylan, a meeting he later described as "disastrous." It was disastrous because Dylan was angry; Hammond, who had accompanied him to Davis's office, was embarrassed; and there was nothing Davis could do to placate either.

In May 1963, Dylan was scheduled to appear on Sullivan's widely viewed family-oriented show, which was broadcast on CBS, Columbia's parent company. He decided he would sing the controversial "Talkin' John Birch Paranoid Blues" rather than, say, the already popular and universally praised "Blowin' in the Wind." CBS's lawyers nixed the idea, arguing that the song was libelous: one of the lyrics suggests that

Birch members condoned Adolf Hitler's version of anti-Semitism. Angered by the censorship, Dylan refused to perform on the show at all.
He still thought he could include the song on his second album, however, and when he found out that the CBS lawyers had nixed that as
well, he blew his top. When he arrived at Davis's office with Hammond
in tow, he demanded an explanation. "What is this? What do you mean
I can't come out with this song? You can't edit or censor me!" Davis
was hard-pressed to deliver a satisfactory answer. "It's all bullshit,"
Dylan reportedly exclaimed, and then stormed out of the room.

Hammond was equally frustrated, telling Robert Shelton some
years later: "The CBS lawyers, not Columbia Records, decided that the
reference to Hitler involved every single member of the John Birch
Society, therefore it was libelous, or some crap like that. I get away
with much worse material with Seeger than was ever on a Dylan
album."

(Both Hammond and Davis discussed the incident in their memoirs. Hammond apparently even went so far as to try to talk Dylan into
belatedly rerecording the song in 1070. Out of the blue, seven years
after the fact, a fan from California wrote Hammond seeking an explanation for Columbia's censorship. Still clearly self-conscious about the
episode, he responded to the inquiry and promised he would try to
persuade Dylan to rerecord the song. Dylan apparently declined.)

Hammond always did his level best to help the artists he signed
maintain their artistic integrity, but even he couldn't avoid losing a battle here and there against formidable opponents like the staff attorneys
at CBS. Nevertheless, in the summer of 1963 there were larger battles
to fight, and he wasted no time in turning his sights elsewhere.

14

JACKSON, MISSISSIPPI—
JUNE 15, 1963

On a sweltering day in June 1963, Hammond and his son Jason, now seventeen, attended the funeral of the slain civil rights activist Medgar Wiley Evers in Jackson, Mississippi. Evers, the field secretary for the Mississippi chapter of the NAACP, had been gunned down in front of his home three days earlier. Jammed shoulder to shoulder with several thousand mourners in a Masonic temple hall on Lynch Street in Jackson's black section, Hammond and the others prayed, sang, and wept. Hammond and Jason were among the few white people in attendance.

"There have been martyrs throughout history, in every land and people, in many high causes," Roy Wilkins declared in his eloquent eulogy. "We are here today in tribute to a martyr in the crusade for human liberty, a man struck down in mean and cowardly fashion by a bullet in the back." Prior to delivering the eulogy, Wilkins, the NAACP's executive secretary, had marched through downtown Jackson accompanied by Martin Luther King, Jr. Wearing matching black suits, the two leaders—one representing the old guard of the civil rights movement and the other the new—spoke cordially despite a widening rift (or perhaps just as accurately described as a rivalry) that was developing between Wilkins's NAACP and King's Southern Christian Leadership Conference.

In another four years that rift would split the civil rights movement down the middle, pitting the old guard against the new in terms of goals, rhetoric, and the pace of progress for black Americans. On that blazingly hot day in Mississippi, however, their respective missions were in step. A picture taken of the two leaders as they marched side by side through Jackson shows them sober-faced amid earnest conversation, their shadows almost nonexistent, an indication that a scorching Mississippi sun was directly overhead.

When Wilkins rose to address the mourners, he cast blame for Evers's death not on a lone assassin but on a society founded on racism:

> The lurking assassin at midnight June 11 and 12 pulled the trigger, but in all wars the men who do the shooting are trained and indoctrinated and keyed to action by men and by forces which prod them to act. The Southern political system put him behind that rifle: the lily-white Southern governments, local and state; the Senators, governors, state legislators, mayors, judges, sheriffs, chiefs of police, commissioners, etc. . . . Not content with mere disfranchisement, the officeholders have used unbridled political power to fabricate a maze of laws, customs and economic practices which has imprisoned the Negro.

If Wilkins's speech angered some in the crowd, the bad feelings dissipated during an emotional rendition of "We Shall Overcome."

Outside the temple thousands of additional mourners, most of them young and black, many of whom had never heard of Medgar Evers until his assassination but were shaken out of their complacency by his death, gathered in the midday sun. Their mood, already angry, grew darker. Chants of "After Medgar, No More Fear" hung heavy in the thick June humidity.

When the service was over, a huge procession formed behind the hearse that carried Evers's casket. Thousands of mourners headed toward Collins Funeral Home a mile or so away, where a private service was to be held. While passing through downtown Jackson, the procession encountered police barricades on Capitol Street, the city's main white commercial district. The barricades were put there ostensibly to control the flow of the crowd, but it was obvious that white city officials feared a riot. The march to the Masonic temple for the funeral had gone without incident. But temperatures and emotions had risen in the hours that had since passed.

John and Jason Hammond joined the crowd of marchers slowly making their way from the Masonic temple to the funeral home at the conclusion of the large public service. Once the horse-drawn hearse reached its destination and the casket was carried inside, thousands of mourners were left standing outside in the street. Many simply bowed their heads in respect for Evers. Some wept; others chanted slogans. Within the larger crowd, a smaller group was forming, numbering perhaps several hundred. These mourners, most of them in their teens or early twenties, were clearly growing agitated, and a number of them headed back toward the barricades on Capitol Street.

Verbal exchanges quickly escalated into physical confrontation, and some of the demonstrators were beaten by cops who refused to cede ground. Others in the mob, many of whom hurled rocks and bottles, were attacked by police dogs. The situation was defused only after the Justice Department official John Doar stepped literally into the no-man's-land between the cops and the demonstrators and successfully pleaded for a halt to the violence. A riot of potentially tragic proportions was narrowly avoided.

Hammond, sensing the growing tension, had pulled out of the procession not long before things nearly spun out of control. "It was really scary," Jason Hammond recalled many years later. In his autobiography, John Hammond, who had come to know Evers at NAACP board meetings over the years, reproached himself harshly for what he referred to as a "foolhardy" decision to attend the funeral, a decision that needlessly placed his son in harm's way. He felt compelled to explain himself: "I have never paused long to weigh the consequences when I felt impelled to do something. Like my mother, I see my duty and I move toward my goal, thinking perhaps, like her, that while others may not agree with me at the time their good as well as my own will be served. That is enough for me." It is a revealing statement both in its overt arrogance and in its acknowledgment of overt arrogance.

At the time of Evers's death Hammond was no longer producing Bob Dylan, having been replaced by Tom Wilson. Nevertheless, Dylan was still viewed within the halls of Columbia Records as a Hammond project. Thus Hammond could only have been pleased at Dylan's treatment of Evers's death in the song "Only a Pawn in Their Game," which appeared on this third album, *The Times They Are A-Changin'*.

Rather than taking the conventional approach of lionizing Medgar Evers as a martyred victim, Dylan considered his violent death from a less obvious point of view: he regarded it from the poverty, fear, and ignorance that put the gun in the hand of the man who shot Evers. In fact, the perspective was similar to the one offered in Wilkins's moving eulogy.

The real enemy, Dylan sings, is not the terrified, simpleminded brute who hid in the bushes outside Evers's home, but rather the politicians, the police, and other branches of the government whose lifeblood is sustained by the status quo, a status quo that thrives on hatred and violence between the races. The song turns the issue inside out, forcing the listener to probe deeper into the more complex reasons for Evers's death and why his killer wasn't immediately brought to justice.

The song was a tour de force of sophisticated dissidence and poetic social commentary, one made all the more striking for coming from a songwriter so young (Dylan was only twenty-two when he wrote it). Yet it was just one of several songs on *The Times They Are A-Changin'* that showcased Dylan's rapid growth as a songwriter. "Only a Pawn in Their Game," "The Times They Are A-Changin'," "The Lonesome Death of Hattie Carroll," and "With God on Our Side," coupled with the touching love songs "One Too Many Mornings" and "Boots of Spanish Leather," went a long way toward convincing the skeptics at Columbia that he might have staying power. Suddenly there was a lot less talk of "Hammond's Folly" around the Black Rock building, Columbia's headquarters on Sixth Avenue.

By the early 1960s Hammond had compiled an impressive list of protégés: Billie Holiday, Teddy Wilson, Count Basie, Charlie Christian, Aretha Franklin, and Bob Dylan all knew what it was like to be swept up into the whirlwind of enthusiasm that was John Hammond. But not all of the artists Hammond championed emerged as cultural icons. Indeed, over the years he stuck his neck out many times for artists he believed in but for whatever reasons never achieved widespread acclaim. For a year and a half in the mid-1960s, the blues guitarist Roy Gaines found himself swept up by Hammond's freight train of energy. All Gaines could do was hold on tight and enjoy the ride.

In September 1963, Hammond headed back on the road, this time to California for the Monterey Jazz Festival. While wandering through the crowd, he happened upon Gaines. The two had known each other for years—Gaines was an established backup musician, having played behind Billie Holiday on some dates late in her career—and Hammond was thrilled to see him again. Gaines was there purely as a spectator, but within a half hour Hammond had arranged with festival organizers for the guitarist to make an appearance onstage.

A few weeks later, after listening to a tape Gaines had sent to him in New York, Hammond told Gaines he wanted to record him for Columbia or one of its subsidiaries. The potential recording contract was just one of several fronts on which Hammond was now working to advance Gaines's career. Hammond also promised Gaines he would contact the organizers of the festival in Monterey to try to get a paycheck for his appearance there. Hammond was also pulling whatever strings he could to get Gaines readmitted to the musicians union—apparently Gaines's union membership had been revoked over some money he owed to a group of union musicians he had hired for a gig but was never able to pay. Hammond even wrote a memo to Columbia brass seeking a three-hundred-dollar advance for Gaines so that the guitarist could pay off the union as well as some other debts. With typical exuberance he wrote, "Roy Gaines is probably one of the most outstanding blues guitarists I have ever heard." Columbia apparently denied the request, and a few weeks later Hammond lent Gaines one hundred dollars out of his own pocket to help him pay for some college courses he was taking. "I'm sorry that I can't afford anything more at this time," Hammond wrote.

Meanwhile, he brought the tape Gaines had already made to executives at Okeh and Epic, two Columbia units that focused on country and blues, in an effort to whet their appetites for Gaines's gutsy guitar work. It took five months of persistent attention, but finally, in February 1964, Hammond convinced Epic to sign Gaines to a one-year contract. Later that spring, he flew to California to record the guitarist. The session yielded at least one potential single, "Katie May," a scorching Lightnin' Hopkins tune that Hammond wanted Epic to release as a single so Gaines could earn some royalties. Gaines wrote Hammond a touching letter shortly after the session: "I'm impress [*sic*] with this whole affair; in as much as, you being one of the most distinguished and notable individuals in my life. I have long needed the motivation given me by you."

Unfortunately for Gaines, the decision makers at Epic didn't share Hammond's enthusiasm for the single, and it was never released. After nearly a year of delays, during which time Hammond lent Gaines another hundred dollars to help him stay in college, Gaines asked Epic to release him from his contract so he could record for a small Australian label. In a letter to Hammond seeking his release from Epic, Gaines expressed no bitterness:

> Sorry things didn't work out with Columbia. I really trying [*sic*] to get something going. I've been trying all my life to get something going for me, and will spend the rest of it trying to reach my goal. I appreciate all you've done for me, for I know you've gone out of your way to help me. That's one reason I've tried so hard on the [recording] dates, and was so determined to make them successful, but you know most of this because I've bent your ear time and time again with the same story.

Gaines ended the letter, "As soon as I can start paying off some of my ruff bills I'm going to start sending you the money you gave me when I need [*sic*] it so badly." Hammond told Gaines not to worry about the money. (No small concession from a man notoriously tight with a dollar. Hammond was known to drive in endless circles around Manhattan in search of a parking space rather than pay the three- or four-dollar fee at a parking garage.)

Gaines never sold out football stadiums, but he made a career for himself. He eventually released several well-received solo albums and toured in the backup bands of such stars as Aretha Franklin, Ray Charles, and Diana Ross, and he remains to this day a fan favorite at blues festivals around the country.

Hammond was returning to his office from a performance of an African choir at a church on the West Side of Manhattan in March 1964 when he suffered his first heart attack. He was fifty-three, an increasingly heavy smoker, and still working an endless round of office days and club nights. It marked the beginning of a long, gradual downward spiral in his health. But after six months at home recovering with his wife, Esme, he was back in his office at Columbia, albeit working at a slightly slower pace.

Not so slow that it kept him from chasing down tips on hot musicians, though.

In late 1965, Hammond got a call from a hardworking manager he trusted and respected, a tough New Yorker named Jimmy Boyd. Boyd began comparing one of his artists, a guitarist named George Benson, to Charlie Christian. Hammond listened to Boyd's praise of Benson with mild amusement but decided to take the manager at his word. A few nights later, he headed uptown to Harlem to hear Benson and his quartet perform at a nightclub called the Palm Café not far from the Apollo Theater on 125th Street. Years later, Hammond would recall two things about that night: Benson's playing, which in his opinion warranted the comparisons to Christian, and the go-go girls who shimmied and shook while Benson's quartet performed.

Benson had received a heads-up from Boyd that someone important was coming to see him. "Sure enough, on the last night [of the gig], a guy came in the door with this elegant lady (Esme Hammond) who had on beautiful clothes and beautiful jewelry," Benson recalled. "Although he was not dressed particularly well, and he had a newspaper under his arm, I could see right away that he was really into the music. He wandered into the middle of the club, found a booth, and sat down, but he couldn't stop shaking his head and tapping his feet. When I saw him, I told the go-go girl to get down, stopped right in the middle of the song, and started playing an uptempo jazz piece. John Hammond, I knew it was him, was going crazy."

Something of a musical prodigy, Benson started singing in nightclubs in his hometown of Pittsburgh as a child. At ten, he recorded several sides for the RCA record label. He got his first guitar as a teenager and promptly formed a rock-and-roll band. But rock and roll gave way to jazz after he had heard the likes of the guitarists Christian and Wes Montgomery.

By the mid-1960s, Benson, now in his early twenties, was leading a jazz quartet and paying his dues in nightclubs up and down the East Coast. According to biographical material on Benson included in Hammond's papers, the group was barely earning enough to buy gas money to make the next show, but Benson seemed to be getting better every night. His chops were remarkable for someone unknown outside of nightclubs, and he was comfortable in any musical idiom, drawing from his experience in a wide range of styles—rock and roll, rhythm and blues, swing, and bebop.

Hammond wasted no time in signing Benson to Columbia and getting him inside a studio. Sessions held in early 1966 yielded the material for Benson's first album, *It's Uptown*. "Jaguar," a groovy instrumental written by Benson, foreshadowed the melding of jazz and rock that would sweep popular music after the release of Miles Davis's *Bitches Brew* in 1969. "Willow Weep for Me," a rangy eight-minute showcase for Benson's tasty jazz licks, meanwhile, could trace its lineage back directly to the Benny Goodman Sextet (featuring Charlie Christian on guitar). And the Latin-tinged "Bullfight," also written by Benson, displayed the guitarist's versatility as well as his virtuosity. Benson sang with aplomb on a couple of tunes, but his voice was clearly taking a backseat to his fret work on these early recordings.

"From a musician's point of view, John Hammond was probably the best kind of producer I could think of," Benson wrote twenty-five years later.

> In those days, artistry was very important, and it took priority over everything else. John Hammond didn't necessarily care about how many records I could sell; his approach was more along the lines of "look at what this talent can do, and I hope you enjoy him as much as I do." This was very important, especially for us, because we had so many ideas, things we had been working on all our lives that we needed to get out, we didn't need anybody hampering them. We needed to let them breathe, and John let us do that.

As usual, Hammond took a personal interest in his new artist. Despite a newly signed contract with Columbia Records, the most powerful label in the industry, Benson and his bandmates were broke. Hammond had to hit up Columbia for a five-hundred-dollar loan for Benson so that the group could buy a used Volkswagen bus to carry their equipment from one show to the next. "I realize that this is a lot of money to advance a new artist," Hammond wrote to a Columbia superior, "but I think we have a tremendous winner in this group, and I would love to help him if it is possible." When Columbia turned down the request, Hammond lent Benson the money out of his own pocket.

Hammond and Benson made another record together, *The George Benson Cookbook*, a satisfying follow-up to *It's Uptown* that featured plenty more superlative guitar playing. But perhaps because the second album was recorded within months of the first, it broke no new ground and would be Benson's last for Columbia.

It's notable that Benson, unlike Hammond's other recent signings, Aretha Franklin and Bob Dylan, relished his time with Hammond in the studio, and the reason is obvious: Benson and his bandmates were day-in, day-out working musicians who needed very little direction. Thus these sessions were similar to the ones Hammond supervised in the 1930s with Teddy Wilson, Benny Goodman, and Lionel Hampton, and again in the 1950s for Vanguard with Mel Powell, Buck Clayton, and Ruby Braff. Hammond could simply arrive at the studio, wave to the musicians, sip a cup of coffee, and read his *New York Times*. The musicians took care of the rest.

Outside the studio, Hammond was working his magic throughout the vast landscape of American popular music—that is to say, he was using all his contacts to make sure that Benson would be heard by as many people as possible. He arranged for Benson to appear at hip nightclubs up and down the East Coast, and he pressed his contacts in the media for articles in the newspapers in cities where Benson was appearing. It was working, and Benson's career began to take off.

Still, despite the higher profile Benson was achieving through Hammond's relentless promotion, the guitarist wasn't making any money. A note from Benson's lawyers in early 1967 alerted Hammond to the disturbing news that Benson owed nearly five thousand dollars in back taxes and needed thirty-five hundred dollars as soon as possible. Ham-

mond asked Columbia to lend Benson the money, but the company refused. "I have just sent a letter . . . explaining the delay in my getting
money for George Benson," Hammond wrote to the guitarist's manager.

> After Columbia turned down George's request for a loan, I tried
> to get a personal loan from CBS so that I could help George out
> personally but I was turned down cold. Since my wife is going
> to the hospital next week and my own financial position is any-
> thing but rosey, I cannot do anything for George personally at
> this time and I am more than sorry that I am unable to help. We
> all have great faith in George and I am mortified that we are un-
> able to help him further at this time.

Once again Hammond was blurring the lines between his professional and his personal life. He would have lent Benson the money
himself if he'd had it. But he didn't have it. Moreover, it hurt him that
this promising young artist should be treated this way by Columbia.

The exact sequence of events is unclear—as are the reasons for
Columbia's apparent lack of interest in such a talented artist—but
around the same time Hammond was angling to get Benson a loan
from Columbia, he received a curt message from his superiors telling
him that Benson had been reassigned to another producer. The memo
all but orders Hammond to help the new producer get up to speed
with Benson's material.

It proved a moot point. A short time later, after Columbia had
made only a lukewarm effort to re-sign Benson, the guitarist decided
to sign with Verve Records, the innovative label founded by Hammond's
old friend Norman Granz. (Benson, of course, would find mainstream
success—superstardom, in fact—in the 1970s with Warner Brothers
after shifting his focus away from the guitar and fully embracing a career as a singer of rhythm and blues and pop songs.)

One long-term relationship Hammond was unable to maintain was his
thirty-year affiliation with the NAACP. The winds of change that had
amounted to little more than a breeze three years earlier at Medgar

Evers's funeral had by 1966 grown into a powerful storm, one that ultimately led to a bitter separation between supporters of Roy Wilkins and the NAACP and supporters of Martin Luther King. The reason for the schism was America's escalating involvement in Vietnam.

Citing his displeasure with Wilkins's leadership and the direction and pace of the NAACP's stewardship of the civil rights movement, Hammond abruptly resigned in the fall of 1966. In a letter to the Harlem-based *Amsterdam News* he wrote, "The NAACP has lost the youth, and when Roy said earlier this year that he wouldn't cooperate with other militant civil rights leaders, I figured this was my exit." The newspaper's editors found Hammond's resignation significant enough to put the story on its front page. (The story referred to him as "John Hammond, millionaire jazz authority.")

In the early 1930s, Hammond had refused to join the NAACP because he didn't believe the nascent civil rights organization shared his fiery commitment to the cause of equality for all people. He eventually changed his mind, seeing Louis T. Wright, then the NAACP chairman, as "an extremely militant leader . . . stimulating and completely compatible with my own understanding of the NAACP's role." For the next three decades he was one of the NAACP's most visible as well as attentive members. Excluding periods of military service and when he was ill, he rarely missed a board meeting for nearly thirty years. Three decades after joining, he resigned from the NAACP because he didn't believe the now-stodgy civil rights organization shared his fiery commitment to the cause of equality for all people.

The move didn't surprise his friends. "John had a passion for justice that may have been his most important trait," said Nat Hentoff. "And he was always consistent. For all the arrogance, he was a man of consistent principle."

The resignation demonstrated more than just Hammond's consistency. It also revealed, once again, his uncanny prescience in forecasting the social moods of Americans. In the past his prescience manifested itself through music. He had been an early supporter of improvised jazz, one of the first to view the medium as an organic expression of American democracy. Later he had championed black artists, predicting correctly that America was ready to hear them perform with white musicians. And he had sensed that folk music, especially as performed by Bob Dylan, could be more than pretty three-part harmonics performed by handsome college boys. It could in fact serve as a catalyst for social change.

In the fall of 1966 he sensed that Roy Wilkins and the NAACP were headed in the wrong direction, and within a matter of months many thousands of others, some of them longtime NAACP supporters, had drawn the same conclusion. By that time, a good six months after Hammond had publicly cut ties with Wilkins, the same concerns that had forced his resignation had moved to the forefront of the American political landscape.

On April 4, 1967, Martin Luther King, Jr., delivered a powerful speech he called "A Time to Break Silence" in New York City's Riverside Church. In it he articulated his view that opposition to America's involvement in the Vietnam War was a logical extension of the struggle for civil rights. King had been an early opponent of the war, seeing it not as a justifiable foreign policy but as a means to export American racism overseas. Now he sought to answer criticism—much of it emanating from the mouths of NAACP leaders—that his antiwar rhetoric was diluting the message of the domestic civil rights movement. He might as well have been addressing Roy Wilkins directly when he admonished his critics: "And when I hear them, though I often understand the source of their concern, I am nevertheless greatly saddened, for such questions mean that the inquirers have not really known me, my commitment or my calling. Indeed, their questions suggest that they do not know the world in which they live."

Wilkins didn't wait long to respond. He gave a speech about two weeks later at Yale University in which he sternly refuted King's assertion that opposition to the war in Vietnam was part and parcel of the civil rights struggle in America. He accused King and his supporters of "downgrading the Negro cause."

Wilkins's strategy backfired badly. His remarks, as well as a resolution adopted around the same time by the NAACP's board of directors which codified the Wilkins doctrine as that of the entire NAACP, drove a wedge down the middle of the organization.

The reaction from the NAACP's rank and file was swift and harsh.

A mother in Cleveland implored: "You are the one that is wrong, but I don't think you will admit it. I am glad Dr. King spoke out and said what so many of us little people believe. I wish you would grow up while some of our black sons are still living. Please open your eyes and not only look but see." A letter postmarked Urbana, Illinois, voiced the sentiments of many once-loyal NAACP supporters:

> It is a known fact that black Americans are dying in Vietnam in disproportionate numbers. This means that Negro GI's also do a disproportionate amount of the killing in Vietnam. This double outrage does not seem to concern you. Instead you berate Dr. King for speaking out boldly against a war, which he has rightly called a blasphemy of all that America stands for . . . I have supported the NAACP in the past. I can do so no longer. From now on my money is on Martin Luther King, Floyd McKissick, Stokely Carmichael and others in the Civil Rights Movement like them.

A lawyer in Paterson, New Jersey, echoed precisely John Hammond's concerns of six months earlier: "Techniques of the NAACP to fight segregation and discrimination through lawsuits and Appellate tribunals, while valid and effective up to a point, are inadequate and too 'status quo' to implement hard won decisions . . . Now, with the repudiation by the National Board of Directors of NAACP of Dr. King's and Stokely Carmichael's stand on the Vietnam war, I feel that resignation is the only way I can express my protest."

Sacks of letters expressing similar anger and disappointment poured into the NAACP's headquarters. Many of them were lengthy in their arguments and eloquent in their outrage. At their core, nearly every one of them questioned Wilkins's decision to repudiate King rather than find common ground.

Thus Hammond had essentially spoken for all in a single sentence months earlier when he told the *Amsterdam News*: "I just couldn't take Roy Wilkins anymore."

As was the case with most of his notable finds, Hammond knew the very first time he met Leonard Cohen that he wanted to sign him to Columbia:

> I had a wonderful two and a half hours with Leonard today and I listened to a whole gang of songs . . . He just wrote one today called "YOUR FATHER HAS FALLEN," which I think will be marvelous for the first album. But, of course, no lead sheet has been made of this as yet. He also sang me "JEWELS IN YOUR SHOULDER" which is a marvelous song, which I think he should do solo with guitar and without instrumental background.

Cohen had come to Hammond's attention via a documentary produced by the Canadian Broadcasting Corporation that focused on his career as a poet. Already well known in Canada, Cohen in 1966 published a controversial novel, *Beautiful Losers*, that earned him a small measure of notoriety in the United States. According to his biographer Ira B Nadel, he turned to music later the same year, at the age of thirty-one, primarily because he thought it might be more lucrative than writing. In any case, Hammond liked what he saw in the documentary and contacted Cohen through his manager. The two met for lunch early in 1967, and then repaired to Cohen's room at the Chelsea Hotel in New York, where Cohen sang a handful of songs. Hammond listened, then reportedly told him, "Leonard, you've got it." A week later Cohen was recording for Columbia in a midtown Manhattan studio.

Signing Cohen was easy. Recording an album with him was not so easy. Cohen had never recorded in a studio before. In fact, according to a biographer, most of his playing up to that point had taken place alone in front of a mirror in his apartment. He had been signed on the quality of his songs, not on the quality of his musicianship. Hammond strove to overcome this obstacle by bringing in an experienced musician—the string bassist Willie Ruff—to record with Cohen and lend an air of musical authority that would help put Cohen at ease. It worked.

Another problem was Cohen's age. At thirty-two, he hardly represented a fresh face to the kids who now made up the lion's share of the record-buying public. This was more of a concern to Hammond's bosses, however, since Hammond was convinced all along that Cohen would do fine as long as the same kids who loved his books and poems also bought his records.

Recording Cohen did present at least one unique situation to Hammond, notwithstanding thirty years of experience in the studio.

Perhaps Cohen was intimidated by the austere surroundings of a recording studio, or perhaps he just liked the ambience created by candles and incense. It was probably a little bit of both. But whatever the reasons, he showed up at Columbia's Manhattan studios one afternoon armed with a box of candles and handfuls of incense. In short order, the recording studio had the feel of the harem tent of some desert warlord. Apparently the dim lighting and heavy reek helped Cohen recreate in the studio the melancholy mood he needed to write the songs in the first place.

Hammond couldn't have cared less. If it put Cohen at ease and helped smoothen the recording process, he was all for it. Besides, Hammond spent most of the time behind a glass partition in a well-lit engineer's booth reading the newspaper. Cohen has said he appreciated Hammond's overt, almost ostentatious nonchalance during his early recording sessions, suggesting by implication that the laid-back demeanor was perhaps staged in order to help Cohen relax. That may have been partly true, but Hammond had been reading newspapers in recording studios for many, many years before Leonard Cohen came along.

Data sheets (notes taken by producers in the studio) from recording sessions in the summer of 1967 reveal Hammond's enthusiasm for Cohen's originality: "excellent, perfect mood, stupendous," he wrote in notes taken during the recording of "So Long, Marianne." During a subsequent session, describing "Master Song," he wrote, "stupendous song, the greatest." He was clearly enthusiastic about Cohen's potential. The good feelings didn't last long, though. Differences arose between producer and artist over how Cohen's music should be presented, and for the third time in less than a decade Hammond's role as producer for a potentially major artist put him at odds with the performer.

In Hammond's version, the rift opened up after Cohen decided well into the recording process that he didn't like how the songs sounded.

Cohen, according to Hammond, wanted to add heavy production devices—layers of stringed instruments and horns—that would help hide what he felt were deficiencies in his singing. Hammond objected to the gimmicks and found himself replaced as producer by John Simon, who had already had great success with Simon and Garfunkel.

A Cohen biographer tells it slightly differently. In this alternate account, Hammond got sick (although nothing in Hammond's writings or papers indicates an illness during this period) and was forced to abandon the project. At that point, a new producer who favored a more lush sound—John Simon—was brought on board. Upon reflection, however, Cohen decided that he disliked the new sound, specifically the superfluous strings and backup choir on songs such as "Suzanne" and "So Long, Marianne." Unfortunately, technology at that time didn't allow for the removal of sound once it had been added to a master track. So the syrupy strings and backup vocals stayed. This version seems less plausible than Hammond's, however, and may be an attempt by Cohen to deflect blame for the overwrought production on some of his early material.

In hindsight, Hammond's instinct to record Cohen with as spare a background arrangement as possible was probably the right one. And Cohen himself seems to have ultimately come to that same conclusion, just a little too late. In any case, there doesn't seem to have been any lasting hard feelings between the two men over their differences while recording—they always spoke highly of each other. But they never worked together again, and Hammond was never credited as producer of any of those early Cohen recordings.

As it turned out, none of the disagreements that arose during the recording of Cohen's first album mattered because *Songs of Leonard Cohen*, released in late 1967, sold fairly well and established him as a rock-and-roll poet almost on a par with Dylan. Like Dylan's, Cohen's influence has since extended well beyond sales of his records, which Columbia has estimated have exceeded ten million. His songs have been covered by literally hundreds of artists, and some of the most popular and influential songwriters of the past three decades, among them Lou Reed, Billy Joel, U2's Bono, and Michael Stipe of R.E.M., have cited Cohen as a primary influence.

Hammond himself concluded: "He was an oddball who paid off because he was unique and because in that unpredictable decade [the 1960s] he had something to say that was important to young people."

By the late 1960s Hammond was spending a lot of time working on projects that leveraged his own status as a music industry legend. For instance, in 1967 he produced a concert at Carnegie Hall to commemorate the thirtieth anniversary of his first "From Spirituals to Swing" concert. George Benson appeared on a bill that also included Count Basie, Buck Clayton, and other stars from a bygone era. ("I don't think I've heard Basie play that relaxed in years and years," Hammond recalled.) Benson was a smash, but the concert did not generate the same excitement as the originals. "The Institute of Jazz Studies [at Rutgers University in Newark] had sort of twisted my arm to do this concert," Hammond told a radio interviewer in 1973. "Unfortunately, it was not a financial success. It cost me a lot of money, personally, as a matter of fact, but we won't go into that." Hammond laughed at the memory in the interview, but it wasn't funny at the time. The show ran a deficit of nearly thirty-five hundred dollars, which Carnegie Hall's management staff sought for over a year to collect from Hammond. It grew ugly. There were repeated threats of a lawsuit before the money was eventually paid, much of it apparently coming from Hammond's own pocket.

There was also the John Hammond Collection, a series of record reissues released by Columbia to commemorate the extraordinary array of talent Hammond had signed to the label. There were several records of Billie Holiday material, a couple more for Charlie Christian, another set for Count Basie, and a whole batch dedicated solely to Bessie Smith. Hammond was proud that these reissues introduced these uniquely American artists to a whole new generation of fans.

And then there were the tributes: luncheons and dinners in his honor held by the numerous organizations to which he had dedicated his time and considerable energy—the New York chapter of the National Academy of Recording Arts and Sciences, the local chapter of the American Federation of Musicians, a youth organization called the Symphony of the New World, among a host of others.

A few years passed without any significant signings, and it looked like things might finally be winding down for Hammond. Then, one day in May 1972, he walked into his office and found a manager named Mike Appel waiting for him. Appel was there seeking an audition for his only client, a singer and songwriter from New Jersey named Bruce Springsteen.

15

A MARVELOUS AUDITION

T here were maybe a dozen people in the Gaslight that night, and that included the bartender, a waitress, John Hammond, and the guy up onstage. It was so quiet that the sound of the performer's fingers squeakily fretting his guitar echoed off the walls of the large club. It was a warm evening in early May 1972, and tourists out for a good time in Greenwich Village wandered in and out. A handful of couples murmured over drinks among the rows of empty tables. Few if any of the bar's patrons were paying attention to the singer, a young rock and roller turned folkie from New Jersey named Bruce Springsteen. More than thirty years later, Springsteen looked back on that evening with equal parts pride and amused astonishment.

The original Gaslight, located around the corner and down a flight of stairs in a cellar on MacDougal Street, had served as practically the epicenter for the urban folk revival that flourished in Greenwich Village in the late 1950s and early 1960s. Allen Ginsberg and Gregory Corso had read their innovative poems there for small groups of admiring beats, and then a few years later Dylan had tried out "A Hard Rain's A-Gonna Fall" and "Masters of War" in the crowded basement club in front of a roomful of his toughest critics—his folk-singing and guitar-picking peers.

But the mood in Greenwich Village—and across the musical landscape—had changed by 1972. Dylan had moved out of the Village around the same time he stopped writing overt protest songs. Earnest folk was no longer the music of choice among American youths who sought a message in their music, having been replaced first by the psychedelic sound of San Francisco and later, in the early 1970s, by the jaded cynicism of New York bands like the Velvet Underground. Over the same period rock musicians had been replaced by rock stars, many of whom were rapidly turning into parodies of themselves—prima-donna junkies who drifted via private jet and stretch limo from one giant arena to the next in a haze of cocaine and heroin. Somehow rock and roll had been subverted by its own subversion. Things had turned upside down, and the music no longer seemed a priority.

The guy onstage at the Gaslight that night in mid-1972 looked a little like Bob Dylan. His scruffy beard and thick curly hair resembled the look Dylan had adopted in the late 1960s and early 1970s. But he had none of Dylan's frailty—there was nothing delicate about this guy. He had piercing brown eyes and his lean, tanned face was dominated by a large nose and strong lower jaw. A gold crucifix hung from a thin chain around his neck. And in scuffed motorcycle boots, ragged blue jeans, and an ill-fitting T-shirt, he looked more like James Dean in *Rebel Without a Cause* or Marlon Brando in *The Wild One* than Woody Guthrie or Jack Kerouac. This was Bruce Springsteen, and he had grown up going to the movies in New Jersey, not reading poetry in Greenwich Village coffee shops.

Assuming Springsteen performed that night as he did on other occasions from that period, performances that were captured on video, the young singer's intensity bordered on startling. He sang each song as if it might be the last chance he would ever get to do so. The veins in his neck and forehead jutted out as he sang. The sinewy muscles in his forearms grew taut as his hands slid with equal parts grace and power up and down the neck of his acoustic guitar. And with his eyes closed tightly and his head leaned far back, he sang full-throated to the ceiling. Hammond, seated nearby, was astonished by the stage charisma of this mild-mannered kid whom he had met for the first time in his office that morning. Springsteen, he recalled, "absolutely amazed his little audience."

Just as startling was the imagery that exploded from Springsteen's songs. These were clearly "Bruce Springsteen's" songs. They were not songs written by Bruce Springsteen in the hope they would sound like someone else. These were passionate, gritty, exuberant songs, and while they mined the universal coming-of-age themes of generations of pop music, the lyrics were somehow devoid of tired pop-music clichés. He sang of uniquely American characters who populated uniquely American landscapes—shady carnival barkers beckoning from the midway, slick uptown playboys in search of their next score, leather-jacketed hoodlum-heroes who broke hearts and rules with equal gusto down on the boardwalk.

During his Gaslight set Springsteen sang a song called "It's Hard to Be a Saint in the City," evidently an optimistically autobiographical number about a young tough who is, among other things, "the king of the alley," "the prince of the paupers," and "the pimp's main prophet." He also sang a personal anthem of rebellion called "Growin' Up"— which Hammond loved—whose protagonist does the opposite of whatever he is told. Instead of sitting down, he stands up. Instead of coming down, he throws up. And instead of pulling down, he pulls up. It's a fresh and clever take on an old idea.

Springsteen also recalled performing a song titled "Arabian Nights" about a young musician who's having difficulty finding his rightful place in the world. The song, its lyrics vivid in surreal detail, is alive with interracial lust, gang fights, and potentially blasphemous biblical references (another Hammond favorite).

The song ends with a knife fight between the devil himself and a gangleader named Duke. Duke wins and sells the devil to "some priest in Pennsylvania to exhibit on his altar Christmas night."

By the time Springsteen had finished his short set of three or four songs, Hammond was beside himself. He fidgeted visibly in his seat, his grin stretched from ear to ear, and his fingers tapped rhythmically and unconsciously on his thighs. Springsteen recalled that when he hopped off the stage, an ebullient Hammond approached him: "That was mah-velous, Bruce. Just mah-velous."

Hammond had made his "discovery" earlier that day when Springsteen, guitar in tow, walked into his office at Black Rock and sat down on the couch. Springsteen had found himself in such enviable environs through the dogged persistence of his manager, a former marine named Mike Appel.

Appel's aggressive personality has become part of the Springsteen legend. Rock-and-roll writers have placed his alleged bluntness almost on a par with Albert Grossman's cagey and secretive ways and Colonel Tom Parker's enigmatic and misleading aloofness on behalf of Elvis. Appel himself has bragged about his methods, and both Springsteen and Hammond have confirmed his pushy ways. "Mike could talk real well," Springsteen recalled three decades later, laughing at his own understatement. "He had relentless energy. But still, you know, he called [Hammond's secretary and aide-de-camp, Liz Gilbert] cold, I believe."

To this day, Springsteen is still amazed that Gilbert put them on Hammond's calendar. Gilbert, Hammond's secretary in the early 1970s, has been described by those who worked with her as the quintessential gatekeeper for the person in the music industry with perhaps the greatest need for a gatekeeper. Hammond's papers at Yale University form a portrait of a trusted assistant on whom Hammond depended to help sift through the hundreds of requests for auditions that poured into his office each week. She seems to have adopted her boss's discerning ear and was frequently called on to write rejection letters to people whose audition tapes didn't measure up. Thus a response from Liz Gilbert, almost always sincere, polite, and articulate, was a response from John Hammond.

On the morning of May 5, 1972, Springsteen took the bus to Manhattan from his home in Asbury Park, New Jersey, where he was living in an apartment over a drugstore. Springsteen and Appel had been introduced the previous November through Carl "Tinker" West, who had managed Steel Mill, one of Springsteen's early bands. Springsteen at the time was looking to forge a career as a solo artist, and West recommended Appel as a possible manager. After two auditions, Appel agreed to represent him. Springsteen subsequently signed a series of contracts between March and May 1972 that called for Appel to serve as both his manager and his producer. (Appel would say later that he reluctantly agreed to act as Springsteen's manager only after the singer asked him to. He said his preference had been to serve solely as Springsteen's producer.)

At the time, Appel had been working in the music business for about a decade with limited success. He had played in bands, written a hit song for the Partridge Family, and produced a mildly successful album for a power trio called Sir Lord Baltimore. Now he wasted no time in making things happen for Springsteen, arranging for the Hammond audition shortly after he and Springsteen had worked out the details of their business relationship.

After arriving at the Port Authority bus station on Eighth Avenue, Springsteen walked up to Appel's lawyer's office on East Fifty-fifth Street, guitar in hand. He and Appel then walked down to Columbia's offices at Fifty-second Street and Sixth Avenue to meet with Hammond.

Thirty years after that audition, Springsteen remained exuberant, even joyful, as he reminisced about how he came to be signed to Columbia Records. He still seemed thrilled that he got in to see Hammond at all, let alone that Hammond liked his music.

"John's secretary said, 'I just had a feeling. I talked to this guy [Appel] on the phone and I just had a feeling.' And [Hammond] let us in," Springsteen recalled, shaking his head at the memory. "I mean, we just came in off the street. It's fascinating that at that point in time, this is the guy, he's one of the vice presidents of Columbia Records, right, discovered all of these major artists, been a key player in sort of the evolution of the music industry—and he's meeting a couple of guys he has [Springsteen's voice rose as he described the encounter] NO IDEA WHO THEY ARE WHO ARE WALKING IN OFF THE STREET! [Then he laughed out loud.] That alone is just something. I don't know if it happens anymore. I'm sure it doesn't happen anymore."

Years later, Appel remembered the phone call that led to his and Springsteen's first meeting with Hammond. "I was trying to see Clive Davis, but Clive Davis was out of town, and so I wondered, Who can I go to next? and I decided, you know, let's see if John Hammond's around. I got his secretary and she just seemed to have a feeling," he said. "I told her, 'You've got Barbra Streisand and you've got Neil Diamond and Chicago. Well, these are acts that are gonna be with your label—they've already been with your label—forever.' I said, 'I have one of those types of acts. He's a real longevity act. He should be with a class label like Columbia Records.' And she said, 'Well, when can you come over?' And I said, 'Whenever you tell us.'"

Appel seemed no less astonished than Springsteen that Liz Gilbert had acquiesced and put them on Hammond's calendar.

According to Appel, once they arrived at Hammond's office, he did most of the talking. After a short wait, they were ushered into a spacious office devoid of any paraphernalia that would indicate its occupant was one of the most powerful men in the music industry. There were no gold records on the wall or pictures of Hammond with recognizable pop-music stars. It might have been a banker's office, Appel said, decorated as it was with low-slung couches on either side of Hammond's desk.

"When we went in, he had his sunglasses set on top of his flattop crew cut. He was very cordial. We walked in and Bruce sits down with his guitar, and I feel it's incumbent upon me to say something. I say to him—and I'll always remember this—'I've grappled with lyrics myself. This guy makes it seem like it's nothing to write reams and reams of poetry.' And [Hammond's] nodding, you know, Okay, okay. Then I said, 'I can't believe he's written as many things as he has in such a short period of time at such a high degree of quality.'"

At that point, according to Appel, Hammond seemed to be growing impatient. "He started to look at me like he thought I was starting to hype. But he didn't say anything, he was just looking. And I said to him, 'In short, you're the guy who discovered Bob Dylan for the right reasons. You won't miss this.' He said to me, 'Please sit down.' So I sat down and I figured, That's it, I've said everything that's on my mind."

Hammond, meanwhile, had slipped his dark glasses down over his eyes, a gesture that made Appel nervous. "I was absolutely panic-stricken in that office after I made that speech. I thought, Gee, I hope I didn't blow it for Bruce by making the guy mad."

Then Bruce, dressed as usual in battered jeans, a ratty old T-shirt, and brown Frye boots, began to play.

Appel recalled: "[Hammond's] glasses were down over his eyes now, because he's mad at me. But then he put his glasses back up on his head, looked at me, and said, 'You were right.' Then he looked back at Bruce. 'Got any more songs, son?' Just like that, he said, 'You were right.'"

After the audition was over and Hammond had made clear his enthusiasm for Springsteen, going so far as to insist on seeing him perform live later that night, Appel and Springsteen were light-headed with glee.

"After we walked out of the building, Springsteen had his guitar case in his hand, and I said, 'Let me hold that guitar.' He just balanced himself on the curb, walking down the street with his arms up in the air, balancing himself. He literally danced on the curb. It was that joyous and that pure a situation. How often do you just walk into a record label cold, the most prestigious record label in the world, with the greatest A&R man in the world, and he says to you, 'Yeah, I love him.'"

Hammond's version of this encounter was essentially the same. In a 1980 interview with a Springsteen fan magazine, he recalled the entire episode:

> It was all very strange. It was wild. It was '72 and I looked on my pad one morning where my secretary had written "Mike Appel—11:00." I had another appointment twenty minutes later so I asked her who Mike Appel was, and she told me that he was a producer who had a couple of things on the charts and that he wanted me to hear a singer. She said, "I think he's been to everyone else at Columbia and no one would see him." So I told her I'd see him. Well, he came in that morning and I must say I didn't like him very much, but behind him was this kid with a guitar. Appel sat down and said, "So you're the guy who was supposed to have found Bob Dylan. I wanna see if you've got ears, because I've got somebody much better than him." I said, "For God's sake, just stop it! You're gonna make me hate you."

Whatever the specifics of their brief exchange, whatever tack Appel took—hard sell, soft sell—it worked. In short order, they were all sitting in Hammond's office, and at some point Hammond looked over at Springsteen and asked him to play. "I just stopped talking to Mike Appel and talked directly to Bruce. I said, 'Bruce, I'm John Hammond. Why don't you open up your guitar, bring it out and I'll listen to you.' Mike was sort of grinning through this whole thing," Hammond recalled.

For his part, Springsteen said he was content to let his aggressive manager speak up for him. He sat off to the side, quietly taking things in. He was just twenty-two years old, and he was about to play the most important gig of his life—for an audience of one. But, by his own account, he wasn't nervous. "Well, you know, I was taking the approach for the day that I had nothing so I had nothing to lose," Springsteen explained. "That was basically my feelings about it."

And why not? He was only twenty-two, but he'd been performing professionally for six years, and he was already a local hero in the bars and clubs along the Jersey Shore. His early bands, Child, Dr. Zoom and the Sonic Boom, and Steel Mill, regularly attracted hundreds of loyal fans to their shows, and witnesses say Springsteen was the primary draw. A fiery guitar player, recognized as probably the best on the Jersey Shore scene, he was also a gifted and magnetic entertainer who clearly relished the visceral give-and-take between audience and performer.

Springsteen said that at the time of his audition he was aware of Hammond's reputation as the man who brought Dylan to Columbia, recalling that he first came across Hammond's name in Anthony Scaduto's biography of Dylan, which was first published in 1971. And, laughing again, Springsteen remembered the film about Benny Goodman in which the Hammond character had been played by an actor who later played Dennis the Menace's father on television. But Springsteen professed to having known next to nothing of the Hammond legacy that dated back to Billie Holiday, Count Basie, and Charlie Christian. No matter. He said he was fully aware of the significance of this audition and what it could mean for his career, and he was determined not to blow it.

So he played with all the confidence he'd acquired since first picking up the guitar in his early teens. "I'd actually been playing for almost ten years by then, you know. I'd played to thousands of people, unbeknownst to most [music industry types] in a very local setting. But I'd collected quite an audience, so I'd built up quite a bit of performance confidence over the years just from playin' so much, you know, when you're a kid. And I had these songs and I thought they were good."

So did Hammond. Springsteen had played just two songs, "It's Hard to Be a Saint in the City" and "Growin' Up," when Hammond abruptly stopped him and said simply, "You've got to be on Columbia Records."

Springsteen laughed at the memory, recalling how he tried to act cool in response to this life-altering remark. "I said to him, 'Oh, I've got some other ones here, too.'"

Hammond recalled, "I was just absolutely knocked out. I can't tell you. It was just ridiculous. I've heard so many hundreds of people and he's the first guy who's ever come through to me this way, much more than Bob Dylan . . . because, I'll tell you, there's an integrity about Bruce that comes through as soon as he opens his mouth."

After performing "It's Hard to Be a Saint in the City," which Hammond loved for its "inner rhyme," and the rebellious "Growin' Up," Springsteen played a melodramatic tune titled "Mary Queen of Arkansas," which Hammond found "a little pretentious." At that point Hammond, curious how far he might be willing to take his lyrics, asked him if he had anything "outrageous," and Springsteen answered with a song called "If I Was the Priest," another iconoclastic tune rife with parodies of sacred Catholic imagery. Hammond loved it. "So then I knew that he had that whole natural gift that you can't learn. You're born with it," said Hammond. "I started writing things down on the desk and listened to a large part of his repertoire. I didn't get out of that office until one o'clock."

Springsteen acknowledged that he hardly lacked for confidence at the time. Nevertheless, he said he was pleasantly startled by the enthusiasm with which Hammond greeted his songs. "I was surprised because, I mean, I had no experience with the music business at all. I'd never met anybody who'd made an actual record with a big record company. So this was a whole other world that I'd never had—I'd never had [Springsteen repeated himself for emphasis] and never knew anyone who'd ever had any contact with, you know."

Having passed the one-on-one audition, Springsteen now moved on to the next step: Hammond wanted to see him perform in front of a live audience—that night. So after a round of handshakes in Hammond's office, Springsteen and Appel headed out into the streets of New York City in search of a venue. Not everyone was interested in hearing him, Springsteen recalled: "We just went down to the Village, and we went into a bunch of places to see if anybody would let us play, you know. I think we went into the Bitter End, and we couldn't get onstage in the Bitter End, and there were a few other places maybe, but we ended up at the Gaslight."

According to Appel, he contacted one of the owners of the Gaslight, either Clarence Hood or his son Sam, and convinced him to allow Springsteen to play a few songs ahead of a group of comedians who were the club's featured performers that night. Apparently Hammond had also made a call to the Gaslight's owners.

In any case, Hammond, after watching the live performance, was convinced, and the next day he and Springsteen got together again at Black Rock to record a demo, on which he sang "Growin' Up," "It's Hard to Be a Saint in the City," "Mary Queen of Arkansas," "Does This Bus Stop at 82nd Street?" and "The Angel," all of which wound up on his first album. Springsteen also played a handful of other songs that didn't make it onto the album: "If I Was the Priest," "Southern Son," "Street Queen," and the colorfully named "Cowboys of the Sea."

During this session Hammond fell in love with the concept of Springsteen alone with his guitar. In interviews years later, he would insist time and again that the recordings made that day were the finest Springsteen had ever made.

Now that Springsteen had passed his auditions for Hammond, there was still the not-inconsequential matter of performing a few songs for Columbia's president, Clive Davis. The live audition for Davis, conducted a few days after Springsteen and Hammond made the demo, may have been a moot point, though, because Hammond had already played the demo for Davis. "Here is a copy of a couple of the reels of Bruce Springsteen, a very talented kid who recorded these twelve songs in a period of around two hours last Wednesday. You've already received . . . a memo about it," Hammond wrote to Davis on May 8, 1972. "I think we better act quickly because many people heard the boy at the Gaslight so that his fame is beginning to spread." Hammond apparently embellished the truth—very few people had heard Springsteen at the Gaslight, and his fame was not beginning to spread—to motivate Davis to move as quickly as possible. But he needn't have worried. Davis wrote back the next day, "I love Bruce Springsteen! He's an original in every respect. I'd like to meet him if you can arrange it."

(Hammond had suggested to Davis in his memo that Springsteen be signed to Epic Records, a Columbia subsidiary, because Columbia was already promoting Dylan and Loudon Wainwright, and Hammond felt Springsteen might get lost in the shuffle. But Appel strongly opposed the idea, and it was dropped.)

On the day he was to meet with Hammond and Davis, Springsteen took the bus from Asbury Park up to Manhattan. For whatever reason (he couldn't recall why), he had to borrow a guitar for the audition. And to make matters worse, the guitar had no case. Thus he had to carry it on the bus and around midtown Manhattan by the neck. "I don't know if you've ever traveled that way, but it's sort of embarrassing sitting there like that, you know," he recalled. Among the sea of suits swarming up and down Seventh Avenue, Springsteen must have looked for all the world like a street musician who had just wandered up out of the subway.

Springsteen recalled that the audition for Davis was just as success-ful as the earlier one for Hammond. During the latter performance, he was helped along in no small measure by Hammond's constant patter of encouragement. "Isn't he mah-velous, Clive? Listen to the imagery. And he's a mah-velous guitar player as well, don't you think?" Davis was as impressed by Springsteen as Hammond had been a few days earlier.

Later that night, alone again on the bus back to Asbury Park, the borrowed guitar stashed in the rack above his head, Springsteen gazed out the window deep into the swamps stretching off into the darkness on either side of the New Jersey Turnpike. Years later, he recalled that he was so excited he could barely sit still. He wanted to shout his good fortune to anyone who would listen. But who could possibly under-stand, let alone relate to his experience? So he peered out the window in silence, trying to make sense of all that had transpired in the last few days. He had met two of the most important people in the music indus-try, two men of unquestioned credentials who had done as much to shape the popular-music landscape in America as any two men alive. And they dug him.

The reason Springsteen's fans identify so strongly with him, why they believe so passionately in the notion of Springsteen as the every-man who has made good, the guy who's up there onstage singing for all of us because he knows our hopes and dreams, becomes a little clearer on hearing his description of that late-night bus ride through New Jer-sey. His astonishment at his own good fortune was as heartfelt and sin-cere as any of his best lyrics.

"It didn't seem real. I don't know if I could even conceive of it all," Springsteen said, his sense of awe still intact. "I went back to Asbury Park the same night, you know, but it was funny because I was on the bus and I said to myself, 'My life has just changed. My life changed today in some [his voice rose] *IMMENSE* way. How can I possibly explain this to anyone?'"

Springsteen's first contract with Columbia called for him to record ten albums in five years for Appel's production company, Laurel Canyon. He got a twenty-five-thousand-dollar advance against future royalties and forty thousand dollars to pay for the recording costs of his first album. But as Dave Marsh has noted, Springsteen hadn't really signed with Columbia; he had signed with Laurel Canyon, and Laurel Canyon had signed with Columbia.

Springsteen wasn't the only one who realized how markedly his life had changed since he had first met Hammond. Hammond also realized it, and he wanted Springsteen to be prepared for what lay ahead. So he did something that, according to other Columbia executives, few other A&R men would have even considered. He sent Springsteen to see an independent lawyer, one familiar with the entertainment business and copyright law but not affiliated with Columbia and therefore carrying no conflicts of interest. The lawyer's name was William Krasilovsky, and from a tiny office overlooking Grand Central Station he advised a number of Hammond's artists on the potential legal pitfalls of the music industry.

Thirty years later, Krasilovsky said he knew right away that Springsteen would one day be sorry he had agreed to Appel's terms in the contracts with him.

One of several significant clauses in the contracts stipulated that Appel, or someone designated by his production company, would act as producer for Springsteen's records. Thus Hammond, who had clashed with Appel from the start, never produced any of the material on Springsteen's albums.

(Columbia's decision to allow Appel's stipulation would later prove costly. Springsteen, as Krasilovsky had predicted, began to chafe under the terms of the contracts and eventually sued Appel, seeking, among other things, to undo the producing arrangement. When Appel countersued, Springsteen was barred from recording for nearly three years, until a settlement was reached that allowed Springsteen to buy himself out of the contracts.)

Springsteen's successful auditions in front of Hammond and Davis led the folks at Columbia, Hammond especially, to assume that he intended to pursue a career as a solo artist, a singer-songwriter in the same vein as Bob Dylan, Leonard Cohen, or James Taylor. And it was as a solo artist that he was signed to the company.

Springsteen, looking back on the confusion, explained that he was between bands and flat broke at the time he wrote the songs he performed for Hammond. He needed to make something happen for himself, he said. So he wrote a batch of songs specifically to "present something that was a fully realized world with just myself and the acoustic guitar."

It worked, and Hammond urged Springsteen to do a solo acoustic record for his debut on Columbia. But Springsteen was determined to follow his own instincts. So after signing the recording contract, he called a number of his old bandmates from the Jersey Shore and told them they were going to make an album together. Both Hammond and Appel were surprised by the turn of events. Eventually a compromise was reached under which Springsteen recorded *Greetings from Asbury Park, N.J.* with a rhythm section—drums and an electric bass—but the electric guitar was used sparingly.

Even after reconciling himself to the idea of recording the first album with a band, Hammond remained uncomfortable with Springsteen and Appel's recording methods. He recalled, "Bruce or Mike or somebody decided to record in Studio 914 over across the river in Blauvelt [in upstate New York], and so I went over there and thought, 'Gee, that's an inconvenient place to record.' But Bruce said he could get unlimited time and unlimited credit. I don't think he knew too much of what was going on."

According to Hammond, after he had made a few suggestions, Appel responded to his input by scheduling the remaining recording sessions for after midnight, long after the increasingly frail Hammond needed to be in bed. (Appel disputes that assertion, claiming that the sessions were scheduled around Springsteen's nocturnal lifestyle.)

Springsteen said he did his best to keep everyone happy while maintaining his musical vision. "That was confusing, and looking back on it, you know, we ended up compromising on the first record," Springsteen explained. "I think John would have preferred me to play completely acoustic alone. Which, looking back on it, I mean, I went back and I heard some of the audition tapes which were just acoustic and they sounded good [he laughed], you know."

In essence, however, John Hammond and Mike Appel, who were trying their level best to steer Springsteen's career in the direction they genuinely believed was in his best interest, didn't know much about his career. According to Springsteen, at the time he began recording *Greetings*, neither Hammond nor Appel had ever seen him perform backed by a full band.

Of course, in the decades to follow, Springsteen, perhaps more than any other rock star, would come to be seen as a band *leader*, the lifeblood, guiding force, musical director, and chief executive officer of the aggregation called the E Street Band. With that in mind, he explained how and why he signed with Columbia as a solo artist, ostensibly to become the new Dylan, but then went about creating the environment in which he was most comfortable making music. "I wrote the music and I went up and I signed as a solo artist because I felt that that music was better than the music I'd been making with the band and better than the stuff I'd done in the past. And it was just the best stuff that I'd ever written. So that was the core of it," he said, referring to the lyric-heavy material on his first album. "But I knew that when it came time to present that [music] that the best way to do it, I felt, was with a group behind me. I wanted to present it that way because I knew I could be exciting onstage and I could get people excited about the music."

One needs only to see firsthand the interplay between Springsteen and his bandmates to realize why he believed he could raise an audience's energy level by presenting his songs backed by a full complement of musicians.

Hammond was never fully convinced that Springsteen wouldn't have made a more powerful statement had he forged ahead as a solo artist, but after seeing Springsteen perform with the whole band at live shows in New York City, he better understood Springsteen's conviction that his music worked better in a band setting. In fact, he became a regular at Springsteen's early club performances.

In keeping with the diversity of his music, Springsteen at the time was performing half of the show essentially alone with his guitar (Danny Frederici might back him on accordion on songs such as "Bishop Danced"). Later he would bring out the whole band. This format helped Springsteen sort out which songs sounded best backed by a band and which ones sounded better using a spare arrangement. "It ended up the best of both worlds," he said. These types of shows, performed at small clubs like Max's Kansas City, eventually convinced Hammond that Springsteen could be successful as a bandleader.

Hammond's professional relationship with Springsteen, as with many of his protégés, was relatively brief. He signed him to Columbia, championed his find in the halls of Columbia's executive suites and among the music media, and then backed away as Springsteen's career took off. But in that brief period—from mid-1972 into 1973—during which Springsteen was finding his way through the dangerous landscape of the music industry, he and Hammond forged a unique relationship. The friendship was unique partly because Springsteen, especially as a young man, was a notorious loner, by his own account preferring the company of his car, a tape deck, and a moonlit highway to the party scene. He had few close friends.

But, according to Springsteen, in Hammond he had found something of a soul mate, notwithstanding the difference in their ages, not to mention their disparate upbringings. Springsteen was the son of a laborer from New Jersey, Hammond a direct descendant of Cornelius Vanderbilt. Yet they connected. In the period just after Springsteen signed with Columbia, he would often show up unannounced at Hammond's office, guitar in tow, to try out a new song or just to shoot the breeze about music. The two men—one a living legend well into his sixties, the other a driven young street poet with a future yet to be determined—would sit and talk over a cup of coffee or a soft drink. Springsteen might pull out his guitar or read Hammond some new lyrics.

"He was somebody I felt that my music was very safe with," Springsteen recalled with obvious fondness. "He just exuded love of music.

The minute he heard something he liked he was capable of expressing such enthusiasm. Physically, his face—he had one of the great smiles of all time—you know, that brush cut and all. You just felt like, you know, the sun was shining on you."

So what was it about Springsteen (and Leonard Cohen and George Benson and Bob Dylan and Aretha Franklin and Charlie Christian and Count Basie and Billie Holiday) that caught Hammond's attention? What were the qualities radiating from Springsteen that day in Hammond's office that burst out at him so clearly and so forcefully? What was it that told Hammond almost immediately that this artist "would last a generation," as he once put it?

"I think he was just instinctive, you know. I think he went with his gut," said Springsteen. "I think that what he sensed in people was a singular voice, you know, that was what moved him. When there were no clichés in the songs, when it's all you, when it's all yours, when he's hearing something he hasn't quite heard before. That's what he looked for. That's what moved him. A singular voice, some sort of distinctive voice that came from someplace particular and spoke with a certain sort of emotional force."

Springsteen paused for a moment, then added, "It was always about the music—the music, the music, the music. Every time we talked it was always about music—my music, somebody else's music, music he'd just heard, music he was looking forward to listening to. He was just steeped in it up to the last time I saw him. I found that inspirational. I found that attention to what the job was supposed to be about very important."

Springsteen's devotion to Hammond was returned. In his memoirs, Hammond paid perhaps his highest compliment to his former protégé. Writing in the mid-1970s, with Springsteen reaching his first peak of fame with the success of *Born to Run* and with simultaneous cover stories in *Time* and *Newsweek*, Hammond made his admiration for the budding superstar abundantly clear. After explaining that their schedules and lifestyles prevented a closer relationship, he wrote wistfully, "I wish I knew him ten times better than I do."

Bruce Springsteen was an anomaly in Hammond's career. Talent usually didn't just walk in the door and sit down on the couch in his office. Usually it arrived in the form of a tape. And more often than not the tapes that arrived at Hammond's office were devoid of talent. Looking back on Hammond's track record through the mid-1970s, one might easily get the impression that everything he touched turned to gold. But that impression would be mistaken. His papers at Yale University reveal the truth. Hammond auditioned hundreds of artists over the years, most of whom were never even offered the opportunity to make a demo tape, let alone an actual record.

Hammond's reputation was based on his ability to spot raw talent long before that talent reached its full potential. Ironically, he was almost equally renowned among his peers in the music industry for throwing his considerable energy behind artists whose talent was questionable at best. The reason for this seeming disparity is that he knew no other way. He either loved what a given musician was doing or hated it. He was criticized for this tendency as a music critic in the 1930s, and he hadn't changed his ways four decades later. Thus there were auditions and demo sessions with groups with names like the Nutty Squirrels and Adrian and the Hatreds.

Mike Kissel, a Hammond protégé in the late 1970s who never attained stardom but nevertheless forged a successful career in the industry as a musician and producer, put Hammond's career into perspective. "Maybe John was right 20 percent of the time. But being right 20 percent of the time in the music business is like hitting four hundred for forty years in the major leagues. No one else in the business had a track record that was even on the same planet."

Hammond's colleagues marveled at his ability to muster enthusiasm for the musicians he was championing, even the mediocre ones. "You just have to watch John listening to a recording by the artist that he's championing at the moment. He's the biggest supporter they will ever have in their life," said Robert Altshuler.

"John did something that every great music man should be doing with his life," Altshuler continued. "From his earliest, earliest years, he made a decision . . . He never knew when and where he would hear something that was unique and original, and that's what he was constantly looking for, something that was unique and original. He had great faith in the grassroots world of music, that it could emerge anywhere at any time, that this country's diversity was its greatest strength in terms of musical creativity. He knew that it could be happening anywhere. That's why John tuned in to long-wave radio, that's why John traveled whenever he got a chance."

And he listened to music constantly.

Scores of tapes from undiscovered artists arrived in the mail every week. After all, what entertainer wouldn't want the opportunity to be heard by the same guy who "discovered" Billie Holiday, Aretha Franklin, Bob Dylan, and Bruce Springsteen? Of course, most of these tapes elicited from Hammond nothing more than a polite letter of rejection.

Some didn't take the rejection well. For example, a bandleader from Providence, Rhode Island, apparently sensing he and his outfit were ready for the big time, sent Hammond a tape and some photographs in the summer of 1974. A few months later, after he hadn't heard from Hammond, the bandleader wrote again. He was getting impatient, and he wanted some word from Hammond as to where their relationship was going. By the end of the year, the bandleader's patience had run out. If Hammond didn't send back all of the material by mid-January, the bandleader wrote, he would be forced to turn the matter over to his "backers." He wasn't specific as to exactly who his backers were, leaving Hammond to speculate. He was very specific, however, about what would happen if his demands weren't met: "I want all said materials by [early 1975] or you're going to be sicker than you ever were in your life . . . It's your choice to stay healthy and mail me all said materials or have an accident, [sic] John accidents happen every day in NY with the people I know."

Never easily intimidated, Hammond ignored the threats. The material in question was returned to the bandleader, and he was never heard from again.

Meanwhile, Hammond could do little more than offer moral support to Springsteen as his first two albums sold poorly and the executives at Columbia began to lose their patience. In a letter to a radio executive written in December 1973, Hammond summed up the situation at Columbia:

Thank you so much for your ecstatic letter about Bruce Springsteen. I agree with your sentiments completely, but am terribly
disappointed in the second album [*The Wild, the Innocent, and
the E Street Shuffle*, which had been released a month earlier].
It seems however that the album has its enthusiasts and I am
enclosing a copy of the review in Sunday's New York Times,
which is nothing less than an unadulterated rave. My reasons
for being disappointed are that Bruce's performances do not
have the ease or the joy of his live appearances and have the
feeling of material being far too carefully worked over. It's all
pretty embarrassing for Columbia since most of us here have
felt that this album doesn't do him justice and are waiting for
what ought to be his major effort—the next album.

A year and a half later, with the release of *Born to Run* in August
1975, Hammond's prediction was proven correct.

According to Springsteen, Hammond was thrilled by his success.
He seemed particularly impressed that Springsteen had achieved stardom on his own terms—that is to say, backed by a band, *his band*, the
E Street Band. "He was just always excited. 'Oh, it's wonderful what
happened to you. It's mah-velous,' yeah, that was his word [Spring-
steen laughed again]. 'Oh, that's mah-velous, it's just mah-velous.' He
was just extremely excited that the whole thing sort of worked."

Hammond officially retired from Columbia in December 1975,
when he turned sixty-five, the mandatory retirement age at the label.
There was the obligatory party and commemorative watch and even a
professionally produced half-hour video in which friends, family, and
colleagues paid tribute. Helen Humes, the jazz singer whom Hammond matched with Count Basie nearly four decades earlier, said with
obvious sincerity, "I used to call him my white father because he was
always there when you needed him." Goddard Lieberson, elegant as
always in a double-breasted blue blazer, recalled, "He was always taking you someplace to hear someone who was wonderful." Count Basie,
Bruce Springsteen, Benny Goodman, and Pete Seeger also contributed a few words each.

Hammond himself provided the high point of the video during
the opening sequence, when he offered up his opinions on everything

from Frank Sinatra ("I never particularly liked Sinatra. He bored me")
to Duke Ellington ("In a class by himself. An absolute genius") to
Richard Nixon ("It's not quotable or printable").

A number of Hammond's friends felt he was treated shabbily by
Columbia at the time of his retirement, suggesting that the company
seemed in a hurry to get rid of the man who had brought to the label
many of the top musical artists of the twentieth century. These supporters were quick to note that Hammond's royalty checks, had he ever
accepted royalties on money generated by the artists he brought to the
label, would have made him easily one of the wealthiest retirees ever to
bid farewell to Columbia.

It's hard to argue the notion that Columbia never paid him nearly
what he was worth. He was making less than fifty thousand dollars a
year at the time of his retirement. Meanwhile, most of his much
younger peers in Columbia's A&R department were making many
times that amount in royalty payments stemming from their work as
producers, a role Hammond never adapted to in the modern sense of
the job. And Hammond was never asked to join the corporate end
of the business, where his opinions regarding the direction of the label
might have held more weight. His title at the time of his retirement
was fancy—executive producer and director of talent acquisition—
but mostly ceremonial. His responsibilities were really no different in
1975 from what they had been sixteen years earlier when he rejoined
Columbia.

But if Hammond felt any bitterness toward his treatment by his
longtime employer, he hid it well. Indeed, he publicly expressed his gratitude to Columbia for offering him a two-year consulting deal that would
allow him to continue to discover and record artists after he retired.

Besides, Hammond didn't enter the music business to make a lot of
money or acquire power as an executive. He was an extremely self-
aware man, one who actively cultivated an image as an eccentric iconoclast who openly disdained the business end of the business. He was
also exceedingly opinionated, and his opinions and the manner in
which he offered them often rubbed people the wrong way. His was
not the type of personality that glided smoothly up the executive lad-
der. And he couldn't have cared less.

So he bid farewell to Black Rock and set up shop in a small office in the New York Coliseum building on Columbus Circle. From there he continued to do what he did best—seek out distinctive talent and fight so that that talent would be heard.

One of his first postretirement projects as an independent producer was a young Polish pianist named Adam Makowicz. He spent the better part of 1976 working to get Makowicz out of Communist Poland so that the pianist could perform in the United States. Makowicz was eventually introduced to American audiences during a six-week run arranged by Hammond at Barney Josephson's Cookery, a successor to the groundbreaking Café Society clubs.

Although Hammond was sixty-five years old, his enthusiasm for the musicians he was championing hadn't diminished a bit. Indeed, Makowicz would eventually echo comments made by many of the artists who had come before him, artists who had also experienced the thrill of being swept up into the Hammond whirlwind.

Makowicz had come to Hammond's attention via Willis Conover, the renowned Voice of America broadcaster who introduced jazz to countless millions of Europeans in the decades after World War II. Conover and Hammond had forged a long-term friendship based on their shared belief that jazz is a musical expression of freedom.

Makowicz said he found in Hammond an integrity that allowed him to trust him unreservedly. He had little choice, after all, since he knew no one in New York and he depended on Hammond for everything from getting an apartment to generating advance publicity for gigs. "The only way I could learn more about this music [jazz] was to leave Europe and I knew that," Makowicz said nearly twenty-five years later. "It was [necessary] to come to New York to play jazz, and Hammond gave me this chance. It was like a dream."

"He was kind of bossy," Makowicz said, laughing, "but he was trying his best to serve the artist and I accepted whatever he suggested. He was only concerned with what was in the best interest of the music and the musician. He was not interested in money. The quality of the music was the most important thing to him."

Makowicz remained astounded a full twenty-five years later at Hammond's ability to open doors and generate opportunities for his artists. Within a year of his arrival in New York in 1977, he had

recorded an album for Columbia Records and shared the stage at
Carnegie Hall with Teddy Wilson, George Shearing, and Earl Hines
during a tribute to the pianist Erroll Garner.

In retirement, Hammond never had work far from his mind, but
some aspects of his new freedom appealed to him. He had spent a lifetime mixing his passions for music and civil rights, frequently using
one to promote the other. These passions left him with little time for
much else. Now, however, he could indulge in a truly frivolous pursuit:
pinball.

Hammond was a walking incongruity, and never more so than
when he was poised in front of a pinball machine inside his favorite arcade on Broadway a few blocks north of Times Square. If he had been
a familiar face at the arcade during his hectic years at Columbia, he
was now positively a regular. His trips to the arcade became something
of a daily pilgrimage. Strolling south on Broadway from Columbus Circle, he would sidle up to a newsstand and, in petulant defiance of his
doctor's orders, purchase a pack of his favorite European cigarettes
and a couple of fancy chocolate bars.

Now he was ready. Consider the image of an elegant if slightly
rumpled looking older man, his handsome face beaming beneath a
flattop crew cut, his shoulders and arms tensed in preparation for his
foe, eyes sparkling and gazing fixedly into the clanging machinery. He
is surrounded by scores of comrades in arms, warriors poised for battle
against a common enemy. Only, the other warriors are teenagers,
smart-aleck kids skipping school or else out-of-towners seeking a brief
repose from their tourist parents. Visually, Hammond stuck out. Spiri-
tually, however, he was right at home.

Hammond also found time to go to the golf course, often with his
old friend Jerry Wexler, who was now a legend himself on account of
his work with Ray Charles and Aretha Franklin. And perhaps best of
all, he got to spend more time with his wife, Esme, and their wide circle
of friends. People who knew the couple described their relationship as
a true partnership, one that thrived not only on their similarities—
boundless curiosity and a passion for music, art, and travel—but also
on their differences. Esme, beautiful (people said she was a prettier
Leslie Caron), graceful, always knowing just the right thing to say to

put people at ease, was the perfect complement to her brash and out-spoken husband.

"They were a fascinating couple," said Ann Slater, who often social-ized with the Hammonds in the 1970s and 1980s. "They were devoted to each other, and they were very in tune to one another's needs."

The Hammonds were still living in the same rented apartment on East Fifty-seventh Street that they had moved into shortly after getting married. In the evening, John and Esme favored Mortimer's for dinner, and Esme was fond of an Irish pub on Fifty-seventh Street between First and Second avenues. After dinner they might drop by the Carlyle to see their friend and neighbor Bobby Short perform his nightclub act. Or maybe they'd take a cab downtown to a jazz club in the Village. On weekends, Hammond drove his decidedly unassuming Toyota Cressida, which he parked in a lot around the corner from their apartment, to the couple's rented cottage in the woods of Weston, Connecticut.

A favorite anecdote from this period, one that captures the essence of John and Esme Hammond, both as a couple and as individuals, orig-inated during a party thrown by a well-heeled society matron at her chic apartment on the Upper East Side of Manhattan. Aware of Ham-mond's professional reputation, the hostess asked him to procure the entertainment for her soiree. On the night of the party, guests munched caviar and sipped champagne while milling about a lovely drawing room equipped with a grand Steinway piano. Word spread that Ham-mond had arranged for the talent, and the room was thick with antici-pation. Maybe Count Basie or one of Hammond's other superstar friends would make a surprise appearance. Or perhaps the guests would be treated to some unknown talent whom Hammond had targeted for stardom. In fact, they were treated to the latter. But it wasn't quite what they had imagined.

At some point, all the guests were asked to be seated. Suddenly a curtain was drawn, exposing a woman standing behind a small table covered with water glasses filled to varying levels. She bowed de-murely, and then proceeded to fill the room with the eerie tonal sound produced by rubbing a finger around the rim of a half-filled glass. Jaws dropped and eyes gaped. Hammond was thrilled. This was the talent he had arranged, and he couldn't have been more excited had Count Basie himself been seated at that magnificent Steinway. "And it was very beautiful," one person who attended the party remembered. "The woman was extremely talented. He just couldn't turn that ear off. It didn't matter whether it was an acoustic guitar or water glasses, John Hammond could hear the genius behind it."

Seated next to her husband, Esme Hammond smiled beguilingly and enjoyed the show.

Every year the Hammonds threw a Christmas party at their apartment for family and close friends. From her apartment building across Fifty-seventh Street, Gloria Vanderbilt, a first cousin of Hammond's, could watch through the window as Esme trimmed the couples' Christmas tree. "They created a wonderful feeling at their apartment," Vanderbilt recalled. "You always felt at home. It was always so warm and comfortable." Esme Hammond, she said, "had a generosity of spirit that was really just lovely."

According to people familiar with the family, Hammond had been less than a doting father following his divorce from his first wife, and his relationship with his two sons suffered over the years. Yet, given his lifestyle, he seems to have done his best to remain involved in their lives, encouraging them to pursue their interests and spending time with them when he could. And despite whatever difficulties existed, he was immensely proud of John Paul's successful career as a musician and equally proud of Jason's success as a carpenter.

Another favorite haunt of Hammond's now that he had more time on his hands was the Century Club, an exclusive redoubt for artists and writers in a Stanford White–designed structure just around the corner from Grand Central Station—and precisely the sort of place a younger John Hammond would never have set foot inside. Hammond's peers during his years of membership in the 1970s and 1980s formed a who's who of intellectual movers and shakers, including the journalist Harrison Salisbury, the writer and editor George Plimpton, the diplomat and historian George Kennan, and the economist Robert Heilbroner. Two of Hammond's frequent lunch mates at the Century Club were the writer Albert Murray, one of the first blacks admitted to the club, and the historian Arthur Schlesinger, Jr.

It was a nod to the many contrasts that defined Hammond that this lifelong champion of the underdog might be found on almost any given day sprawled luxuriously in an overstuffed leather chair, sipping a martini in the Century Club's billiard room. There, one long leg swung over the other and surrounded on all sides by oak-paneled walls adorned with original landscapes by the painters of the Hudson River school, Hammond would hold forth on his favorite topics—music, (liberal) politics, and civil rights.

"He was an intellectually stimulating person," Arthur Schlesinger, Jr., recalled. "He had a great talent for friendship. He was the kind of person whom [upon seeing him] when you entered a room your spirits rose." Hammond's engaging personality and high-profile notoriety as the man who had discovered so much rich American musical talent made him an extremely popular member, according to Schlesinger. Groups of serious, dark-suited, gray-templed men, each one an eminence in his field, would crowd around him to hear his latest exploits scouting new talent at some nightclub in Harlem or recording some rock star in a midtown studio.

He also worked on his memoirs, which were published to mostly warm reviews in 1977. "Here's the most informative and most informed book ever written about jazz," read a headline in the *Toronto Star*. Alden Whitman wrote in *The New York Times*, "Few men have been quite so near to the pulse beat of jazz and swing as Mr. Hammond. In this anecdotal and graceful account of his life and exploits, written with the help of Irving Townsend, he displays an admirable modesty, while describing his career with candor and perspective." The *New Yorker* review was long and lukewarm: "John Hammond's autobiography . . . is the reverse of what one expected. It is frank and buoyant about his family and background and low-voiced and defensive about his place in jazz music and civil liberties. Moreover, the book . . . is delivered in a styleless, store-bought monotone that is the direct opposite of Hammond's ebullient, superlative-spattered self."

But cocktail parties, fancy private clubs, and memoirs were an amusement, something to pass the time now that he actually had time to pass. He would have preferred otherwise. And when an old friend came to him with a proposal to start a small music label, he jumped at the chance.

16

SRV

Hank O'Neal first met John Hammond shortly after leaving the Central Intelligence Agency in the late 1960s. O'Neal, a jazz buff, came to New York from Washington, D.C., hoping to start a new career as a record producer. A mutual friend suggested he call Hammond, and the two quickly hit it off, but no opportunities arose for them to work together. A decade passed during which O'Neal founded and subsequently sold his own small record company, the influential Chiaroscuro label. Then, in 1980, he decided it was time to start another one. He and his partner, a Wall Street financier named John Moore, were looking for a third partner, preferably an insider in the music business, when they thought of Hammond. "John was thrilled because he had sort of been just put out to lunch [by Columbia]," O'Neal recalled. "He was enthusiastic about becoming involved because, quite frankly, what we were suggesting was, 'Hey, we're gonna raise some money and let you make some records that would be fun.' He thought that would be terrific because nobody else was letting him do that and hadn't let him do it for a long time."

Hammond Music Enterprises was launched in January 1981. The partners threw a party at Sardi's, that most famous of show-business watering holes. Many of Hammond's friends showed up, among them Count Basie, Buck Clayton, Vic Dickenson, Barney Josephson, and Jerry Wexler. At first things seemed promising. Hammond and his partners were able to raise about $250,000, and Hammond used his connections to get the fledgling label a distribution pact with Columbia. Office space was rented on West Fifty-seventh Street. Meanwhile, Moore was making arrangements on Wall Street for the company to raise additional money by selling shares of its stock to the public. "The game plan was to use the quarter of a million dollars to go public," O'Neal said. "Everything was looking real good. John was having a ball, people were coming in, we were looking at new artists and new acts."

Hammond was especially keen on recording Allen Ginsberg. The two had grown friendly over the years, with their shared sentiment of the activist. Hammond loved Ginsberg's poetry, the forcefulness of the words, and they way Ginsberg used those words as an agent of change.

But things fell apart quickly, according to O'Neal. In the spring of 1981, Hammond Music Enterprises switched accounting firms, delaying its initial public offering. Later that year the stock market fell into a prolonged decline as the federal deficit soared under President Ronald Reagan's domestic policies of tax cuts and increased military spending. "Nothing ever went anywhere . . . and by January of '82 everything had gone south with the company," O'Neal said. It would take another two years for the company to regroup enough to sell some shares to the public. But by the time the company had changed its name, Hammond's health had deteriorated, and he was no longer actively involved.

It was an embarrassing episode for an industry legend, and, more important, Hammond lost a good deal of money, further complicating his already-fragile financial situation. But he was able to take some solace in the fact that of the handful of albums released by Hammond Music Enterprises, one of them was a two-record collection of poem-songs by Allen Ginsberg titled *First Blues*. Hammond had recorded a number of the songs in the years just after his retirement from Columbia, when he was working as an independent producer under Columbia's auspices. But, according to Hammond, Columbia allegedly refused to release the songs because of numerous sexual and scatological references. Hammond was only too happy to release the controversial material through his own label when the chance arose.

Bruised egos notwithstanding, the foundering of Hammond's record company did nothing to diminish his reputation. The name John Hammond remained a magnet for unique voices hoping to be heard. Thus in the winter of 1982, as the future of Hammond Music Enterprises was growing increasingly precarious, a tape arrived in the mail. It had been sent by the manager of a blues guitarist from Austin, Texas, named Stevie Ray Vaughan. The tape contained a recording of a performance by Vaughan and his band, Double Trouble, broadcast on the radio from Steamboat 1874, one of Austin's top live music venues. The tape was addressed to Hammond, but O'Neal was the first to hear it. "I took the tape home with me and played it in the car," O'Neal recalled. "And then I went back to work the next morning and I told everyone to bet the ranch on this kid."

Vaughan and his bandmates had been scuffling around the live music mecca of Austin for several years before anyone outside of Texas started to pay attention. Vaughan had followed his brother, the guitarist Jimmie Vaughan, down to Austin from their hometown of Dallas as a teenager in the early 1970s, and he had virtually grown up honing his chops on the stages of the Armadillo World Headquarters, Soap Creek Saloon, and the Continental Club. He played in bands with names like Krackerjack, the Nightcrawlers, and the Cobras. But it was onstage at Antone's that Vaughan's legend began.

Antone's opened downtown on Sixth Street in the summer of 1975 as the dream of the blues enthusiast Clifford Antone. In short order, word had spread as far north as Chicago that there was a club down in Texas that catered exclusively to the gutsy, flamboyant style of electric blues favored by regional guitar slingers like Buddy Guy, Albert Collins, and Albert King. Antone recruited men like Hubert Sumlin from Howlin' Wolf's band; Luther Tucker, an ex-sideman of Muddy Waters's; and Eddie Taylor, who'd once played with Jimmy Reed. Finally, even Waters himself came down from Chicago to see what all the fuss was about. One of Vaughan's biographers put it aptly when he wrote that Vaughan and the rest of the blues musicians who congregated in Austin used Antone's as their very own "University of Soul."

By 1978, when Double Trouble was formed, the twenty-three-year-old Vaughan was recognized as the best young guitarist in Austin.

Double Trouble's lineup changed a few times early on, but things began to stabilize when a drummer named Chris "Whipper" Layton joined. Slightly built at perhaps five feet eight and 145 pounds, Layton could kick up a hurricane with his sticks. The group was complete early in 1981 when a tall, soft-spoken bass player named Tommy Shannon signed on. Shannon, some ten years older than Vaughan, was akin to a genuine rock star in Austin, having played Woodstock as a member of Johnny Winter's band. Moreover, he and Vaughan shared a taste for cocaine and Crown Royal whiskey.

Things started to look up for the band in early 1982 after the producer Jerry Wexler heard Vaughan jamming with a who's who of Austin guitar heroes at the Continental Club during an album-release party for Lou Ann Barton, who had once sung with Vaughan. Wexler, in town from New York, was so impressed with Vaughan that he hung around Austin another day to hear him play with Double Trouble. Afterward, he used his considerable influence to arrange for Double Trouble to appear at the Montreux Jazz Festival in Switzerland.

If the Vaughan legend began at Antone's, it was cemented at Montreux on July 17, 1982. Early on, the European audience seemed unsure about this brash young guitarist and his high-decibel attack. But Vaughan won them over, charming them with his charisma and astounding them with his chops. He mixed technical wizardry with flashy rock-and-roll gimmicks, fingerpicking jazzy arpeggios one minute and playing the guitar behind his back the next. And it worked. By the end of the set the crowd was riveted.

Among the crowd were a handful of rock royalty, including David Bowie, who watched the Double Trouble performance from backstage. Bowie liked what he saw and asked Vaughan to play on his next album. Jackson Browne also saw the performance, and he was so knocked out he offered the band free recording time in his California studio. Vaughan accepted both invitations, and within a few months of the Montreux show he had contributed some scorching leads to Bowie's next album, *Let's Dance*, gaining invaluable exposure in the process, and the band had traveled to California, spending three days recording ten songs at Browne's Down Town Studio in Los Angeles.

Meanwhile, Double Trouble's manager, Chesley Millikin, was sending tapes of the band's live performances to influential music industry types in New York City. One of those was heard by Hank O'Neal at Hammond Music Enterprises.

All of this activity brought Vaughan to Hammond's attention, and he liked what he heard. Eventually, through Millikin, Hammond got hold of a copy of the demo Double Trouble had made at Jackson Browne's studio, and with that demo in hand he started the ball rolling as only John Hammond was capable of doing. Realizing that his independent label couldn't do justice to the kind of future he foresaw for Stevie Ray Vaughan and Double Trouble, Hammond took the demo to a friend and colleague at Epic Records, a Columbia subsidiary. The friend, Gregg Geller, head of A&R at Epic, took one listen and was just as hooked as Hammond.

Epic, facing competition from Elektra and MCA Records, signed Vaughan in early 1983 and gave him sixty-five thousand dollars to touch up the album he had recorded at Browne's studio the previous summer. In short order, the band was ensconced at Media Sound Studios in Manhattan remixing those recordings. During the remixing process, Hammond finally got a chance to see Vaughan and Double Trouble play live at a performance arranged to showcase the band for CBS executives at the Bottom Line in New York. According to a biography of Vaughan, the guitarist was nervous during his sound check. "That's all right. You'll do fine," Hammond told him. Vaughan settled down and blew away an audience sprinkled with record company honchos and rock stars, including Mick Jagger, Johnny Winter, and Billy Gibbons of ZZ Top.

With a bit of polish (but not much) the album *Texas Flood* was released in June with John Hammond credited as executive producer. Vaughan and his bandmates, with a hand from an Austin friend, a sound engineer named Richard Mullen, actually produced the songs. In truth, Hammond hadn't done much work on the album, in part because he liked the raw sound Vaughan, Layton, and Shannon had achieved during the three days of hurried recording in California. Hammond's chief role on *Texas Flood* may have been making sure Vaughan and the others didn't clean the songs up too much such that they lost all their raw emotion. The album was essentially a collection of live performances recorded inside a studio rather than a theater or a nightclub—in other words, exactly the kind of album Hammond preferred.

The seventy-two-year-old Hammond took an immediate shine to these three young bluesmen from Texas. And the feeling was mutual. So much so, in fact, that Double Trouble chose for the rear cover of the album a photo of the three band members seated in the studio alongside Hammond. Vaughan is looking sideways at Hammond and laughing at something, perhaps his good fortune. Chris Layton is leaning over Hammond's shoulder as if about to tell him something in confidence. Tommy Shannon is taking it all in in his quiet way. And Hammond, in his ubiquitous tweed coat and skinny tie, is grinning, the same grin that, according to Bruce Springsteen, "kinda washed all over you."

Texas Flood filled a vacuum. When the album was released early in the summer of 1983, popular music was mired in one of its periodic cycles during which style takes precedence over substance. Contrived bands whose look was more memorable than their sound sat atop the charts. Certainly Flock of Seagulls is remembered more for the band members' distinctive hairstyles than for any lasting contribution to the musical landscape. Duran Duran, another chart topper of the period, with a lineup consisting of several male models turned musicians, seems to have been formed specifically to fill the growing need for music videos. And Boy George, another cultural icon of the period, became a star less for his music than for his brassy androgyny. Even the unique sound of the Police, whose *Synchronicity* album yielded a number of intelligent and catchy hits, and Michael Jackson's *Thriller* lacked the sort of gut-wrenching passion the punk bands had brought to music just a few years earlier.

Also missing in action were the guitar gods of the 1970s: Jimi Hendrix and Duane Allman were long dead, Johnny Winter was dealing with addiction, Eric Clapton was making pop records, Jeff Beck was mired in obscurity, and Jimmy Page apparently had nothing left to say.

Into that void stepped Stevie Ray Vaughan and Double Trouble. Their swaggering hybrid of traditional blues and contemporary rock and roll was reminiscent of the best power trios of the late 1960s, Cream and Jimi Hendrix (most especially Hendrix). Vaughan's fret work was phenomenal, enabling him after just one album to accomplish the ultimate guitar-hero achievement—that of having an immediately identifiable sound. Layton and Shannon behind him provided the foundation on which Vaughan strutted his stuff. "He brought back a style that had died, and he brought it back at exactly the right time," Hammond is quoted as saying in a Vaughan biography. "The young ears hadn't heard anything with this kind of sound."

Prompted by extensive radio airplay of the single "Pride and Joy" and impassioned live performances at increasingly larger venues around the country, *Texas Flood* sold well—500,000 copies by the end of 1983. Soon it was time for the band to get to work on a follow-up album. So in January 1984 Vaughan, Layton, and Shannon squeezed some time out of their relentless touring schedule to return to New York to begin laying down the tracks for what would become *Couldn't Stand the Weather*.

Meanwhile, Vaughan's unexpected success prompted Columbia Records to reach out to Hammond and extend an offer to return to the company as a salaried consultant. He jumped at the opportunity. After nearly ten years as an independent producer with little to show for that time save a failed record company, he was thrilled to rejoin the most powerful name in the business, one that had the ability to take the raw talent he specialized in and provide a forum for that talent to be heard. Columbia even gave him a new office at Black Rock. He felt like he had come home again.

As significant as his new salary and office was a royalty arrangement he had agreed to at the insistence of none other than Stevie Ray Vaughan. In five decades, Hammond had never accepted a penny of royalties from the sale of any of the records he produced for the company. He was virtually alone among his peers in his belief that money generated by the sale of records should go to the artists who wrote and performed the music heard on the record. (Hammond did receive royalties on reissues that he helped compile for Columbia, collections of songs from artists such as Mildred Bailey, Robert Johnson, and Bessie Smith.)

Vaughan and Hammond had struck up a unique friendship, not un-like the bond that had formed between Hammond and Springsteen a decade earlier. Each saw in the other a rare integrity. Exactly how Vaughan got Hammond to agree to accept part of the band's royalties is a mystery. But everyone—Stevie Ray Vaughan, Chris Layton, Tommy Shannon, and Hammond himself—was pleased with the deal. Not long after Hammond returned to Columbia, he wrote a note to his lawyer: "Things are going very well for me here at CBS, and I'm finally getting some sizable royalties as a producer from one of my new artists. It's made me realize what I have given up in the past with people like Dylan and Springsteen, but I think this is right and I have no regrets."

Barely an hour into the first recording session for the songs that would appear on *Couldn't Stand the Weather*, the band's engineer, Richard Mullen, asked the musicians to play something, anything, so that he could adjust his dials to the sound of their instruments. Vaughan, Layton, and Shannon had been busy piecing together their equipment since arriving at the studio a short time earlier. Now they got ready to play. Hammond, meanwhile, was sitting off to the side of the engineer's booth hidden behind that day's *New York Times*.

"I don't remember if anybody called it off or what, but I did that roll on 'Tin Pan Alley,' you know, that sort of rumble," Layton recalled. "We kinda just did a pass at that and [Mullen] had the tape rolling. I don't even know why we did that song. As I recall, it was the very first thing we did."

When the musicians had finished playing, Hammond's voice came over the cue mix. "That's the best you'll ever get that song," he said. "That sounded wonderful." Then came the sound of rustling newspa-per, and Hammond disappeared again. Vaughan, Layton, and Shannon trusted Hammond implicitly, but after digesting his remark, they looked at one another a little skeptically. They had barely noticed Hammond was present, let alone that he was listening to what they had considered little more than a sound check.

Layton recalled: "I thought, 'Well, we can get a better one than that, let's keep it rolling.' But we never did. We tried to cut it six, seven more times, but it never sounded better than that. It's pretty interesting that he was that certain of that. He was just so connected to the spirit of what we were doing. He had that intuition. While we were all pretty certain that we could play that song better than that, he sensed something about the whole feel of it that he felt it was probably the truest nature of what we were all about. That's how I took it. Because we did it again, and it never sounded better. I thought, 'How could he know that?'"

Vaughan died tragically in a helicopter crash in 1990, a star on the order of Beck and Clapton. Before his death, he and his bandmates had climbed to the very top of the music business. But more than a decade after Vaughan's death, Layton and Shannon say that no phase of their career was more meaningful to them, more satisfying to them as musicians and artists, than the days spent holed up in the studio working with Hammond.

"You know what really struck me about him that I always appreciated was that what we had was like a family," said Layton. "Stevie was such an incredible talent that no matter what situation he played in, whatever group of musicians, he still always shined, he just shined. So I'm not the world's greatest drummer. We're probably not the world's greatest band, but we all love each other, we care about each other, and John recognized that immediately."

Layton and Shannon were no fools. They knew very well that some music industry types would have shed them in a heartbeat in order to establish Vaughan as a solo artist along the lines of a Clapton or Beck. But Vaughan would have none of that. And Hammond, no doubt intuitively because no one in the band ever brought it up, picked up that vibe immediately and from the very start never treated Double Trouble as anything but a three-person band.

Shannon remembered: "He had the insight to realize that we were a band. That's how we played. It wasn't like Stevie was over here and we were over *here*. It was part of his genius that he saw that. Just being around us for a few minutes he realized that. Nothing slipped past him."

Hammond, according to Layton and Shannon, arrived every day at the studio in a tweed coat and a skinny tie. He brought with him a cup of coffee, that day's *New York Times*, and his lunch in a brown paper bag. And he arrived each day more ebullient than the last. "How is everyone today? Ohh, that's mah-velous, mah-velous. Okay, well, you know, whenever you guys want to go, you just go ahead."

"It was just such a nice spirit," Layton observed.

There was just one matter on which Hammond and the musicians weren't in sync with each other. With success often comes excess, and as Vaughan, Layton, and Shannon grew famous, they ratcheted up their use of whiskey and cocaine. "We were out of our fucking minds on dope and alcohol, that was the thing," said Layton.

Picture a recording studio cluttered with microphones and wires, a drum set, and numerous stands holding an array of guitars and electric basses. In the corner stands a Steinway piano. Inside the engineering booth, which is separated from the studio by a glass partition, a couple of soundmen are fiddling with knobs, busying themselves while the musicians take a break. Hammond is also in the booth, sitting cross-legged at the knee, his face behind a newspaper, as usual.

The lid of the Steinway is open, and three men—Vaughan, Layton, and Shannon—are huddled behind it. One of them holds a mirror on which several grams of powdered cocaine have been poured and cut into lines. One by one, the musicians lean over and ingest those lines through a rolled-up twenty-dollar bill. Each line is chased with a healthy shot of Crown Royal whiskey.

According to Layton, these breaks might last for fifteen minutes, a half hour, or an hour. Then they were ready for another few takes.

"But, you know, we're there and we're doing all these drugs and we're drinking and John's in there reading the paper and kind of listening and we're trying to cut the song and some of the shit's just not sounding good and some of it is sounding good," said Layton. "I don't know how long this goes on for, two weeks or something like that. We cut some particular track and we're all kind of standing there and we're listening to the playback and of course it's really loud and I'm thinking John may not really want to hear the music this loud. The song gets done and he stopped the tape."

At this point in the anecdote Layton began to (affectionately) mimic Hammond's Brahmin accent. "'Ya know,' he goes, 'yeahs ago I worked with this mahvelous musician, he was just a wondahful, wondahful musician. His name was Gene Krupa. The nicest man you'd ever want to meet. Ya know, there was one thing, though, that Gene did. He liked to smoke pot, marijuana. When Gene smoked pot, his timing would go all to hell on the drums. A brilliant player, but his timing would just go all to hell on the drums when he smoked that marijuana. I guess ever since then I guess I just never really had much use for drugs at sessions.'"

"And then," Layton concluded, "he picked up the paper and started reading again."

Hammond never mentioned the drug issue again, and while it would be another few years before the band members cleaned up their acts, the message had been sent. Among top-notch musicians, drugs were not only a senseless distraction; they were a detriment to the only thing that really mattered—the quality of the music.

After the recording sessions for *Couldn't Stand the Weather* were completed, Vaughan and Double Trouble hit the road again. It was the last time they would work with Hammond, and to the band members' dismay their nonstop touring schedule allowed for few occasions to visit with him.

One exception was an extraordinary concert at Carnegie Hall on October 4, 1984, during which Vaughan and, it seemed, practically every musician he had ever played with in Austin took over that celebrated stage.

It's doubtful that in the nearly one hundred years since the steel magnate Andrew Carnegie dedicated what he hoped would become the premier concert venue in the world, one he predicted would "intertwine itself with the history of our country," the hallowed venue at the corner of Fifty-seventh Street and Seventh Avenue had ever seen a crowd quite like the one that came to see Vaughan that night. The tweed, wool, and cardigan that were the norm on a typical fall evening at Carnegie Hall had been replaced by flannel, denim, and leather. This crowd hadn't bustled in from a pretheater dinner in a bistro on Restaurant Row, warmed by a cocktail or two and a bowl of onion soup. Hardly. This crowd, eyes bloodshot from too many beers and blackberry brandy chasers, stumbled in from the seedy bars along Eighth Avenue.

The hall was buzzing with anticipation when, at about eight o'clock, Ken Dashow, a disc jockey from WNEW-FM, stepped onstage from behind a curtain. He introduced himself to distracted applause. And then he called out John Hammond from behind the same curtain, introducing him to the rowdy audience as "one of the most prime forces in rock and roll." Hammond was now seventy-three years old, and a handful of heart attacks over the past two decades had altered his once-energetic gait into something more akin to a shuffle. But illness and age couldn't dim the enthusiasm and pride he felt that night. He was fairly bursting with excitement, and the broad grin on his face was clearly visible from even the rear balcony.

"Hello, everybody," he called. "Thank you for Stevie Ray Vaughan and Double Trouble. Double Trouble is Chris Layton on drums and Tommy Shannon on bass. They're gonna do a whole first half of the show and it's gonna be smoking." (The few people in the audience actually listening to Hammond cheered his prophecy.) "And I think perhaps that . . ." Hammond now apparently sensed the crowd's growing impatience, and he stopped himself mid-sentence. "I promised I wouldn't go on for more than a half a minute [loud cheers from the audience], so I want to introduce to you one of the greatest guitar players of all time, Stevie Ray Vaughan."

A moment later, barely enough time for Hammond's voice to fade out, an earsplitting explosion of notes burst from the wall of amplifiers at the rear of the stage as Vaughan detonated the opening salvo of a bluesy rocker called "Scuttle Buttin'." An instant later the guitar was joined seamlessly by Layton's precise drumming and Shannon's steady bass line. The explosion of music happened so suddenly it caught many in the audience off guard, leaving them startled by the surge of power.

Hammond made his way back across the stage, passing just in front of Vaughan. The guitarist, resplendent in a custom-made mariachi outfit and black bandito hat, was bowed over his battered Stratocaster, his face clenched in concentration. As Hammond walked past, Vaughan glanced up from beneath his hat, and the two men exchanged quick smiles.

In the spring of 1985, John Hammond was working on a demo tape with a young singer-songwriter he had recently anointed as the next coming of Bob Dylan and Bruce Springsteen. The kid's name was Ned Massey, and he was talented but probably not going to live up to those lofty expectations. In any event, Mikie Harris, Hammond's aide-de-camp for the last decade of his life, recalled that Hammond looked a little pale that morning, a little out of sorts. But Hammond was excited about Massey's future and looking forward to working with him in the studio. As usual, he walked from his office at Columbia over to the studio on the West Side, where he was recording Massey. But after working for an hour or so, he told Massey that he wasn't feeling well and that they would have to cut short that day's work. Concerned, Massey called Harris and she hurried over to the studio.

By the time she arrived, Hammond was slurring his words and slumping forward in his chair. He was obviously very ill. A taxi was summoned, and Massey carried Hammond down several flights of stairs to the street. The cabdriver was instructed to find a jazz station and turn the volume way up for the drive across town to Lenox Hill Hospital, where Hammond's primary physician practiced. Esme Hammond met them there.

All of their worst fears were confirmed by Hammond's doctor—he had suffered a massive stroke. Now seventy-four years old, he had been in declining health for some time, and he never fully recovered. He could get around with a walker, but most of his time was spent in a hospital bed that had been installed in his apartment on East Fifty-seventh Street.

Friends say that while the stroke buckled Hammond's knees, the knockout punch came a year later, when Esme passed away. Like her husband, she had been in declining health for some time, having been diagnosed with breast cancer a few years earlier. Radical surgery successfully fought off the cancer for a time, but complications set in. A blood transfusion had infected her with the AIDS virus. She died on May 19, 1986, at the age of sixty-six. Her obituary in *The New York Times* listed the cause of death as pneumonia.

Her funeral service, held at St. Jean Baptiste Roman Catholic Church on Lexington Avenue, was a beautiful affair, according to people who attended, a celebration befitting one of Manhattan's lead-ing ladies.

Esme may have been gone, but Hammond didn't die alone. He made too many friends along the way. Friends who couldn't visit made their feelings known in other ways. At Christmastime in 1986, for in-stance, visitors passing through the front hall of his apartment had to make their way around a giant poinsettia sent by Bruce Springsteen.

And there were lots of visitors in the final months—Allen Ginsberg, Arthur Schlesinger, Jr., Bruce Lundvall, Hank O'Neal, among many others. Hammond tried to get dressed for their brief stays, but it grew more and more difficult. He watched a lot of CNN to keep abreast of the news and read voraciously.

Ginsberg took a picture of Hammond not long before he died. It is perhaps the last photograph of him. It shows a man bedridden and gaunt, his eyes haunted. A man who isn't yet ready to die. "The last thing that happened that I remember very vividly was that John was bedridden and he was dying and I went to see him," remembered his old friend and colleague at Columbia Bruce Lundvall. "He had a nurse, and John was in bed and we had this wonderful conversation. He said to me, 'Bruce, on top of the bureau there's a cassette. Could you get it down? I want you to hear this woman who's very talented.'" Lundvall laughed and shook his head at the memory. "He was playing a new artist for me that he'd discovered on his deathbed. And I think within days he died."

He passed quietly on July 10, 1987. Legend holds that he was lis-tening to Billie Holiday when he slipped away for good. It's entirely possible, even probable. His beloved *New York Times* sent him out in grand style, putting his obituary on the front page the following day. "John Hammond, a critic, talent scout and record producer whose mu-sical discoveries ranged from Billie Holiday to Bob Dylan and who had an extraordinary influence upon the history of American popular music, died yesterday at his home in Manhattan," read the article. Family members were pleasantly surprised that the most influential newspaper in the country saw his death as front-page news. A few days later, a private funeral was held in Manhattan attended by family and close friends.

Hammond is interred in the section of the Vanderbilt mausoleum on Staten Island reserved for extended family. He lies next to his parents and his son Douglas, who died in infancy. He took with him for the journey, stashed inside his favorite cloth satchel (a freebie he had received for making a donation to public television), a pack of cigarettes and a recent edition of one of his favorite magazines, *Mother Jones*. His friends would recognize him when he arrived.

EPILOGUE

I am still a New Yorker who owns no house, who thrives on city weekdays and country weekends. I still would change the world if I could, convince a nonbeliever that my way is right, argue a cause and make friends out of enemies. I am still the reformer, the impatient protester, the sometimes-intolerant champion of tolerance. Best of all, I still expect to hear, if not today then to-morrow, a voice or a sound I have never heard before, with something to say which has never been said before. And when that happens I will know what to do.

Those lines, articulate and self-aware, closed Hammond's 1977 memoirs. Ten years later, they were reprinted on the program cover for a memorial service held in his honor a few months after his death.

Conducted at St. Peter's Church (known as the "jazz chapel" for its jazz vespers service held every Sunday at 5:00 p.m.) at Fifty-fourth and Lexington Avenue in Manhattan, the memorial was well attended by Hammond's family and many friends, old and new alike. By one esti-mate, some four hundred people crowded into the church's amphi-theater.

Seated cheek by jowl on the tiered wooden rows that surround and rise away from the sanctuary, a who's who of the music industry gath-

ered to pay their respects and reminisce. Streaks of fading autumn sun-
light fell on the faces of Ahmet Ertegun, Jerry Wexler, Mitch Miller,
and Pete Seeger, among others.

Highlights included remarks by John's sister Adele, who, according
to family members, overcame a lifelong aversion to public speaking in
order to address the gathering. And one of Hammond's oldest friends,
the rabbi Edgar Siskin, whom he had met nearly six decades earlier at
Yale and who conducted the services at his first wedding, had flown in
from Israel to offer remarks commemorating Hammond's life.

Arthur Schlesinger, Jr., whom Hammond had befriended over
cocktails at the venerable Century Club during the last decade of his
life, spoke of how Hammond's "endearing smile, enthusiastic manner,
crewcut hair, gaudy tweed or madras jacket" had provided the often-
stodgy club with a desperately needed breath of fresh air. With an elo-
quence and sincerity befitting one of America's most respected historians,
Schlesinger covered the highlights of a life lived with joy and purpose:

> Others today are better qualified to discuss John's contributions
> as a zestful pioneer on the frontiers of American music; the per-
> formers he discovered; the music he rescued; the recording ses-
> sions he incited; the distillation he encouraged and preserved of
> a race's and a nation's work and woe and joy—sounds he heard
> that no one had quite heard before, voices saying, as he himself
> put it, things that no one had quite said before.
>
> His wonderful instinct for creativity in others made him a
> vast creative force himself, and he established the canon for
> the serious popular music of our lifetime. This alone would have
> fulfilled a career. But he combined his genius as a music man
> with a passion for fairness and for equal rights—the passion that
> led him well over half a century ago, long before Presidents and
> preachers and politics and press had embraced the cause, into
> the still unfinished struggle for racial justice.
>
> What one remembers most about John Hammond is his
> sense of expectation. Every day was a new adventure for him.
> He began each morning with anticipatory delight, "setting out,"
> as he wrote, "to discover the world all over again." He experi-

enced his share of grief and tragedy, but his capacity for wonder and hope and possibility remained. He communicated this divine expectancy to all who knew him and he was therefore a life-saver and a life-giver.

Schlesinger's words were as evocative as any prose can be. But the most fitting and moving tributes were, naturally, paid in song. The gospel singer Marion Williams performed a cappella, and the theater came alive as Hammond's legacy was brilliantly articulated through her passionate delivery. The pianist Adam Makowicz performed a piece titled "Blues for John," and there was not a dry eye left in the chapel.

Then Bruce Springsteen walked to the microphone set up near the sanctuary. Dressed formally in a dark suit and visibly moved, he slipped an acoustic guitar over his shoulder. He collected himself for a moment, then mustered a smile and spoke to the gathering. "Here's a song by another young fellow John gave a break to." Softly, he began to sing Dylan's "Forever Young." He closed with the lines:

> May your heart always be joyful,
> May your song always be sung,
> And may you stay . . . forever young.

After finishing, he paused briefly, then looked skyward. "Thanks, John," he said.

It would be easy to measure Hammond's influence purely through the prism of the artists with whom he is most closely identified. By that measurement, his influence has probably never been greater than it is today.

Try listening to the radio for a few minutes without coming across one of his protégés. There's Aretha Franklin singing "Respect" on the oldies station. There's Bob Dylan singing "Like a Rolling Stone" on, of all places, the local college radio station. (*Rolling Stone* magazine recently named "Like a Rolling Stone" the best song of all time, and a whole new generation has apparently discovered his music.) There's

George Benson singing "On Broadway" on the easy-listening station. There's Bruce Springsteen singing "Born to Run" on the classic-rock station. There's Stevie Ray Vaughan singing "Texas Flood" on a Sunday morning blues show.

Now put aside their hits for a moment and consider each of those artists purely as American icons. Franklin, like Billie Holiday before her in jazz, has arguably set the standard by which all women pop singers are now judged. After forty years, she remains the "Queen of Soul." Dylan is credited with nothing less than changing how we define popular music. His influence on American popular culture over the past four and a half decades is immeasurable. Benson became a household name as a rhythm and blues and pop singer, yet Hammond tabbed him—correctly—as one of the finest jazz guitarists of his generation. He has mastered each of those genres. Springsteen's career rivals that of Dylan's. His music remains relevant and his popularity enormous. Vaughan, too, set a new standard, one by which all up-and-coming blues-rock guitarists are measured. After his death in 1990, a statue was erected in his honor in his adopted hometown of Austin, Texas.

Hammond's earlier protégés are no less iconic. Consider Billie Holiday and Charlie Christian, two of the rare examples of jazz figures from the swing era whose popularity has grown since they stopped making music. Holiday, revered today as much for her tragedies as for her musical talent, established the archetype for the tortured artist too sensitive for this world. And Christian's status now approaches that of the almost-mythical Robert Johnson. Meanwhile, other prominent figures from that period—Benny Goodman, Artie Shaw, Glenn Miller, Woody Herman—cannot say the same.

But to view Hammond solely through the prism of the talent he supported would be to sell short his true legacy: that of almost singlehandedly integrating the music industry. His efforts in the mid-1930s— which went mostly unnoticed outside jazz circles—might be viewed as the first domino to fall in a sequence that later included Jackie Robinson's 1947 admission into major-league baseball; the Supreme Court's 1954 ruling in *Brown v. Board of Education of Topeka, Kansas*; the bus boycott in Montgomery, Alabama, in 1955 and 1956; and the Civil Rights Act of 1964.

About a year before Congress enacted the civil rights bill, John Hammond was replaced as Bob Dylan's producer by Tom Wilson, a black man. And no one gave it a second thought. That was because by then, as is the case today, integration within the music business was taken for granted. And that might be the greatest testament of all to Hammond's legacy.

NOTES AND DISCOGRAPHY

1. THE BASEMENT ON EAST NINETY-FIRST STREET

Hammond wrote about his introduction to the music of African-Americans in his autobiography, *John Hammond on Record* (New York: Ridge Press/Summit Books, 1977), and spoke of his childhood and early forays into Harlem in numerous interviews, notably during a television interview (circa 1981) with Dick Cavett, segments of which were used in a 1990 PBS documentary on Hammond produced for the American Masters series titled *From Bessie Smith to Bruce Springsteen*.

Nearly all of Hammond's recollections of his childhood were corroborated by his sister Rachel Breck, whom I interviewed on numerous occasions and without whose memories of her and her siblings' unique childhoods the early portions of this book would have been woefully lacking. Mrs. Breck regaled me with detailed descriptions of the Hammonds' homes, both in Manhattan and in Westchester, as well as with vivid portraits of her parents and their relationships with their children. Understanding Hammond's dynamic relationship with his mother would have been difficult without the context provided by Mrs. Breck. She was also apparently more capable than her brother of painting a broader picture of Hammond's often-distant relationship with his father.

Hammond's cousin Frederick Field wrote about growing up as a Vanderbilt in his autobiography, *From Right to Left* (Westport, Conn.: L. Hill, 1983). A thorough history of the Vanderbilts can be found in *Fortune's Children: The Fall of the House of Vanderbilt* by Arthur T. Vanderbilt (New York: Morrow, 1989). The information on Henry Sloane Coffin, as well as the history of Harlem, came from *The Encyclopedia of New York City* (New Haven, Conn.: Yale University Press, 1995). *The WPA Guide to New York City* (New York: New Press, 1992) was also helpful. The early story of jazz is told in many books, but the best may be Nat Shapiro and Nat Hentoff's seminal oral history, *Hear Me Talkin' to Ya* (New York: Dover, 1955). A history of the Hotchkiss School can be found in *Hotchkiss: A Chronicle of an American School* by Ernest Kolowrat (New

York: New Amsterdam, 1992). The book was given to me as a gift by Jennifer Olmquist on a visit I made to Hotchkiss in October 2001. While there, I reviewed yearbooks from each of the years Hammond attended the school, an opportunity that presented invaluable insights into his personality as a teenager.

COMPANION LISTENING

One of the best compilations of James P. Johnson's music is a 25-song collection called *Harlem Stride Piano: 1921/1929* on the French label EPM Musique. Other good introductory compilations are *Stride Piano Summit: A Celebration of Harlem Stride & Classic Piano Jazz* on the Milestone label, and *The Very Best of Fats Waller* on the RCA label. For a broader introduction to jazz, Louis Armstrong's Hot Five and Hot Seven recordings are essential.

2. AN EDUCATION

Hammond's work as a reporter in Maine at the *Portland Evening News* is covered in his autobiography. Ernest Gruening's life, including his efforts to revive the *Evening News*, is told in Robert David Johnson's *Ernest Gruening and the American Dissenting Tradition* (Cambridge, Mass.: Harvard University Press, 1998). The Depression-era story of the Harvard students is probably nothing more than an urban legend, and its origins are uncertain. Frederick Field dismissed the anecdote as false in his autobiography.

Katharine Graham discussed Hammond's penchant for iconoclasm at length one morning in November 2000 at her home in Georgetown near Washington, D.C. She and Hammond were neighbors growing up in Westchester County, and they corresponded frequently throughout their lives. Mrs. Graham was kind enough to sit with me for several hours, and later sent me a package containing several pieces of correspondence between her and Hammond.

Hammond's early career as a record producer is recounted in his autobiography, as well as in his first columns for *Melody Maker*. Indeed, most of his early magazine columns were little more than diary entries, describing in detail the studios where he spent his days, the nightclubs where he spent his evenings, and the records he was listening to.

COMPANION LISTENING

Garland Wilson's recordings have been compiled on a 24-track CD on the Classics Jazz label titled *Garland Wilson, 1931–1938*. There are numerous Fletcher Henderson compilations. One that includes the 1933 Hammond-produced records is titled *Fletcher Henderson and His Orchestra, 1932–1934*, also on the Classics Jazz label.

3. AN EMERGING VOICE

On the first of many visits to Rutgers University's Institute of Jazz Studies in Newark, I was introduced by Dan Morgenstern to Otis Ferguson's brilliant profile of Hammond, which was first published in the September 1938 edition of the magazine *Society Rag*. It's unlikely that anything written about Hammond since then has captured him as accurately. Friends of his told me that he himself acknowledged as much. The piece not only described his frenetic lifestyle as a critic, producer, and impresario but also captured his sometimes-difficult personality. Yet on the whole it was a sympathetic profile.

Hammond began promoting projects in which he had a financial stake in his early *Melody Maker* columns. The habit attracted criticism, but his motives were rarely if ever driven by financial gain. It was enthusiasm, not money, that attracted him to the job at WEVD.

Hammond's version of the trip to the Kentucky coal mines in his autobiography is not markedly different from Edmund Wilson's version in *The Thirties* (New York: Farrar, Straus and Giroux, 1980). Wilson's perception of Hammond was valuable to me, however.

One of the most authoritative accounts of the Scottsboro trials can be found in *Scottsboro: A Tragedy of the American South* by Dan Carter (New York: Oxford University Press, 1971). Hammond's articles for *The Nation* are referenced in the book.

Hammond's friendship with Benny Carter is recalled in Carter's biography *Benny Carter: A Life in American Music* by Edward Berger (Metuchen, N.J.: Scarecrow Press, 1982). Hammond also discussed his relationship with Carter in a 1973 radio interview with the disc jockey Ed Beach.

COMPANION LISTENING

Hammond's recordings of Benny Carter and Spike Hughes are compiled on one CD titled *1933: Spike Hughes & Benny Carter* on the Challenge label.

4. DISCOVERY

Which brings me to the Ed Beach tapes. In February 2001, as I was finishing an interview with the producer Frank Driggs, a man arrived at Driggs's door in the Flatlands section of Brooklyn. As I recall, Driggs and the man were working on a project together related to Driggs's particular expertise, Kansas City jazz. The man asked what I was working on, and when I told him, he complimented me on my selection of Hammond. Then he asked if I had heard "the Ed Beach tapes." I had not, so he explained that in the early 1970s Hammond had sat for a series of interviews with Ed Beach, at the time the dean of New York jazz disc jockeys. The man then gave me Dan Forte's name and said Forte could probably get me a copy of the tapes. Forte, who was then working as an archivist at the Blue Note in Greenwich Village, put me in touch with Ed Beach. Within two weeks, Beach had sent copies of the interviews, about fourteen hours in all, to Forte, who turned them over to me. They were an invaluable resource. Hammond discussed in detail with Beach virtually every aspect of his career. Billie Holiday was the topic of one of the earliest interviews. He also discussed his work with Teddy Wilson and Bessie Smith during the first few interviews.

Mr. Beach graciously spent several hours on the phone with me talking about his method for conducting the interviews and Hammond in general.

During a brief telephone conversation I had with Whitney Balliett, he told me many people believed Hammond had been tipped off to Billie Holiday by the jazz singer Mildred Bailey. Hammond never confirmed that version, though. Spike Hughes wrote of his trip to New York in his *Melody Maker* column. Hammond's columns in the same issues also mentioned the trip.

Gunther Schuller's *The Swing Era: The Development of Jazz, 1930–1945* (New York: Oxford University Press, 1989) was a valuable source for all of the chapters on Hammond's contribution to swing jazz. Thanks to my friend Rich C. for alerting me to its existence and getting me a copy.

Lewis A. Erenberg's *Swingin' the Dream: Big Band Jazz and the Rebirth of American Culture* (Chicago: University of Chicago Press, 1998) contains a lucid description of the American mind-set during the swing era.

Other sources for this chapter include Hammond's autobiography; two books on Holiday, the unreliable *Lady Sings the Blues* by Billie Holiday and William Duffy (Garden City, N.Y.: Doubleday, 1956) and the more reliable *Billie's Blues: The Billie Holiday Story, 1933–1959* by John Chilton (New York: Stein and Day, 1975); Michael Brooks's fine liner notes for *Lady Day: The Complete Billie Holiday on Columbia Records, 1933–1944*, Sony, 2001; two biographies of Benny Goodman, *Benny Goodman and the Swing Era* by James Lincoln Collier (New York: Oxford University Press, 1989) and *Swing, Swing, Swing: The Life and Times of Benny Goodman* by Ross Firestone (New York: Norton, 1993); Goodman's autobiography *The Kingdom of Swing*, co-written with Irving Kolodin (New York: Frederick Ungar, 1939); Teddy Wilson's memoirs, *Teddy Wilson Talks Jazz*, by Wilson with Arie Ligthart and Humphrey van Loo (New York: Cassell, 1996); and *Bessie* by Chris Albertson (New York: Stein and Day, 1972).

The Danny Barker quotation on Bessie Smith is from *Hear Me Talkin' to Ya*.

COMPANION LISTENING

Hammond's recordings with Bessie Smith can be heard on *Bessie Smith: The Collection*, a Columbia Records compilation. There are countless Billie Holiday compilations. For her complete Columbia recordings, there is a 10-CD set titled *Lady Day: The Complete Billie Holiday on Columbia (1933–1944)*. A broad compilation of Teddy Wilson's music, including his first recordings with Hammond, can be found on *The Elegant Mr. Wilson, 1933/1945* on the EPM Musique label.

5. CONVERGENCE

Dan Carter's *Scottsboro: A Tragedy of the American South* and Hammond's articles for *The Nation* were the sources for the early portion of this chapter. Descriptions of Hammond in the studio were gathered during numerous interviews with musicians and producers who worked with him, among them Jerry Wexler, Ahmet Ertegun, Mike Kissel, Hank O'Neal, Chris Layton, Tommy Shannon, and Ned Massey.

The material on Chick Webb was drawn from several sources already cited, including *Hear Me Talkin' to Ya*; *The Swing Era: The Development of Jazz, 1930–1945*; and *Swingin' the Dream: Big Band Jazz and the Rebirth of American Culture*.

Hammond described Irving Mills's business practices and his brief tenure as one of Mills's employees in his autobiography.

The story of the black and white all-star band that never materialized was drawn primarily from Hammond's columns in *Melody Maker* and *Down Beat*. Context was provided by *Swing, Swing, Swing: The Life and Times of Benny Goodman*. The story of Goodman and Wilson's jam session at Mildred Bailey's home in Queens is recounted in all of the Goodman books cited above. The story of the 1936 concert for the Chicago Rhythm Club at which Goodman and Wilson first played together in public was drawn from the same sources.

Hammond's articles for the *Brooklyn Eagle* were also used to complete this chapter, specifically his controversial piece titled "The Tragedy of Duke Ellington," which was reprinted several weeks later in *Down Beat*. The quote from Albert Murray was taken from an interview with the author on June 1, 2001. Ellington responded to Hammond's criticism four years later, also in the pages of *Down Beat*. The articles can also be found in *The Duke Ellington Reader* (New York: Oxford University Press, 1993).

COMPANION LISTENING

Hammond's recordings with Chick Webb can be found on *Chick Webb: Rhythm Man* on HEP Records. A good collection of Teddy Wilson and Billie Holiday collaborations is *Teddy Wilson and His Orchestra with Billie Holiday: Fine & Dandy*, also on HEP Records. There are countless Benny Goodman compilations. I recommend the 1938 *Carnegie Hall Jazz Concert (Live)* on Sony; also *Original Benny Goodman Trio and Quarter Sessions, Volume 1: After You've Gone* on RCA. The Mildred Bailey recordings can be heard on *Mrs. Swing: Mildred Bailey*, a boxed set from Proper Records.

6. FURTHER AND FURTHER AFIELD

Hammond described his trip to Kansas City to hear Count Basie first in his *Down Beat* column, and later in his autobiography and in interviews with Ed Beach. Basie recalled the visit in his autobiography, *Good Morning Blues* (New York: Random House, 1985). My description of Kansas City in the mid-1930s was drawn from several sources: old editions of *The Call*, Kansas City's black newspaper, which I perused at the Kansas City Public Library; *Kansas City . . . and All That's Jazz* (1999), a publication of the Kansas City Jazz Museum; and *Reading Jazz: A Gathering of Autobiography, Reportage, and Criticism from 1919 to Now*, edited by Robert Gottlieb (New York: Pantheon Books, 1996). The Mary Lou Williams quotation is from *Reading Jazz*. *The Swing Era: The Development of Jazz, 1930–1945* was the source for most of the information on territory bands. I also drew on information given to me during a visit to the Oklahoma Historical Society. Basie described his time in a territory band in his autobiography. Hammond and Basie told the story of Basie's ill-advised contract with Decca in their respective memoirs.

In late December 2000 I was fortunate enough to interview Lionel Hampton. I spent several hours taping his recollections in his apartment in Manhattan, and his memory was remarkable. He recalled in vivid detail the circumstances that led him to join Benny Goodman's band, and he was firm in his opinion that Hammond's successful efforts to integrate popular music in the 1930s opened the door for Jackie Robinson to join major-league baseball a decade later.

The author Albert Murray, who helped Basie with his memoirs, described for me Hammond's role in shaping the Basie band. During a long talk in his apartment in Harlem, he explained that while Basie trusted Hammond, he did not allow Hammond to arbitrarily replace his musicians.

Billie Holiday's ill-fated tenure with Basie's band is described by Basie in his memoirs. The Claude Williams quotation is from an interview he did with a historian affiliated with the Oklahoma Historical Society. The Basie quotation, "That John, he's been so good to me," is from *The Big Bands* by George Simon (New York: Schirmer Books, 1981).

Other sources for this chapter include *Hamp: An Autobiography* by Hampton and James Haskins (New York: Amistad Press, 1993); *Buck Clayton's Jazz World* by Buck Clayton (New York: Oxford University Press, 1987); and *Lester Leaps In: The Life and Times of Lester "Pres" Young* by Douglas Henry Daniels (Boston: Beacon Press, 2002).

COMPANION LISTENING

Count Basie's recordings supervised by Hammond, including the 1936 sessions for the Vocalion label, can be found on *America's #1 Band! The Columbia Years*, a boxed set on Columbia. But since most of Basie's earliest recordings were for Decca Records, I also recommend *The Complete Decca Recordings: 1937*, a boxed set from Verve. A good sampling of Lionel Hampton's work with Goodman can be heard on *Lionel Hampton: Small Combos, 1937–1940* on the Giants of Jazz label. Columbia/Legacy released a collection of Billie Holiday–Lester Young collaborations titled *Billie Holiday & Lester Young: A Musical Romance*.

7. A MINOR REVOLUTION

The show at the Dallas Exposition was recounted using Hammond's *Down Beat* columns and Lionel Hampton's personal recollections. Goodman's biographers also told the story, as did Goodman in his autobiography. Hammond told the story of organizing "From Spirituals to Swing" in his autobiography and in interviews with Ed Beach. Other sources for this chapter were Hammond's clips under the pseudonym Henry Johnson in *New Masses*; his article on "From Spirituals to Swing" written for *The New York Times*; and the program from the concert, reproduced by Vanguard Records for a release of the show on compact disc. I used the CDs to describe the concert itself.

The discrepancy between Hammond's version of Bessie Smith's death and what is now understood to be the truth was pointed out to me in an interview in February 2001 with Smith's biographer Chris Albertson, who was a colleague of Hammond's at Columbia Records.

Otis Ferguson's marvelous profile has been cited earlier in these notes.

COMPANION LISTENING

Vanguard recently reissued the complete "From Spirituals to Swing" concerts on three CDs.

8. CAFÉ SOCIETY

In addition to Hammond's own recollections of "From Spirituals to Swing" and his activities later that night at Café Society, his sister Rachel Breck recalled the memories of their sister Alice, who had attended the show with Hammond's parents. An employee of the theater troupe that now uses the basement where Café Society was housed gave me a tour of the space. Nothing remains of the famous murals or, for that matter, any other evidence that a seminal nightclub once thrived there.

Sources for information on Barney Josephson, his nightclub Café Society, Communism's popularity among intellectuals during the 1930s and 1940s, and Communism's relationship to jazz were drawn from *Whistling Girl: Candid Confessions of a Chameleon*, a little remembered but richly detailed account of Hammond's intellectual circles in the 1940s by Helen Lawrenson (Garden City, N.Y.: Doubleday, 1978); David Margolick's intriguing *Strange Fruit: Billie Holiday, Café Society, and an Early Cry for Civil Rights* (Philadelphia: Running Press, 2000); *Swingin' the Dream: Big Band Jazz and the Rebirth of American Culture*; Joe Klein's *Woody Guthrie: A Life* (New York: Knopf, 1980); Lena Horne's autobiography, *Lena* (Garden City, N.Y.: Doubleday, 1965); and Hammond's recollections to Ed Beach and material contained in his papers at Yale University.

The *New Yorker* profile of Milt Gabler was found in Hammond's file at the Institute of Jazz Studies in Newark. Jerry Wexler shared his views on the song "Strange Fruit" and many other subjects related to Hammond in a long telephone interview in the spring of 2001. But the quotation in this chapter is from Margolick's book. The history of CBS's purchase of Columbia Records was found in William Paley's autobiography *As It Happened* (Garden City, N.Y.: Doubleday, 1979).

Goddard Lieberson's professional relationship with Hammond was described to me by Robert Altshuler, who worked at Columbia throughout the 1960s and knew both men well. Evidence of Lieberson's affection and respect for Hammond can be found among Hammond's papers at Yale University.

Most of the Charlie Christian material was drawn from a two-day trip I made to Oklahoma City in December 2002. During my stay I had the good fortune to meet the historian Anita G. Arnold, as well as Margretta Christian Downey, Christian's girlfriend and the mother of his only child. Ms. Arnold gave me copies of her privately published books *Charlie and the Deuce* (1994), *Charlie Christian Photo Collection* (1995), and *Legendary Times and Tales of Second Street* (1995). Mrs. Downey spent an entire afternoon recalling the shy young man who left Oklahoma City to join Benny Goodman's band. For me, the afternoon with her was one of the most enjoyable experiences of this project.

Other sources were *Charlie Christian*, a slim biography by Peter Broadbent (Newcastle upon Tyne, U.K.: Ashley Mark, 1997); "Flying Home," an essay by Rudi Blesh in *Reading Jazz: A Gathering of Autobiography, Reportage, and Criticism from 1919 to Now*; *The Swing Era: The Development of Jazz, 1930–1945*; and an interview with the music historian Michael Brooks.

The Ralph Ellison quotation was taken from material provided by the Oklahoma Historical Society.

"Strange Fruit" can be found on any number of Billie Holiday compilations. A fine sampling of the boogie-woogie piano of Meade "Lux" Lewis, Albert Ammons, and Pete Johnson can be found on *The Boogie Woogie Boys*, from Magpie Records. Sony's Legacy label recently reissued all of Charlie Christian's recordings on a four-CD package titled *Charlie Christian: The Genius of the Electric Guitar*.

9. A FAMILY

Much of the information related to Hammond's relationship with Jemy was drawn from an interview with Isobel Fisher in Ardsley, New York, in September 2002. Fisher described in detail Hammond's visit with his wife to Albuquerque in the winter of 1942. The Basie quotation on Paul Robeson is from Basie's autobiography. Harold Leventhal spoke to me of many things during several interviews in the spring of 2001, including Hammond's efforts to integrate commercial radio. The bassist Milt Hinton wrote of Hammond in *Bass Line: The Stories and Photographs of Milt Hinton* (Philadelphia: Temple University Press, 1988). I obtained Hammond's FBI file with the help of my friend Randy Herschaft, the Pulitzer Prize–winning researcher for the Associated Press. The material on Hammond's relationship with Goodman after the bandleader married Alice was drawn from the previously cited Goodman biographies. Rachel Breck provided invaluable insight into Hammond's relationships with his sister Alice and his brother-in-law Goodman. The Spike Jones and the George Avakian quotations were taken from *Swing, Swing, Swing: The Life and Times of Benny Goodman*.

The tribute to Joe Louis performed by Paul Robeson and Count Basie was recently included on a CD titled *Joe Louis: An American Hero* on Rounder Records. In the early 1940s, Hammond supervised a series of sessions for *Metronome Magazine* that included contributions from Harry James, Benny Goodman, Count Basie, Jack Teagarden, Charlie Christian, Gene Krupa, Benny Carter, and Cootie Williams, among others. The recordings, known as the Metronome All-Star sessions, have been compiled on a CD titled *Summit Meetings 1939–1950* from Fremeaux & Associates, a French label.

10. AT WAR AT HOME

Hammond's activities as a member of the NAACP were traced through records I reviewed during three days of research at the Library of Congress in October 2002. Information on the Legal Defense Fund is available in numerous histories of the NAACP. I supplemented my book research with an interview in January 2003 with Jack Greenberg, former director-counsel of the LDF. All of the information pertaining to Hammond's rift with Roy Wilkins was drawn from the NAACP archives at the Library of Congress.

Isobel Fisher recalled for me Jemy Hammond's account of the death of the couple's second son.

The letter written by Hammond to Phil and Katharine Graham was given to me by Mrs. Graham. The letters written by African-American soldiers stationed on U.S. military bases during World War II were found in the NAACP's archives at the Library of Congress. Other sources for this chapter included *The Life of Langston Hughes, Volume II* by Arnold Rampersad (New York: Oxford University Press, 1988); a *Chicago Defender* article on King Kolax, which I found in Hammond's papers at Yale University; and *Swingin' the Dream: Big Band Jazz and the Rebirth of American Culture.*

11. VANGUARD

Isobel Fisher described her sister's domestic unhappiness following Hammond's return from the Army. Hammond's career moves after leaving Columbia in 1946 can be traced through his autobiography, his interviews with Ed Beach, and his papers at Yale University. Some of the material on his trip to Prague in 1947 was drawn from a visit I made to Prague in the spring of 2002.

The "John could be difficult" quotation came from Isobel Fisher. Yet several people who knew him intimately, including his sister, made similar statements. Fisher's account of her sister's relationship with Robert Capa is corroborated in *Robert Capa*, a biography by Richard Whelan (New York: Knopf, 1985).

Hammond's sister Rachel Breck corroborated all of the material related to his personal life after his marriage to Esme O'Brien. She described for me in detail her mother's relationship with the Moral Rearmament movement and the family's attempts to discourage that relationship. Mrs. Breck could only speculate on the amount of money her mother turned over to Frank Buchman and his movement. Hammond mentioned his financial difficulties frequently in his personal correspondence, although he rarely used specific figures.

Accounts of the 1953 Goodman tour are included in all of the Goodman biographies, but I emphasized Rachel Breck's version because she had no agenda and was close with Goodman and his wife at the time.

Both Elaine Lorillard and George Wein were kind enough to recount for me the origins of the Newport Jazz Festival. There were some minor discrepancies between their versions regarding Hammond's role in the first festival held in 1954. For instance, Ms. Lorillard said his role was significant in 1954, whereas Mr. Wein said it grew over time. Nevertheless, both praised his efforts. The descriptions of the first festival were drawn from my interview with Ms. Lorillard, from newspaper clippings from July 1954, and from Hammond's own accounts in various interviews. Hammond praised Ms. Lorillard in an undated newspaper clip she gave me.

Some of the material for Hammond's work with Vanguard was drawn from a *New Yorker* article included in his file at the Institute of Jazz Studies. It seems likely that Whitney Balliett was the author, but he couldn't recall writing the article in a brief conversation we had. Other sources included interviews with Nat Hentoff, Seymour Solomon, and especially, the inimitable Ruby Braff.

The John McLellan article critical of Hammond seems to have been written around 1957. I found it in Hammond's file at the Institute of Jazz Studies.

COMPANION LISTENING

A good sampling of songs recorded at early Newport Jazz Festivals has been compiled on *Happy Birthday Newport: 50 Swinging Years* on Sony's Legacy label. Hammond's recordings for Vanguard have all been reissued by Vanguard on CD. Highlights include Ruby Braff, *Linger Awhile*; Ellis Larkins and Ruby Braff, *Duets*, Volumes I and II; *The Basie Bunch: Too Marvelous for Words*; *The Essential Buck Clayton*; Vic Dickenson, *Nice Work*; *The Essential Joe Jones*; Mel Powell, *It's Been So Long* and *The Best Things in Life*; *The Essential Jimmy Rushing*; Sir Charles Thompson and the Hawks, *For the Ears*; and Joe Williams, *A Night at Count Basie's*.

12. A SECOND ACT

Hammond's career from 1959, when he returned to Columbia Records, until his death in 1987 was traced through his papers at Yale University, where I spent much of the summer of 2003. Ken Crilly and his staff at the Yale Music Library were enormously helpful, providing space, pencils, and copies upon request. Much of the material in the final five chapters was drawn from those papers. I also used that material to either corroborate or provide alternate versions of incidents involving Hammond that have found their way over the years into the public record.

Hammond wrote of his experience with the Abyssinian Baptist Gospel Choir in his memoirs and spoke of it with Ed Beach. The liner notes to a 1991 reissue of the recording were also helpful. Dave Marsh wrote a short biography of Alex Bradford for All Music Guide, an online music database.

All of the material on Ray Bryant was drawn from Hammond's papers. The material on Columbia was drawn primarily from Clive Davis's memoir, *Clive: Inside the Record Business*, written with James Willwerth (New York: Ballantine Books, 1976). The Aretha Franklin material was drawn from Hammond's papers, and also from *Aretha Franklin: The Queen of Soul* by Mark Bego (New York: Da Capo Press, 2001). Interviews on Hammond's professional relationship with Franklin were conducted with Jerry Wexler, Ahmet Ertegun, and Robert Altshuler. Hammond's quote about signing Pete Seeger is from Anthony Scaduto's *Bob Dylan* (New York: Grosset & Dunlap, 1972), pp. 94–95.

Pete Seeger told me about Pete Seeger, as only Pete Seeger can. Harold Leventhal was also helpful on this material.

Bob Dylan's memoir *Chronicles, Volume One* (New York: Simon & Schuster, 2004) was something of a revelation. His account of his first meeting with Hammond at a rehearsal at Carolyn Hester's apartment in September 1961 was similar to other accounts already in print. Yet his praise of Hammond was effusive and quite touching. Carolyn Hester sent me a wonderfully written e-mail describing in detail how Dylan came to be at that rehearsal. In a phone interview, she spoke warmly of her days as a Hammond protégée. Other sources for this material included *Bob Dylan* by Anthony Scaduto; *No Direction Home: The Life and Music of Bob Dylan* by Robert Shelton (New York: Beech Tree Books, 1986); and *Positively 4th Street: The Lives and Times of Joan Baez, Bob Dylan, Mimi Baez Fariña, and Richard Fariña* by David Hajdu (New York: Farrar, Straus and Giroux, 2001). The quotations from George Avakian came from several interviews we did during the winter of 2001. I interviewed Nat Hentoff twice, once in April 2001 and again in the summer of 2002.

COMPANION LISTENING

Sony has reissued the Abyssinian Baptist Choir recordings under the title *Shakin' the Rafters: The Abyssinian Baptist Gospel Choir Under the Direction of Professor Alex Bradford*. Most of Ray Bryant's Columbia recordings have been compiled on a CD titled *The Madison Time* on the Collectables label. Many of Pete Seeger's Columbia recordings supervised by Hammond are included on *Pete Seeger's Greatest Hits*, a 16-track CD from Sony. I also recommend *We Shall Overcome: The Complete Carnegie Hall Concert*, a 1963 live album produced by Hammond that has been re-issued in an extended version on CD. Carolyn Hester's self-titled first album for Columbia (the one on which Bob Dylan made his first appearance on record) has been reissued by Sony on the Legacy label.

13. THE A&R MAN

My interview with Ahmet Ertegun in June 2002 in his office at Atlantic Records was one of the most enjoyable conversations I've had as a journalist. He is certainly one of the classiest men in the music industry, and he shared his thoughts on Hammond with great candor and humor.

Much of the material for this chapter was drawn from the same sources as the previous chapter: the same books on Franklin and Dylan, including Dylan's memoirs. Hammond's personal correspondence with Franklin is included in his papers at Yale. Although I interviewed Jerry Wexler, the quotation in this chapter is from his autobiography, *Rhythm and the Blues: A Life in American Music* (New York: Knopf, 1993).

Hammond's version of the contract dispute with Dylan was drawn from his papers, in particular an October 9, 1962, memo to his bosses in which he described his proposed solution to Dylan's request to renegotiate his contract.

Other sources for this chapter included interviews with the former Columbia executives Robert Altshuler and Bruce Lundvall.

COMPANION LISTENING

Aretha Franklin's first two albums for Columbia, the ones produced by Hammond, are titled *Aretha* and *The Electrifying Aretha Franklin*. Sony has reissued many of these recordings, most recently on a boxed set titled *The Queen in Waiting: The Columbia Years, 1960–1965*. Dylan's first two albums for Columbia are titled *Bob Dylan* and *The Freewheelin' Bob Dylan*.

14. JACKSON, MISSISSIPPI—JUNE 15, 1963

Hammond described his trip to Jackson, Mississippi, for Medgar Evers's funeral in his memoirs. His son Jason corroborated his account and added a few details in an interview. Other sources used were material from the NAACP's archives at the Library of

Congress, and the books *For Us, the Living* by Myrlie Evers-Williams with William Peters (Garden City, N.Y.: Doubleday, 1967) and *Coming of Age in Mississippi* by Anne Moody (New York: Dell, 1968), both of which include detailed descriptions of Evers's funeral.

Robert Altshuler recalled for me the change in attitude toward Dylan by Columbia's executives as Dylan's albums began to sell and his prowess as a songwriter became evident. The Roy Gaines material was drawn entirely from Hammond's papers at Yale. The Benson material was also drawn primarily from Hammond's papers, but Benson's quotations were taken from liner notes on reissues of his two Columbia albums that were rereleased on compact disc.

Hammond's split with the NAACP was reported in November 1966 in the *Amsterdam News*. Martin Luther King's speech at Riverside Church was reprinted in *The Eyes on the Prize Civil Rights Reader: Documents, Speeches, and Firsthand Accounts from the Black Freedom Struggle, 1954–1990* (New York: Penguin Books, 1991). Wilkins's response and the subsequent outcry from NAACP members were documented through materials found in the NAACP's archives at the Library of Congress. The Nat Hentoff quotation on page 258 was taken from an interview with the author on April 13, 2001.

The material on Leonard Cohen was drawn from Hammond's memoirs, his papers at Columbia, and *Various Positions: A Life of Leonard Cohen* by Ira B. Nadel (Toronto: Random House of Canada, 1996). Hammond described his disappointment with the thirtieth-anniversary "From Spirituals to Swing" concert in his papers and in an interview with Ed Beach. His debts resulting from the show were found in his papers.

COMPANION LISTENING
"Only a Pawn in Their Game" is on Dylan's third album, *The Times They Are A-Changin'*. Hammond did not participate in the album's production. *Gainelining* is a hard-to-find album by Roy Gaines. It's worth the effort. An easier-to-find collection is called *Bluesman for Life*, on JSP Records. George Benson's work with Hammond can be found on his first two albums for Columbia, *It's Uptown* and *The George Benson Cookbook*. Sony recently reissued both albums with liner notes by Benson. Hammond's sessions with Leonard Cohen can be heard on Cohen's first album, titled *The Songs of Leonard Cohen*.

15. A MARVELOUS AUDITION

Bruce Springsteen was the primary source for this chapter. He was elaborate and animated in his descriptions of his first several meetings with Hammond. He also fondly recalled the unique relationship that emerged between them. I want to thank Tammy McGurk and Barbara Carr for making the interview happen. Tammy exhorted me to keep the faith, assuring me that Bruce wanted to do the interview and that he eventually would. And Barbara treated me like one of the crew on the night I sat down with Bruce in Providence, Rhode Island.

I spent two delightful hours with Mike Appel in a midtown Manhattan restaurant talking about John Hammond, Bruce Springsteen, rock and roll, and life. I'm grateful to him for his time and candor. I also used material from *Down Thunder Road: The Making of Bruce Springsteen*, (New York: Simon & Schuster, 1992), a book by Marc Eliot that Appel collaborated on, apparently in an effort to set the record straight regarding his split with Springsteen. The book contains depositions and other documents from their legal battle, which were helpful to me.

William Krasilovsky expressed to me in an interview his legal opinion that Springsteen's contract with Appel was flawed. He said he tried to convince Appel and Springsteen to rework it long before Springsteen began to make a lot of money but that, for whatever reason, they ignored his advice. Other sources include the transcript of an interview Hammond did in 1980 for *Backstreets*, a Springsteen fan magazine, which I found in Hammond's papers at Yale. Ample evidence that Hammond would have preferred that Springsteen remained a solo artist was also in his papers.

Other sources for this chapter included *Born to Run: The Bruce Springsteen Story* by Dave Marsh (Garden City: N.Y.: Doubleday, 1979), and interviews with Mike Kissel and Robert Altshuler. I also used a video prepared by Columbia for Hammond's retirement in 1975 given to me by Bruce Lundvall. The material on Adam Makowicz was drawn from a February 2002 interview with him.

Mikie Harris, Hammond's assistant, was an invaluable resource for information on the last decade of Hammond's life. I owe her a huge debt of gratitude for her help and support. I interviewed Gloria Vanderbilt in October 2001 and Ann Slater in March 2002. Ms. Slater recalled the incident with the water glasses at the society party. And I shared a steak au poivre and some *frites* with Arthur Schlesinger, Jr., in an Upper East Side bistro in July 2002—another highlight of this project.

COMPANION LISTENING
Four of the dozen or so songs Springsteen recorded with Hammond for a Columbia demo tape were included on *Tracks*, a collection of previously unreleased material from Sony. (Hammond's voice describing the demo session opens the collection.) Adam Makowicz's recordings for Columbia are difficult to find. Try his *A Tribute to Art Tatum* on VWC Records and *Swiss Encounter: Live at the Montreaux Jazz Festival* on Atlantic.

16. SRV

Hank O'Neal was the primary source for information on Hammond's unsuccessful attempt to start a record company. He was also an important source for Hammond's initial contact with Stevie Ray Vaughan. But most of the material on Vaughan came from Chris Layton and Tommy Shannon. Beverly Howell, who arranged for the interview, told me Chris and Tommy would be happy to participate in a conference call with me. But I insisted that I wanted to meet them in Austin, and they were only too happy to oblige. I spent an entire day in a hotel room around the corner from Antone's talking about the business of rock and roll, the blues, Stevie Ray Vaughan, and John Hammond with the two of them. I've rarely enjoyed myself as much as I did that day. Additional material on Vaughan was drawn from *Stevie Ray Vaughan: Caught in the Crossfire*, a wonderful biography by Joe Nick Patoski and Bill Crawford (Boston: Little, Brown, 1993). I attended the Vaughan show at Carnegie Hall in October 1984.

Mikie Harris and Ned Massey were the primary sources regarding Hammond's breakdown in health, his final decline, and the circumstances of his burial. Other sources included interviews with Jerry Wexler and Bruce Lundvall.

COMPANION LISTENING

Hammond's work with Stevie Ray Vaughan can be found on *Texas Flood* and *Couldn't Stand the Weather*, both released on Epic Records. Hammond is heard introducing Vaughan on a live recording of the Carnegie Hall concert titled *Live at Carnegie Hall*, from Sony.

EPILOGUE

Mikie Harris, Rachel Breck, and Arthur Schlesinger, Jr., recalled for me Hammond's memorial service. Mr. Schlesinger was gracious enough to send me a copy of his comments that day. Springsteen can be heard singing "Forever Young" at the end of *From Bessie Smith to Bruce Springsteen*, a PBS documentary on Hammond.

ACKNOWLEDGMENTS

On a spring day in 2000 I was walking up Fifth Avenue on my way to work when I bumped into a friend of mine and a fellow writer, Erik Simon. He asked how things were going at my job. He listened for a while, and then, apparently unimpressed, asked, "What else are you working on?" When I told him that for several months I had been working on a biography of John Hammond, he insisted I call his agent. Next he helped me prepare a proposal. Then he helped me edit the entire first draft of the book. More valuable than his expertise with the written word, however, was his support. Until he came aboard, I wasn't sure I had it in me to write a book. He laughed at my misgivings, and for that I am grateful.

Thanks especially to Rachel Breck, who spent many, many hours with me discussing her brother. Her frank assessments provided insight I certainly could not have obtained otherwise. After Mrs. Breck had praised a few of my chapters, I knew I was heading in the right direction. Meeting her was one of the great joys of this effort.

When I began work on this, I had in mind three specific goals. I wanted to interview Bob Dylan, although I figured it was unlikely to happen. (I was right.) I wanted to interview Bruce Springsteen, which I figured might happen. (I was right again.) And I wanted to interview Tommy Shannon and Chris Layton, Stevie Ray Vaughan's bandmates.

Two out of three isn't bad, and I'm extremely grateful to Bruce,

Tommy, and Chris for taking the time to meet with me, as well as to their extended staffs who worked out the arrangements.

Thanks to Paul Elie and his affable and capable assistant, Kevin Doughten, at Farrar, Straus and Giroux for seeing Hammond as I see him, and thanks to my agent, Martha Kaplan, for knowing whom to call.

Finally, thanks to my parents for everything I am.

INDEX